"I am excited to recommend this important new work on servanthood and leadership. Graham Hill's book offers important insights and correctives to all of us and our views of leadership. Together the contributors help move us from the board room, back to the role of the bowl and the towel."

—Terry Walling
Adjunct Professor
Fuller Theological Seminary

"Christian leaders in North America are hearing competing voices as they struggle to understand the relationship between leadership, servanthood, and the mission of the church. Graham Hill's book is a clarion call to servantship, a fresh and needed approach for existing and emerging leaders."

—Harry Gardner
President, Acadia Divinity College
Dean of Theology, Acadia University

SERVANTSHIP

Servantship

Sixteen Servants on the Four Movements of Radical Servantship

Edited by
GRAHAM HILL

Foreword by Lance Ford

WIPF & STOCK · Eugene, Oregon

SERVANTSHIP
Sixteen Servants on the Four Movements of Radical Servantship

Copyright © 2013 Graham Hill. All rights reserved. Except for brief quotations in critical publications or reviews, no part of this book may be reproduced in any manner without prior written permission from the publisher. Write: Permissions, Wipf and Stock Publishers, 199 W. 8th Ave., Suite 3, Eugene, OR 97401.

Wipf & Stock
An Imprint of Wipf and Stock Publishers
199 W. 8th Ave., Suite 3
Eugene, OR 97401

www.wipfandstock.com

ISBN 13: 978-1-62032-824-8

Manufactured in the U.S.A.

Scripture taken from the Holy Bible, Today's New International Version™ TNIV®
Copyright © 2001, 2005 by International Bible Society®. All rights reserved worldwide.

For my great-grandfather, John McKittrick, whose deep love for Jesus shaped his compassion for the vulnerable and his tireless ministry among the broken, the despised, the forgotten, and the outcast. His enthusiasm for mission found its source in prayer and in reliance on the Spirit of Jesus Christ. He was selflessly missional "because of his great love for his Lord and his untiring 'passion for souls.' From this source flowed his infinite capacity for caring."

John McKittrick exemplified the missional zeal and deep compassion of outwardly focused, radical servantship.

Servantship is essentially about following our Lord Jesus Christ, the servant Lord, and his mission—it is a life of discipleship to him, patterned after his self-emptying, humility, sacrifice, love, values, and mission. Servantship is humbly valuing others more than yourself, and looking out for the interests and wellbeing of others. Servantship is the cultivation of the same attitude of mind Christ Jesus had: making yourself nothing, being a servant, humbling yourself, and submitting yourself to the will and purposes of the triune God. Since servantship is the imitation of Christ, it involves an unreserved participation in the missio Dei—the trinitarian mission of God. Servantship is the movement from hierarchical leadership to radical service, from shallow pragmatics to dynamic theological reflection, from abstract theories to courageous practices, and from forgetfulness to transforming memory. Servantship recognizes, in word, thought, and deed, that "whoever wants to become great among you must be your servant, and whoever wants to be first must be your slave—just as the Son of Man did not come to be served, but to serve, and to give his life as a ransom for many."

—GRAHAM HILL

Contents

Contributors   xi

Foreword by Lance Ford   xv

1   The Theology and Practices of Self-Emptying, Missional Servantship—*Graham Hill*   1

Movement One
From Leadership to Radical Servantship

2   For the Son of Man Did Not Come to Lead, but to Be Led: Matthew 20:20–28 and Royal Service—*Darrell Jackson*   15

3   Nothing Leadership: The Locus of Missional Servantship—*Roger Helland*   32

4   Sacrifice and Succession: Rethinking Servantship and Missional Community—*Simon G. Rattray*   42

Movement Two
From Shallowness to Dynamic Theological Reflection

5   Forming a Missional and Trinitarian Church—*Graeme Anderson*   63

6   Participating in God's Mission—*Christine Redwood*   75

7   Responding to the Missional Context—*Lynette Edge*   85

8   Exploring Theological Bearings—*Paul Winch*   97

9   Seeing Mission as Organizing Function—*Grae McWhirter*   111

10   Recalibrating Church in Post-Christendom—*Peter Ong*   123

11   Considering Emerging Innovations—*Jim Collins*   135

12   Rediscovering Community—*Steven Rodda*   147

Movement Three
From Theories to Courageous Practices

13   Shaping Missional Churches and Associations—*Graham Hill*   165

14   Deepening Discipleship—*Graeme Anderson*   178

Contents

	15	Nurturing Missional Modes of Servantship—*Christine Redwood*	190
	16	Exploring Servantship and Cultural Shifts—*Jamie Freeman*	201
	17	Welcoming Multiculturalism—*Christine McGowan*	211
	18	Cultivating Narrative and Storytelling—*Christine Redwood*	222
	19	Disturbing the Present and the Status Quo—*Lynette Edge*	232
	20	Challenging Cyber-spaces—*Paul Winch*	243

Movement Four
From Forgetfulness to Transforming Memory

	21	Caring for the Broken and the Vulnerable—*John McKittrick*	257
	22	Epilogue: Following Our Servant Lord and His Mission —*Graham Hill*	291

Bibliography   293

Contributors

Graeme Anderson grew up as a missionary kid in the highlands of Papua New Guinea. He taught as a Middle School specialist before beginning to work as a pastor for St Philip's Anglican Church on Sydney's North Shore. He is currently working towards a Master of Arts in Ministry at Morling College, Sydney, and has recently completed studies with the Renovarè International Institute for Christian Spiritual Formation. He is currently serving as lead pastor for Northside Baptist Church in Sydney.

Jim Collins is the State Officer for Family Voice Australia in Tasmania. Originally from the United Kingdom, Jim has a background in corporate advisory and business analysis work. After retraining at Morling College, Jim has worked as a Christian speaker and writer, including a role as assistant pastor at Seaforth Baptist Church in Sydney. He recently co-authored a photo-story book, *Love in Action: Taking Action against Poverty*.

Lynette Edge is a Salvation Army Officer currently working in the heart of Sydney at a church called Sydney Congress Hall. Previously she has also taught mission at the Salvation Army Booth College, church planted in inner-city Sydney, and worked as a chaplain in Paris. Lynette is passionate about creating real connections for faith and the contemporary world.

Lance Ford wrote the Foreword for this book. Lance is the co-founder of the Sentralized Conference in Kansas City, and has over two decades experience as a pastor and church planter. Lance holds a Masters degree in Global Leadership from Fuller Theological Seminary and is an adjunct professor at Biblical Seminary, Hatfield, PA. He is co-author of *Right Here Right Now: Everyday Mission for Everyday People* and *Missional Essentials: A Guide for Experiencing God's Mission in Your Life*. Lance recently published *Unleader: Reimagining Leadership . . . and Why We Must*. He serves on the National Leadership team for Forge America Missional Training Network.

Jamie Freeman is the lead pastor at H3O Church in Dee Why, Sydney—a new missional community cultivating a holistic expression of faith in order to reach Sydney's beach culture with the good news of Jesus. His servantship role includes providing strategic direction, team development, teaching, and coaching. He has served on staff at Gymea Baptist Church and Soul Survivor Ministries.

Contributors

Roger Helland is district executive coach of the Baptist General Conference in Alberta, Canada. His mission is to help establish and empower missional, disciple-making leaders and churches. Roger holds a DMin in missional leadership and spiritual formation from Trinity Western University and has over twenty-five years experience as a pastor, Bible college and seminary instructor, and denominational leader. He is co-author of *Missional Spirituality*, and author of *Magnificent Surrender*. For his blog and contact see: http://missionalspirituality.com.

Graham Hill is a practical theologian, teacher, and speaker, with twenty-five years experience in local church, denominational, and theological college servantship. He is a leader in the field of missional servantship and ecclesiology, and has a PhD in theology from the Flinders University of South Australia. Graham teaches at Morling College in Sydney, where he is Senior Lecturer in Applied Theology, Coordinator of Postgraduate Coursework and Ministry Research, and heads up the Centre for Leadership Studies. Graham travels widely teaching in churches, seminaries, and universities, and speaking at conferences. Graham is the author of *Salt, Light, and a City: Introducing Missional Ecclesiology*. For his ministry website and contact see: http://www.grahamhillauthor.com

Darrell Jackson has served as a Baptist pastor, a National Mission Advisor to the Baptist Union of Great Britain, as the Executive Researcher in European Mission for the Conference of European Churches, and more recently as the founding Director of the Nova Research Centre and Lecturer in European Mission, Redcliffe College, England. He graduated in 2009 with a ThD in missiology from the University of Birmingham. Darrell is a member of the Lausanne Movement's Leadership Council, a member of the WEA Mission Commission, and a member of the International Association of Mission Studies. He now serves as Senior Lecturer in Missiology at Morling College, Sydney.

Christine McGowan serves as an associate pastor at West Ryde Baptist Church, a multi-generational, multi-ethnic church in Sydney. Her passions and primary responsibilities include discipleship, preaching, and ministry to women. She holds a Bachelor of Ministry and is currently working towards her Master of Arts in Ministry at Morling Theological College, Sydney.

John McKittrick was born on 17 March 1903, in Glasgow, Scotland, and came to faith in Jesus Christ in 1924, while on a ship bound for Australia. He began serving with Sydney City Mission in 1933, and from 1933 to 1982 he gave himself completely to serving the mission of Jesus Christ (especially in Sydney), among the addicted, the vulnerable, the despised, the violent, the abused, and the forgotten.

Contributors

Grae McWhirter is the senior pastor of Blakehurst Baptist Church in the southern suburbs of Sydney where he has served for the past ten years. He is also Vice Chairman of the Morling College Board of Directors. Grae has an education background, having worked as a primary school teacher. He has a Bachelor of Ministries and is currently working towards a Master of Arts in Ministry.

Peter Ong is a cross-cultural missionary serving as a youth ministry coordinator with SIM (Serving in Mission) in Malawi. His main role is to assist in discipleship and training of youth leaders in the Africa Evangelical Church, SIM's partner church in Malawi. He has served in youth and young adult ministry for a number of years, primarily working with Australian-born Chinese youth and international students. His postgraduate research focuses on Malawian youth culture, and the implications of this culture for discipleship and servantship development in Malawi.

Simon G. Rattray was born and raised on the mission field amongst the headhunters of western Borneo. Simon is a disability advocate and Bible teacher who interprets culture from a Christian world view. Simon has served as a pastor and a church planter, and is the founder and team leader at the Jump Network, a consultancy that specializes in social research and servantship development for churches and corporations. Simon's brother Paul Rattray was instrumental in developing the notion of Sacrificial Succession with him. For his ministry website and contact see: http://www.thejumpnetwork.com.au

Christine Redwood is an associate pastor for Hornsby Baptist Church, Sydney. Her primary responsibility is the evening congregation, which consists mostly of young adults. She holds a Bachelor in Communications and a Master in Divinity, and is currently working towards her Master of Arts in Ministry. In 2010 she was the preaching intern for Morling College.

Steven Rodda is a pastor of fourteen years experience in Canberra and Sydney. He is currently senior pastor at Hornsby Baptist Church, a multi-ethnic, semi-urban church in the north of Sydney, where he has served for the last nine years. More recently, Steven has also been working with theological students and younger pastors to develop a resilient and down-to-earth approach to ministry for the long haul.

Paul Winch is serving with a college mission group called *Credo*, and since 1998 has been the Campus Director for the Australian Fellowship of Evangelical Students (AFES) at the University of Technology, Sydney. He grew up in West Papua, Indonesia, where his parents were missionaries, and now resides in the inner western suburbs of Sydney with his wife and three children.

Foreword

IF YOU ARE A parent you are familiar with the frustration of giving instructions to your children, only to be ignored. Furthermore, Mums and Dads know the frustration of being ignored, reiterating the instruction, and being ignored yet again. Inevitably the parent says to the child, "Did you hear a word I said?" When it comes to the subject of leadership I wonder how often Jesus must say this to us. As often as he said, "Whoever has ears to hear . . ." he must now be saying, "Obviously they don't have ears to hear what I was so clear on regarding hierarchy and leading."

Leadership has become the number one subject among those who are called as servants in Jesus's church. I do not believe it is an overstatement to call it an addiction, an all-out obsession. Despite the fact that in the entire New Testament "leader" is used eight times at most—by only one contemporary translation I have been able to identify—and "leadership" is not even used one time by most translations, leader and leadership are the prevailing concerns for the overwhelming majority of pastors and denominational guides today.

As soon as I saw the title of this book was going to be *Servantship* I could not wait to read it. The word "servant" is used across the entire New Testament—well over a hundred times. It is the favorite word the Apostle Paul uses to describe himself. It was the way our Lord described himself. This should give us all serious pause as to how we have arrived at the place we are in the church today. The idea of *servantship* has been swept under the *leadership* rug in the past few decades of church growth obsession.

In our search for identity we have grasped for that which Jesus shunned. We have fashioned and formed our identities as leaders—all the while Jesus and the writers of the New Testament clung to the identity of *servant* of the Lord. Indeed, we need the church to be led. The book you are reading now in no way says the church is not to be led. But it doesn't need *leaders*. As much of a contradiction as that sounds, stay with me. The church needs servants—women and men who lay down the staff and crown and pick up the towel and basin as they answer the bidding of the Lord and Master. What Jesus forbids is for us to have our identity shaped by the leadership culture of this world. He says clearly, "*Do not be called leaders; for One is your Leader, that is, Christ*" Matthew 23:10 (NASB).

Lance Ford
Author of *Unleader: Reimagining Leadership . . . and Why We Must*
Kansas City, Missouri

1

The Theology and Practices of Self-Emptying, Missional Servantship

Graham Hill

Do nothing out of selfish ambition or vain conceit. Rather, in humility value others above yourselves, not looking to your own interests but each of you to the interests of the others.
In your relationships with one another, have the same attitude of mind Christ Jesus had:

Who, being in very nature God,
did not consider equality with God something to be used to his own advantage;
rather, he made himself nothing
by taking the very nature of a servant,
being made in human likeness.
And being found in appearance as a human being,
he humbled himself
by becoming obedient to death—
even death on a cross!
Therefore God exalted him to the highest place
and gave him the name that is above every name,
that at the name of Jesus every knee should bow,
in heaven and on earth and under the earth,
and every tongue acknowledge that Jesus Christ is Lord,
to the glory of God the Father.[1]

---

1. Philippians 2:3–11.

Servantship

On May 1, 1957, the *Mission Herald* reported the following things about the servant ministry of John McKittrick,

> He was a boxer in his day . . . this gentle-spirited inoffensive servant of all, whose gracious presence has brightened many a sick room; whose faith has infused hope to the hopeless and comfort to the dying. Incidentally he tells me that his experience in the ring is useful occasionally if one of the guests of the City Night Refuge needs a firm hand. But strong-arm tactics are not the usual method employed by missionary John McKittrick in this most heart-breaking ministry of his. I quote the advice that he gives always to young Christian workers as his own rule of life: "Work hard and pray much!"
>
> Work hard? John McKittrick rises before five each morning; spends a hallowed time "in the secret place" and is at work soon after five, superintending the preparation of breakfast for his overnight guests. This, of course, is the famous McKittrick wholemeal porridge with bread and jam. At 9.30am the men leave and the missionary's day is spent replenishing stocks from the markets etc., and attending to the continual cleaning operations of the Refuge. At 3.30pm the men return again, waiting in the Assembly Room until their tea of stew and rolls is served before they retire at 6.30pm. One-hundred-and-fifty have breakfast, two-hundred-and-seventy are provided with tea, and one-hundred-and-six beds are provided each night. Quite a family, you will agree.
>
> Though religion is not handed out with the soup, John McKittrick assures me that each man is quietly spoken to about the Lord Jesus Christ and his power to lift the fallen, a Scripture booklet given to all. On Sunday evenings a gospel service is held in the dining room. I suggested that the work must be depressing and frustrating and his reply was characteristic of the man: "Over and over again when I have talked to the men about salvation and find they are interested only in receiving a shirt, a razor, a meal or a bed, I go to my room and fall on my knees to cry to God for the souls of these poor beaten men." Oh yes, he works hard and prays much, practicing always what he preaches.[2]

While so many grasp after leadership in church and society, not enough follow Jesus's model of servantship, as did John McKittrick. John took the words of Matthew 20:25–28 seriously, and sought to practice a servantship modeled after the Son of Man.

Here's my definition of *servantship*:

> Servantship is essentially about following our Lord Jesus Christ, the servant Lord, and his mission—it is a life of discipleship to him, patterned after his self-emptying, humility, sacrifice, love, values, and mission. Servantship is humbly valuing others more than yourself, and looking out for the interests

---

2. The *Mission Herald* reporting on the life and ministry of John McKittrick, as quoted in McKittrick, *Just One of God's Servants*, 38–39.

and wellbeing of others. Servantship is the cultivation of the same attitude of mind Christ Jesus had: making yourself nothing, being a servant, humbling yourself, and submitting yourself to the will and purposes of the triune God. Since servantship is the imitation of Christ, it involves an unreserved participation in the *missio Dei*—the trinitarian mission of God. Servantship is the movement from hierarchical leadership to radical service, from shallow pragmatics to dynamic theological reflection, from abstract theories to courageous practices, and from forgetfulness to transforming memory. Servantship recognizes, in word, thought, and deed, that "whoever wants to become great among you must be your servant, and whoever wants to be first must be your slave—just as the Son of Man did not come to be served, but to serve, and to give his life as a ransom for many."

This book seeks to make clear some of the important connections between leadership (I prefer the word *servantship*), servanthood, church, culture, and the mission of God. Although I have been in ministry for close to twenty-five years, it has only been recently that I have begun to appreciate the deep connections between our theologies of church, culture, servanthood, and the mission of God and his church. Lesslie Newbigin made these connections explicit. He understood that discipleship and witness are about partnership with Jesus in his servanthood and mission. "To share in the servanthood of Jesus means also to be his witness."[3]

In this book sixteen followers of Jesus describe the four movements of radical servantship. They detail the characteristics of servantship within each of these four movements.

At the end of each chapter there are *Individual and Corporate Servantship Practices* and *Questions for Reflection and Discussion*.

The four movements of radical servantship are:

1. From secular, hierarchical, and unbiblical notions of *leadership* to biblically based, self-emptying, downward missional, and *outwardly focused servantship*;

2. From shallow leadership and ecclesial *pragmatics* to life-giving, *dynamic theological reflection*;

3. From abstract *theories* to community-formed, locally-shaped *courageous practices* and stories;

4. From historical amnesia and spiritual *forgetfulness* to *transforming memory*, witness, and imitation.

These movements aren't sequential—they're simultaneous.

Let's take a moment to consider *the key characteristics of servantship*, which are developed in the following chapters by our sixteen contributors.[4]

---

3. Newbigin, "Jesus the Servant and Man's Community," 32.

4. In these summaries I intentionally use the words of these contributors, to represent their thought accurately and to do their contributions justice.

Movement One: From Leadership to Outwardly Focused Servantship

Servantship is the cultivation of *a deeply biblical imagination*. It is characterized by practices forged upon the imitation of Christ. It does not dismiss notions of *leadership* or *servant leadership* altogether, but it does evaluate these concepts as well as contemporary notions of power, authority, and control.

In chapter 2, Darrell Jackson considers the way in which "the Son of Man did not come to lead, but to be led: Matthew 20:20–28 and royal service." Jackson examines the biblical evidence for the notion of servant leadership. He shows how Scripture "redefines the concepts of greatness and status within the kingdom of God with reference to the hallmarks of service and humility." He demonstrates that Jesus "initiates a revolution of ruling and leadership" characterized by service and humility. Jackson writes, "Far from the throne-rooms and boardrooms, the "scum" of the earth (1 Corinthians 4:13) are exercising a ministry of service and humility that is frequently regarded with contempt, is typically accompanied by sacrificial suffering, yet which is capable of a revolution of cosmic scale, for it is a call to royal service in a kingdom against which the gates of Hades will not prevail (Matthew 16:18)."

Servantship cultivates a biblically informed practical theology of leadership that takes adequate account of our theologies of the church, servanthood, Christology, discipleship, eschatology, and the mission of God. Jesus re-conceives status in the kingdom of God as bonded service. Such service is accompanied by the forfeiture of social status and personal freedom, and characterized by utter reliance on the one to whom bonded service is being rendered. Christian servantship reflects the Spirit of Jesus Christ when it is saturated in the characteristics of servanthood revealed in Philippians 2:1–11 (and in other biblical treatments). The metaphor of servanthood, and our understanding of the mission of Jesus Christ, must shape our practice of Christian servantship. Only then will it truly be outwardly focused Christian *servantship*. In Jesus's church, those with spiritual authority and status need to be led by those in the congregation every bit as much as they need to lead them.

Servantship is the cultivation of *self-emptying or downward missional leadership*. It is the cultivation of self-emptied, outwardly focused discipleship. In Philippians 2:7 we read that Jesus intentionally "made himself nothing," he "emptied himself." In chapter 3, Roger Helland shows how servantship is movement away from selfish ambition, pride, and narcissism, and movement toward the same attitude as that of Jesus, intentionally emptying oneself, being a servant, humbling oneself, and becoming obedient to death. Self-emptied discipleship is oriented toward the mission of God, since the chief orientation of the self-emptied Son of God through the incarnation was *mission*. Helland helps us see that the ultimate characteristic of servantship is love leadership. I can serve people but not love them. However, I cannot love people and not serve them. The central point of the incarnation was love, and missional servantship is characterized by love. Missional servantship founded on *nothing leadership* is marked by love.

Servantship is the cultivation of *sacrificial succession*. It re-imagines the concepts of leadership and servantship through a theology of sacrificial succession. Only the sacrificial succession exemplified by Jesus will be sufficient, if the church is to faithfully pursue the mission and example of Christ. In chapter 4, Simon G. Rattray reveals how an incumbent ministry cannot stop with servant leadership alone—servantship takes the next step, which is sacrificial succession. The incumbent must establish their true understanding of servantship through mediatory sacrifice for their successors. It was the altruistic laying down of Jesus's life for his friends that most fully demonstrated this example. Thus, for a sacrificial succession to occur, a leader must lay down their leadership ambitions for the success of their successors. Rattray notes that a genuinely sacrificial succession cannot occur unless the sacrifice by incumbent for successor outweighs the sacrifice of successor for their succession. Servantship cannot be properly understood outside the context of sacrificial succession, which is the faithful application of Christ-centered servantship. The mediatory sacrifice of Jesus and his ongoing advocacy for his successors following a ministry of successor preparation are the perfect illustration of succession and the answer to the contemporary leadership crisis.

Movement Two: From Shallowness to Dynamic Theological Reflection

Servantship is the cultivation of *a trinitarian missional ecclesiology*. Outwardly focused servantship cannot be separated from a missional theology. Servantship remains superficial and inwardly focused without an authentic missional understanding of God and, as a consequence, of the gospel and the church. In chapter 5, Graeme Anderson demonstrates how this biblical and theological view of the church and its mission is formed around particular questions. The primary question is, "What is a missional vision of the church?" The secondary questions are: "What are current challenges to this vision?", "What is the foundation of this vision?", and "How might the church move towards this vision?" The foundation of a missional view of the church and servantship is a trinitarian missional ecclesiology that is shaped after the nature of the triune God. This trinitarian and missional imagination leads to a life of discipleship to Jesus, a truly incarnational church, and a Christ-imitating servantship. In chapter 6, Christine Redwood argues that the church and its leaders must approach worship, discipleship, and mission with recognition that their mission is part of the wider mission of God. God's mission must be the foundation and starting point for servantship, churches, and their mission in a rapidly changing world. Rather than conforming to the values and practices of surrounding cultures, servantship embraces dynamic, missional theological reflection.

Servantship is the cultivation of *a responsive posture within missional contexts*. It develops a practical theology of contextual responsiveness and proactive contextual engagement. In chapter 7, Lynette Edge sketches some key areas of cultural identity and change, before moving on to explore the biblical call to missional contextualization. Servantship understands that issues such as diversity, spirituality, relationship building, cultural dynamics, and social concern shape our missional responses and theology.

Servantship is the cultivation of *dynamic biblical and theological bearings and reflection*. In chapter 8, Paul Winch describes how the transformation to a missional-mode church and servantship is dependent on at least three key theological foundations—*missio Dei*, a *peculiar people*, and *integral discipleship*. *Missio Dei* reminds us that God is on mission—he is a missionary God. It is part of God's intra-trinitarian nature that he is sender and sent, the Father having sent the Son in the power of the Spirit to complete his work, and the Father in turn sending the Spirit through the Son. Missional-mode churches and leaders assume and expect God to be active in their community and society. An understanding of God's church as a *peculiar people* calls the church to be salt, light, and a city on a hill—recognizing their identity as a witnessing people who are, and always were, elected for service. Winch also emphasizes *integral discipleship*. Held together, a biblically informed view of humanity and of evil points to an integral discipleship, where becoming "more human" not less is what is required. Mission is the redemption of the world of which we are a part, not redemption from it. These three theological pillars work together to lay robust foundations for a missional mode of being for servantship, discipleship, and the church.

Servantship is the cultivation of *mission as organizing function*. In chapter 9, Grae McWhirter constructs a theology of the church that has mission as the organizing function. Churches and leaders who are authentically missional allow the mission of Jesus Christ to catalyze their worship, discipleship, community, and mission. These churches operate as unique reflections of their context and culture and, therefore, do not necessarily bear similarities in form and method to each other. However, the commonality of mission as the organizing function places such churches in the best position to impact their communities with the demonstration and proclamation of the lordship of Jesus. Quoting Michael Frost, Grae McWhirter shows us that the challenge to the missional community, the call to live an "incarnational life, to serve as Christ did, and to lead others into the risky vocation of following the *missio Dei*, is not a simple or easy task. It is a lifelong calling to service, sacrifice, selflessness, and effort. It will be worked out in neighborhoods and people groups around the world, and fuelled and led by the least likely saints."[5]

---

5. Frost, *The Road to Missional*, 21.

Servantship is the cultivation of *a radical post-Christendom recalibration.* The western world is rapidly changing, and the church in the west finds itself on the margins of post-Christendom cultures. In chapter 10, Peter Ong calls the church to a thoroughgoing missional recalibration in post-Christendom. In order for the church to be relevant and effective in the service of her King, it must reflect theologically on the mission of God and engage passionately in this mission within post-Christendom contexts. This post-Christendom missional recalibration is informed and shaped by our theology of the *missio Dei* and, subsequently, our theologies of Christ, culture, church, and the "last things." Ong asserts that the main challenge facing the western church is cultural captivity, and the western church must recalibrate itself in the light of the gospel and the *missio Dei*—if it is to become a missional church within post-Christendom, as evidenced by its rhythms, characteristics, practices, and servantship.

Servantship is the cultivation of *mission-shaped innovations.* In chapter 11, Jim Collins constructs a provisional ecclesiology for the emerging-missional church movement. Servantship creates an environment in which mission-shaped innovations thrive, and fosters churches that are Jesus-centered, praxis-focused, missional, and community-oriented, and that adopt holistic approaches to spirituality. Without diminishing concerns some have raised about emerging-missional theological innovations, Collins demonstrates why Christian leaders can learn from courageous emerging-missional responses to postmodern, twenty-first century, post-Christendom challenges. Mission-shaped innovations are necessary in the church's servantship approaches, structures, worship, discipleship, spiritual formation, mission, pastoral and ministry training, and so on. Collins says that such servantship-led innovations require clear, Jesus-centered biblical foundations.

Servantship is the cultivation of *community.* The church is called to be a radical, counter-cultural, alternative society. In chapter 12, Steven Rodda explains the importance of Christian leaders nurturing missional, Bible-shaped, storytelling, spiritual, connecting, and journeying communities. Only churches that endeavor to build innovative communities of disciples, rather than static institutions of tradition, will meet the challenges of rapid and discontinuous change in the twenty-first century. Openness, spirituality, storytelling, and vulnerability will enable the contemporary church to speak a language postmoderns understand. A missional identity shaped by the Scriptures rather than modern methodology, and a willingness to embrace approaches that are relevant and that emerge from the margins of society, will gain greater ground than a Christendom model. Rodda writes that churches and leaders need to learn the arts, outlooks, and practices of cross-cultural missions in their own settings. Our culture is rapidly changing, and we are called to be a particular kind of community that witnesses to the redemptive and transforming Person and gospel of Jesus Christ.

Movement Three: From Theories to Courageous Practices

Servantship is the cultivation of *courageous practices*. Chapters 13 through 20 provide space for seven Christian leaders to tell provocative stories—stories that illustrate how they are moving from mere theory to courageous servantship practice in their own settings. Graeme Anderson, Christine Redwood, Jamie Freeman, Christine McGowan, Lynette Edge, Paul Winch, and I tell stories about our own attempts at servantship.

Among other things, we learn from these stories that *servantship is*:

- Shaping missional churches and associations
- Proactively deepening discipleship
- Nurturing missional modes of discipleship and servantship
- Intrepidly exploring the possibilities within cultural shifts
- Welcoming multiculturalism, difference, and the "other"
- Fostering narrative and storytelling
- Disturbing the present and the status quo
- Challenging new and emerging social spaces (including cyberspaces)

These, of course, are just a few examples of leaders' efforts to nurture the concrete practices of Christ-imitating, outwardly focused servantship in their settings. The courageous practices of servantship are being demonstrated at this very moment across the globe. Many other stories might be told, if space were to permit.

Movement Four: From Forgetfulness to Transforming Memory

Servantship is the cultivation of *transforming memory*. In an age that easily forgets those who have gone before, servantship nurtures the kind of memory that transforms lives and communities. We remember our spiritual and servantship heritage. We remember the courage, sacrifice, passion, servantship, achievements, sufferings, and so forth of those who have gone before. We remember Jesus Christ—incarnate, crucified, resurrected, glorified, returning, and reigning. We remember the work of the triune God in human history. We remember the courageous acts of historical faith communities. We remember the example of fellow disciples who have gone before. We throw off, run with perseverance, fix our eyes, consider Jesus Christ, and, by his grace and Spirit, do not grow weary or lose heart. "Therefore, since we are surrounded by such a great cloud of witnesses, let us throw off everything that hinders and the sin that so easily entangles. And let us run with perseverance the race marked out for us, fixing our eyes on Jesus, the pioneer and perfecter of faith. For the joy set before him he endured the cross, scorning its shame, and sat down at the right hand of the throne of God. Consider him who endured such opposition from sinners, so that you will not grow weary and lose heart."[6]

Servantship is the cultivation of *compassionate care for the broken, despised, and vulnerable*. In chapter 21, John McKittrick provides a challenging example of a life dedicated to serving among the "least of these." As we remember others who have given up much to serve Jesus when he was hungry, thirsty, a stranger, naked, sick, or in prison, we pray that this memory might be transforming—that it might lead to a servantship that images Christ as it serves him. "For I was hungry and you gave me something to eat, I was thirsty and you gave me something to drink, I was a stranger and you invited me in, I needed clothes and you clothed me, I was sick and you looked after me, I was in prison and you came to visit me . . . Truly I tell you, whatever you did for one of the least of these brothers and sisters of mine, you did for me."[7]

Servantship is the cultivation of *imitation and witness*—the imitation of Jesus Christ, and the passionate, obedient witness to him. It is characterized by a transforming memory, that is, by a redemptive meditation on the Person, work, and mission of our Servant Lord. The goal of such meditation is imitation, submission, worship, and witness.

To help you contextualize this chapter in your own setting, Simon G. Rattray and I offer the following *practices* and *questions*.

Individual and Corporate Servantship Practices

- Most people have some awareness of the church's marginality and issues of cultural distance; initiate spaces that encourage the fermentation and articulation of your parishioners' feelings about their dislocation from secular community. Help them discover fresh ways to serve in those settings.

- Cultivate ways of engaging people in dialogue and discussion that bring to voice their experiences and locate them within the narrative of the *missio Dei*. Help them see how their servantship participates in the service of Jesus Christ and in the salvation history of the triune God.

- Frequently confront the church with God's broad agenda for mission, such as global suffering, local community injustices, and cultural inequality and segregation. Balance majority world incentive with local mission concern. Develop a culture of missional service.

- Through corporate and private prayer networks, identify and pray for the "men

6. Hebrews 12:1–3.
7. Matthew 25: 35, 36, and 40.

Servantship

and women of peace" (Luke 10), the "younger brothers" (Luke 15), and the "Samaria" (John 4) in the church's immediate cultural orbit.

- In your preaching, emphasize the Gospels and narratives over the exposition of abstract systematic theological concepts. Allow stories of service to inspire and catalyze contemporary servantship.

- Teach people the biblical significance of the incarnation beyond mere doctrine; emphasize the call to activism and service and social concern, teaching them how to reinterpret Scripture through a missional hermeneutic—and a hermeneutic of service.

- Concentrate on interactive preaching; do not merely experiment with dialogical over monological approaches but encourage members to be involved in the formation of sermons. Their stories may provide the best illustrations of lives and churches shaped by service in the way of Jesus.

Questions for Reflection and Discussion

- What are practical ways in which you can demonstrate *self-emptying* or *downward missional servantship*?

- Does your church have a *sacrificial succession* plan, and how does this plan reflect your biblical theology of servantship?

- Would you agree that for servantship to be sustained, pastors must insist upon allocating a portion of their time to specific community activities and activism endeavors, and make these conditional upon appointment or reappointment? Discuss your objections.

- Missionaries sometimes spend years serving and developing relationships before the first official service or "meeting." What are some of the implications of this statement for (1) how we adopt an attitude of listening to our community; (2) our assumptions about evangelism and mission; and (3) how we discern what our community is responding to . . . what are they resisting and why?

- Does your church have a *transforming memory*? Whose courage, sacrifice, passion, servantship, achievements, sufferings, and love do the people in your congregation remember, and take hope and inspiration from?

> It was just before the Passover Festival. Jesus knew that the hour had come for him to leave this world and go to the Father. Having loved his own who were in the world, he loved them to the end.
>
> The evening meal was in progress, and the devil had already prompted Judas, the son of Simon Iscariot, to betray Jesus. Jesus knew that the Father had put all things under his power, and that he had come from God and was returning to

God; so he got up from the meal, took off his outer clothing, and wrapped a towel around his waist. After that, he poured water into a basin and began to wash his disciples' feet, drying them with the towel that was wrapped around him.

He came to Simon Peter, who said to him, "Lord, are you going to wash my feet?"

Jesus replied, "You do not realize now what I am doing, but later you will understand."

"No," said Peter, "you shall never wash my feet."

Jesus answered, "Unless I wash you, you have no part with me."

"Then, Lord," Simon Peter replied, "not just my feet but my hands and my head as well!"

Jesus answered, "Those who have had a bath need only to wash their feet; their whole body is clean. And you are clean, though not every one of you." For he knew who was going to betray him, and that was why he said not every one was clean.

When he had finished washing their feet, he put on his clothes and returned to his place. "Do you understand what I have done for you?" he asked them. "You call me 'Teacher' and 'Lord,' and rightly so, for that is what I am. Now that I, your Lord and Teacher, have washed your feet, you also should wash one another's feet. I have set you an example that you should do as I have done for you. Very truly I tell you, servants are not greater than their master, nor are messengers greater than the one who sent them. Now that you know these things, you will be blessed if you do them."[8]

---

8. John 13:1–17.

Movement One

From Leadership to Radical Servantship

My friend Lance Ford has recently published a book called *Unleader: Reimagining Leadership . . . and Why We Must*. In this important book Ford helps us understand why we must reject hierarchical and self-serving models of leadership, and embrace an authentic servant leadership modeled, redefined, and recalibrated after Jesus Christ. In an article in *ChurchLeaders.com* Ford writes the following about the movement from unbiblical and toxic models of leadership to radical, Christ-like, missional servantship.[1]

> Our churches and ministry organizations are filled with "top level" leaders who personify the very attitudes and actions that Jesus clearly stated were not to be allowed in his tribe.
>
> *And Jesus called them to him and said to them, "You know that those who are considered rulers of the Gentiles lord it over them, and their great ones exercise authority over them. But it shall not be so among you. But whoever would be great among you must be your servant." Mark 10:41–43*
>
> Many of those who are reading this article have served in ministries with a leadership culture that has been formed with the very principles and practices of corporate America. Upper tier leaders treat lower tier staff members in controlling, sometimes demeaning, and even abusive ways and tones. The entire leadership culture within many evangelical churches carries the scent of the world . . . Jesus set aside his privileges, took on the status of a slave, and lived a selfless life. If we stake the claim that we are followers of Jesus then it means we follow his pattern. We follow Him—The Way. Any form of leadership that clings to privilege, eschews the posture of a slave, and lives selfishly is denying the true Christ. Churches with leadership cultures fueled by a privilege-taking few are being led by people that are not following Christ

---

1. Ford, *Unleader*; Ford, "Do Some Churches Suffer from Leadership Immunity?"

Movement One—From Leadership to Radical Servantship

> from the very epicenter of who he is . . . Jesus told us all that his kingdom is different. It is different from the world around us. And the way of leadership would be upside down—not just on paper but also in practice.

Servantship stands in contrast to the leadership principles and practices of the global corporate age. Servantship is shaped after the humility, sacrifice, and values of the suffering servant, our Lord Jesus Christ. Servantship is the cultivation of *a deeply biblical imagination*. There is no value in dismissing notions of *leadership* or *servant leadership* altogether. Yet we need to recalibrate and evaluate these concepts in the light of our theologies of the church, servanthood, discipleship, eschatology, Jesus Christ, and the mission of God. Our understanding of servanthood and its relationship to the mission of Jesus Christ must shape our practice of Christian leadership. Only then will it truly be outwardly focused Christian *servantship*. Servantship is the cultivation of *self-emptying* or *downward missional leadership*. It is the cultivation of self-emptied, outwardly focused discipleship. Missional servantship founded on *nothing leadership* is marked by love. Finally, servantship is the cultivation of *sacrificial succession*. A servant-disciple (we have become accustomed, possibly unhelpfully, to calling these "leaders") must lay down their ambitions for the health and missional vitality of their congregations and successors. Controlling, corporate, or Christendom models of leadership will not solve the contemporary leadership and missional crisis. We need a servantship formed within a deep biblical imagination and the authentic imitation of Christ. This servantship will be characterized by a self-emptying and downward missional commitment. It will evidence a sacrificial succession characterized by love, hope, and self-sacrifice. "Whoever would be great among you must be your servant." Authentic service is the first movement in radical servantship.

2

For the Son of Man Did Not Come to Lead, but to Be Led

Matthew 20:20–28 and Royal Service

Darrell Jackson

*"Servanthood with no rights or status is,
for the Christian, the height of greatness."*[1]

Several years ago the Christian organization for which I worked hired a new colleague. As we got to know her, we discovered that a cousin of hers was a footman at Buckingham Palace and, therefore, worked for Queen Elizabeth. It was probably the closest degree of separation with royalty that any of us would ever have and it was the talk of the office for quite some time. Unsurprisingly, we were never party to any royal tidbits or morsels of gossip—her cousin was clearly a discreet and loyal servant of the monarch.

Reflecting, years later, on her cousin's service as a royal footman, I now understand something of what it means to be in royal service. Let me explain. Royal footmen are as rare as hens' teeth. The chance of getting a job as a royal footman is probably one that many young men and women would jump at. For starters, it's going to look great on your resume. Secondly, it's an amazingly privileged position to be in. It's a job with high social status. In comparison, bankers, brain surgeons, and basketball coaches are relatively commonplace. Each of them would be lining up to swap stories and contacts with a royal footman. A royal footman could quickly come to be a person of influence

---

1. Goldsmith, *Matthew and Mission*, 148.

as a consequence of his position in royal service. But, and note this well, he or she remains a servant.

Now, the analogy is far from perfect, but it offers a potentially new way into a fifty-year-old conversation about a style of leadership that is known as "servant leadership." We'll return to the analogy towards the close of this chapter. Before that, however, I'm going to take a closer look at the way that Christian authors and leaders have mined the apparently endless seam of leadership theories and practices.

Christian Leadership and Christ's Lordship

It's a widely observed fact that there are numerous theoretical perspectives relating to leadership, whether secular or specifically faith-based.[2] A cursory examination of Christian leadership literature soon unearths an absence of any coherent theoretical grounding for the various discussions of Christian leadership. That is not to say that these authors have studiously avoided the use of Scripture as an appropriate place to begin. Clearly that is not the case. However, even here there seems to be little agreement about which passages or individuals might be the most helpful or suggestive: Abraham, Nehemiah, Moses, Samson, David, John the Baptist, Jesus, Barnabas, Paul, or one of several alternatives? An alternative is to develop a synthetic approach, drawing principles from the leadership displayed by the collection of biblical leaders I've just listed. Or should we instead prioritize the example of Jesus with what we might call a *Christocentric* approach? Frustratingly, none of these approaches is without its hermeneutical or exegetical challenges.

Despite these unanswered questions and uncertainties, the fact remains that many Christians find themselves in situations where they are required to exercise leadership and some of these are keen to exercise their leadership as a disciple of Jesus of Nazareth. What resources are there to help church and other Christian leaders struggling with this question?

The New Testament leaves little room for doubt that Jesus came to understand himself as fulfilling the messianic prophecies of the Old Testament. His self-identification as a servant, "I am among you as one who serves," underlines this simple observation. Running throughout passages such as Matthew 20:20–28; Mark 10:35–45; and Philippians 2:1–11 is a theme of service and we find these and other New Testament authors making frequent allusions and references to Old Testament passages describing a "suffering servant" (Isaiah 49–53). Verses from Isaiah 53 are, in fact, cited over thirty-five times in the New Testament.

However, the frequent use of "servant" by Jesus merely serves to deepen the apparent paradox whereby the early church arrived at its confession of Jesus as "Lord"

---

2. See Northouse, *Leadership*; Northouse, *Introduction to Leadership*; Yukl, *Leadership in Organizations*, for helpful summaries of the range of leadership theories in use.

(in the Greek this is the word *kurios*). This appears to have been used by the early church as an alternative to the oath of loyalty required by the imperial Roman rulers: "Caesar is Lord!" The early church readily embraced the Lordship of Jesus as a central feature of its liturgical life and worship. The Christology of the early church, what it believed about Jesus, implies a limitation of imperial authority over the lives of those who saw themselves as citizens of another kingdom. More obviously, it is a clear rejection of Caesar's claim to divinity. The early church worshipped Jesus, not Caesar, as the Lord; the true Lord of life whose authority extends over every aspect of human life.

The extent to which we may understand Jesus as both "Servant" and "Lord" lies at the heart of attempts to use his life and legacy as a resource for modern leadership theory and practice. The way that Jesus, the servant, reacted to the oppressive exercise of imperial Roman power has provided contemporary Christian leaders with a resource for framing their own understanding and practice of leadership. However, this is certainly complicated by the fact that, according to James Edwards, "At no place do the ethics of the kingdom of God clash more vigorously with the ethics of the world than in the matters of power and service."[3] In seeking to clarify leadership practices against this complex background, a cue has been taken from biblical passages dealing with power and service given the prominence over the last fifty years of the theory and practice of servant leadership. A brief discussion of the origin of this view of leadership will be helpful and to that task we now turn.

Servant Leadership and Robert Greenleaf's Work

The study of leadership typically oscillates between analysis and artistry. During periods of leadership crisis, the former is typically given more attention. During periods of leadership confidence, the latter tends to receive more attention. However, Robert Greenleaf (1904–1990) faced the uncertainties framing the period of his own career as an AT&T director of management research in order to develop a durable and creative approach to understanding the nature of leadership.[4] Greenleaf was a committed Quaker and introduced the concept of "servant leadership" into the discussion of organizational leadership during the late 1960s and 1970s on the back of a successful managerial career.

Robert Greenleaf's understanding of servant leadership emerged intuitively whilst reading the novel *Journey to the East* by Hermann Hesse in which the leadership of a mythical group of pilgrims is finally revealed to have been in the hands of their servant, Leo. Hesse's writings were heavily inspired by Buddhism and Greenleaf's Quaker beliefs readily accommodated insights from Hesse.

---

3. Edwards, *The Gospel According to Mark*, 325.
4. Greenleaf, *The Servant-Leader Within*.

After Robert Greenleaf's death, the consulting and publishing business he established has continued to attract attention within the not-for-profit and the commercial sectors. An edited collection of his private writings demonstrates clearly his essentially religious worldview.[5] Stephen Prosser notes the extensive use that Greenleaf made of the Old and New Testaments in his reflections.[6]

The attraction of Robert Greenleaf's work to practitioners and students of Christian leadership is obvious. He was comfortable with the language of spirituality and faith (albeit in a Quaker accent). Secondly, his attention to the servant nature of leadership resonates with Old Testament passages that make reference to the servant nature of the Messiah as well as to New Testament understandings of the person and ministry of Jesus of Nazareth. Thirdly, he was encouraged and invited to address his thinking directly to Christian organizations, including theological colleges and seminaries.

Robert Greenleaf found quite a number of willing and active collaborators within various Christian organizations and churches. Among these we might mention Professor Stephen Prosser and Bishop Bennett Sims.[7] Sims collaborated with Greenleaf in establishing the *Institute for Servant Leadership* in North Carolina. In Greenleaf's model, these Christian leaders and others like them found a convincing alternative to existing models which imagined a leader with superhero traits and capacities; models that elevated the individual leader with positional authority. These models were becoming increasingly difficult for some Christian leaders to adapt with authenticity and integrity. They consequently turned to Greenleaf's work on servant leadership for a more convincing expression of specifically Christian leadership.[8]

The use of the servant leadership metaphor by Christian leadership practitioners and writers, whilst mostly rooted in Robert Greenleaf's work, has continued to adapt and modify his insights. This has been undertaken without consistency of methodological approach, scriptural defense, and in the absence of a thoroughgoing philosophical or epistemological foundation.[9] So, let's take a look at a broadly representative sample of that work.

The Use of Servant Leadership Models and Greenleaf's Work by Christian Leadership Practitioners and Authors

Each of the authors surveyed here is concerned primarily with the dyad of leadership and service, given their acknowledged (and occasionally unacknowledged) reliance upon Robert Greenleaf's work. J. Robert Clinton offers only a brief discussion of

5. Fraker and Spears, *Seeker and Servant*.
6. Prosser, *To Be a Servant-Leader*, 5–7.
7. Ibid., 10; Sims, *Servanthood*, 11–12.
8. See Prosser, *To Be a Servant-Leader*, 7–9 for a brief overview of other Christian authors also influenced by Greenleaf.
9. Wallace, "Servant Leadership: A Worldview Perspective," 1.

servant leadership but it demonstrates the early engagement that Christian leaders in the late 1980s were beginning to have with Greenleaf.[10] Initial Christian responses to Greenleaf's work began with an exploration of the likely applicability of his model for specifically Christian leadership.[11] David Young makes direct references to Greenleaf and notes that he established close organizational links with Greenleaf's center.[12] J. David Lundy and Stephen Prosser refer to Greenleaf's work.[13] Indeed Prosser admits to being "inspired by what I read" and Efrain Agosto draws attention to Greenleaf's use of the Bible in developing his servant leadership model.[14] Although Scott Rodin and Lance Ford are critical of the concept of servant leadership, they both concede that no other leadership model has been "embraced as much by the Christian community as servant leadership."[15]

Several authors locate the dyad within the nature or character of God whilst others regard Jesus as a role model, an exemplar, a prototype, or the paradigmatic servant-leader who, in some instances, may even embody servant leadership.[16] The biblical passages they discuss in support of the concept of servant leadership include Isaiah 49–53; Matthew 20:20–28; Mark 10:35–45; Luke 22:24–30; John 13:1–17; and the epistle of Jude. From these passages, several lists of either qualities or principles of servant-leadership are derived. These include seven qualities found in the "suffering servant" chapters of Isaiah;[17] five principles drawn from Jude and a further nineteen aspects of a theology of biblical leadership;[18] eight biblical principles of servant leadership;[19] and the wider range of traits outlined by Stephen Prosser.[20]

Given the differing lists of qualities and principles it seems that discerning the "Who?" and the "What?" of a servant leader is a fraught exercise; arguably more of an interpretive art than an exegetical science. This requires further comparative work and is something for another day. Of more immediate concern is the way in which those authors writing about servant leadership outline and define the dynamic and relationship that exists between the notions of service and leadership. Several begin

---

10. Clinton, *Leadership Perspectives*, 74–76. See Clinton's reference to Kilpatrick, *A Theology of Servant Leadership*, on page 75 of Clinton, *Leadership Perspectives*.

11. Sims, *Servanthood*, 9–12; Prosser, *To Be a Servant-Leader*, 4–9.

12. Young, *Servant Leadership for Church Renewal*, 18.

13. Lundy, *Servant Leadership*, 97; Prosser, *To Be a Servant-Leader*, viii.

14. Ibid., 3; Agosto, *Servant Leadership*, 6.

15. Rodin, *The Steward Leader*, 81; Ford, *Unleader*, 85.

16. Sims, *Servanthood*, 13; Rodin, *The Steward Leader*, 34; Blanchard and Hodges, *The Servant Leader*, 13; Prosser, *To Be a Servant-Leader*, 7; Sims, *Servanthood*, 16; Lundy, *Servant Leadership*, 45–46; Agosto, *Servant Leadership*, 199; Russell, "A Practical Theology of Servant Leadership," 4.

17. Young, *Servant Leadership for Church Renewal*.

18. Wright, *Relational Leadership*, 11.

19. Kilpatrick, *A Theology of Servant Leadership*.

20. Prosser, *To Be a Servant-Leader*, 13–22.

with caveats such as "the Bible is not exactly a book about leadership,"[21] some explicitly avoid biblical exposition in the search for leadership terminology and ideas,[22] and at least one studiously avoids the use of the title "leader" on the basis that Jesus rejected all such titles.[23]

By this point, the astute reader may have begun to wonder whether there is in reality a coherent basis for carrying the discussion any further. If this were in any doubt, it only requires us to examine more carefully the way that the concepts of "servant" and "leader" shape each other, particularly when used in the hyphenated construct "servant-leader."

Early leadership theories argued that effective leaders demonstrate a number of universal *traits* and values. Among these, at least for Christian writers, service and stewardship are to be found.[24] Some writers see service as a *quality* of leadership and use servanthood and servant-leadership interchangeably.[25] Yet others have tried to distinguish the *role* of leader from the *identity* of servant.[26]

A sizeable cluster of writers tries to integrate the role of servant with that of the leader. Several commonalities exist within this cluster, including a core conviction that "leadership *is* an act of service."[27] Not all servants serve as leaders though they may become leaders and servant-style leading may become leadership.[28] Some from this group state it quite bluntly— "leadership is for servants, for serving not ruling"[29]— whilst others put it more prosaically, "Leaders who are servants first will assume leadership only if they see it as the best way they can serve."[30]

A smaller cluster of authors attempts to open up the existing evangelical status quo regarding servant leadership by calling for a thorough-going discussion of "servantship" free from its association with "leader."[31] If there is no willingness to do this, they insist, the concept of servant leadership will remain inevitably and unhelpfully paradoxical as a metaphor for Christian leadership. Few writers seem to acknowledge that the paradox rests in the hyphenation of two terms derived from quite different sources. Service and servanthood are well attested in various biblical passages and are evaluated there in an almost universally positive fashion. A growing and increasingly diverse body of theoretical literature, in contrast, shapes the practice of leader-

21. Agosto, *Servant Leadership*, 1.
22. Prosser, *To Be a Servant-Leader*, viii.
23. Ford, *Unleader*, 51.
24. Clinton, *Leadership Perspectives*, 16.
25. Sims, *Servanthood*, ix.
26. Ibid., 18.
27. Blanchard and Hodges, *The Servant Leader*, 12. *Emphasis mine.*
28. Young, *Servant Leadership for Church Renewal*, 19, 28.
29. Wright, *Relational Leadership*, 11.
30. Lundy, *Servant Leadership*, 230.
31. Ford, *Unleader*, 11.

ship. In addition to this, leadership has a troubled scriptural career and its practice is frequently regarded with ambivalence by the biblical authors. Servant leadership has been championed as one way of alleviating the impact of those critical voices. Whether it successfully continues to do this remains an open question.

> Over the past forty years the idea of servant leadership entered the church leadership conversation. But leaders could not bear the concept of "servantship" as a stand-alone term. "Leadership" had to be added to the equation. Being a servant is the form of leadership urged upon us by Jesus [and] the ethos of leadership is not a posture but a result.[32]

Attending to "servant leadership" is primarily a study of leadership whilst an investigation of service, or stewardship, is primarily a study of divine call.[33] This insight is primarily an insight into methodological approach or, if you prefer, our theoretical starting point. Discussions of servant leadership are primarily conducted by Christian authors with reference to the wider leadership literature whilst discussions of service and servanthood by them are mostly conducted with reference to the theological perspective of the biblical texts. Such a statement isn't intended to limit the potential value of leadership literature to leaders in the Christian churches or their related agencies. It's intended simply to reveal the complexity of integrating leadership theory and biblical theology. Several potentially destructive consequences flow out of this complex relationship where it is not given adequate or careful attention. These can all be found among the authors reviewed above and three of these follow immediately.

The first, though least common, consequence is illustrated in the work of Kenneth Blanchard who appears to commit to Jesus-*like* servant leadership yet who goes on to integrate it with his own model of *Transactional Leadership*. He sees in this an effective way of determining when the servant leader must choose to delegate, support, coach, or direct.[34] A second consequence is to underestimate the relevance of the "call to service" for all church and Christian leadership,[35] typically reserving it for individuals ordained to church ministries or those commissioned for overseas mission service. The third is to accept uncritically the theoretical grounding of servant leadership and merely unearth biblical passages that are alleged to support leadership models outlined elsewhere. This is the most common consequence and underscores the need for a more robust discussion of the biblical material that is regularly cited by Christians writing about servant leadership.

---

32. Ibid., 85–86.
33. Rodin, *The Steward Leader*, 76.
34. Blanchard and Hodges, *The Servant Leader*, 73–83.
35. Rodin, *The Steward Leader*, 76–83.

Movement One—From Leadership to Radical Servantship

Where Are the Servant Leaders in the Bible?

The most extensive biblical treatments of servant leadership include those of Walter Wright, who discusses the model with reference to the Epistle of Jude, and that of David Young who outlines six qualities of a servant leader that he claims to have distilled from the portrait of the suffering servant depicted in Isaiah chapter forty-nine onwards. Much of the biblical exposition found elsewhere is more cursory than these two instances. However limited the breadth or scope of the biblical exegesis or exposition, the conclusions may go on to gain unwarranted significance when they pass into what may be described as the "canon" of biblical reflection on servant leadership.

Robert Russell is another writer who tackles several biblical passages in a more than cursory fashion and his work deserves particular attention as we turn now to the Gospels of Matthew and Mark.

Robert Russell implies that there is a broader biblical witness to servant leadership than the number of biblical texts seems to actually warrant. He describes Matthew 20:20–28 and Mark 10:35–45 as "among the important scriptures" and discusses other passages (the Servant Songs in Isaiah, Luke 22:25–30, and John 13:1–7) as "among the important supplementary scriptures reviewed."[36] The rather disingenuous way he refers to his selection of passages conceals the fact that these passages pretty much exhaust the biblical passages that may be construed as referring to servant leadership, or at the very least to "service" and "greatness."

Robert Russell's reading of Matthew 20:20–28 and Mark 10:35–45 is informed by a prior commitment to servant leadership. "The primary purpose of this article is to examine the biblical texts that relate to the concept of servant leadership and thereby build a theological foundation for the leadership theory."[37] This is not necessarily an unhelpful way of reading these texts, but Russell adopts an unacknowledged hermeneutic shaped by this prior commitment and as a consequence his hermeneutical approach is insufficiently self-critical and results in some startling statements.

For example, at the outset of his textual investigation, Robert Russell confidently asserts that "the aforementioned passages directly address the issue of leadership. They clearly indicate that Jesus saw himself as a servant leader."[38] Russell does not substantiate these assertions from the text of the passages he examines; he simply states a conviction that he has already assumed to be the case. Elsewhere he concludes (with reference to the Isaianic passages) that it is in his *leadership* role that Jesus restores "both Jews and Gentiles to relationship with God through salvation."[39] This is a clumsy construction at best and theologically misleading at worst. The problem that lurks at the heart of Russell's statements here is that they sideline the contributions

---

36. Russell, "A Practical Theology of Servant Leadership," 1.
37. Ibid., 1.
38. Ibid., 4.
39. Ibid., 6.

of Jesus' service and sacrifice to human salvation. Writing about Mark 10, James Edwards observes, "The economy of God's kingdom is not based on power and control but on service and giving, for the latter are not only the ethics of the kingdom but the *means of redemption*."[40]

Robert Russell believes that Jesus' alleged demonstration of servant *leadership* in these passages is a response to his disciples seeking elevated status in the anticipated kingdom announced by Jesus. Reflecting on the interaction of Jesus with his disciples, Russell casually concludes that "Jesus acknowledges there would be exalted places of leadership."[41] The text of the passage actually says, *contra* Russell's misinterpretation, "to sit at my right or left is not for me to grant" (Matthew 20:23). It is probably more accurate to interpret this phrase as inferring positions relating to the coming judgment (compare this with Matthew 19:28; 25:31–46). To be on the right and left may indicate a position of honor, held by loyal individuals in royal service. It does not necessarily suggest a "leadership" position for James and John. Whatever it is that is sought by James and John, the right to grant these positions is clearly not held by Jesus, despite his authority as a purported servant leader. A less committed interpretation by Russell would have allowed a less constrained interpretation of the text of Matthew.

Central to Robert Russell's analysis of these passages are claimed to be "three critical components that support the concept of servant leadership."[42] In the first, according to Russell, Jesus identifies the oppressive nature of imperial Roman rule. In the second, Jesus equates the greatness of his messianic rule with humility and service. In the third, he identifies himself as a servant. Russell summarizes by insisting that these, taken together, "directly indicate that Jesus saw himself as a servant *leader*."[43] One does not have to reject Russell's identification of these central components in order to disagree with his conclusions relating to Jesus' servant *leadership*. Russell's singular focus obscures the fact that these texts clarify an understanding of *service and servanthood* whilst, secondly, lending undue weight to the view that they clarify an understanding of *leadership*. Indeed, the examples of "ruling" referred to in Matthew 20:25 are despotic and autocratic examples of imperial Roman rule. In this respect, if such examples of imperial Roman rule could be described as leadership in any way, they would be judged as *inauthentic* leadership, at least according to the conventions of most contemporary leadership theories.[44]

---

40. Edwards, *The Gospel According to Mark*, 321. *Emphasis mine.*
41. Russell, "A Practical Theology of Servant Leadership," 3.
42. Ibid., 3.
43. Ibid., 4.
44. See Northouse, *Leadership*, 384, and Bass and Riggio, *Transformational Leadership*, 15.

Movement One—From Leadership to Radical Servantship

Reading Matthew in Context

So, what might there be in these texts, especially Matthew 20:20–28, for church and Christian leaders looking for deeper insights into their leadership roles? An immediate point to note is that Matthew is writing as an acknowledged authority within the early church, as one of the evangelists, one of the witnesses to the good news about Jesus. He probably understood himself as a "servant of Christ" (as did Peter, in 2 Peter 1:1; James, in James 1:1; and Paul, in Romans 1:1). Matthew surveys the churches, which acknowledged his apostolic credentials, from a similar perspective to that of many contemporary church leaders. He is to be found among them, an elder with authority, and he frames the gospel narrative in a way that addresses what he sees as the immediate pastoral concerns for the churches of the first century.

Robert Gundry grounds his hermeneutic in the pastoral concerns of Matthew and suggests that Matthew is warning against the presence of false, authoritative leaders in the early church (Matthew 7:21–23; 23:1–36).[45] Matthew argues that ecclesiastical leaders must reject honorific titles (Matthew 23:8–10), they must humble themselves (Matthew 18:4; 23:12). Through service, as opposed to self-seeking, they must adopt the position of little people in the church (Matthew 18:3; 23:11). In other words, they must be meek, like Jesus, the persecuted teacher of righteousness who gave himself for others (Matthew 20:20–28).[46]

Barclay Newman draws attention to the *persecution* faced by Matthew's readers (10:16–23, 25; 20:22), which the disciples, including James and John, can't hope to escape given that their master has already suffered a self-giving death.[47] Graham Stanton suggests, on the other hand, that Matthew is writing in response to conflict in the *synagogue* between the followers of Jesus and those of traditional Judaism; a view adopted by most commentators.[48] J. Andrew Overman suggests that the focus is a *conflict within the church* due to recent arrivals provoking a crisis of authority and leadership.[49] Consequently, Matthew sets out "to cast further doubts about the dominant leadership" patterns being introduced.[50] Warren Carter bases his interpretation on the view that Matthew's primary context is one in which *imperial Roman rule* was being experienced as brutish and oppressive.[51] Matthew's Gospel is thus written to a church under the pressure of persecution and is a reminder of the need to remain loyal to the messianic rule of Jesus.

---

45. Gundry, *Matthew*, 6.
46. Ibid., 7.
47. Newman and Stine, *A Handbook on the Gospel of Matthew*.
48. Stanton, *A Gospel for a New People*.
49. Overman, *Church and Community in Crisis*.
50. Ibid., 20–21.
51. Carter, *Matthew and the Margins*; Carter, *Matthew and Empire*.

Noting the scholarly discussion, it may be worth heeding R.T. France's caution against too narrowly determining the purpose of Matthew's Gospel and recognize that this caution may be just as relevant when it comes to identifying the context for his Gospel.[52] It is likely that Matthew intended it to be read in any one of several diverse contexts, albeit with some common elements present in those contexts. Among the latter we may expect that imperial Roman rule, discrimination, and persecution, and questions of leadership within the community were enduring issues for the early church. We'll take these up as we begin a closer examination of Matthew and Mark without limiting too narrowly the focus or context for our investigation. That being said, the contextual commonalities sketched here do deserve serious consideration. The dialectic between imperial Roman rule and messianic rule is sufficient cause alone for explaining the generation of hostility and persecution against the Christian citizens and subjects of the Roman Empire. It's equally possible to speculate that a consequence of hostility towards the early church would be a growing uncertainty among the believers concerning leadership in the early church. They can be imagined wondering whether the leadership was sufficiently expedient in the stance it had adopted towards the imperial authorities. In such situations, the moral authority of leadership may typically emerge as an inevitable casualty.

Warren Carter's commentary is a clear and persuasive reconstruction of the imperial Roman context in which the early church grew and spread.[53] He argues that Matthew's Gospel carries a bold critique of the sovereignty of the Roman Empire, issuing a social challenge, with its alternative vision of community, and a theological challenge that outlines a vision of the coming sovereign rule of God. Commenting on Matthew 20:29, Carter writes, "Imperial rule . . . does not accomplish God's purposes. It subverts God's/Jesus' life-giving purposes and empire in bringing poverty, misery, political control, and, above all, death to God's agent."[54]

Jesus, in Matthew 20:25, "exposes the nature of the present [imperial system] as a world in which sinful, brutish, and death-bringing power operates."[55] As an alternative to this trend, "Jesus' resurrection shows that that is not the only way in which power can be used, that God's life-giving power overcomes abusive imperial power." Warren Carter then highlights the manner in which the claims of Jesus in Matthew 20:25 are radicalized through the use of "Lord" with reference to Jesus. This becomes an assault on the "lording" of the imperial powers. As the "Lord," Jesus has "life-giving authority" over judgment and other human authorities (Matthew 7:21–22).[56] For Carter, the "ruling over" of Matthew 20:25 is inevitably destructive and remains a pervasive theme throughout Matthew's Gospel.

52. France, *Matthew*, 119–22.
53. Carter, *Matthew and the Margins*; Carter, *Matthew and Empire*.
54. Carter, *Matthew and the Margins*, 403.
55. Ibid., 406.
56. Ibid., 403.

Movement One—From Leadership to Radical Servantship

Servants and Slaves with Status and Importance

Correctly understanding the dialectic of imperial rule versus messianic rule is key to interpreting the use that Jesus makes of μεγας ("great") and πρωτος ("first") in Matthew 20 and elsewhere. The Greek word μεγας (lit. *megas*) in this context can be taken to mean "a person of importance," normally used of a prince or governor. It is used less commonly as a contrast with "younger" (Luke 22:26) where it is used in the case of somebody who has "grown to maturity" (Hebrews 11:24). Intriguingly, Jesus describes John the Baptist by saying "among those born of women there has not risen anyone greater than John the Baptist," yet he states that even John is surpassed in greatness by μικρος ("little ones" or "small ones") who exercise humility and service in the kingdom of God (Matthew 11:11).

Service and servanthood are clearly major themes of Matthew 20, given its repeated references to διακονος ("servant") and δουλος ("slave"); its response to status and authority; and its pre-figuring of Jesus' messianic rule. Perhaps unsurprisingly therefore, few commentators seem as convinced as is Robert Russell that the text refers to servant *leadership*. Russell may not be wholly unjustified in seeing these elements as helping to define contemporary notions of leadership but it is false logic on his part to argue that leadership is therefore *the* theme of the passage.

Jesus uses "great" elsewhere in Matthew's Gospel (see Barclay Newman and Philip Stine for the following summary).[57] It is used to discuss importance and rank within the kingdom of heaven (18:1). To understand Jesus' use of "great," a change of attitude is required; a readjustment to how one understands authority and power (18:3). Those who are truly "great" will be as unconcerned about their status, rank, and importance as will the little children they are called to emulate (18:4, esp. NRV and TEV). Matthew writes pastorally, implying that the nameless members of the congregations that he knows well are the "great ones" in the kingdom of God.

The mother of James and John shows respect for Jesus as one of the "greats," with power to "promise," "grant," "give orders," or even "command" (Matthew 20:21). Matthew's use of προσκυνειν (Matthew 20:20) indicates petition or submission before one of high authority.[58] This heightened sense of dramatic expectation merely serves to underline the apparently deflationary response from Jesus that he does not possess the authority sought by the mother.

Of course, this may be intended to deflect her use of the imperative "Grant!" or "Declare!" (Matthew 20:21). The tone of deference she has shown in Matthew 20:20 recedes and reveals clearly that she and her sons fail to understand the nature of God's empire. In it there can be no domination, prestige, and importance, only service and humility.[59] Jesus states bluntly that he cannot promise, grant, give orders, or com-

---

57. Newman and Stine, *A Handbook on the Gospel of Matthew*.
58. Gurtner, *Jesus, Matthew's Gospel and Early Christianity*, 56.
59. Carter, *Matthew and the Margins*, 402.

mand.⁶⁰ This authority belongs to the Father alone and the Father *will* reserve places of honor for the truly "great." Furthermore, we should expect to see some people sitting in the seats of greatness who are currently not free to make decisions on their own behalf, let alone on behalf of any followers, for among the "greats" will be servants and slaves (Matthew 20:23). In matter of fact, greatness may be as much on display in the glorious accomplishments of death as much as through the glorious accomplishments of life (Matthew 20:28). Messianic humility and service carry a commitment to the "giving of one's life as a ransom for others. It points up the extreme to which service may attain—and did."⁶¹

With the shift in language of Matthew 20:27, "great" becomes "first" and "servant" becomes "slave." This illustrates another tricky aspect of interpretation. "Great" and "first" are generally interpreted as shorthand for leadership by Robert Russell and other servant leadership writers. However, this assumes that greatness and status in these passages can be sufficiently redeemed and, therefore, sought after aspects of the general social order. Greatness and status are thereby located firmly in the secular world (of imperial rule) whilst service and slavery continue to be seen as reasonable, or desirable, only within the realm of the kingdom of God. If that is true, then authentic greatness or leadership that serves and empowers (Matthew 20:26) can be contrasted with inauthentic rule, or leadership, which is self-serving and authoritarian (Matthew 20:25). The first may be welcomed as messianic with the second being dismissed as imperial.

However, we have suggested that an essential dialectic in this passage exists in the tension between the messianic rule of Jesus and the imperial rule of Caesar. That suggests an alternative interpretation of the way that Jesus intends us to understand "greatness." If "great" and "first" are to be primarily understood with reference to the messianic rule, then what is required is a new way of talking about "greatness" and "status." This requires us to redefine greatness and status with reference to his messianic rule and to our life in the messianic community. Quite simply, there can be no biblically authentic definition or expression of greatness and status that moves beyond the twin domains of "service" and "humility." To put it another way, all there is to be said about Christian leadership can be said with reference to just these two words. Humility and sacrificial service are not steps to greatness; they *are* the greatness that is the hallmark of the kingdom of God, of Jesus' messianic rule.

This insight is vital for it is a necessary way of avoiding the temptations to lust and power that accompany all forms of imperial leadership and ruling (Matthew 20:21,24,25). Mark's use of κατακυριεύειν ("exercising authority") in Mark 10:42 is, for example, used in the sense of "gaining mastery or power over others," "to subdue," or "to function as a despot."⁶² The only alternative narrative for negotiating authentic

---

60. Ibid.
61. Gundry, *Matthew*, 404.
62. Edwards, *The Gospel According to Mark*, 325.

positional authority "comes from Jesus' own biography" (Matthew 20:22). J. Andrew Overman notes that Matthew's retention of hierarchical language may be ironic, given that wherever it is used it provokes jealousy and rivalry.[63] He does not thereby imply that Matthew rejects hierarchy, leaders, or authority out of hand, but he reminds us that the use of honorific titles (as was common in Jesus' day) is to be rejected (Matthew 23:8–12). We can only understand Matthew's eschewal of such titles if we understand this: even the title of "Rabbi," used only twice by Matthew of Jesus, is found both times on the lips of Judas.

Royal Servants of the Messianic Household

In referring to the Gentile rulers' abuse of power (Matthew 20:25), Jesus re-conceives status in the messianic community or kingdom (20:21) as bonded service (20:26). Such service could be entered into willingly with the prospect of seeking release from a debt owed in the fullness of time. However, it was accompanied by the forfeiture of social status and personal freedom. It also implies utter reliance on the one to whom bonded service was being rendered. Thus, if it is service in the kingdom, rendered to the messiah, it is not inconceivable that we are to understand this as "royal service." The concealed "drive for power" inherent in the ambition for money, fame, and influence is beyond the reach of the bonded slave.[64] Status in the messianic community, though granted to servants and slaves with no prospect of imperial or commercial success, is nevertheless the status of royal servant.

The messianic rule of Jesus in the kingdom, of God, is one that honors him with the status of κυριος ("Lord"). Christopher Wright points out that it is a transliteration of the Hebrew *Adonai,* used when reading references to *YHWH* in the biblical text.[65] In this respect, the concept of "Lord," when used of Christ, would appear to be a reference to his divinity rather than a reference to any leadership that he might be understood to have exercised.

Warren Carter suggests that the human experience of slavery (lived at the social margins between the point of entry into slavery and the hoped for manumission or release) parallels the Christian self-understanding of life as a slave. The experience of a slave, despised by others, is one through which great honor could accrue to the slave by his or her association with a great household. This has its parallel in the final promise of "eschatological vindication." The slave metaphor applies to all disciples; there are to be no "masters" claiming ownership over members of the messianic community. Instead of hierarchy there is equality. "Enslavement to God, not domination of others, marks their identity and the social structure of this community which embodies God's

---

63. Overman, *Church and Community in Crisis*, 288.
64. Stott, *Calling Christian Leaders*, 40.
65. Wright, *The Mission of God*, 108.

empire."[66] Matthew characteristically describes the disciple as a learner, over whom Jesus has all authority.[67] Service and humility in the royal community of the Messiah are patterned on a Messiah who does not insist on being served (Matthew 20:28). His service to others, beyond the point of death, involves their being sprung free from captivity to the bondage of sin.

Commenting on Mark 10, James Edwards notes that, "All servants of Christ serve, some may lead."[68] Servants appear to be pre-eminent in the kingdom of God because the sole function of a servant is to give and giving is of the essence of God. Edwards continues, "the ideas that Jesus presents regarding rule and service are combined in a way that finds no obvious precedent in either the OT or Jewish tradition" and this despite the references in Isaiah 49 depicting a "servant to rulers."[69] In attempting to find parallels with the linking of service and ruling (see Matthew 20:26–7) Warren Carter directs our attention to the Hellenistic tradition of the ideal king as the servant of his people, exemplified in Plato's *Republic*.[70] He also notes that the school of philosophers known as the Cynics used the idea to describe a philosopher-ruler—described in Seneca's *Epistles*.

Jesus as the humble servant of God is the model for the Matthean communities. They are the "little ones," the "meek," the "poor in spirit," and the "unlearned ones" whose cause will be vindicated at the future coming of the Son of Man himself (Matthew 25:31–46). Matthew maintains a certain tension between Jesus as the humble and meek "chosen servant" and the glory of his future coming as Son of Man and judge. Stanton suggests that all forms of Christian leadership ultimately seem to sit somewhere in the pivot between humility and glory.[71] We have tried to suggest, rather, that the more authentic forms of Christian leadership sit at the pivot between humility and *service*.

Some Tentative Implications for Missional Leadership

In choosing the title "Your Will Be Done: Mission in Christ's Way," the 1989 Conference on World Mission and Evangelism of the World Council of Churches pointed to new images of mission that eschewed power and violence.[72] In preparing for this conference, evangelicals issued the Stuttgart Statement which acknowledged that mission in Christ's way required "humility" on the part of "unworthy servants, earthenware vessels" entrusted with the priceless treasure of the gospel.[73]

66. Carter, *Matthew and the Margins*, 404.
67. Gundry, *Matthew*, 594–97 on Matthew 28:18–20.
68. Edwards, *The Gospel According to Mark*, 325.
69. Ibid.
70. Carter, *Matthew and the Margins*, 403.
71. Stanton, *A Gospel for a New People*, 381.
72. Wilson, *The San Antonio Report*; Samuel and Hauser, *Proclaiming Christ*.
73. Ibid., 212.

Movement One—From Leadership to Radical Servantship

I assume that Christian leadership is a helpful way of describing the nature and function of cooperative activity by individuals working towards the common goals they share as royal servants within the community of the Messiah, Jesus the Lord. My insistence that "leadership" concepts are absent in Matthew 20:20–28 is not to be taken that I have a problem with Christian leadership *per se*. Nor do I believe that the metaphor and practice of servanthood is of no value to contemporary leadership. On the contrary, if we are to adequately deal with the temptations towards the abuse of power and authority, these texts are vital to a proper appreciation of the contribution that Christian virtues (humility, patience, kindness, diligence, chastity, abstinence, and liberality) can make to a contemporary understanding of authentic, moral leadership.[74] Understanding this will allow the development of a biblically informed, practical theology of leadership that takes adequate account of service and humility.

Of course, this discussion has left unexamined the detailed discussion of how the concepts of service and humility shape the contemporary practice of Christian leadership. What it has sought to do, instead, has been to investigate what the mission of Christ, especially through his service of others, means for a contemporary discussion of Christian leadership models. As Craig Keener argues with reference to Matthew 20:20–28, ". . . in Philippians 2:1–11 the evangelists treat their audiences to this summary of Jesus' mission . . . to provide an active model for Christian living."[75] Understood in this sense, the notion of missional service and humility extends across the totality of the Christian life and experience, including those areas where the Christian may be required by circumstances, or other people, to exercise leadership, individually and corporately.

If Christ came to serve others in humility, rather than to be served, then perhaps we might at least countenance for a moment the notion that, in like fashion, he did not come to lead, but to be led. In turning the metaphor on its head in this way we may see more readily the subversive intent of Jesus in John 13:1–17.[76] This is the impact intended by Stephen Cottrell's turning of familiar metaphors upside down. He pictures leadership differently by referring to the need to "jump off the bandwagon," to "hit the ground kneeling," to "let the grass grow under your feet," to "state the obvious," to "spoil the broth," to "count your chickens before they're hatched," and to "reinvent the wheel."[77]

By redefining the concepts of greatness and status within the kingdom of God with reference to the hallmarks of service and humility, Jesus initiates a revolution of ruling and leadership. This is a vital insight for those who lead churches and Christian organizations. It is also a much-needed corrective for the kind of evangelistic leadership that is frequently little more than imperialism, building "human empires instead

---

74. See Wallace, "Servant Leadership: A Worldview Perspective," 2.
75. Keener, *A Commentary on the Gospel of Matthew*, 488.
76. Russell, "A Practical Theology of Servant Leadership," 6.
77. Cottrell, *Hit the Ground Kneeling*.

of the kingdom of God."[78] This all-too-frequent experience has led some missiologists to call for new metaphors of mission and missional leadership that shun imperial images in favor of those describing "God's eternal reign."[79]

Far from the throne-rooms and boardrooms, the "scum" of the earth (1 Corinthians 4:13) are exercising a ministry of service and humility that is frequently regarded with contempt, is typically accompanied by sacrificial suffering, yet which is capable of a revolution of cosmic scale, for it is a call to royal service in a kingdom against which the gates of Hades will not prevail (Matthew 16:18).

Individual and Corporate Servantship Practices

- Look at the Christian leadership books on your self. Make a list of those influenced by servant leadership models and Greenleaf's work. Write some notes about the influence of these writings on these books.

- Read Isaiah 49–53; Matthew 20:20–28; Mark 10:35–45; Luke 22:24–30; John 13:1–17; and the epistle of Jude. Have your ministry team discuss what these passages tell us about servanthood, discipleship, and ministry.

- In a preaching series, focus on the themes in these passages and their implications for your church and its mission in the world.

- Spend time learning about the discipline of service. Engage in this learning individually and with others. Consider how this discipline shapes your discipleship to Jesus.

Questions for Reflection and Discussion

- What new images of leadership and mission does the church need if we are to eschew power and violence?

- How do Christian virtues (humility, patience, kindness, diligence, chastity, abstinence, and liberality) contribute to a contemporary understanding of authentic, moral leadership?

- How do we develop a biblically informed, practical theology of leadership that takes adequate account of service and humility and Christian virtues?

- How does redefining the concepts of greatness and status within the kingdom of God, with reference to the hallmarks of service and humility, initiate a revolution of ruling and leadership?

---

78. Stott, *Calling Christian Leaders*, 41.
79. Skreslet, *Picturing Christian Witness*, 15–18.

3

Nothing Leadership

The Locus of Missional Servantship

ROGER HELLAND

[He] made himself nothing.[1]

Leadership is a hot topic these days. There are legions of books, seminars, courses, and graduate degrees offered in both secular and Christian leadership circles. I typed in the word "leadership" on Amazon.com only to learn that the word appears in over eighty-nine thousand book titles. There's everything from "Monday Morning Leadership" to "Primal Leadership" to "Leadership and Self-Deception" to "The Leadership Secrets of Santa Claus!" Let me suggest another type of leadership, "Nothing Leadership." What's nothing leadership? It's the type of leadership compressed into one word in one verse concerning one Person in Philippians 2:7. We could also call it "self-emptying" or "downward missional" leadership. The Greek word *kenosis* for "made himself nothing" in Philippians 2:7 simply means, "to empty." It's a mystery whose meaning is not comprehended. But understand that mystery is not the absence of meaning, but the presence of more meaning than we can comprehend.

Of what did Christ empty himself? He emptied himself of *himself*. Notice Paul wrote that Jesus *made* himself *nothing*. He made an intentional and willful choice. To become a *nothing* leader means I will seek to have no selfish ambition, practice humility toward others, cultivate the same attitude as that of Jesus, intentionally empty myself, be a servant, humble myself, and become obedient to death. Quite a challenge! The chief orientation of the self-emptied Son of God through the incarnation was

---

1. Philippians 2:7.

mission—to become an obedient servant of God, a servant who would die on a cross! Look at the fuller context of Philippians 2:3–8,

> Do nothing out of selfish ambition or vain conceit. Rather, in humility value others above yourselves, not looking to your own interests but each of you to the interests of the others. In your relationships with one another, have the same attitude of mind Christ Jesus had: Who, being in very nature God, did not consider equality with God something to be used to his own advantage; rather, he made himself nothing by taking the very nature of a servant, being made in human likeness. And being found in appearance as a human being, he humbled himself by becoming obedient to death—even death on a cross!

During the last sixty years, numerous cultures have been transitioning into what many scholars call *postmodernity*—namely, the cultural quest to move beyond modernity. At its heart, modernity focuses on *reason*; postmodernity focuses on *relationship*. Authenticity is a core value for postmoderns. Postmoderns are not simply attracted to leaders who lead by position, power, and prestige, or lead through hierarchy, rank, or control as business or spiritual CEOs or CFOs. Len Hjalmarson writes,

> Postmoderns reject authority in position in favor of authority in relationship. They do not buy into hierarchies, and they tend to assign authority only when it is earned. They don't respect leaders who are "over" but not "among." This aligns with the NT teaching on the priesthood of believers and Jesus's teaching that "the greatest among you must be the servant of all."[2]

The postmodern context is ripe for *nothing* leaders who are among us as servants. I interviewed a twenty-seven-year-old pastor of student ministries. Leslie is a sharp, intelligent, and deeply spiritual postmodern leader. I asked her what she felt were some of the key qualities that she would admire and want to be as a leader in the postmodern context. Here is her reply:

> Postmodern leadership means that I shift from walking in front of you to walking beside you, shoulder to shoulder. When I try to be "the leader," the students don't follow me. My leadership has to be about relationship leading to respect leading to trust. We must share life together, connecting, and helping students belong, believe, and become, in that order. I must not be afraid to allow people to wrestle with faith issues and explore deep theological questions like, "Could I ever stop being a Christian?" Narrative is important. Sharing life together is important. Spiritual leadership is more informal.

I also interviewed another postmodern young adult. Steven is a twenty-one-year-old university student who understands the modern–postmodern conversation. He said, "My brain is like a dysfunctional family trying to run a convenience store."

---

2. Hjalmarson, "Post-Modern Possibilities," 11.

Movement One—From Leadership to Radical Servantship

When I asked him what he felt were the characteristics of a good leader he would follow or would be attracted to, he replied,

> Honesty—the postmodern assumption is that we are going to be lied to and be deceived. Authenticity and integrity. Someone who is iconoclastic, meaning, someone like John Stewart of the "Daily Show" who is anti-institutional, who does what he believes is right and will do what is right rather than do what he is expected to do, and willing to challenge the status quo. Someone who is fearless. Will speak on the same level as me and not talk down to me, treating me as an equal, as a friend, relating to me; one who is a servant leader who will lead with me on a mission.

Servant Leadership

In 1977, Quaker management consultant Robert Greenleaf published a foundational secular leadership book entitled *Servant Leadership*.[3] Greenleaf developed his ideas while he was an executive at American Telephone and Telegraph (AT&T), and lectured at such prestigious schools as Massachusetts Institute of Technology (MIT), Harvard Business School, and Dartmouth College. The subtitle is very telling: *A Journey into the Nature of Legitimate Power and Greatness*. Greenleaf reveals that he got his idea of servant leadership from reading Hermann Hesse's *Journey to the East*.

Peter Block expands the theme of servant leadership by replacing leadership with *stewardship*—where leaders are willing to be accountable for choosing service over self-interest.[4] Greenleaf's book has influenced many Christian writers on leadership who point to its validity for missional church leadership. Robert Webber remarks,

> This recovery of servant leadership in the church is not just incidental. It is *missional* in nature. The church is not just a "saving station," it is a place for spiritual formation, for healing, for the formation of a countercultural community, a locality where people live under the reign of God. When relationships are structured on mutual servanthood and not power, the world sees a glimpse of heavenly reality. Jesus's lordship of structures calls us to live and work with each other by the servant leadership, which Jesus modeled. He was not the CEO of the disciples; he was their servant.[5]

However, leaders can serve in a functional way, as a style or as a strategy, not genuinely based on a self-emptying missional foundation. *Nothing* leaders will be *servant* leaders. They are servants first rather than leaders first. Those served willingly consent to give power to the servant leader. Nothing leaders are servant leaders

---

3. Greenleaf, *Servant Leadership*.
4. Block, *Stewardship*.
5. Webber, *Younger Evangelicals*, 149.

who empty themselves in their leadership. They will not assert their own ambition or interests but will be servants in their attitudes and actions toward others. True servant leaders will empower others and help them succeed. They will not rule over people. I wonder if we should concentrate less on "leadership" and more on "servantship?" The word "servant" is used far more than "leader" in the Bible.

The Gospel of Mark highlights the idea of *nothing* leadership expressed in self-demoting missional service. Notice what's important to Jesus and the missional goal of his servantship,

> You know that those who are regarded as rulers of the Gentiles lord it over them, and their high officials exercise authority over them. Not so with you. Instead, whoever wants to become great among you must be your *servant*, and whoever wants to be first must be *slave* of all. For even the Son of Man did not come to be served, but to serve, and to give his life as a ransom for many.[6]

Whoever wants to become great must be a *servant*. The Greek word used here is where we get the words *deacon* and *minister*. The Greek term has associations with waiters at table and of servants to a king. "And whoever wants to be first must be *slave* of all." The word *slave*, also translated as *servant*, is the same word used in Philippians 2:7. Slaves are servants whose service and mental models are not based on rank, position, power, or control. Stacy Rinehart writes,

> This classic passage in Mark brings us to a fork in the road called leadership. The fork gives us two directions, or models, and each will lead us to entirely different outcomes. One route relies on power, authority, and control. The other path—one that follows in Christ's footsteps—is a road of humility and of putting others first . . . Each of us has a mental model of leadership, and that model defines how we operate, how we go about ministry. A leadership model that rests on the power inherent in the position will eventually hinder the task of releasing and empowering others for ministry. A servant leadership model helps equip and liberate others to fulfill God's purposes for them in the world.[7]

It's one thing to practice servant leadership. It's quite another thing to be a servant leader, where serving others is the essence of leadership. The missional goal of Jesus was to give his life as a ransom. This isn't based on a corporate or military chain of command and control but a subversive self-emptying humility based on love and obedience to the missional reign of God. Jesus only did what he saw his father doing. His food was to do the will of him who *sent* him and to finish his work.[8] Greenleaf taught, "Good leaders must first become good servants." Jesus implies it's OK to be great. How we become great is the issue. As Bill Hybels wrote, we must *descend into greatness*. That descent is by the way of love.

6. Mark 10:42–45. Emphases added in italics.
7. Rinehart, *Upside Down*, 29.
8. John 4:34.

Movement One—From Leadership to Radical Servantship

Love Leadership

What's the quality that will ultimately characterize me as a servant/slave leader? Henri Nouwen expresses it for me:

> Here we touch the most important quality of Christian leadership in the future. It is not leadership of power and control, but a leadership of powerlessness and humility in which the suffering servant of God, Jesus Christ, is made manifest. I, obviously, am not speaking about a psychologically weak leadership in which the Christian leader is simply the passive victim of the manipulations of his milieu. No. I am speaking of a leadership in which power is constantly abandoned in favor of love. It is a true spiritual leadership.[9]

The ultimate characteristic of servant leadership is love leadership. I can serve people but not love them. However, I cannot love people and not serve them. The central point of the incarnation was love. God so loved the world that he gave his son. God is love. *God is a servant.* When I was in Bible College I read a little book by Francis Schaeffer entitled *The Mark of the Christian*. I expected some deep theological exposition on the mark or secret of what it really means to be a Christian. I was surprised to discover that the mark of the Christian is love.

Missional servantship founded on *nothing leadership* is marked by love. Christian leadership is *relationship* not just function. Love guarantees godly relationship through spirituality. We are spiritual to the degree that we love. The great commandment to love God and neighbor is both the substance and structure of a *missional spirituality*, which seeks to embody and express God's love from the inside out.[10] Spirituality is *relational*. Notice the following texts,

> The only thing that counts is faith expressing itself through love.[11]

> But the fruit of the Spirit is love, joy, peace, patience, kindness, goodness, faithfulness, gentleness and self-control. Against such things there is no law. Those who belong to Christ Jesus have crucified the sinful nature with its passions and desires. Since we live by the Spirit, let us keep in step with the Spirit.[12]

Leadership that's spiritual (marked by the Spirit) comes from leaders who love. A while ago, my wife Gail and I were out in our backyard working in her flowerbeds. I was installing some wood borders for a new flowerbed that required sawing, nailing, and dumping in new soil. Normally, I don't like yard work. While I was working, she queried, "Why are you doing this? I usually have to talk you into something like this."

---

9. Nouwen, *In the Name of Jesus*, 63.

10. For a discussion of this theme with theological foundations and practices see my book: Helland and Hjalmarson, *Missional Spirituality*, co-authored with Len Hjalmarson.

11. Galatians 5:6.

12. Galatians 5:22–25.

I replied, "Well, I'm doing this for you. Instead of only doing what I want, I need to do what you want. That is part of love." I also recently sold a car that I loved and she didn't and bought a car that she would love and I might! When I put her interests above my own and serve her needs, I practice love leadership.

When it comes to my job as a district pastor, I'm called to love our pastors and churches. If my mental model is a top-down, power-based, "follow my vision and respond to my agenda" type leader, then I'll have to expend enormous amounts of energy trying to control people and align the structures accordingly. It's even possible that "visionary leadership" or so called "vision casting" can be just another way to use dominance or power that will incite people to follow me or implement *my* vision.[13] If my mental model is a servant/love leader, I'll spend energy cultivating shared ownership of mission, and help others succeed as I direct them to the reign of God and the indwelling Spirit, for the sake of others. Our mission is to establish and empower missional, disciple-making leaders and churches. The result of effective missional servantship is *trust*, the basis of all relationships, forged by love. It doesn't matter how compelling our vision, strategy, or ministry sounds or looks on paper. If we lack the hidden element of trust—working quietly like a computer operating system—our leadership won't run well. Nothing leaders will inspire trust. Patrick Lencioni shows how the absence of trust is the foundation for a dysfunctional team.[14] We must love others with leadership integrity.

Leadership Integrity

Kevin Mannoia, in his book *The Integrity Factor*,[15] writes that leadership performance flows out of the unseen foundation of our *being*. Using Moses and Jesus as models of spiritual leadership, Mannoia offers his thesis that the process of building integrity between who one is and what one does is the way to grow as a spiritual leader. He calls this "leadership formation" centered on "the integrity factor"—a balance between identity and performance.

For Mannoia, the unseen foundation of leadership is like the 80 percent invisible part of an iceberg under water, which gives stability to the 20 percent visible part of an iceberg above water. If I intentionally concentrate on my unseen foundation of *character*, that will have a dramatic influence on my *conduct* as a leader. I will always behave out of my identity. For Mannoia, the central unseen foundation and identity for effective Christian leadership is self-emptying humility and servantship described in Philippians 2:5–11. Spirituality and leadership must intersect in the soul and practices of the missional leader, where the leader must give up any inadequate human resources

---

13. I am indebted to Leonard Sweet for this insight: Sweet, *Summoned to Lead*, 17.
14. Lencioni, *The Five Dysfunctions of a Team*.
15. Mannoia, *The Integrity Factor*.

to gain spiritual ones. Alan Nelson remarks, "The closer we get to understanding that our power as spiritual leaders comes from God, the more secure we'll be allowing us to fulfill servant roles as leaders."[16]

Permit me to be brutally honest. There are times when I feel like I am playing the pastoral game: put on a happy face, be nice to everyone, exude passion for God, cast vision for spiritual formation and mission, show up at key events so people will notice I am there "doing my job being a leader." Then conceal the fact that sometimes my thought life, my family life, and my spiritual life seem like the cavern full of snakes that Indiana Jones (Harrison Ford) fell into in the movie *Raiders of the Lost Ark*. Then I read books like *A Tale of Three Kings*,[17] and realize that I can live a very double life—one that's "spiritual" and another that's "carnal." I can be a so-called good pastor but still be a bad person in need of spiritual formation or leadership formation.

I feel confident, however, that there are times when my identity and my performance are aligned. There's freedom and fulfillment. But there are times when I have to preach or teach or give spiritual counsel in my office or lead a meeting with a group of leaders only to wish that I could stay home and forget the charades, knowing that my life and doctrine don't match.[18] How can I be on mission with Jesus if my walk does not match my talk, if my life message doesn't embody the gospel message? I must become the change I want to see in others.

It all boils down to a very practical and personal Christology that orients the process of spiritual formation (sanctification). "Spiritual formation," as Jeffrey Greenman defines it, "is our continuing response to the reality of God's grace shaping us into the likeness of Jesus Christ, through the work of the Holy Spirit, in the community of faith, *for the sake of the world*."[19] Spiritual formation is trinitarian, relational, and missional. The Spirit will shape me into a servant, patterned after Jesus, for the benefit of other people—this is a *missional spirituality*.

Lately, I've been reflecting on what it means to be a *nothing* leader who must discover how to experience Philippians 2 in practical and intentional ways where I surrender *my* ambition and *my* agenda. I'm contemplating what it means to be a slave and servant to my family, to my friends, and to my flock. It's not about *doing* servant leadership stuff but *being* a servant leader. It means serving subversively in kingdom ways, like the parables of yeast or the mustard seed. Great leadership in God's kingdom comes from great servantship. God exalted Jesus for being a self-emptied servant who surrendered to God even to the cross. Notice the word "therefore,"

> Therefore, God exalted him to the highest place and gave him the name that is above every name, that at the name of Jesus every knee should bow, in heaven

---

16. Nelson, *Spirituality and Leadership*, 64–65.
17. Edwards, *A Tale of Three Kings*.
18. Cf. 1 Timothy 4:16.
19. Greenman, "Spiritual Formation in Theological Perspective," 24, italics mine.

and on earth and under the earth, and every tongue acknowledge that Jesus Christ is Lord, to the glory of God the Father.[20]

This is quite an astonishing reward, therefore, for someone who *made himself nothing*.[21] Reflect for a moment on the notion that Jesus abandoned his eternal place in glory to become implanted in the womb of a young woman in Israel, to grow into a tiny baby inside her womb for nine silent and solitary months and then is born. He then nursed on her breasts as an infant while he soiled whatever kind of diapers they used then. He grew up as a boy and as a teenager (imagine Jesus Christ as a fifteen year old!), and then he finally became a young adult man who was shamefully crucified on a rugged Roman cross. How much faith and focus would it take to navigate such a profound path of self-emptying, service, and surrender? Because of what Jesus did, I must die to entitlement and privilege, self-centeredness and self-governance.

Nothing leaders must establish themselves with a deeply *theological* grounding in Christology—the person and work of Christ. They will practice a "magnificent surrender" to Christ Jesus as Lord, their model of missional servantship. They will *receive* (welcome) him but will also continue to *live* in him.[22] There's a deep fascination in seminaries and summits these days with *modernist* American secular business, military, and sports models of leadership, often based on power and vision. However, the world and the church need secure and spiritual leaders who lead from the inside out—from spiritual *presence* rather than from organizational *position*. Christian leaders can accomplish church tasks without a foundation of a missional spirituality, but *the spiritual life is the surrendered life* to Christ Jesus as Lord.

This requires that we reform and reorient our *identity* in Christ to that of a slave and a servant before that of a Christian leader or pastor. The moment we play the "I'm the leader" card, we aren't. Scott Bessenecker remarks, "The words *doulos* (slave) or *diakonos* (waiter, servant, or one who performs menial chores) show up in every single letter attributed to Paul in the New Testament as pictures of what it means to follow Jesus."[23] The New Testament speaks to *discipleship* and *servantship* enormously more than it speaks to so-called "leadership." Granted, the New Testament uses the word leader and mentions the gift of leadership. However, anything that we label or teach as "Christian leadership" or even "servant leadership" must place Jesus Christ as the central model and means of what this is and what it looks like. We must *adopt* the missional leadership and servantship of Jesus and the New Testament before we *adapt* whatever leadership there is in the business and corporate worlds.[24]

---

20. Philippians 2:9–11.

21. Philippians 2:7.

22. Colossians 2:6. For a discussion of this with theological and practical reflections through the book of Colossians, see my book: Helland, *Magnificent Surrender*.

23. Bessenecker, *How to Inherit the Earth*, 96–97.

24. For a book-length treatment of these issues, see: Ford, *Unleader*.

Movement One—From Leadership to Radical Servantship

Servantship and virtue are first, then leadership. Leaders can lead from the dark side because fear, control, performance, ambition, or power, drives them. How do we become leaders who are self-emptied, broken, *nothing* leaders who resist the temptation to be powerful? How do we avoid the temptation to be "super-apostles" who have voracious ego needs?[25] Henri Nouwen suggests, "Power offers an easy substitute for the hard task of love."[26] We must shift from a paradigm of being "professionals" to that of being servants and slaves.[27] Perhaps the common clergy title should also be senior servant rather than Senior Pastor! All God's people are being built into a spiritual house, chosen and ordained to the holy and royal priesthood of the believing community, who live as *servants* of God.[28]

Let me leave you with a story. Arturo Toscanini was a famous Italian symphony conductor, specializing in the works of Beethoven. One night in Philadelphia, Pennsylvania, Toscanini conducted the Philadelphia Symphony Orchestra in a program that included the Ninth Symphony—one of the most difficult pieces to direct. It was so majestic and so moving that when the piece was completed, the audience stood for round after round of applause. Toscanini took his bows again and again. He turned to the orchestra; they bowed. The audience continued to clap and cheer. The orchestra members themselves were smiling and clapping. Finally, Toscanini turned his back to the audience, and spoke only to the orchestra. He said, "Ladies and gentlemen—I am nothing. You are nothing. Beethoven is everything."[29] May I announce to my readers, "Ladies and gentlemen. I am nothing. You are nothing. Jesus is everything." I really do want to practice *nothing leadership*, because it really is something—wouldn't you agree?

Individual and Corporate Servantship Practices

- Approach your role from the paradigm of servant first and leader second.
- Daily, in your relationships with others (especially those of a lesser state), foster the same *attitude* of Jesus Christ—namely, *make yourself nothing* and *humble yourself*.
- Seek to put the interests and success of others above your own, starting with your family.
- Foster and choose to lead by *spiritual presence*, without power, coercion, or control.

---

25. 2 Corinthians 11:5–6.
26. Nouwen, *In the Name of Jesus*, 59.
27. Mark 10:41–45.
28. 1 Peter 2:4–16.
29. Cited in Tenney, *Prayers of a God Chaser*, 135.

- As a daily rule of life, orient yourself and resolve to love the Lord your God from all your heart, soul, mind, and strength, and your neighbor as yourself.
- As a daily rule of life, seek to practice a "magnificent surrender" to Christ Jesus as Lord and the missional reign of God in your life, *for the sake of others.*

Questions for Reflection and Discussion

- Read Philippians 2:3–8 in two translations and consult at least two commentaries. What insights into "nothing leadership" emerge from your study of this passage? How does Christology inform your understanding of how "nothing leadership" is the locus of "missional servantship?"
- Read Mark 10:42–45 in two translations and consult at least two commentaries. What insights into "servant leadership" (*servantship*) emerge from your study of this passage? What are the main points of contrast between the rulers of the Gentiles and the disciples and Jesus?
- How do the dynamics of leading by control, power, and position, as well as leading without the integrity factor between identity and performance, affect your capacity to be a servant leader who cultivates trust? What is the alternative and how?

4

Sacrifice and Succession

Rethinking Servantship and Missional Community

SIMON G. RATTRAY

One of the greatest issues facing leadership today is the mushrooming Generation Y or Millennial population, not only in terms of their personal and social challenges, but also the weakness in certain contemporary leadership approaches, in particular, the capacity to hand over leadership to them. The following project will be presented in two stages. The first addresses the Generation Y dilemma, and discusses a number of significant factors and practices which have contributed to the current leadership succession crisis in both corporations and in churches, arguing for a re-imagining of the concepts of *Servant Leadership* through *Sacrificial Succession*. The conclusion stresses that both sacred and secular research affirm the need for more sacrificial approaches. However, only the sacrificial succession exemplified by Jesus will be sufficient.

The second section is written for those pastors who have a deepening desire to see missional transition take place. More specifically, I appeal to those church leaders who seek to empower and release the next generation of leaders. Not only is our situation calling for an intellectual reprogramming around a fresh posture of servantship, it is also imperative that leaders, especially church leaders, realize the essential importance of the time and place where servantship must now be modeled, practiced, and authenticated. The final part of this discussion will examine the critical tension between a private and a corporate call to ministry and include a number of practical suggestions to ensure that the church remains faithful to its mission.

A Personal Note to Leaders

Becoming someone who practices sacrificial servantship is not easy as it runs counter-clockwise to many of the widely held assumptions and practices of leadership in Christian circles today. Much of the contemporary leadership literature criticizes leaders who interpret power as the securing of position and control. Yet conclusions still encourage leaders to excel in their own capacity and skills (gifts) whereas succession is all about sacrificing self-interest and investing in the skills and capacities of others. Max Dupree makes the point that "we need to care more about faithfulness than success, about the potential of communities than individual accomplishment."[1] I advise a number of large corporations both Christian and secular. I have also served as a pastor and as a church planter, so I am well aware of and sensitive to the looming challenges many leaders face, particularly pastors who are trying to implement cultural change at a congregational level. I realize that not all corporate leaders or pastors will have the permission or the freedom to apply all of these findings and suggestions within their leadership settings. But my goal and passion is to encourage every leader to find fresh inspiration and hope as they pursue their calling, taking courage from the Apostle Paul who with unmistakable certainty pronounced, "God made me a servant" (Eph 3:7, Col 1:25).

Part 1: Servantship and Sacrificial Succession

"A society grows great when old men plant trees whose shade they know they shall never sit in."—Greek Proverb

A Crisis of Millennial Proportions

In the last ten years an increasing interest in the topic of leadership has emerged. In both the corporate world and the world of the church the resurgence of leadership as a dominant theme is not surprising. Historically, people turn to leaders in times of crisis. The last decade has been marked as a period of rapid change and widespread uncertainty, leading to serious cultural and sociological anxieties.[2] The most notable contributors have been 9/11 and the subsequent war on terror, and the appalling examples of leadership and management that led to the near demise of the world banking system in 2008. Educators and theorists are struggling for clarity about how leadership should now be exercised in society and institutions.[3]

---

1. Quoted in Banks and Ledbetter, *Reviewing Leadership*, 132.
2. Roxburgh, *Missional Map-Making*, 24–32.
3. Behrstock and Clifford, *Leading Gen Y Teachers*, 8.

Movement One—From Leadership to Radical Servantship

Two issues have become of great concern to researchers: the first is the burgeoning Generation Y or Millennial population (those born between 1980 and 1994) and the second is the absence of adequate leadership modeling by the Baby Boomer generation (those born between 1945 and 1964)—in particular, ineffective succession planning. Unlike Generation X (those born between 1965 and 1979), Millennials are not as interested in debating truth—they want to change the world. In fact Millennials have more in common with Baby Boomers. This is why they have been referred to as "boomers on steroids." So why are Boomers finding it so difficult to include Millennials in leadership and pass on leadership to them? The following enquiry will, in part, attempt to answer this question.

Defining Terms

Before beginning an evaluation, we need to form some definitions. For the purposes of this review, *succession planning* is defined as follows: a structured process involving the identification and preparation of a potential successor to assume a new role. Andrew Garman says, "By the term 'structured,' succession is referred to as a process having some reliable structure and/or custom, thereby excluding from the definition the more ad hoc or 'just-in-time' identification of successors."[4]

The term *Sacrificial Succession*, coined by Paul Rattray, can be defined as the direct consequence of the faithful application of Christ-centered servantship. Paul Rattray says, "A ministry of servanthood and sacrificial succession are unnatural. They stand in sharp contrast to the dynastic and corporate successions commonly observed as succession norms today in many churches and ministries. Sacrificial Succession is the genuine outworking of servant leadership through the sacrificial handover of leadership by incumbent for successor success."[5]

Millennials and the Challenge for the Church

Whilst people are living longer, the birth rate is surpassing older generations—in some countries at an alarming rate. Today the average age in China and India is mid-twenties. In the next fifteen years, over half of the world's population will be twenty-one years old or younger. Christian research has unearthed some alarming statistics. Timothy Tennent, president of Asbury Theological Seminary, suggests that in the US now, only 7 percent of Millennials have any Christian orientation. It is sobering to note that this is only 2 percent away from Millennials being classified as an *unreached* people group or a *lost tribe*.[6]

---

4. Garman and Glawe, "Succession Planning," 2.
5. Rattray, "Sacrificial Succession," 8.
6. See Timothy Tennent's blog here—http://timothytennent.com/blog/.

Millennials and the Challenge for Servantship

The name Jeffrey Nielsen has become synonymous with Generation Y research. In *The Myth of Leadership: Creating Leaderless Organizations*, Nielsen argues that our understanding of leadership is, for the most part, a myth that justifies the significance we place on our inherited concepts of management and control. Nielsen wasn't the first to propose the move from rank-based to peer-based leaderless thinking in organizational management but he has certainly done so with more preciseness and provocation than most before him.[7] Some Millennials have argued that the revolution in Egypt in February 2010 is an example of Nielsen's theory as it was successful because it had no leaders—only coordinators of bottom-up energy.[8] However, these findings do nothing to prove that there was no leadership. Robert J. Banks makes the point that such conversations merely reaffirm the elusiveness of leadership; "Leadership often expresses itself through a variety of forms, some of which are not easily discernible."[9]

Whilst there is insufficient evidence to argue that Millennials necessarily endorse views such as those espoused by Nielsen, it is clear that they are discouraged by command-and-control or rank-based leadership, as they often quickly move on from jobs where these attitudes prevail. This is one reason why many organizations are being left with an ageing work force. Jasmine Boatman's research concludes that less than 18 percent of organizations currently have a workable plan to fill the gaps in their leadership pipeline. When asked why, time and again they cited a lack of focus, strategy, and the absence of a succession plan.[10]

Boomers and the Succession Vacuum

The American researcher George Barna argues that far too few young pastors are entering the ranks of church leadership. Reasons include: (a) more Builder pastors are often staying on to pastor well into their eighties; (b) an unusually high share of Boomer pastors are not retiring or planning to retire in their mid-sixties; and, (c) most importantly, Barna's findings suggest that succession planning is a glaring weakness in most Protestant denominations.[11] If a succession occurs it is often reactive rather than proactive.

---

7. Nielsen, *Myth of Leadership*, 14–20.
8. Nikravan, "Ask a Gen Y," http://blog.clomedia.com.
9. Banks and Ledbetter, *Reviewing Leadership*, 17.
10. Boatman and Wellins, "Global Leadership Forecast," 36.
11. Barna, "Gracefully Passing on the Baton," 6.

Dependency on Importation

So why are Christian Boomer pastors so poor at handling succession? Historically, succession is not a topic that has been taught well. Most churches are still highly dependent on the importation of pastors from denominational pools, mostly occupied by Builder and Boomer pastors. Whilst some individual churches and ministries have long prepared and empowered leaders from within the organization, it is not a common practice. In his substantial review of corporate leadership Jim Collins concluded, "Ten out of eleven of the 'good to great' leaders came from inside the company."[12]

The Power Inertia

It is often stated that Millennials are selfish narcissists, but this all depends on perspective. George Barna argues that "Whilst Boomers are likely the richest generation the world has ever encountered, they are also its most selfish. Despite being brilliant strategists and tacticians, Boomers find it extremely difficult to hand over leadership. The sticking point is their core value: power. Most Boomers have no intention to relinquish it."[13]

The Decline of Social Significance

As fewer people associate Christianity with their world view, pastors have more to lose. David Fitch says, "Outside of the church, pastors no longer enjoy significance within society like they once did. As ageing pastors struggle to interact meaningfully with their social environment, they tend to retreat from change. This has contributed to an internal battle developing among clergy in the West, which has led to a significant psychosocial hurdle."[14] Fitch's conclusions may help to explain why some pastors have distanced themselves from the emergent/missional conversation, suspicious of empowering younger leaders who may advocate such an agenda.

The Erosion of Self-sacrifice

Many Christian denominations in fact have succession plans. However, the research concludes that: (a) plans are either insufficient for the context; (b) they are rarely implemented appropriately; or (c) they are influenced by dynastic and corporate

---

12. Collins, *Good to Great*, 32.
13. Barna, "Gracefully Passing on the Baton," 8.
14. See David Fitch's article here http://www.reclaimingthemission.com. For more on this see Fitch, *The End of Evangelicalism?*

succession principles.[15] Increasingly leadership studies are recognizing the need for more altruistic (sacrificial) approaches. Howard M. Bahr argues that the concept of sacrifice used to be a dominant theme in social scientific theorizing. But he says, "It is now so neglected that recent work speaks of the need for a recovery of sacrifice. The absence of a language of sacrifice and love limits our ability to give voice to our experience, and the professional neglect of these concepts diminishes our understanding of the processes they name."[16] Bahr goes on to say, "The anthropologist Victor Turner identified sacrificial love as the 'basal principle of all human relationships.' Following Turner's work, anthropologist Merlin Myers was convinced that one's willingness to sacrifice—or rather, the experience of having sacrificed, and been sacrificed for—was the essential glue of a moral society."[17]

A Preoccupation with Servanthood not Sacrifice

To quote Paul Rattray again,

> Many Christian leaders demonstrate genuine servant leadership throughout their ministry careers. These leaders honestly work hard to put the needs of their followers before their own. They treat their teams and their parishioners with respect and love. However, when it comes to the handover of leadership to successors, most of these leaders' successions are in crisis, with the dynastic handover to kin or a corporate reshuffle the most likely outcome. As I pondered these successions, I questioned why so many of these leaders who are serving sacrificially, by "serving rather than being served," as Jesus commanded in Matthew 20:28a, are failing to sacrificially hand over leadership to their successors as Jesus did by "giving his life as a ransom for many" as the second part of this verse so clearly emphasizes.[18]

Servant Leadership and the Mystic Impulse

Part of this dilemma could be what Jack Neiwald calls "Pelagian inward-directedness." For Neiwald, Servant Leadership theory, in particular the influence of Robert Greenleaf, stresses the interior mental and spiritual processes of the leader as the means by which outward change is affected. He argues "servant posture often presents itself as the means by which both the leader and the follower find their human fulfillment, apart from the transforming power of Jesus Christ. Servant leadership seems to say that it is the process of choosing servanthood over alternative pursuits that affects the

---

15. Singh and Krishnan, "Self-Sacrifice and Transformational Leadership," 261–71.
16. Bahr and Bahr, "Families and Self-Sacrifice," 1231.
17. Quoted in ibid., 1232.
18. Rattray, "Sacrificial Succession," 14.

life-changing experience of individuals and organizations. In true existentialist fashion, this choosing renders the leader's existence authentic, and such existence, whatever it may mean, is alone efficacious for organizational well-being."[19] Under such an arrangement, it makes no difference whether our guide is Jesus, Gandhi, or Buddha. Robert Greenleaf, though a Quaker, acknowledges that his inspiration for Servant Leadership theory arose from the work of Herman Hess, who was a self-confessed Eastern Mystic.[20] In his 1951 book *Christ and Culture*, H. Richard Niebuhr prophetically concluded that existentialism will continue to shape leadership language well into the future.[21] The true altruistic nature of Christ's leadership is indeed missing from much Christian leadership literature. The research affirms that succession planning is not uncommon. What are uncommon are incumbents: (a) handing over leadership in a timely manner; (b) personally preparing successors; (c) sacrificing leadership for successors; and (d) advocating for successors post succession.[22]

The Sacrificial Succession of Jesus

Within the servantship of Jesus we see all four of the principles mentioned above occurring intentionally. The example of succession that Christ teaches is clearly brought to bear in Matthew 20:1–28 and the other Gospel parallels: Mark 10:17–45, Luke 22:24–28, John 13:1–15, 14:26, 15:9–17 and 26–27. In the parable of the Vineyard Workers (Matthew 20:1–16), the first principle of Christ's succession plan emerges. In verse 16, Jesus teaches that the choice of successors should not be based on performance and tenure. On the contrary, "the last will be first and first will be last." The recognition of Paul as the apostle to the Gentiles, despite his "unnatural birth" (1 Corinthians 15:8–9), is evidence of this truth in practice. Three key phases of sacrificial succession are clearly identifiable in the servantship ministry of Jesus.

Ministry of Preparation

As the time for the Lord's departure draws closer, Jesus reminds his disciples of his impending death for a third time. Here we see Jesus clearly preparing his successors for their succession prior to it occurring. It is crucially important to recognize the fact that Jesus makes the timing of the servantship transition clear. Jeffrey Sonnenfeild notes that a glaring weakness within corporate successions is that the transition

---

19. Niewold, "Beyond Servant Leadership," 126.
20. See Greenleaf and Spears, *Servant Leadership*, 28.
21. Niebuhr, *Christ and Culture*, 26.
22. For a deeper examination see, Harrison and Fiet, "New CEOs Pursue their Own Self-Interests," 308–14.

phase is often very unclear.[23] In John 15:15, Jesus explains this successional truth by considering his successors as friends rather than servants. Jesus makes everything he has learned from his Father known to them. Peter's acceptance as leader by the early church and Jesus's apparent reference to him as successor (Matthew 16:18–19, John 21:16), reinforce this important pre-succession truth.

Following the example of Jesus, a sacrificial pre-succession ministry involves preparing successors, appointing a successor, and predicting the timing of a succession well in advance of it occurring. Many potential successors serve sacrificially yet with selfish ambitions. This often occurs because systematic successions are corporately inclined and modeled on papal "conclaves."[24] In Matthew 20:20–23 and Mark 10:35–40, the mother of James and John asks Jesus if her sons may receive favored treatment in his succession. Jesus rejects the request and in verses 25–28 he warns against the worldly standards seen in the corporate and dynastic successions of the day. Also, see Mark 10:42 and Luke 22:25.

Ministry of Sacrifice

An incumbent's ministry cannot stop with servant leadership alone. The incumbent must establish their true understanding of servantship and example through mediatory sacrifice for their successors. It was the altruistic laying down of Jesus's life for his friends (John 15:13) that most fully demonstrated this example. Thus, for a sacrificial succession to occur, a leader must lay down their leadership ambitions for the success of their successors. This is the principle missed by much of the leadership literature. The spiritual and practical truth underpinning Jesus's sacrifice for us is maintained through sacrificial succession and authentic servantship. We are saved by grace not works (Ephesians 2:8–9), meaning that sacrificial successors are more than mere servant leaders who "give up to go up"—a phrase coined by John Maxwell.[25] Incumbents willingly and expressly sacrifice their leadership for the success of their successors. A genuinely sacrificial succession cannot occur unless the sacrifice by incumbent for successor outweighs the sacrifice of successor for their succession.

Ministry of Advocacy

The final aspect of sacrificial succession modeled by Jesus is his advocacy on our behalf through the ministry of the Holy Spirit. The example here is that Christ voluntarily limits himself so that he can work through us. Jesus promises his disciples that he will not leave them to face things alone (John 14:18) and, through the advocacy

---

23. Sonnenfeld, "Good Governance," 112.
24. Konrad and Skaperdas, "Succession Rules and Leadership Rents," 623.
25. Maxwell, *21 Irrefutable Laws of Leadership*, 225.

of the Holy Spirit, he will continue to remind them of his instructions (John 14:26). The success of Jesus's successors, so to speak, was very much tied to their "abiding" in him (maintaining relationship) (John 15:5) and to the ongoing ministry of the Holy Spirit. This important spiritual truth applied practically in a post-succession context involves the replaced leader staying on as advocate for their successor. In staying on post-succession, the replaced leader maximizes successor success, by teaching and reminding their successors about the importance of sacrificial succession, by helping them to prepare the next generation of successors, and by continuing to model Christ-like servantship. Succession literature has often argued that it is unhealthy for an incumbent to remain present in any capacity once the transition process is complete.[26] However, when leaders understand the sacrificial nature of succession modeled by Jesus, a different set of priorities will begin to emerge.

Insights from Paradigm Theory

In his *paradigm shift* theory, Thomas Kuhn argues that the history of scientific discovery affirms that a new paradigm will not gain traction until the old paradigm has been fully rejected.[27] Unfortunately we have become acclimatized to the subversive charms of pluralism where juxtapositions are frequently left unchallenged. Whilst this does not hold true for all Boomer pastors—some are prepared to relinquish inherited methods, for example—Kuhn's prophecy appears timely and true. Emerging research suggests that Millennials will not be willing to maintain Boomer-type institutional church structures. George Barna argues that the "only way forward will be for Boomer pastors to not just allow but even encourage the emergence of new models of ministry that either improve or completely replace many current models and methods."[28]

Proving their Capacity for Succession

Ecclesiastes 2:21 reminds us that succession is particularly difficult when a person "must leave all they own to others who have not toiled for it." Moses instructed Joshua to lead a comprehensive reconnaissance mission to explore the Promised Land prior to invading it (Num 13:18–20). Moses realized that if Joshua was to lead the nation of Israel, he needed a series of progressively responsible assignments. We are working towards helping Boomers cultivate potential Millennial leaders by giving them developmental assignments so that they can prove themselves in a number of contexts before they receive promotion. We are trying to make sure that a process is firmly in place before the need for a transition to succession begins. This approach is also

---

26. Sonnenfeld, "Good Governance," 110.
27. Kuhn, "The Structure of Scientific Revolutions," 77.
28. Barna, "Gracefully Passing on the Baton," 6.

helping Boomer leaders begin to think proactively about the required transition process well in advance.

Intentional about Deconstruction

The author is encouraging Boomer leaders to walk beside Millennials and familiarize them with the necessary corporate parameters whilst making sure Millennials do not wither under the immensity of it all. At the same time, it is encouraging to note that Boomer leaders are realizing that deconstructing the unnecessary corporate processes often requires Millennial intuition and involvement. In my dealings with Boomer leaders I encourage them to allow Millennials into board meetings not merely as observers but as advisors and to be prepared to take their suggestions seriously. This will increase Millennials' self-motivation and problem-solving skills. Feedback throughout this kind of process will enable better tracking of where Boomers are at with their alignment to inherited methods and their preparedness to begin a required transition. More importantly, feedback helps establish whether or not Boomers understand the practical implications of sacrificial succession.

Nurturing a Servantship Culture

Millennials thrive on being appreciated, involved, and trusted.[29] We want to recognize their desire to understand their role and we want to find creative ways to nurture their need to see how their role supports the needs and the ongoing life and direction of our organization. In my effort to help organizations develop processes of sacrificial succession, I am forming a program that will act as a progression to a larger plan for the nurturing of a servantship environment where all staff will be given training on servantship theory and assignments where these can be applied. They will also be given opportunities to understand how their personality and skill set can further benefit the organization at a wider level.

Reverse Mentoring

We also want to give Millennials opportunities to familiarize Boomers with the Millennial lingo and lifestyle. Introducing these strategies will show Millennials that Boomers are genuinely serious about healthy interdependency and co-learning environments. We are already seeing examples where mutual respect and confidence are increasing. We are talking through how to apply strategies where Millennials can mentor Boomers in the social and contemporary arts, and the science of modern technology. We are looking for ways to genuinely appreciate Millennial contribution

---

29. McCrindle, "Emerging Trends, Enduring Truths," 7.

at this level, possibly even paying them or rewarding them as pseudo consultants for their services. Aside from being greatly rewarding for Millennials, this process gives Boomer managers more insight into the benefits of keeping Millennials engaged. Stephen Abram suggests that by "implementing policies that reflect their need for connection to the world outside of work, such as flex time, telecommuting, and volunteer opportunities," Gen Ys will demonstrate greater commitment.[30] We hope also to see developing confidence in the Boomer manager's capacity to meaningfully relate to Millennials at both a personal and a professional level. Boomers may also develop a greater capacity to bridge some of the social hurdles through a deeper appreciation of the need to adapt to the changing context. In time this will hopefully free them from some of the fear of approaching change.

Closing the Cognition Gaps

Millennials can think critically, but more through the design of their environment than by learning how to analyze matters effectively. Eric Metaxas provides recent research suggesting that "Millennials tend to find it difficult to reason their way through issues. Their responses are often not the result of who has the best argument but whether or not they feel comfortable with the proposed outcome."[31] Angela Weilar suggests that we must "implement programs to help Millennials develop greater problem solving skills—skills that they often failed to develop in their educational experiences. Filling the gap in their cognitive processing abilities is essential for helping Millennials succeed in meeting the demands that leadership will place on them."[32] We are encouraging Boomer managers to approach these matters intentionally but sensitively. The success of our servantship will be partly measured by how well future leaders can discern, evaluate, and critique.

Applying Sacrificial Succession

For a number of our projects we apply *The Seven Steps of Sacrificial Succession*. For churches and other Christian organizations that are interested in applying *Sacrificial Succession* to their servantship transition, the seven main steps are laid out here. These sacrificial succession steps are grouped into three transitional phases. Phase one is the pre-succession ministry of preparation of successors for succession. Next is the mediatory sacrifice by incumbent for successor, which defines the succession event. The final post-succession phase is a mastery of advocacy by replaced leader for successor.

---

30. Abram, Managing Generation Y in the Workplace, http://www.stephenslighthouse.com, 1.
31. Metaxas, "Imagination, Culture, and Politics," 2.
32. Weiler, "Information-Seeking Behavior," 49.

Ministry of Preparation (Three and a Half Years)

- Choose and prepare sacrificial servants and ministers as potential successors.
- Minister sacrificially by clearly predicting the timing and terms of a succession.
- Appoint a successor with a proven track record of ministering sacrificially.[/BL]

Ministry of Sacrifice (Six Months)

- Ensure incumbent's sacrifice outweighs that of successor by handing over servantship sacrificially.
- Mediate a sacrificial handover of servantship midway through a transition.

Mastery of Advocacy (Three Years)

- Stay on to teach and remind successors of sacrificial succession.
- Master by advocating with the organization's governing group for successor success.

The Old Testament makes it very clear that when leadership development and succession planning were performed poorly or neglected the Israelites suffered through a succession of leaders who lost sight of the mission, oppressed God's people, and reverted to idol-worship. The worse curse, which occasionally came to pass, is uttered in Isaiah 3:4: "I will make mere youths their officials; children will govern them."[33] It would be tragic if this prophecy came true for the church in the next generation. Many leaders serve sacrificially yet they are failing to hand over leadership to Millennial successors. The first clause of Matt 20:28 is often applied whilst the second is usually neglected. This has occurred because servant leadership in both secular and sacred institutions has been highly influenced by existentialism. Servantship cannot be properly understood outside the context of sacrificial succession, which is the faithful application of Christ-centered servantship. There is undeniable power in sacrificial succession. Secular research confirms both the reciprocal power of sacrifice by leaders for followers and the need for more genuinely sacrificial approaches. The mediatory sacrifice of Jesus and his ongoing advocacy for his successors following a ministry of successor preparation provide the perfect illustration of succession and the answer to the contemporary leadership crisis. *Sacrificial succession*, in the context of authentic, Christ-like, *missional servantship*, is the answer to what many consider to be a "leadership crisis."

---

33. Woolfe, *The Bible on Leadership*, 196.

Movement One—From Leadership to Radical Servantship

Part 2: Servantship and the Shaping of Missional Community

"The place God calls you to is where your deep gladness and the world's deep hunger meet."—Frederick Buechner[34]

Reversing Perceptions

What does the seedbed for a sacrificial succession of leadership look like in a church setting? How do leaders begin planting and nurturing these principles in a volunteer environment? Over the last several decades a number of unscriptural assumptions have powerfully shaped Servant Leadership theory. These have had the effect of encouraging some leaders to push on with tight-lip resolve whilst leaving others disillusioned and confused about the way forward. Before we can progress into a thoroughly Christological design of servantship, a number of these subversive influences must be addressed.

Whilst the imposition of Christianity is no longer practiced as a social and ethical program, the largely attractional endeavors that were central to *Corpus Christianum* are proving difficult to shake. These, for the most part, only serve to recycle the already churched, and attract the semi-churched and those with nostalgia for Christianity. The de-churched, the un-churched, and the anti-church, who make up the increasing majority, are not only indifferent to these approaches, they are in fact becoming more hostile and they are withdrawing further from the church because of them. Churches that cannot escape the appeal of congenial, monocultural, middle-class community building and conventional forms of American-style evangelism and outreach do little to reverse the average Australian's perception that Christianity is oppressive, moralistic, and hypocritical. In fact the world economic crisis and its severe impact on our working class and underclass families, both morally and socially, have thrown the church into a much deeper challenge in terms of its cultural distance than many leaders realize.[35] For the most part, denominational leaders acknowledge that we are now in a cross-cultural missionary situation, not unlike, say, Indonesia or Africa—however, many of our theories about how to invoke and cope with change still operate from within the twin assumptions of Modernism and Christendom. Darryl Guder warns us, "The reclamation of the church's missional vocation is not an easy process; the mind-set of Christendom is much more resilient than its crumbling

---

34. Buechner, *Wishful Thinking*, 57.

35. The concept of *cultural distance* was designed by pioneering missiologist Ralph Winter for the purpose of measuring how far a specific people group is from a meaningful engagement with the gospel. See Winter and Koch, "Finishing the Task," 509–24.

structures."[36] It seems that within many leadership contexts the terms *missional* and *emerging* still refer more to a dissonant state of mind than a daring paradigm shift at the servantship level.

From Information to Imitation

Perhaps the greatest pitfall of leadership evolving from the modernity era of the eighties and nineties was the uncritical borrowing of management structures from other systems, especially those that are highly deconstructionist and pragmatic in nature. They have stayed with us, continuing to shape our habits. Alan Roxburgh argues that, "The challenge we face as leaders is that we find ourselves in a new space where we are trying to navigate with maps that represent a reality that no longer exists."[37] The many pastors who have been coached in these leadership models are struggling to adapt to the complexities of our time. They are finding it extremely difficult to transition to a more agile form of church servantship where outcomes are not as easy to manipulate. Operational theories of leadership worked well during the *come-to-us* mode of Christianity where everyone was assumed to be Christian and church attendance was the accepted norm.[38] But these principles don't work so well in a situation that requires a *go-to-them* missionary stance. We need to close the gap between the current skill set and the skill set required if we are to adequately adapt our servantship to our changing context.[39]

Behavior is rarely changed by instruction in theory alone. You can't be what you can't see! Our situation calls for a radical recalibration around the incarnational servantship example of Jesus. Servantship in the Bible always flows from an orthopraxic discipleship design.[40] This ensures that the impulse for multiplication is not only imbedded into the DNA of all who aspire to servantship, but into all who will be disciples. In the West today we have access to more discipleship tools and resources than at any other time in the history of the church. But the church is in decline because not enough leaders are actually modeling discipleship. Jews have a blessing that beautifully expresses the commitment of a disciple to follow their spiritual mentor: "May you always be covered by the dust of your rabbi." That is, "May you follow him

---

36. Guder, "Walking Worthily," 254.

37. Roxburgh, *Missional Map-Making*, 11.

38. Sometimes referred to as tactical or transactional leadership, *operational leadership* is employed by organizations and institutions which exist within economic and political environments that are relatively stable, where leaders can pass on knowledge through a network of a pre-existing repertoire. There is usually an expectation of a reasonable degree of predictability and control during the foreseeable future. *Adaptive leadership* does not fear chaos or threatening contexts, but invites these so that people develop multiple forms of experimentation.

39. McNeal, *The Present Future*, 126.

40. *Orthopraxy* refers to correct action (activity) compared to *orthodoxy*, which emphasizes correct adherence to beliefs and creeds as a means of authenticating one's faith.

so closely that the dust his feet kick up cakes your clothing and lines your face."[41] The central idea is that observation moves to application. This is what John N. Williams calls "true succession."[42] Jesus always exercised his ministry in close proximity to his disciples. Even when Jesus refers to God as "Our Father in heaven," he is doing more than providing an epithet by which to refer to God. He is inviting us to acknowledge an important part of our relationship with God. In Jesus's time, sons would often observe their fathers every day at work. Jesus said, "My Father is always at his work to this very day, and I too am working." And, "the Son can do nothing by himself; he can do only what he sees his Father doing, because whatever the Father does the Son also does" (John 5:17,19). "Here Jesus is suggesting that he has learned his Father's trade from a young age by observing God in action."[43]

From Positional Authority to Moral Persuasion

This shift in the role and activity of a pastor is of essential importance in a social environment where the vast majority of those outside the church are disillusioned with authority and aristocratic roles, and the typical parishioner does not possess the perspective and the language required for an abiding presentation of the "good news" of Jesus to their lost neighbors, friends, and colleagues. Alan Hirsch reminds us that the example Paul urges us to imitate was not characterized by charismatic presence but by empowerment and suffering.[44] Pastors in the emerging era can no longer rely on congenital roles or positional authority as their leadership paradigm; they must lead by moral persuasion and example. One issue most authors on change and transition miss, almost without exception, is the importance of context and circumstance: the time and place (or today, space) where servantship is actually modeled and practiced. We live in a time when the gospel message has lost a great deal of its credibility within western cultures. Whilst I agree that people can only come to a saving knowledge of Christ through a divine encounter with the gospel message, Evangelicalism remains strong on proclamation and pronouncements, and weak on persuasion, powerlessness, and suffering. (Note, when I speak of persuasion I am not merely referring to the apologetic kind of rhetoric used in debating truth claims.) The central issue for pastors to take from this conversation is the reality that authority these days no longer comes from one's title or position so much as from one's authenticity and currency in the community. Authority is earned as we lead by example and show our congregations how to live a Christ-centered incarnational life, and a form of servantship modeled by Jesus Christ. I also note that the Queensland Baptist Code of Ethics encourages pas-

---

41. Bieschke, "Five Succession Planning Values," 3.
42. Williams, "Confucius, Mencius, and the Notion of True Succession," 158.
43. Frost, *Exiles*, 182.
44. Hirsch, *The Forgotten Ways*, 164.

tors to be "salt and light in society, involving themselves in social justice initiatives and . . . showing concern for the moral as well as the spiritual needs of the community."[45]

Revealing the Manifold Wisdom of God to the World

In Ephesians 3:3–12, the Apostle Paul wrestles with the vital tension between a personal and a corporate call to ministry. His personal call from Christ is to reveal the mystery of the gospel to the lost, yet he recognizes that personally, even as a top leader, he cannot reveal the manifold wisdom of God to the principalities and powers (which influence people). Only the church, the *ecclesia*, can fulfill this corporate calling by example. Top leaders, especially corporate pastors, who attempt to do both, often miss this point. This tension is relevant to the dilemma Christian servantship faces today, because it requires change at the personal level to be obedient to a calling toward pastoral and pioneering ministry whilst empowering the church to make known the manifold wisdom of God to the world. Unless both personal and corporate ministry requirements are met, spiritual and structural change are unlikely.

Donald McGavran explains how a denomination moves through various stages of development in its mission: (1) the early exploratory period, (2) the establishment of mission stations and their ministries, and (3) the development of an indigenous church—finally it is now ready for (4) the continuing challenge of wider evangelism within its society. Churches in this final stage of development will continue to decline until they rediscover their apostolic mission.[46] The identity crisis facing many Protestant denominations is, sadly, an inevitable consequence of their place on this continuum. Christian leadership in the western tradition has always struggled to find a safe balance between empowering the collective conscience of the priesthood and satisfying its fixation with clerical modes of leadership. Yet if the latter remains fundamentally unchallenged at the operational level, this exercise will prove to be counterproductive to discerning the will of God, releasing his people for works of service, and cultivating Christ-like servantship.

The pastor-teacher gift of leadership as it has been so far understood is simply not able to rise to meet the servantship challenges facing Christianity today. Churches don't need better managers, they need better missionaries; apostolic-type, servant-disciples who understand the cross-cultural situation and have the capacity to begin to reconcile the church's marginality. In his delightful commentary on the Gospel of John, Lesslie Newbigin emphasizes that Jesus commissions Peter as both a pastor *and* a missionary.[47] The gift of pastor must flow out of and be inspired by the missionary instinct. The twenty-first century landscape requires a pastor with a skill set and a

---

45. Queensland, *Queensland Baptist Code of Ethics*, 1, Section 1.5.
46. McGavran, *Ethnic Realities and the Church*, 225–27.
47. Newbigin, *Light Has Come*, 279.

capacity to pioneer and innovate new forms of servantship. This will require pastors to relinquish many inherited assumptions and learn new skills, as they model an incarnational life and ministry outside the church, nurturing dangerous discipleship so that "works of service" are recognized beyond as well as within the Christian community.

Denominational and Corporate Servantship Practices

Whilst the implications of the shift to a missional ecclesiology are as daunting for theological education as they are for pastoral practice, seminaries must initiate changes to college curricula ensuring that more core electives move beyond mere propositional theology to a theology of social consciousness and political engagement.

- Seriously reconsider the preoccupation with brands of evangelism that do little to reverse the negative perceptions of western people, and that inhibit Christians from speaking with relevance into the burgeoning social issues of our time.
- Initiate structural changes at the denominational administrative level that renounce bias toward corporate, one-dimensional, pastor-teacher models and permit the manifestation and the recognition of other apostolic modes of servantship.
- Reimagine ecclesiology to support the shift to pioneering lay servantship, and the shift to leaders who are not encumbered by clerical restraints but released to model incarnational servantship within the local community.
- Widen discussion about how to empower individual believers missionally so that the individual's competency and the untrained layperson's capacity to discern God's will contribute to servantship direction in a more enduring way.

Individual and Pastoral Servantship Practices

- Embrace songs, prayers, and liturgies from the world church. Read out testimonies and prayers from persecuted and imprisoned Christians. Prevent worship from becoming escapist and consumptive.
- Seek to dismantle the mental separation between justice as an outward political program and righteousness as an inward and spiritual state.
- Look for concrete ways to engage personal and pastoral concerns with incarnational action.
- Encourage servantship teams and cell (life) groups to make a habit of meeting outside church buildings or the safe home environment. Rather, meet somewhere in proximity to the needs of the local community.
- Seek out spaces where Christians and non-Christians can meet and interact

meaningfully together. For example, take the church servantship and ministry teams undercover and meet non-believers together, or just sit and listen to and identify with the rhythms and sounds of the culture. Discuss what the Spirit might be saying and what the implications could mean for a servantship vision and agenda.

- Dispel the inertia of attractional evangelism and find creative ways to enable the congregation to grasp the long-term commitments required to minister in a cross-cultural environment.

- Be intentional about setting limits on expenses for maintenance and increase expenditure on local mission. Be prepared to fund local secular establishments and initiatives, realizing that God is already on mission there.

Questions for Reflection and Discussion

- Would you agree there is a need to empower lay leaders—not merely interns and seminary students but members of the congregation—to share the preaching, baptisms, Eucharist, dedications, etc., so the pastoral team is not always seen to be the performers of the sacred and sacramental?

- Would you agree that there is an exclusivity and elitism that often comes with the preaching role? If so, how would you go about helping your congregation realize you are not the only one who gets to speak for God and that you genuinely value the priesthood of all believers (a multi-voiced community)?

- Would you be willing to take familiar courses such as Alpha, Christianity Explained, and Pathways outside the church context into public spaces such as community centers, pubs, and bowling clubs? How would you reframe these courses, releasing them to speak significance into the lives of unchurched people? If you disagree with this approach, what other options would you consider?

- How would you begin to communicate the idea that "cross cultural" should no longer be understood in merely ethnic terms but as a sociological phenomenon?

- In his letter, James challenges us to authenticate our religion by caring for "orphans and widows" in their distress (1:27). Are these orphans and widows only other believers? Or should we be identifying the equivalent to "orphans" and "widows" in our immediate cultural context? If so, who falls into the vulnerable classes in your church's social orbit? What are their names and what foretastes of the kingdom of God are they longing for?

- Would you agree that a genuine affirmation of the priesthood of all believers would mean writing into the constitution a renouncing of bias towards the gifts of pastor-teachers? How would you approach this endeavor if you were: (1) Baptist, (2) Pentecostal, or (3) Presbyterian?

Movement One—From Leadership to Radical Servantship

- How would you begin the process of allocating a budget for the payment of a multiple part-time laity within the church?

- As a pastor can you identify any de-churched, un-churched, and anti-churched persons in your ministry connections? If not, would you agree that as a leader, it is essential that you cultivate relationships with these people?

- In the New Testament, ministry happened . . . on a mountainside (Mat 5:1), in a boat (Mat 13:1), as a dinner guest (Luke 14:15), within the temple precincts (Acts 2:5), in a chariot (car) (Acts 8:31), in the marketplace (Acts 17), at university (Acts 17). Where does the majority of your ministry happen?

Movement Two

From Shallowness to Dynamic Theological Reflection

One of the reasons why unbiblical, self-serving, or controlling models of leadership are embraced in the church is because pastors and their churches have traded dynamic theological reflection for shallow pragmatism. Servantship demands biblically grounded and self-reflective theological thought. It demands ministry practice rooted in the biblical narrative, the mission of God, and *the dynamic theological imagination of the people of God*. This theological imagination is not restricted to the academy—it finds its fullest expression in a living conversation between scholars, leaders, churches, the gospel narrative, traditions, theologies, and cultures. A vibrant theological reflection forms the practices and perspectives of servantship.

Henri Nouwen reflects on the importance of theological reflection in ministry, and on the role of theological reflection in helping us avoid the temptation to be powerful, when he writes,

> Few ministers and priests think theologically. Most of them have been educated in a climate in which the behavioral sciences, such as psychology and sociology, so dominated the educational milieu that little true theology was being learned. Most Christian leaders today raise psychological and sociological questions even though they frame them in scriptural terms. Real theological thinking . . . is hard to find in the practice of ministry. Without solid theological reflection, future leaders will be little more than pseudo-psychologists, pseudo-sociologists, pseudo-social workers. They will think of themselves as enablers, facilitators, role models, father or mother figures, big brothers or big sisters, and so on, and thus join the countless men and women who make a living by trying to help their fellow human beings to cope with the stresses and strains of everyday living. But that has little to do with Christian leadership because the Christian leader thinks, speaks, and acts in the name of Jesus, who came to free humanity from the power of death and open the way to eternal life. To be such a leader it is essential to be able to discern from

Movement Two—From Shallowness to Dynamic Theological Reflection

> moment to moment how God acts in human history and how the personal, communal, national, and international events that occur during our lives can make us more and more sensitive to the ways in which we are led to the cross and through the cross to the resurrection . . .[1]

A theology of servantship is built upon our understandings of theology, culture, and the mission of the triune God and his church. Servantship occurs when a set of postures, understandings, and practices are cultivated through a missional theology and practice of church. This involves discipleship to our Servant Lord, and participating in his redemptive, cosmic, eschatological mission in the world and in human history. The contributors to this section of the book show how a vigorous theological outlook on church, mission, and servantship involves the cultivation of a missional responsiveness, the formation of dynamic theological bearings, the pursuit of mission as organizing function, and the radical post-Christendom recalibration of the church and its servantship. Servantship creates an environment in which mission-shaped innovations thrive, and fosters churches that are theologically vibrant, Jesus-centered, mission-shaped, and community-oriented. Out of this vivacious life churches develop rhythms, community, faith, theology, and mission and ministry practices. It is time for disciples to develop authentic and robust theological thought. Such theological reflection is the second movement in radical servantship.

---

1. Nouwen, *In the Name of Jesus*, 65–66.

5

Forming a Missional and Trinitarian Church

Graeme Anderson

This chapter seeks to develop an authentic and practical missional ecclesiology. In order to do this, the nature of the church and mission are initially discussed. Following this, the current challenges and changes to church and culture are briefly examined. From this place an approach to missional ecclesiology is developed. The foundation of this approach, termed *trinitarian missional ecclesiology*, is the nature of a triune God. The vision and primary expression of this approach, a life of discipleship to Jesus, is described and discussed. Finally, the implication or outcome of a trinitarian missional ecclesiology is outlined—that is, the expression of a truly incarnational church. The chapter concludes by stating that an incarnational missional community seeks both to embrace the present Christ and be present in the community to which they have been sent.

Constructing a Missional Ecclesiology

> *Follow me . . .*[1]
>
> *Let it be the most important thing we do, then, to reflect on the life of Jesus Christ.*[2]

It seems the theological foundation of the church is currently in a phase of formation and reformation. Jürgen Moltmann states, "Today one of the strongest impulses towards the renewal of the theological concept of the church comes from the theology

---

1. Jesus, the Christ.
2. Kempis, *The Imitation of Christ: In Four Books*, 1.

Movement Two—From Shallowness to Dynamic Theological Reflection

of mission."[3] There seems to be something about the concept of "mission" that invites individuals and communities to think outside the traditional walls of space and understanding and to envision something more, and perhaps even something new. This is a process that must begin with who God is. As Darrell Guder states, "We do not end up with mission, as the precipitate of all our theologizing; we start with God's mission and work our way through the theological agenda of the faith."[4]

The biggest risk in a movement such as this (and indeed, a study such as this) is to focus on the symptoms of mission and what a "missional church" might look like. This chapter will endeavor to resist that temptation, heeding the words of the great Scottish thinker, George MacDonald, "Nothing is so deadening to the divine as an habitual dealing with the outsides of holy things."[5] This chapter shares Ray Anderson's concern—for a deeper ecclesiology and spirituality rather than a superficial and consumer-oriented religiosity stimulated by innovative and spectator-oriented methods.[6]

The central assumption of this chapter can be stated as follows,

> The aim of God in history is the creation of an all-inclusive community of loving persons with God himself at the very center of this community as its prime Sustainer and most glorious Inhabitant.[7]

The aim of this chapter is to form a biblical and theological view of the church and its mission. This view will be formed within the reality that there are various challenges and changes taking place within western culture. The primary question is then, "What is the missional vision of the church in western culture?"[8] The secondary questions will be: "What are current challenges to this vision?" "What is the foundation of this vision?" and "How might the church move towards this vision?"

In order to begin, the primary question will be examined in two parts. Firstly, the nature of the church will be commented upon—the ecclesial question. Following this, the concept of the term "missional" will be discussed—the missional question. From this foundation, the secondary questions will be entered into.

Depending on one's upbringing and/or experience, the church might be seen as a building, collective noun, concept, reality, and even a visible community of God. There seems to be consistent confusion over precisely what the church is and what (or who) the church exists for. Much of this confusion is the fault of the church. "As Christians we say we believe in truth and in the practice of truth, and yet we face

---

3. Moltmann, *The Church in the Power of the Spirit*, 7.
4. Guder, "Missional Theology for a Missionary Church," 7.
5. Macdonald, *Thomas Wingfold, Curate*, 27.
6. Anderson, *An Emergent Theology for Emerging Churches*, 56.
7. Foster, *The Life with God Bible*, 1.
8. This in no way diminishes an international and developing world missional ecclesiology, it is merely the focus of this chapter.

much untruth in the visible church."[9] The result of this is that what is seen is not understood. Dan Kimball also points out the dynamic difference between what is said and what is done. "Whatever our church's vision of mission statement, the fact is we hire most of our staff to support the weekend event."[10] The problem then becomes that worship services in which we participate every Sunday morning remain devoid of genuine human contact,[11] when what is truly needed is the presence of relationship.

This being the case, the foundation of the church must be clearer. The mission of the church must be re-understood. The nature of the church is to exist as the missionary people of God.[12] Understood from this lens, "Mission does not come from the church; it is from mission and in the light of mission that the church has to be understood."[13] As Ray Anderson states, ". . . there is a theological priority belonging to mission as determining the nature of the church and its relation to the mission of God for the world."[14] This reality leads to the discussion of mission.

Lesslie Newbigin points towards the implication of a church understood from the perspective of mission. "The church is the bearer to all the nations of a gospel that announces the kingdom, the reign, and the sovereignty of God."[15] This mission is the ". . . acting out by proclamation and by endurance, through all the events of history, of the faith that the kingdom of God has drawn near."[16] As a result, mission is ". . . not meant to call men and women out of the world into a safe religious enclave but to call them out in order to send them back as agents of God's kingship."[17] The church is not doing mission or deciding to be involved in mission; by its very calling and nature, the church *is* mission—it exists as the sent people of God.[18] This sending is to be seen in all of the facets of what it means to be a church—a present taste of the kingdom of God. "Church must follow mission."[19]

There is a significant difference between a church that is involved with, or supportive of, mission and a church that is missional. The former will often send out members or sponsor others who are stationed in other parts of the country or overseas areas that are not yet "churched." Often this operation is outsourced to a parachurch mission society or the like. A missional church, on the other hand, "is a unified body of believers, intent on being God's missionary presence to the indigenous community

---

9. Schaeffer, *The Church before the Watching World*, 7.
10. Kimball, *Emerging Worship*, 32.
11. Moltmann, *The Open Church*, 29.
12. Anderson, *An Emergent Theology for Emerging Churches*, 32.
13. Moltmann, *The Church in the Power of the Spirit*, 10.
14. Anderson, *An Emergent Theology for Emerging Churches*, 186.
15. Newbigin, *Foolishness to the Greeks*, 124.
16. Newbigin, *The Open Secret*, 39.
17. Newbigin, *Foolishness to the Greeks*, 124.
18. Guder, "Missional Theology for a Missionary Church," 5.
19. Hirsch, *The Forgotten Ways*, 143.

Movement Two—From Shallowness to Dynamic Theological Reflection

that surrounds them..."[20] The primary question for the missional church is no longer one of sending people out in order to attract people in. The primary questions have become, "What is God up to in this neighborhood?" and "What are the ways we need to change in order to engage the people in our community who no longer consider church a part of their lives?"[21]

An authentic missional church will resist the temptation to put "new clothes on old trends." This is what has been seen in the seeker-sensitive movement and the church-growth movement, for example.[22] The foundation of a missional church will necessarily be biblical, historical, contextual, eschatological, and practical.[23] Stated simply, a missional church will be, "... a group of people called missionaries who already organize their corporate life around a story that is told in a book and is continually re-enacted by word and sacramental action in their liturgy."[24]

Challenges Encountered by the Missional Church

Now that the ecclesial and missional questions have been examined, the ecclesial and missional reality must be encountered. This chapter will now briefly outline challenges that will be encountered by the missional church, particularly in the areas of change and culture.

It seems that one of the foremost challenges of any church is that of involvement. Whether this is seen through the lens of membership, attendance, or association, churches must consist of people. Jamieson comments on the "... steady stream of people who were leaving churches ..." This was as a result of feeling "... they could no longer stay and continue to develop in their Christian faith."[25] Darrell Guder points out that the passing of Christendom has revealed the "reductionistic and culturally diluted" western gospel. One of the symptoms of this is the focus on individual and personal salvation as the "sole purpose of the gospel."[26] This could be described as "line theology," where the purpose of mission is to ensure people cross the line between "unsaved" and "saved." When this is the foundation of mission, it is difficult for the "convert" to move on from this point and grow in faith.

Significant changes have been taking place within the church and church communities. Dan Kimball states that this change is inevitable and that there is a "critical need" for it.[27] Alan Hirsch outlines the practicalities of this necessary change,

20. MacIlvaine, "What Is the Missional Church Movement?" 91.
21. Roxburgh, *Introducing the Missional Church*, 20.
22. Billings, "What Makes a Church Missional?" 56.
23. Guder, *Missional Church*, 11–12.
24. Newbigin, *Foolishness to the Greeks*, 42.
25. Jamieson, *A Churchless Faith*, 8.
26. Guder, "Missional Theology for a Missionary Church," 7.
27. Kimball, *Emerging Worship*, x–xi.

> What we need now is a new set of tools. A new "paradigm"—a new vision of reality: a fundamental change in our thoughts, perceptions, and values, especially as they relate to our view of the church and mission.[28]

The issue here is that change is difficult, particularly amongst communities and institutions. Change can be slow and, as a result, there is a loss of sight of the initial vision for change. Change threatens the sense of control. Due to this reality, those who have a sense of power within church communities may well resist losing the sense of control and resist the new paradigm Alan Hirsch outlines. It must be noted as well, that while this change is focused on local mission, it must take place within the context of global mission. "If by 'missional' we neglect the church's responsibility to other nations, then we introduce a new kind of cultural imperialism—deciding that our culture's spiritual needs are more important (or just as important) than that of other nations."[29]

Culture, as always, is in the process of change. The way in which the church interacts with culture must also change. There seems to be a fear that this change in approach will necessarily interfere with the message of the mission. This fear can often leave churches lagging behind cultural changes by some decades. Gordon Lynch states that popular culture involves the environment, resources, and practices of everyday life. This being the case, those who are involved in the study and communication of contemporary religion must be involved in popular culture.[30] This is a useful relationship to be aware of as it aids the clarification of understanding how churches function and the issues raised by religious responses to popular culture.[31]

Perhaps the most significant change in culture can be explained through the transition from modernism to postmodernism.

> Pure modernism held to a single, universal worldview and moral standard, a belief that all knowledge is good and certain, truth is absolute, individualism is valued, and thinking, learning, and beliefs should be determined systematically and logically. Postmodernism, then, holds there is no single universal worldview. All truth is not absolute, community is valued over individualism, and thinking, learning, and beliefs can be determined nonlinearly.[32]

This transition has left many with a modern mindset in fear. This fear is that the "gospel" as they have understood it might change. Indeed it might, but only if the gospel they have been preaching is the reductionist one designed to get adherents across "the line." Missionary techniques of arguing the historicity of the Gospels, the apologetics of doctrine, and the logic of the substitutionary atonement are no longer

---

28. Hirsch, *The Forgotten Ways*, 17.
29. Scott, "A Theological Critique," 345.
30. Lynch, *Understanding Theology and Popular Culture*, 22.
31. Ibid., 27.
32. Kimball, *Emerging Church*, 57.

Movement Two—From Shallowness to Dynamic Theological Reflection

viable.[33] The long-term effectiveness of these approaches is now being seen in a church that is stilted. Thankfully, this change of approach in postmodernism, ". . . endorses the resurgence of spirituality, reflects the loss of confidence in rationalism and science, and urges pursuit of authentic humanity."[34]

Forming a Trinitarian Missional Ecclesiology

The nature of church and mission has now been defined. The reality of the situation has been commented upon. It is now possible to form an ecclesial missiology. This missiology will be founded upon a trinitarian model. The model that has briefly been commented upon in this chapter thus far is a sin-focused missiology. That is, the sin of the individual must be dealt with. This has formed the foundation of mission. However, as God does not deal with people on the basis of their sin, then mission does not need to either. All this sin-focused approach does is emphasize behavior modification. The gospel, as a result, is focused upon sin and the management of sin.[35]

On the contrary, each of the Gospels in the canon is framed through the lens of the Trinity.[36] Lesslie Newbigin describes mission as proclaiming the kingship of God the Father, the presence of God the Son, and the hope in the action of God the Spirit.[37]

The great strength in this approach is that rather than building a church on doctrine, the church is founded on the person and work of Jesus Christ, which is a perfect revelation of who God is and the nature of his Spirit. Doctrine can then be viewed for what it is, a way towards understanding the nature of God. This is where the nature of the church, and therefore its mission and ministry, must have its source—the life of the triune God.[38] *Missio Dei* is understood to be derived from the nature of God. As a result, it makes sense for it to be found in the context of the doctrine of the Trinity, not of ecclesiology or soteriology.[39] The church is a picture of God the Father, Son, and Holy Spirit sending the church into the world.[40]

This trinitarian foundation is seen clearly in the closing words of Jesus in the Gospel according to Matthew. Jesus commissions his followers to go and make disciples, baptizing them in the name of the Father, and of the Son, and of the Holy

---

33. This is not to state that these areas of study are not important. These areas are vitally important—they simply no longer need be the primary focus of evangelism.
34. Murray, *Post-Christendom*, 13.
35. Willard, *The Divine Conspiracy*, Ch. 2 "The Gospels of Sin Management."
36. Bryan Smith, "Why Christians Should Be Strange."
37. Newbigin, *The Open Secret*, 56.
38. Anderson, *An Emergent Theology for Emerging Churches*, 32–33.
39. Bosch, *Transforming Mission*, 390.
40. Guder, "Missional Theology for a Missionary Church," 5.

Spirit.[41] Graphically, in the Gospel according to John, Jesus says to his disciples, "As the Father has sent me, I am sending you." Jesus then breathed on them and said, "Receive the Holy Spirit."[42]

As has already been stated, ecclesiology is largely driven by the theology of mission. Mission, in turn, is driven by, "a Christology that unfolds the missionary character of the Triune God."[43] As Ray Anderson states, "Central to an emerging church theology is a view of God's mission through the Spirit by which the Spirit of God in creation is united with the Spirit of God through Christ seeking the restoration of the whole of God's creation."[44] This is the reality of the kingdom of God come. The redemptive reign of God in Christ "gives birth to the missional church through the work of the Spirit."[45]

> The real point is not to spread the church but to spread the kingdom . . . The missionary concept of the church leads to a church that is open to the world in the divine mission, because it leads to a trinitarian interpretation of the church in the history of God's dealings with the world.[46]

How might the church move towards this vision? This trinitarian missional ecclesiology involves the disciples of Jesus being sent out in the name of Jesus, by the power of the Spirit, for the purpose of the kingdom of God. What are the implications of this missional ecclesiology? The first and primary implication is that authentic, growing discipleship is integral to the mission of the church, ". . . to show forth the love of God and the holiness of God *simultaneously*."[47]

In the Gospels, Jesus is continually heard saying, "*Follow me*."[48] This invitation involves the whole life of the disciple. On one occasion, Jesus follows this invitation to the fishermen Simon Peter and his brother Andrew with the words ". . . *I will make you fish for people*."[49] The "fish for people" phrase is often used as the catch-cry of the missional church. It would seem that the earlier two clauses of "follow me" and "I will make you" are foundational to the outcome. As a result, it would be a grave mistake for communities to merely focus on the outcome. Dan Kimball is aware of this danger, ". . . the danger of focusing on ministry methodology without understanding and addressing foundational issues that are far more important."[50]

41. Matthew 28:19.
42. John 20:21–22.
43. Bliese, "The Mission Matrix," 245.
44. Anderson, *An Emergent Theology for Emerging Churches*, 34.
45. Van Gelder, "Rethinking Denominations," 33.
46. Moltmann, *The Church in the Power of the Spirit*, 11.
47. Schaeffer, *The Church before the Watching World*, 54.
48. Matthew 4:19; 8:22; 9:9; 10:38; 16:24; Mark 1:17; 2:14; 8:34; 10:21; Luke 5:27; 9:23; 9:59; 14:27; 18:22; John 1:43; 10:27; 12:26; 21:19; 21:22.
49. Matthew 4:19.
50. Kimball, *Emerging Church*, 14.

Movement Two—From Shallowness to Dynamic Theological Reflection

> The emerging church must redefine how we measure success: by the characteristics of a kingdom-minded disciple of Jesus produced by the Spirit, rather than by our methodologies, numbers, strategies, or the cool and innovative things we are doing.[51]

Alan Hirsch as well seems to comprehend the importance of this point.

> When dealing with discipleship . . . we are dealing with that single most crucial factor that will in the end determine the quality of the whole—if we fail at this point then we must fail in all the others.[52]

The truth is, as Lesslie Newbigin points out, "Our knowing is not separate from our being."[53] This "knowing" must be far more than knowing about God, it must involve interactive relationship with him.[54] As our knowledge of God grows, our faith in him will grow also.[55] This kind of day-to-day discipleship is what Dallas Willard has called "the great omission from the great commission."[56]

Dan Kimball laments, however, that the "systems" used to teach believers how to be disciples of Jesus "are not connecting with them."[57] It would seem that this "system" for Kimball involves what is essentially the involvement in weekly smaller groups for the purpose of Bible study and mutual encouragement.[58] This model of discipleship will never work as it simply teaches people how to act like disciples. What the true missional church must be interested in are people who genuinely *are* disciples—their knowledge and their being are one and the same. The alternative is a paralysis that has been seen throughout all expressions of church.

> The Pharisees were in many respects the very best people of Jesus's day. But they located goodness in behavior and tried to secure themselves by careful management at the behavioral level . . . Hence, the Pharisee always fails at some point to do what is right, and then must redefine, redescribe, or explain it away—or simply hide it.[59]

The approach to discipleship here is through what has been called "spiritual disciplines." These could also (more accurately) be termed "soul training exercises."[60] Alan Hirsch reflected on the value of these habits and stated that each small group in

---

51. Ibid., 15.
52. Hirsch, *The Forgotten Ways*, 102.
53. Newbigin, *Discovering Truth in a Changing World*, 18.
54. Willard, *Knowing Christ Today*, Ch. 1.
55. Ibid., 156.
56. Willard, *The Great Omission*, xiv.
57. Kimball, *Emerging Worship*, xii.
58. Ibid., 52.
59. Willard, *The Great Omission*, 15.
60. Bryan Smith, *The Good and Beautiful God*.

the community he led was engaged in a "healthy diet" of spiritual disciplines. He states they are, "the only way to grow in Christlikeness that we were aware of."[61] There is a danger here; these exercises must not be treated as ends in and of themselves. They merely create space in the person for the Spirit of God to work within the whole of life. Should these activities be given more weight than this, they will quickly become legalistic and over-spiritualized.

This is the kind of practice that draws (understandable) criticism from other expressions of church community. Ray Anderson states that these traditional forms of spirituality tend towards the "individualistic" and "pietistic." He is nervous of the apparent lack of criticism extended towards these disciplines within contemporary Protestant spirituality as they can ". . . tend more toward the human spirit than the Holy Spirit . . . and an internal rather than an external form of spiritual devotion."[62]

While Ray Anderson does have a point here, it seems what he is commenting on is a caricature of the practice of spiritual disciplines. An authentic expression of this approach to discipleship will ideally take place within community. The purpose of this is to grow in Christ. Growth in Christ necessitates the characteristics of the Trinity—mutual submission, mutual accountability, and generosity.

This discipleship is integral to a trinitarian missional ecclesiology. The visible church must be an authentic expression of the kingdom of God. This involves the whole life of each person within the community. "Scriptures teach that we must *practice*, not just *talk* about, the purity of the visible church."[63] Francis Schaeffer states that this purity consists of two principles, "The principle of the practice of the purity of the visible church in regard to doctrine and life and . . . the principle of the practice of an observable love and oneness among *all* true Christians regardless of who and where they are."[64]

This purity does not come about simply by meeting together as a community. It is also not a natural by-product of missional work. Charles MacIlvane states that missional activity motivates individuals towards change and spiritual growth.[65] This is simply not the case. This motivation does not persist through trials and confusion. Disciples of Jesus need to make plans to become the people Christ is forming them to be.[66]

---

61. Hirsch, *The Forgotten Ways*, 47.
62. Anderson, *An Emergent Theology for Emerging Churches*, 61.
63. Schaeffer, *The Church before the Watching World*, 53.
64. Ibid., 7–8.
65. MacIlvaine, "What Is the Missional Church Movement?," " . . . if a Christ-follower determines to be '"on mission,"' he or she will become highly motivated to grow and change." 106.
66. Willard, *The Great Omission*, 29: "We should not only want to be merciful, kind, unassuming, and patient persons but also be *making plans* to become so."

Movement Two—From Shallowness to Dynamic Theological Reflection

Focusing on Discipleship

This chapter has endeavored to outline the importance of a trinitarian missional ecclesiology. This approach acknowledges the cultural and philosophical changes in the contemporary western world without shying away or aiming to convert persons to a merely cultural Christianity. The focus of this approach is on discipleship. This focus does not in any way detract from a missional perspective. On the contrary, it enhances, empowers, and directs it. Discipleship is of the individual, in community, and for the sake of mission. As Dallas Willard states, "The church is for discipleship and discipleship is for the world."[67] The evidence of this approach and focus is what could be termed an "incarnational" church or community.

> . . . The incarnation is an absolutely fundamental doctrine, not just as an irreducible part of the Christian confession, but also as a theological prism through which we view our entire missional task in the world.[68]

As Ray Anderson states, "The mission of the church is to embody in its corporate life and ministry, the continuing messianic and incarnational nature of the Son of God through the indwelling of the Holy Spirit."[69] This will only take place within a plan for authentic discipleship that maintains a vision on the kingdom of God here and now. As disciples grow in Christ, the incarnational nature of the church grows. Michael Frost continues,

> . . . the incarnation provides us with the missional means by which the gospel can become a genuine part of a people group without damaging the innate cultural frameworks that provide that people group with a sense of meaning and history.[70]

The promise of Jesus is to be with his disciples to the end of the age.[71] This promise can become the cornerstone of all missional activity. Regardless of the form, style, personality, presentation, or reception of a missional expression, the presence of Jesus Christ is what must inform, inhabit, and inspire the message. He is literally to become the substance of the missional church. This is the expression of an incarnational faith—the knowledge of God becoming substance (tangible reality) in the life of the disciple. A church in mission cannot rely on anything other than the beauty of a believable God revealed in the person of Jesus.

The incarnational expression grows as a community of disciples creates space for the Spirit of Christ to act. As Richard Foster states, "The really crucial decision comes,

---

67. Willard, "The Gentle Art of Making Disciples."
68. Frost, *The Shaping of Things to Come*, 35.
69. Anderson, *An Emergent Theology for Emerging Churches*, 32.
70. Frost, *The Shaping of Things to Come*, 37.
71. Matthew 28:20.

not when we decide to be a pastor rather than a biologist, but when we decide to allow our entire life to be a channel of divine love."[72] A sign of an authentic incarnational church will be what takes place when disciples are in their homes. Foster continues, "The most basic place of our sacramental living is in our marriages and homes and families."[73] This is the reality Jean Pierre du Cassade describes as the sacrament of the present moment; that is, growing in the knowledge of what it means to receive and live within the presence of Christ in each moment of each day.

This sacrament of the present moment allows individuals and communities not only to embrace the presence of Christ, but also to be authentically present with those around them in each moment. An incarnational church is truly present in and for the community they are within. This community will see what is needed, will hear what is actually being said, will touch those who are the last, the lost, the least, and the dead.[74] This community will express the love of Christ through being present in each moment and learning how to serve the community to which they have been sent.

As David Bosch states, "The church-in-mission is, primarily, the *local* church everywhere in the world."[75] The local church must continue to learn what it means to be a sent people. This does not mean merely modifying the exterior. "Being missional is not about *doing church* in a better way, nor is it about the *church* itself. There is much more."[76] The "much more" that is mentioned here is the need for authentic discipleship to shape missional communities. This approach, couched in the real and eternal presence of the triune God gives meaning, purpose, and depth to the message of hope and life the church is sent with. As a result, it is the message that shapes the church, rather than the church endeavoring to shape the message. Jürgen Moltmann states, "The meaning of life gives us a strong heart and this in turn shapes our external way of being in the world."[77] God is achieving his purpose of the formation of an all-inclusive community of loving persons. God is at the center of this community. God is the prime sustainer and most glorious inhabitant of this community. This truth brings freedom to all who are sent in his name.

The freedom of this truth leads communities of disciples towards the "other." The freedom of this truth empowers communities of disciples towards faith, hope, and love. The freedom of this truth envisions communities with the present kingdom of God.

---

72. Foster, *Streams of Living Water*, 224.
73. Ibid., 218.
74. Capon uses this phrase throughout his series on the parables. Capon, *Kingdom, Grace, Judgement*.
75. Bosch, *Transforming Mission*, 10.
76. Roxburgh, *Introducing the Missional Church*, 72.
77. Moltmann, *The Open Church*, 37.

Movement Two—From Shallowness to Dynamic Theological Reflection

> The truth can only be known through incarnation, through the actual presence of God in history, the presence of the one in the midst of history, who calls upon us with the words: "*Follow me!*"[78]

Individual and Corporate Servantship Practices

- In a preaching series, focus on the themes surrounding living in the light of the present kingdom of God (for example, The Sermon on the Mount, The Parables, or the book of James).
- Spend time reading the Gospels and inviting Jesus to reveal himself to you through them.
- As a servantship group, read chapter 9 of *The Divine Conspiracy* by Dallas Willard ("A Curriculum of Christlikeness").[79]
- Develop a "Curriculum of Christlikeness" for yourselves and share these with each other.
- Engage with this curriculum with a goal to create space for the Holy Spirit to work in your life.
- Spend time learning about the discipline of silence. Read chapter 3 of Dietrich Bonhoeffer's *Life Together* ("A Day Alone").[80]
- Engage in times of silence.
- Take time to intentionally listen to those around you.

Questions for Reflection and Discussion

- In what ways might your missional community experience a tension between what is said and what is done?
- How does your understanding of the Christian gospel express itself within and therefore shape your missional community?
- To what extent might a movement towards "the sacrament of the present moment" form the foundation of a missional community?

---

78. Newbigin, *Discovering Truth in a Changing World*, 19 (italics added).
79. Willard, *Divine Conspiracy*.
80. Bonhoeffer and Doberstein, *Life Together*.

6

Participating in God's Mission

CHRISTINE REDWOOD

This chapter argues that both from a biblical and theological perspective the church must begin by knowing that its mission is actually part of the wider mission of God. God's mission must be the foundation and starting point for local churches and their mission into a rapidly changing world. God's mission is for his reign to come upon the world. Jesus, through his messianic vocation, ushers the kingdom in calling people to respond and follow him. This mission is universal and each church needs to take up God's mission wherever they are situated. A missional and ecclesial challenge facing the western churches is the effect of Christendom. Many churches have forgotten the full mission of God and have too often conformed to the culture around them. In the last century this has been the modernist world view. Biblical resources are emerging for the western church to equip them in these practical challenges. The church must contextualize and present an alternative as it lives out God's kingdom purposes in the western context. In this way the church can continue God's mission.

The Church's Mission Originates in God

There is strong biblical and theological support for arguing that mission originates in and from God. In God's mission the church has a central role to play as it participates in his plans for all of creation. The Bible reveals God's mission, which is to bring his salvific reign to all the nations. This salvation comes through the sending of God's Son into the world. Jesus at his ascension leaves his disciples with the task to continue his mission by spreading the gospel forward into a swiftly changing world. Thus the church is born. Today there are pressing ecclesial and missional challenges in western churches that need to be addressed if the church is to continue in its God-given

Movement Two—From Shallowness to Dynamic Theological Reflection

mission. Western culture has rejected Christendom, and in some ways has become immune to Christianity because of the effects of Christendom. Western culture is also rapidly transforming into a postmodernist society. Unfortunately the church is too often ignoring the changes. Yet there are rich biblical resources that can enable churches to practically engage in this new western culture. The church needs to be both incarnational and prophetic. The challenges in western culture have the potential, if churches are prepared to wrestle with these challenges, to see new disciples of Jesus being made and the mission of God continuing. If they do not, the church in the west will continue to decline.

There is a theological imperative to form churches centered on the mission of God. This has been rediscovered throughout the last century. First, mission itself began to be redefined as God's mission. David Bosch notes that Karl Barth was one of the first theologians "to articulate mission as an activity of God himself."[1] The church had often conceived itself as the "sending agency" with certain people known as missionaries sent out, rather than understanding itself as the "sent agency" of God.[2] Missiologist Karl Hartenstein built on this theological suggestion by coining the term *missio Dei* to capture the idea that the triune God is on mission, and that he fulfills this mission through a "series of sending acts"; the Father sends the Son, and the Son sends the Spirit in order to send the church into the world.[3] There would be no mission or indeed church if the triune God had not acted.[4] This "theocentric reconceptualization" reorients the church that had previously approached mission as one "activity the church does" rather than God's ultimate project.[5] A key biblical text which supports this theological thesis is John 20:21 when, Jesus talking to his disciples after his resurrection, says, "As the Father has sent me, I am sending you." Wright argues that it is not just a few key proof texts but the whole Bible that reveals and invites people into the mission of God.[6] At a local level each church's mission must align with God's mission. A biblical view of the church is that it is called into the mission of God.

God's mission can be traced right through the Bible. The word *shalom* or the phrase *kingdom of God* are often used to describe God's mission, which is to see all of creation worshipping him and living as they were intended—redeemed and brought into a new life where "justice, peace, (and) wholeness" reigns.[7] The Old Testament traces the story of "creation, fall, and redemption"—throughout the Scriptures God, out of his grace, initiates a plan to see the whole world renewed.[8] The Old Testament

---

1. Bosch, *Transforming Mission*, 389.
2. Stevens, *The Other Six Days*, 197.
3. MacIlvaine, "What Is the Missional Church Movement?" 96.
4. Ott et al., *Encountering Theology of Mission*, 74.
5. Guder and Barrett, *Missional Church*, 4.
6. Wright, *The Mission of God*, 48.
7. Spellers, "The Church Awake," 33.
8. Van Gelder, "From Corporate Church to Missional Church," 440.

covenants, particularly with Israel, were always driven by God's purpose that all the nations might come to worship him—yet Israel was unable to fulfill this mission due to their own unfaithfulness and sin.[9] Into this context Jesus entered announcing that the kingdom of God was now coming.[10] Throughout Jesus's life in his teaching and miracles he claimed that the kingdom was "being unveiled through his own presence," he gave people a taste of what the kingdom is like, and ultimately opened up the way for people to enter God's kingdom through his death and resurrection.[11] He acted with authority, performing functions that belonged to Yahweh and in so doing revealed God more completely.[12] After the death and resurrection of Jesus the New Testament shows how many people responded to Jesus's call to follow and believe in him.[13] They formed communities around him and saw themselves as part of God's unfolding kingdom purposes spreading throughout the world.

The church is called to participate in the mission of God as revealed in Christ Jesus. The church's mission is rooted in the identity of Jesus's mission.[14] Jesus repeatedly calls his disciples to be his *witnesses*.[15] Through Christ's "redemptive victory" he gathers a "kingdom community" that is to proclaim the good news in both word and deed that God's reign is bursting into this world through Christ.[16] An often quoted verse which supports the centrality of God's mission in and through the church is the commission of Jesus to his followers, "Go and make disciples of all nations, baptizing them in the name of the Father and of the Son and of the Holy Spirit, and teaching them to obey everything I have commanded you."[17] The one imperative in that sentence is "to make disciples." Jesus's followers are to create a community of people who recognize Jesus as both Savior and Lord, who seek to reflect the rule of God breaking into their lives.[18] In order to do this, churches need to be communities committed to being "Jesus-shaped people," not just simply believing in Jesus, but having their lifestyles transformed by the Spirit of Jesus.[19] Christology should shape missiology, which in turn should shape our ecclesiology.[20] Christians' "primary relationship with

---

9. Ibid., 441.
10. Matthew 4:17, Mark 1:15, and Luke 4:18–21.
11. Wright, *The Challenge of Jesus*, 38.
12. Wright, *The Mission of God*, 122.
13. Acts 2:41, 8:12, 11:26, 20:28, 1 Corinthians 1:2, 16:19, and Revelation 1:4.
14. Wright, *The Mission of God*, 66.
15. Matthew 10:18, Luke 24:48, and Acts 1:8.
16. Glasser, *Announcing the Kingdom*, 234.
17. Matthew 28:19.
18. Glasser, *Announcing the Kingdom*, 234.
19. Frost, *ReJesus*, 41.
20. Ibid., 43.

Movement Two—From Shallowness to Dynamic Theological Reflection

God is through the mediation of Jesus the Messiah," thus his mission is central to the identity of missional churches.[21] Missional churches need to be grounded in Jesus.

A Biblical and Cultural Imperative

This mission that Jesus gives the church is universal. The disciples are called to go to the nations. Bauckham describes the mission of the church as situated between the particularity of Jesus and his work, and the "universal coming of God's kingdom" that is the eschatological goal.[22] It is in the particular, the local church, from which the gospel goes forth into the world. God initiates this movement at the first Pentecost after the ascension of Jesus. There the Holy Spirit comes upon the gathered church, and they are filled with power to speak the gospel in many different languages to those around them.[23] This becomes the pattern throughout Acts as the Spirit leads and empowers the church in the mission of God to the nations.[24] The Bible teaches that the mission of the church is always in the context of changing world cultures.[25] The church needs to grapple with how both to engage in the particular culture it is situated in, and challenge that culture with the gospel. Drawing the biblical material together in an ecumenical statement, the World Council of Churches affirms, "It is at the heart of Christian mission to foster the multiplication of local congregations in every human community."[26] The biblical foundation affirms that all churches are called to reach out into their continually changing culture with the gospel of Christ.

There is not only a biblical imperative to form missional churches, but also a cultural imperative. The mission of God is "always clothed in culture and comes to expression through particular people." This means that churches have to understand their particular culture.[27] This is crucial in western society, which has seen the decline of churches. For instance, I minister within the Baptist Churches of New South Wales and the Australian Capital Territory (Australia). These churches have, in the last ten years, "Experienced zero aggregate numerical growth, and aged significantly."[28] There are many reasons given for this decline. Industrialization and secularism are two great forces which have impacted western culture and, by implication, the church. Steve Bruce argues that the social changes brought by industrialization led to the decline of religious organizations as the breakdown of community and the equalizing of ideas

21. Frost and Hirsch, *The Shaping of Things to Come*, 112.
22. Bauckham, *Bible and Mission*, 10.
23. Acts 1:7—2:47.
24. Hedlund, *The Mission of the Church in the World*, 201.
25. Ibid., 205.
26. Churches, "Appendix," 18.
27. Van Gelder, "From Corporate Church to Missional Church," 442.
28. Pratt, "Awake O Sleeper," 6.

led to "general relativism that supposes that all ideologies are equally true."[29] He sees people in the west as being primarily indifferent when it comes to religion, and declares that God is dead.[30] Christians would disagree that this is the end of the mission of God, but for those who are prepared to face the facts they must examine the culture around them and respond appropriately.[31] This begins by realizing that "everywhere the churches are in missionary situations."[32] For too many years western churches believed they had accomplished God's mission and lived in a "Christian" society. A significant change in western culture is the demise of that idea known as Christendom.

A missional challenge for the western church is the shift from Christendom to a post-Christendom society. Stuart Murray defines post-Christendom as the "culture that emerges as the Christian faith loses coherence within a society."[33] At its height "the church was the entire society and the entire society was the church," nations were shaped to an extent around the Christian story and called Christian nations.[34] For centuries Christendom has flourished with a close partnership between church and state dominating the culture.[35] That is crumbling. Yet the established churches in the west have been unprepared to face the challenge because many are still living as if Christians are "protected and privileged."[36] When the churches have a Christendom mindset there is less critical reflection of the culture as churches maintain the status quo and mission is not urgent.[37] The Christian church has never lived in a post-Christendom culture. Mike Riddell speaks about the indifference and anger that exist in sections of western culture where people have dismissed Christianity, or at least the version of Christianity Christendom churches have presented.[38] The church as an institution is perceived negatively.[39] There needs to be an engagement with these ecclesial and missional challenges facing western churches so that they may continue to be involved in the mission of God.

An ecclesial challenge facing western churches concerns the way many churches in the twentieth century embraced modernity's values. John Drane names it the *Mc-Donaldization* of the church, to describe how the church embraced the tenets of modernity with its commitment to efficiency, logic, and sameness, and in the process it

---

29. Bruce, *God Is Dead*, 117.
30. Ibid., 240.
31. Riddell, *Threshold of the Future*, 1.
32. Churches, "Appendix," 25.
33. Murray, *Post-Christendom*, 19.
34. Hanciles, *Beyond Christendom*, 84.
35. Murray, *Post-Christendom*, 84.
36. Guder and Barrett, *Missional Church*, 6.
37. Murray, *Post-Christendom*, 200.
38. Riddell, *Threshold of the Future*, 29.
39. Hay, *Something There*, 232.

lost some of the gospel.[40] Yet in a rapidly changing western culture which is rejecting modernism the church seems to be slow to change. Mike Riddell proposes that the western church has become the "biggest barrier" to the gospel as it has conformed to the middle-class, modernist way of life, in the process losing the heart of Jesus's teachings.[41] Lesslie Newbigin also highlights how the mission of the church has been compromised as the church took on modern assumptions such as the split between science and faith, public and private, words and deeds.[42] Dan Kimball, examining the contemporary church in the USA, notes how the church tries to reach people through media presentations, relevant music, and stripping back visible signs of the Christian faith. Taking many aspects of the culture around them they have had great success, yet as the culture again shifts, this way of doing things will fail to connect with a new generation.[43] The modernist paradigm is no longer connecting to many people who are becoming postmodern.

Western culture is rapidly changing and this process is often referred to as postmodernism. Postmodernism is described as a world view that "holds there is no single universal worldview"; it reacts against the overarching metanarratives of modernity, and instead champions diversity, community, creativity, and non-linear thinking.[44] The church needs to engage with what is happening, both at academic and popular levels. The church needs to listen and understand its context, as Jesus did, so it can tell the gospel in a way that "is relevant to the people" whom the church encounters.[45] This is a difficult time, for everything is transitioning, and nobody is sure what new culture or church will emerge.[46] Yet there are hopeful signs and opportunities as people turn to the Bible to be equipped afresh and resourced.

An Alternative Model of Church

There are both scholars and practitioners who are engaging practically with the ecclesial and missional challenges for the church in such a context. The incarnation of Jesus has proven to be theologically rich in this regard.[47] God became a human being in order to fulfill his salvific mission. Alan Hirsch describes it "as an act of profound affinity" with humanity.[48] If this is how God fulfilled his mission, then it follows that as his people the church should be following in the footsteps of Jesus and likewise being

40. Drane, *The McDonaldization of the Church*, 156.
41. Riddell, *Threshold of the Future*, 39.
42. Newbigin, *A Word in Season*, 112.
43. Kimball, *The Emerging Church*, 48.
44. Ibid., 57.
45. Detweiler and Taylor, *A Matrix of Meanings*, 27.
46. Fillebrown, "The Church Meets the Postmodern Era?" 83.
47. John 1:1–18.
48. Hirsch, *The Forgotten Ways*, 132.

incarnational. This means a "genuine identification and affinity" with the people in their particular context.[49] Churches have done this in the past to some extent, as they identified quite strongly with a modernist culture. The problem is then they imported that model of church around the world.[50] This particular model of church also tended to stifle a large proportion of the church, because it emphasized professional people doing mission rather than the whole people of God engaging in God's mission.[51] Churches have often created consumerist subcultures of so-called Christianity that have also alienated people.[52] There is, however, an alternative model emerging.

Churches are discovering how to embody the whole gospel in their lives. Every Christian needs to be "recognized and supported in the communal life of the church" as people in God's mission.[53] Then mission becomes part of "the ordinary rhythms" of people's lives becoming contextualized, as individual Christians see themselves as the church going out to the people, rather than focusing their energy into recruiting people to church to listen to the professionals share the gospel.[54] For established churches Tom Sine gives practical advice, encouraging people to "start small," and begin by discerning with a small group where God is working in the local context before experimenting.[55] As the church joins God's mission it should be renewed and guided by the Holy Spirit.[56] As the church lives incarnationally it begins to wrestle theologically with the questions of that culture.[57] Alongside the incarnational motif churches also need to remember who they are before God.

The church cannot totally identify with culture—the church needs to form strategies around the mission of God. The church is called to be a community that "lives out the reign of God in their lives and society."[58] It is not the kingdom in full, but an "anticipatory sign."[59] Rodney Clapp argues that the church is called to be a "political body" that presents an alternative way of living in line with Jesus.[60] Rob Bell agrees, highlighting how the early church was a "countercultural society" working with God to create a "new kind of culture" right in the midst of the mighty Roman Empire.[61] Therefore the church is called to invite people to be part of this "alien people,"

---

49. Ibid., 133.
50. Guder and Barrett, *Missional Church*, 4.
51. Stevens, *The Other Six Days*, 208.
52. Kimball, *The Emerging Church*, 82.
53. Stevens, *The Other Six Days*, 210–11.
54. Hirsch, *The Forgotten Ways*, 135.
55. Sine, *The New Conspirators*, 277.
56. Anderson, *An Emergent Theology for Emerging Churches*, 186.
57. Kimball, "The Emerging Church and Missional Theology," 89.
58. Engen, *God's Missionary People*, 110.
59. Ibid.
60. Clapp, *A Peculiar People*, 126.
61. Bell, *Velvet Elvis*, 165.

Movement Two—From Shallowness to Dynamic Theological Reflection

expressed not just by proclaiming right belief, but also by living out the way of God.[62] Many people are spiritually open and looking for a community to belong to—unfortunately the church is often not seen as a spiritual community. John Drane suggests the church has the opportunity, as it rediscovers what it means to be a distinct culture, to offer such people a home.[63] For the church to sustain such a mission requires imaginative and biblical resources.

There is an abundance of biblical resources to draw on for contemporary mission in western culture. Bernard Scott points to how Jesus re-imagined the world through the use of parables.[64] Preaching needs to become prophetic. Walter Brueggemann defines the prophetic voice as, "Offering an alternative perception of reality and letting people see their own history in the light of God's freedom."[65] Leaders need fresh biblical resources. A biblical metaphor that Brueggemann suggests as a practical resource for the western church in this time is to see itself as an exile like Jeremiah, Ezekiel, and Isaiah.[66] There are also exilic narratives like Daniel and Esther which show God's people navigating between living in a foreign culture and also being distinct from that culture.[67] Apart from the parables, Jesus's teaching (particularly the Sermon on the Mount) is a rich resource that has been neglected as being unrealistic when the church tried to settle and conform to the world. Now, however, this teaching in the Gospels offers a new ethical vision of what it means to be "citizens of a new kingdom" in a "visible, practical form."[68] The church needs to be able to dwell in the eschatological story of God and live it out. Then it will be better able to cultivate a discerning spirit as it engages with the culture around it.[69] Coupled with biblical teaching will need to be spiritual formation and relational discipleship, to form such missional communities.

The church needs to embody the gospel of God in both words and deeds. This has practical appeal to a post-Christendom, postmodernist culture. David Hay traces the ways that spirituality is expressed in western cultures—though it is often denied, there is awareness of a relational consciousness.[70] He suggests that churches need to embrace the holistic mind-set of the current culture and engage in prayer forms that are more contemplative in nature.[71] Christian discipleship, according to Dan Kimball, is "practicing the presence of Jesus and arranging our lives" as he calls us.[72]

62. Hauerwas and Willimon, *Resident Aliens*, 24.
63. Drane, *Do Christians Know How to Be Spiritual?* 142.
64. Scott, *Re-Imagine the World*, 150.
65. Brueggemann, *The Prophetic Imagination*, 116.
66. Brueggemann, *Cadences of Home*, 131.
67. Frost, *Exiles*, 18.
68. Hauerwas and Willimon, *Resident Aliens*, 87.
69. Clapp, *A Peculiar People*, 155.
70. Hay, *Something There*, 248.
71. Ibid., 232.
72. Kimball, *The Emerging Church*, 224.

To live this out, churches need to practice ancient disciplines for spiritual formation that then spills out into action.[73] Christians are rediscovering that the gospel that Jesus proclaimed is not simply about where our souls might go once we die, but that salvation is *holistic*, meaning God is saving us to *a way of life* that can begin right now and continue into eternity.[74] Even that does not go far enough—it is not just for the individual finding wholeness in life, but the mission of God is concerned about the whole of creation, and so should the church.[75] Story is a powerful medium to express God's kingdom purposes. Many in western cultures are tired of logical propositions, and yearn for a more relational response. Stories are a way to express that, bridging the gap between our own personal story and God's story.[76] Engaging with the missional and ecclesial challenges of the speedily changing western cultures might in fact revitalize the church and its theology by returning to the mission of God.

Participating in God's Mission

The church has a mission. It is involved in the triune God's mission. The whole Bible traces this mission to see God glorified as his kingdom comes to the nations, and indeed the whole of creation. In Jesus Christ this mission becomes clearer, and the church is born. The church in the power of the Holy Spirit is called to invite the nations to become disciples of Jesus and join the mission of God. Theological and practical engagement is needed in keeping churches focused on this mission, especially because the cultures in which churches are set are always changing. There are massive ecclesial and missional challenges for the western church which is in decline. This is due to many different forces, such as the demise of Christendom and the shift away from a modernist world view. Churches need to be incarnational, affirming what is good, and communicating the gospel in understandable ways. Churches also need to present a prophetic alternative to their culture, a community in line with God's mission. There are many biblical resources for this new challenge. There is also a growing excitement that the western church is again taking God's radical mission seriously.

Individual and Corporate Servantship Practices

- Invite a small group of people to be trained over a lengthy period of time. Spend time teaching and modeling with them what it means to be disciples of Jesus. Give people projects and hands-on experience so that they in turn will be able to become better equipped to be a disciple-maker.

---

73. Ibid., 215.
74. Bell, *Velvet Elvis*, 107.
75. Anderson, *An Emergent Theology for Emerging Churches*, 195.
76. Bausch, *Storytelling*, 17.

Movement Two—From Shallowness to Dynamic Theological Reflection

- Preach and teach regularly on Jesus and his mission.
- Celebrate the fact that the gospel is for all peoples and nations—for instance celebrate Pentecost. Hold a party where food is welcomed from all nations, involve people of other ethnic backgrounds to participate, have them share their faith, and pray in their mother tongue.
- Spend time in your local community and neighborhood. Visit the same stores, eat out, talk to people, hear their stories, and pray that God might help you to discern what the needs are for this community.
- Teach people the spiritual disciplines in order that their faith might have impact in their everyday life.
- In your language, behavior, and servantship model that the gospel is holistic, both words and actions.
- Remind the congregation regularly of God's mission that unites them to be a community for God.

Questions for Reflection and Discussion

- Does your church understand itself as the sent agency of God? How is this reflected in its structures and servantship?
- In your own words, what is the mission of God?
- How does your church engage with culture? Are they hostile? Heavily influenced? Indifferent?

7

Responding to the Missional Context

Lynette Edge

Brian McLaren provocatively suggests, "If you have a new world, you will need a new church. You have a new world." By doing so he sets the theme and tone for this chapter.[1]

It is the intention of this chapter to explore the context I live in (the Australian context), before going on to explore some dimensions of missional ecclesiology that might emerge in response to this context.

This chapter is specifically interested in exploring the Australian context for mission and ministry. Whilst one might be able to identify trends across western cultures in general, this chapter is specifically interested in focusing on the Australian context. I do this well aware that this focus itself requires making generalizations that, by necessity, simplify the complex nature of the issues that we confront today.

Whilst there is much merit in looking at trends across the broad sweep of western cultures, this chapter has chosen a national focus because "Australian Christianity needs locally grown approaches." It has been suggested that bringing in missiological theory and practice uncritically from other countries, even other western countries, can be like what happens to strangler figs when they take root in their host tree before going on to take them over completely.[2]

This chapter attempts to sketch some key areas of national identity and contemporary change, before moving on to explore the biblical call to missional and ecclesiological contextualization.

---

1. McLaren, *Church on the Other Side*, 5.
2. Cronshaw, *Credible Witness*, 160.

Movement Two—From Shallowness to Dynamic Theological Reflection

I then explore, in broad terms, some specific ways our missional ecclesiology might be shaped by these issues—such as diversity, spirituality, relationship building, and social concern.

The Australian Context Today

We know that this is a time of great change and cultural transformation, and this is true not only in all western settings but specifically here in Australia. Perhaps Australia's most prominent social researcher, Hugh Mackay, suggests that in Australia we are having our own cultural revolution. He quotes one of his respondents as saying, "You feel as if you're on a runaway train, speeding out of control. You're too scared to jump off because you know you'll be left behind, so you hang on, but you have no idea where this is taking you."[3]

There are a variety of areas in which Australian culture is undergoing rapid cultural change, and this chapter uses the work of Hugh Mackay, Mark McCrindle, and other social research and theological writers to explore these changes further.

The nature of relationships is changing and this is something that Hugh Mackay calls the gender revolution. This has ushered in changes in ways that women and men function on a daily basis. There are more divorces, fewer marriages, and households are shrinking.

> More than 50 percent of households now contain only one or two people and the single-person household is our fastest-growing household type. While this adds to feelings of loneliness and isolation for involuntary singles, it is a symbol of new-found freedom and independence for others.[4]

Economics is another area of change, challenging our traditional ways of understanding the place of work in our lives. This was true long before the Global Economic Crisis of 2008/2009, but the change to increasingly part-time and casual work, as well as the growing divide between rich and poor, are only truer as a result of the GFC.

Information technology has redefined the way we live, work, communicate, inform, and entertain ourselves. According to the Australian Bureau of Statistics, "the rate of household internet access has quadrupled over the past eight years, from 16 percent in 1998 to 64 percent in 2006/7."[5] Australia has one of the highest levels of home internet usage in the world. Social networking sites have created a new world of global and local connections.

Another major area of change is our sense of our identity and our selves. The term "un-Australian" is used by social commentators and politicians, and assumes a knowledge of what we agree constitutes "Australian" identity, so that we might

3. Mackay, "Australia and the World."
4. Ibid.
5. Government, "Australia."

compare this with that which is "un-Australian." However, it would appear that there is no clear consensus on what an Australian cultural identity is today.

It is interesting to note that recently both major Sydney Sunday papers ran front-page banner headlines about our search for a national identity. The *Sun Herald* headline was "Identity Crisis: Our Cross to Bear."[6] Our search for a national sense of self is squarely on the agenda today.

One thing is true—any historic sense of a monoculture Australian character is a thing of the past. We live in one of the most multicultural countries in the world with 22 percent of our population being born overseas—and yet there is a sense of unease with what that means for an Australian identity. There also exists the ongoing question of reconciliation and closing the gap between indigenous and non-indigenous Australians. The question of asylum seekers also looms large on our agendas, often with an overstated fear that people arriving in boats will swamp us. Paul Keating, a former Prime Minister, pressed on us that we were part of Asia, and yet often those cultures remain an enigma to us and we feel apprehension at the instability of our region. "We perceive the world beyond the front gate as a rougher, tougher place than it used to be. We exaggerate our fear of crime and violence; we become more protective of our kids; we welcome, more than ever, the escape into sport and showbiz."[7]

These things, of course, are not all bad news, and "the good news is that when the focus turns inwards, we begin to examine what we see. The present mood of disengagement may well give way to a more contemplative mood as we become more interested in the quality of our lives, and in the ways we express the values we claim to espouse. This explains the rise of interest in spirituality; the so-called 'sea-change' fantasy ('if only we could move to a little place up the coast'); the urge to simplify and down-shift; the dream of 'balance.'"[8]

Gary Bouma is another academic who has explored the current Australian situation, especially in terms of faith and spirituality. He suggest that in the 1970s "secularism was in its heyday, universities its temple, and professors of philosophy and sociology among its high priests."[9]

However, he suggests we have moved as a nation from those days. He borrows a phrase from Manning Clarke as his thematic statement to explain Australian spirituality today, when he suggests we have a "shy hope in the heart."

> There is a profound shyness—yet a deeply grounded hope—held tenderly in the heart, in the heart of Australia. It is not characteristically Australian to trumpet encounters with the spiritual like some American televangelist. That would be an obscene dealing with what is so precious. Australians hold the

---

6. Dart, "Identity Crisis."
7. Mackay, "Australia and the World."
8. Ibid.
9. Bouma, *Australian Soul*, 1.

spiritual gently in their hearts, speaking tentatively about it. The spiritual is treated as sacred.[10]

Spirituality in Australia is growing and increasingly popular. Among those religious groups growing are Buddhism, Islam, Hinduism, Pentecostalism, "nature religions" (including Paganism and Wicca/witchcraft), and Scientology. Australia's religious and spiritual life is increasingly diverse and less tied to formal organizations. The *Australian Communities Report* found that one in two Australians do not identify with a religion, 40 percent consider themselves Christian, 31 percent do not identify with any religion or spiritual belief, and 19 percent say they are spiritual but not religious (the categories "no religion" and "spiritual but not religious" have been the huge growth area in Australia in recent times).[11]

A recent survey commissioned by the *Sydney Morning Herald* drew these headline conclusions: "God is not dead in Australia. Rumours of his failing powers are exaggerated. Disbelief is growing, but God thrives. The default setting of this country is faith. We are not the rational country we thought we were. More Australians believe in miracles, angels, heaven and ESP than in Darwin's theory of evolution."[12] This survey found that 68 percent of Australians believe in a God, 53 percent in a life after death, and 51 percent in angels.

While Australians are not as devout as their North American counterparts, they are more religious than citizens of many other western nations, such as the United Kingdom and Sweden. "Many evangelical Christians who have come to Australia from the USA quickly form the impression that Australia is spiritually dead and that Australia is ripe for conversion."[13] In contrast to the brash, mega-industry of the right-wing Christianity in the United States, it is considered un-Australian to "trumpet encounters with the spiritual like some American televangelist," and a gentler but nonetheless profound expression of faith is to be found here.

The Call to Contextualization

We have just explored some of the cultural conditions in contemporary Australia. These are important insights as they are fundamental to an understanding of how the gospel might be incarnated in the Australian setting today. This chapter will now

10. Ibid., 2.

11. McCrindle Research, 2011, *Australian Communities Report*: http://www.mccrindle.com.au/resources/Australian-Communities-Report_McCrindle-Research.pdf. For more information on spiritual and religious shifts in Australia, see the online McCrindle Research papers: "Christianity in Australia" http://www.mccrindle.com.au/Infographic/Christianity-in-Australia_Infographic.pdf, and "The Spiritual Attitudes of the New Generations" http://www.mccrindle.com.au/resources/whitepapers/Emerging-Trends-Enduring-Truth_The-Spiritual-Attitudes-of-the-New-Generations.pdf.

12. Marr, "Our Faith Today."

13. Bouma, *Australian Soul*, 32.

move on to briefly explore how missional ecclesiology needs to respond to the biblical call of contextualization.

> The Christian faith is intrinsically incarnational. Therefore, unless the church chooses to remain a foreign entity, it will always enter into the context in which it happens to find itself.[14]

Orlando Costas further contends that the gospel cannot be defined at all without reference to context, since "the context is the stage where all comprehension takes place. It is the reality that ties together and therefore shapes all knowledge . . . We participate in it, actively or passively. Not one of us can claim to stand outside it. The question is whether or not we can consciously and critically incorporate it into our efforts to interpret and communicate the gospel. This is what we do in contextualization."[15]

The apostle Paul certainly models contextualizing the gospel when he was preaching to the philosophers in Acts 17. This text is a profound example of someone entering and understanding the culture in which they wish to share the gospel, and then uses the culture's places, symbols, narrators, and stories to introduce people to Jesus.

Charles Kraft further explores the place of contextualization in the Bible. He suggests four ways in which we might see it.

- Our God . . . is mainly a God of dialogue who interacts with us, not simply a God of monologue who makes pronouncements above us.
- God's method of communication is to use familiar ways.
- God's self-disclosure is participatory.
- We observe God's revelatory activity in the Scriptures to be situation-specific.[16]

In the past we may have thought that contextualization was the domain of cross-cultural missionaries who went to work in foreign countries. Today, however, "it is necessary for the church to rethink its stance entirely and to become a missionary church within the west."[17]

This is not a task we can take lightly. "There is urgency and force in God's direction towards the world, and if religion is no longer successful in carrying forwards this divine power into the world, then God may be behind the so-called demise of religion. God may be saying to us, 'I will take away the traditional vessels from you, and see what creativity may arise. I will break the religious clichés and images, and see whether something new can be fashioned from the direct experience of spiritual life.' God is serious about spiritual mission, and serious enough to take action if religion

---

14. Bosch, *Transforming Mission*, 190.
15. Costas, *Christ Outside the Gate*, 5.
16. Kraft, *Christianity in Culture*, 24.
17. Robinson, *To Win the West*.

appears to be falling short of the mark... The spirit of God wants to lead us on, and yet our attachment to old forms may be preventing this spirit from being realized."[18]

In light of that, we now turn our attention to the question of exploring the ways in which a missional ecclesiology might be shaped by our context today.

Towards a Missional Ecclesiology for Australia Today

It is important to note that this chapter will not attempt to develop a full ecclesiology for today, but rather explore some specific ways in which our ecclesiology should respond to the Australian context in which we find ourselves—much as Paul did in Athens in the first century.

Ecclesiology could be defined as the theology of the church, the sense of our own self-understanding as the church, or our ways of operating as the people of God.

> In the ecclesiocentric approach of Christendom, mission became only one of the many programs of the church... but it has taken us decades to realize that mission is not just a program of the church.[19]

Mission is not one more job for the church, but in fact is at the heart of the nature and activity of God. *Missio Dei* is a Latin term that can be translated as the "sending of God." David Bosch has been vital to our recent understanding of *missio Dei*. He says "Our mission has no life of its own: only in the hands of the sending God can it truly be called mission. Not least since the missionary initiative comes from God alone."[20]

In attempting to flesh out the *missio Dei* concept, it is important to understand that mission is not primarily an activity of the church, but an attribute of God. "It is not the church that has a mission of salvation to fulfill in the world; it is the mission of the Son and the Spirit through the Father that includes the church."[21] "The church ... must run to catch up with what God is already doing in the world. We are invited to look for where God is working in the world and to join him there."[22]

If this is true, then our ecclesiology, by definition, should be a missional one.

Church in Its Diversity

We noted that Australia is one of the world's most multi-cultural societies, with 22 percent of its population born overseas.[23] The challenge for the church and its ser-

---

18. Tacey, *The Spirituality Revolution*, 192.
19. Guder and Barrett, *Missional Church*, 6.
20. Bosch, *Transforming Mission*, 390.
21. Moltmann, *Church in the Power*, 64.
22. Cox, *God's Revolution*, 24.
23. Australian Government, "Australia."

vantship in Australia today is to reflect that diversity. This is not only true of ethnic diversity, but of cultural groups, and social interests which make up Australian society today.

> The relationship between church and society has been changing for some time. The church finds itself no longer at the center of uniform and clearly recognized culture—the situation that has pertained for many years. Society itself is becoming more diverse. This means that it is no longer enough to imagine that the Christian church can change in one particular direction and so move with the times. That may appeal to some, but it will alienate others. Different parts of our culture are actually moving in different directions.[24]

The Anglican church in the United Kingdom has responded to this increased diversity in their culture by advocating a "mixed economy of church," where variety will be expressed in the very fabric of the Christian communities. These are as diverse as café churches, school or professionally linked congregations, locally shaped community initiatives, and alternative worship congregations.

The Archbishop of Canterbury opened the way for Anglican churches in the United Kingdom to embrace this diversity, when he said that "if church is what happens when people encounter the Risen Lord Jesus and commit themselves to sustaining and deepening that encounter in their encounter with each other, there is plenty of theological room for diversity of rhythm and style."[25]

Australian churches are far from being a "mixed economy" of diverse faith communities and expressions of worship. There is a great challenge here to not only embrace, but also actively create diverse expressions of church in Australia today.

> The church is a dynamic cultural expression of the people of God in any given place. Worship style, social dynamics, liturgical expressions must result from the process of contextualizing the gospel in any given culture.[26]

If the challenge to genuine contextualization of the gospel were taken up in Australia, we could not only foresee more diverse ethnic groups in our churches, but a variety of churches around social groupings such as sport, professional interests, children, or social causes (such as the environment). It has been noted that Australia has one of the highest levels of pet ownership in the world. Is this a point of connection that could draw a group of people together to explore faith, who would not normally be attracted to our traditional, uniform, or mono-cultural churches?

To embrace radical diversity will require leaders who can think outside the box in terms of how church communities function. In a recent article in *Servantship Journal*, Alan Hirsch reflected upon a time when he questioned what sorts of leaders were

---

24. Croft, *Mission-Shaped Questions*.
25. Williams, *Mission-Shaped Church*, vii.
26. Hirsch, *The Forgotten Ways*.

being trained for ministry in Melbourne, Australia. He said, "we needed a new type of servantship, one with the courage to question the status quo, to dream of new possibilities, and to innovate new ways of being the people of God in a post-Christian culture. We needed missionaries to the west, but our seminaries were not producing them."[27]

It has been suggested that Christian leaders today will need to have a holy discontent, embrace subversive questioning, take more risks, and be able to create a climate of change.[28]

This presents a real challenge for church, theological, and denominational leaders in the process of both attracting and training leaders for our churches in Australia today.

Church Nurturing Connection with God

It has been widely recognized that there is a spiritual awareness in Australia today, demonstrated, for instance, by the Darling Harbour *Mind, Body, Spirit* festival. This spiritual festival is one of the largest of its kind in the world.[29] The time is ripe in Australia for the church to reclaim its role as spiritual guides who can nurture a connection with God through their lives and worship.

Darren Cronshaw calls the church to fulfill the role of spiritual companion in Australia today, to help people connect with the sacredness of their situations. He goes on to suggest that "the anti-religious temperament of Australian culture is like a radical Protestantism, an attack on religious orthodoxy, a resistance to authority, a clearing away of icons, not to get rid of God, but to know God more directly."[30]

Michael Frost and Alan Hirsch employ another metaphor to call the church to this task today. They suggest we need to learn to be "whisperers to the soul" as we connect with the deepest longings of not-yet-Christians today.[31]

People today process information holistically. This is the antithesis to the propositional teaching that the church has done so well in the past. We must engage people in an "all-of-life spirituality."

However we envisage the role, the call to the church is clear. Many people in Australia today are open to the things of God, to mystery and wonder, to spirituality and prayer. The church has largely not been the place they have turned to in search of an encounter with the Divine, but a call remains for us to be that place as we share the spiritual journey with Australians today.

---

27. Hirsch, "Three Over-Looked Leadership Roles."
28. Frost and Hirsch, *Shaping of Things to Come*, 192.
29. http://www.mbsfestival.com.au/index.htm.
30. Cronshaw, *Credible Witness*, 24.
31. Frost and Hirsch, *Shaping of Things to Come*, 99.

Church as Community

We reflected earlier on the fact that the single-person household is our fastest-growing household type in Australia. This might suggest a period of increased social isolation and relational dislocation. However, Hugh Mackay points out "it may also turn out to be good news for communities: the human herd instinct won't be denied and when it is not satisfied by the domestic herd, we look elsewhere—to the coffee shop, the book club, the adult-education class—for the sense of belonging that is vital to our personal, social, and moral health."[32]

Biblically, the metaphor of the church as family communicates that we are to be a place of belonging, care-giving, and mutual value (see Galatians 4:1–7). This place of care and connection is a gift we can, and should, be offering to our society, since these things are less available in our contemporary domestic lives.

A study quoted in the *Sun Herald* a few years ago entitled "Hardwired To Connect: The New Scientific Case For Authoritative Communities," suggested that the human brain is "biologically hardwired for enduring attachments to other people and for moral and spiritual meaning."[33] They reported that the decline in social connectedness, the loss of civic and community groups, and falling church attendance, are thought to contribute significantly to childhood problems. "If religion does protect adolescents, Australians are in trouble" said Miranda Divine in response to these findings. "Fewer than 10 percent of Australians now attend church regularly. As churchgoing slumped, so did children's emotional wellbeing."[34]

Australian churches today are in a position to offer a place of security, of deep relationships, and of meaning-making through connection with God and with others in real community. This cannot be an optional extra for any church—it must be at our very heart.

Church as a Prophetic Voice and Caregiver

As previously mentioned, the wealth and power gap in Australia is growing. "The top 20 percent of households earn 45 percent of the income and hold 60 percent of the wealth."[35] This growing gap is a challenge to the Australian notion of a classless egalitarian society where there is a "fair go" for all, but, more importantly, it is not a matter on which the church can be silent since it goes to the heart of issues of justice. The gospel has much to say about how we respond to poverty and injustice. The question is, "will the church lead the way in addressing the growing gap between rich and poor?"

32. Mackay, "Australia and the World."
33. Divine, "Church and Family."
34. Ibid.
35. Mackay, *Advance Australia—Where?* 84.

Movement Two—From Shallowness to Dynamic Theological Reflection

This is a challenge in Australia where the wider community sees the churches negatively as the moral "police," while, at the same time, expecting the church to be helpers of the poor and needy.[36]

A challenge exists for the church to consider how meeting and challenging community expectations fit with our prophetic task. "The path of peace is well understood by the churches, yet also stands the warning of Jesus, 'Woe to you when all speak well of you, for that is what their ancestors did to the false prophets.' Luke 6:26."[37]

We are a country that traditionally loves an "underdog" and champions the "little battler," so this role of advocating and caring for the marginalized should be widely embraced in our culture. Sadly, we know that is not so, as evidenced by the statistics of poverty and indigenous disadvantage here. The church must step up and be that voice for the voiceless, however politically costly that is.

So there is a prophetic role for the church in Australia today, but there is also the call to care for the direct needs of the disadvantaged amongst us. Matthew 25:40 reminds us that the church is to demonstrate Christ through our acts of service to those in need. James 1:27 adds that "religion that God our Father accepts as pure and faultless is this: to look after orphans and widows in their distress."

The need for the church to stay engaged in direct involvement with the needy is embodied in this story of William Stead, who was a friend of the Salvation Army in its early days in London. He was jailed for his involvement in the Salvation Army's campaign to raise the age of consent. He said, "Do you know what I think Jesus Christ would do if he came now? He would go to church and chapel ever so many times and listen, and no one would speak to him. He would look to see who sat round him and he would see no ragged people, no thieves, and no harlots—only respectable people. And he would hear all these respectable people singing hymns to Christ, and giving all the glory to Christ, and then after standing it a long time, Jesus would stand up some day in the middle of the church and say just two words, 'Damn Christ!' and then he would go out and go down some slum and put his arms round the neck of some poor lost orphan girl, who was having a bitter cry, and say 'Come unto me, all ye that are weary and heavy laden, and I will give you rest.'"[38]

The church today is called to care for the needy through acts of compassion, and through being a prophetic voice calling for an end to systemic injustice in our society.

At the outset of this chapter we read Brian McLaren's bold statement that "If you have a new world, you will need a new church. You have a new world."[39]

We then went on to explore some ways in which the nation of Australia is developing and thus becoming, in Brian McLaren's words, a new world. There is rapid

36. Langmead, "The Best of Times, the Worst of Times."
37. Kaldor, "The Role of the Churches in Australia Today."
38. Cleary, "Boundless Salvation," 77.
39. McLaren, *Church on the Other Side*, 5.

change in areas such as relationships, economics, information technology, a sense of identity, and spirituality.

In light of this social context for faith and ministry, we explored the question of contextualization before moving on to develop a missional ecclesiological response for Australia today. Our cultural context has profound implications for the church, for our missiology, our ecclesiology, our evangelism, and our social action.

This chapter has attempted, in very broad terms, to explore some of those implications for the church in Australia today. In so doing, I have tried to shape some questions we face regarding our diversity, our spirituality, our relationship building, and our social concern. These are areas that call from us change, so that we will be able to be Jesus Christ in this new world in which we live, as his salt and light.

Individual and Corporate Servantship Practices

- Approach your local council or community center to obtain community analysis data for your neighborhood. Present that information to your faith community and discuss how it reflects your church and your ministry engagement. Listen to what God is saying to you through that information.

- If your faith community does not have a website or cyber presence, consider if an on-line engagement would help you connect with your community. Surf the web and look at other church or faith community websites and let yourself be inspired or challenged by them.

- Search YouTube for examples of the *Fresh Expression* movement and see what is happening there.

- Attend a spirituality expo, such as *Body, Mind, Spirit*, and as you engage with the spiritual seekers there ask how God is at work in this space?

- Walk around your community with your eyes open and ask where are people meeting here? Ask yourself how God is present in those spaces.

- Consider what justice issue God is laying on your heart and how he might be calling you to respond prophetically to that issue. If you are not already active in this area, find something small and practical you can do to get started.

Questions for Reflection and Discussion

- Harvey Cox says the church must "run to catch up with what God is already doing in the world." How do you respond to this quote? What might it mean to "catch up with God" in your local context and in your servantship?

- Michael Frost and Alan Hirsch challenge us to be "whisperers to the soul" as we

Movement Two—From Shallowness to Dynamic Theological Reflection

respond to people today. How do you understand the term "whisperer to the soul"? Imagine someone was whispering to your soul, what would you like to hear?

- People are seeking a sense of connection and belonging. What does community mean to you? What does it look like in your church or faith context? How might your sense of community be strengthened?

- How does servantship practiced in the Spirit of Christ strengthen community?

8

Exploring Theological Bearings

Paul Winch

Our western society is a very different one than it was just fifty years ago, and the rate of change only seems to be escalating. As a people sent into that world, the church needs to rapidly change too, in order to adequately and faithfully respond to such changes.

> Every now and again, dramatic changes in culture and media, new findings in scholarship, and discoveries in science enable a new transformation to take place in the way the Christian church lives out its mission to embody the love of God to the world.[40]

Such an assessment of our times is commonplace in academia. Yet these opportunities described by Joshua Moritz are hard to actualize. For a start, the changes are so profound and ongoing that they are still undetermined. There is dispute about whether such changes herald a new era of history called *postmodernism*, because many thinkers within a postmodern stream would dispute even the assumptions that would lead to such a linear analysis of history. Nevertheless, epoch marking or not, changes are substantial and need to be faced, whether we have the wherewithal to analyze them adequately or not.

Where Are We Now?

Here is a brief survey of some of the changes that the church is still grappling with.

---

40. Moritz, "Beyond Strategy, Towards the Kingdom of God," 34.

Movement Two—From Shallowness to Dynamic Theological Reflection

Cost of Housing: The real affordability of housing in many western markets has worsened over the last few decades. According to the Property Council of Australia, affordable housing is measured by the purchase price to household income ratio being 3.0 or less. Up until the 1980s this was the case in most English-speaking western countries. However, house prices escalated rapidly from then on. According to the Property Council's most recent report, the housing affordability in Sydney was measured at 9.1 in 2009, the second highest in nearly three hundred major English-speaking markets around the world.[41] Anything over 5.0 is considered "severely unaffordable," which is a category that twenty-two of twenty-three major markets in Australia fall into. In many markets of the western world, fewer and fewer people can afford to purchase their own home. If they do purchase their own home, making loan repayments takes several incomes through multiple jobs or a highly paid, dual income family. People's lifestyles have invariably shifted to cope. While domestic duties over a similar period have become vastly easier and less time consuming due to mechanization, discretionary time and money have still shrunk for those with mortgages or working towards purchasing a home. However, discretionary time and money for many churches are often exactly what they rely on for volunteer programs and ministries.

Mobility: While people face discretionary time and money pressures, at the same time changes in industry, transport, and residential options have all facilitated a massive social mobility. Tenure is now generally unheard of in the workplace. A lifetime career in an industry, let alone a single company, would be considered unusual. When I recently took out a first-home-owner's mortgage, the lender was genuinely shocked that I have been continuously employed in the one organization for seventeen years. Travel opportunities, both domestic and global, facilitate rapid mobility, with companies keen to keep experienced employees brokering international workplace transfers where they can. Often economic considerations enforce workplace moves as companies seek economic advantage. And, of course, travel is much easier these days because of transport advances. My wife's grandparents travelled to India as missionaries by boat, and were gone for a decade. Today, my church supports missionaries in India who return home by airplane about once a year for holidays in Australia. Growing up in the one house, at the same school, and so forth, is not as commonplace as it used to be. According to the Australian Bureau of Statistics, "Of the 5.3 million people aged 18 years and over living in NSW, 1.6 million people had changed their usual residence, or moved," during the three-year period prior to October 2008.[42]

---

41. See the *6th Demographica International Housing Affordability Survey* (January 2010) accessible at http://www.propertyoz.com.au.

42. See the report released from the Australian Bureau of Statistics in October 2008 entitled *3240.0—Residential and Workplace Mobility, and Implications for Travel*, available from http://www.abs.gov.au.

This social mobility means that community and neighborhood relationships, so often the lifeblood of church outreach and ministry, are often in a state of flux, if they exist at all.

Worldview Questions: While technology has been a large contributor to the changes surveyed above (which represent just two of the significant developments),[43] the shift in cultural values and world view has been occurring over a longer period, say the last century.[44] This shift has been occurring for many decades, even though popular awareness of postmodernity has only been a feature of the last two decades. "Incredulity toward metanarratives" is perhaps the most widely regarded simple definition of postmodernism, although John Drane makes a strong case for modifying that definition slightly—"incredulity towards *Enlightenment* metanarratives" being more accurate.[45] Autonomous individualism, "objective" rationalism, scientific positivism, and technological pragmatism—these values of the Enlightenment metanarrative have been rejected for a metanarrative that values respectful and attentive world view dialogue, collective tolerance, communitarian knowledge, mystery, and pessimism (or even cynicism) about progress.[46] "The modern notion of freedom remains in postmodern culture, [but] . . . it has shifted from an extrinsic orientation to an intrinsic one."[47]

---

43. Other important ones not surveyed here include:

    a) communications and connectivity
    b) genetically modified food
    c) the extension of life expectancy
    d) the prospect of pandemics similar to or worse than SARS, bird flu, and swine flu
    e) the changing demographic with the aging of the "boomers" (although this is not as pronounced a problem in Australia as elsewhere in the west)
    f) the "war on terror"
    g) environmental issues including climate change.

    For an extensive interaction with most of these issues see Sine, *Mustard Seed Vs. Mcworld*.

44. Postmodernism ". . . emerged in the arts around the turn of the [twentieth] century, in deliberate rejection of the world shaped by Enlightenment and Romanticism, i.e., of the world otherwise called 'modern.'" (Jenson, "How the World Lost Its Story," 19). Two world wars in the first half of the twentieth century also contributed to an increasing lack of confidence in "the world that instrumental and critical reason built." (ibid., 20).

45. "Popular culture is not rejecting the possibility that there might be such a story, but is rather searching for a new one that more closely approximates to the realities of everyday life." (Drane, "Contemporary Culture and the Reinvention of Sacramental Spirituality," 55). See also Drane, "The Globalization of Spirituality."

46. These four categories are slight variations on those proposed by Engen, "Mission Theology in the Light of Postmodern Critique." Another characterization of postmodern values includes that they are non-optimistic (skeptical), non-religious (but spiritual), non-segmental (holistic), non-elitist (inclusive), non-univocal (dialogical), non-objective (subjective), non-totalizing (tolerant), non-propositional (narratival), and non-foundational (mystical). Sellers, "Is Mission Possible in a Postmodern World?"

47. Stanley, "Speaking Credibly?" 25.

Movement Two—From Shallowness to Dynamic Theological Reflection

Globalization: With the shift after the cold war of most of the world's central economies to capitalist ones, along with the requisite political commitment to the opening of free trade, the effect of globalization has arguably become the biggest indicator of change in society. "It is my contention that the number one force that will shape the future of our lives, families, congregations, and the larger world is globalization."[48]

Globalization could be seen as the height of the Enlightenment dream, a feature of late modernity. Yet when freedom from "external constraints" has largely been met by the modern project, the options of a consumerist culture present themselves to those postmoderns looking for internal needs, as agents for differentiation or satisfaction. "In the quest for intrinsic freedom, postmodernity has turned to the resources of the global economy."[49]

Globalization fits well with postmodernism. The commercial forces of globalization and the influence of postmodernity combine in the marketing of new identities, including spiritualities.

> There is an intrinsic connection between the fact that Western people have begun to take seriously other cultures and their spirituality only at the point when the Western world view is trivializing and relativizing all culture.[50]

When there was high confidence in the west, other views were regarded simply as wrong. Now, with an evaporating confidence in metanarratives in the west, other world views are tinkered with consumeristically, but are regarded as meaningless within a postmodern epistemology. All that is left is personal choice, a consumerist's nirvana, such that "openness" to other cultures is often a masquerade for a mix-and-match commercialization (especially of eastern views and practices).

> Postmodernity is oft expressed as the consumer quest for emancipation from intrinsic authority . . . Religion is consumed in ever-new special effects of our own making that conform to our insatiable quest for "shock and awe."[51]

Internal Decay: While the situational context for the church in the west is one of great flux, the organizational reality fares no better. The decline in church attendance has been consistent and gradual throughout the last forty years, and there are few signs that this could change, even with the growth of the Pentecostal movement, which has so often been lauded as a panacea in the rate of decline (at least in the west). The figures of decline are truly alarming and therefore the situation is absolutely urgent.[52]

---

48. Sine, *Mustard Seed Vs. Mcworld*, 49.
49. Stanley, "Speaking Credibly?" 25.
50. Drane, "The Globalization of Spirituality," 13.
51. Stanley, "Speaking Credibly?" 26–27.
52. In 1960, 41 percent of the Australian population attended church at least *monthly* and by 2000 this was closer to 20 percent, and falling. Between 1996 and 2001 *weekly* church attendance fell by 7 percent. Source: see http://www.ncls.org.au.

By and large the church has not coped with these changes, and has not been able to retain adherents. People move, whether by choice or otherwise, and drop out of congregational life as relationships are severed. The pressures of life, with shrinking discretionary time and money, leave little room for additional engagements—something that many volunteer organizations apart from the church have experienced. Modes of church operation are still largely based on Enlightenment values, which seem strange to many in our society—these people are often reacting against such narratives of structural and organization progress, and looking for something more organic. Others have drunk long at the well of globalization and consumerism, and approach church involvement in the same consumerist way. For all these reasons and more, the decline of the church has continued unabated in the western world.

Are There Signs of Hope?

There are a number of reasons to be optimistic for a potential reversal—apart from the obvious theological imperative to hope in the resurrected Christ to build his church. The social situation within which the church operates presents many opportunities.

> . . . though the meaninglessness of metanarratives has been questioned, the very existence of New Spirituality is evidence that the personal search for some bigger story that might be worth giving one's life for has not diminished but has actually intensified.[53]

Quite simply, people want to make sense of the change and difficulty of their life.

Internally, there are also signs of life and renewal in such things as the *emerging-missional church movement*, which is incredibly diverse (and therefore notoriously difficult to analyze).[54] There is also hope in the *fresh expressions* movement in the United Kingdom,[55] which is much more intentionally and denominationally organized than typical emerging churches, as well as hope to be found in the numerous church-planting and missional-leader networks springing up in western cultures.[56]

---

53. Drane, "The Globalization of Spirituality," 18.

54. Probably the best survey I have read of the emerging church, based on ethnographic research, is by Gibbs, *Church Next*. However, the rate of change within the emerging church is such that this book is likely now already out of date.

55. See http://www.freshexpressions.org.uk, which is partnered by the Methodist, United Reformed, and Church of England denominations in an institutional attempt to create a "mixed economy of churches"—with encouraging early signs.

56. Some of these include:
    a) OzReach—see http://www.ozreach.org
    b) Next1000—see http://www.next1000.org
    c) Geneva Push—see http://www.thegenevapush.com
    d) Forge Mission Network—see http://www.forge.org.au
    e) en:trust church planting network—See http://www.rice.entrust.thereformission.net
    f) Inspire Network—see http://www.morling.nsw.edu.au/tinsley_institute.

Movement Two—From Shallowness to Dynamic Theological Reflection

Much of this potential has not eventuated by accident, but through a thoroughgoing evaluation of contemporary change and a careful consideration about how the church should deal with it. The church must embrace change. New ways of being and doing missional churches have to be conceived and forged. One of the key conceptual grids through which this reorientation is analyzed and explained is by comparing a *Christendom-mode* church with a *missional-mode* church.

Michael Frost and Alan Hirsch describe the typical Protestant church in the west as inheriting a Christendom-mode of being. This is where the church claims for itself a central and intrinsic role in the life of the community. This was true even after the Reformation, when the papal monarchical system had been repudiated, because, for example, in Luther's two-kingdom theology, the state and the church were still profoundly related. In Australia, which has never had a state church, and which could perhaps be regarded as resistant to deep church/state relations, the church nevertheless made presumptions about its role within the wider society. Many still call Australia a "Christian nation"—with (tenuous and ambiguous) census figures to back the claim up.

Within an Enlightenment world view, which increasingly threw off the "superstitious shackles" of religion in the "freedom" of rational enquiry and empirical science, such a Christendom-mode of being was able to survive within the church, and perhaps even thrive. This was because the Christendom approach mirrored modernity's optimistic progression to its "manifest destiny."

> In the past, because the church believed it was the repository of the only plausible "big story" or metanarrative, our forebears were able to assume not only that they spoke on behalf of everyone, but also that they had an unassailable right to speak to everyone. In some way or another, we were all "Christian," because that was perceived as the only world view that made sense of things.[57]

The Christendom-mode church has been surprisingly resilient throughout the machinations of the Roman Empire, the Byzantium Empire, the Holy Roman Empire, the Reformation, the Enlightenment, and even places such as Australia.

> Anabaptists—and the Free Churches generally—rejected the coercive aspects of Christendom, but still operated on the underlying Constantinian notion of a culture that would be directed and owned by Christians.[58]

Today, a Christendom-mode church "plants itself within a particular community, neighborhood, or locale, and expects that people will come to it to meet God."[59] Such churches work hard to provide the "best events" or "deepest relationships" for the community, even marketing these within the community so that as many as

---

57. Drane and Drane, "Breaking through into Dynamic Ways of Being Church," 146.
58. Drane, "Looking for Maturity in the Emerging Church," footnote 27.
59. Frost and Hirsch, *Shaping of Things to Come*, 18.

possible will "come." If people get used to being at the church premises, so the strategy goes, they will have the opportunity to hear an engaging speaker explain the gospel. This end might be good, but the premise is usually wrong, as Michael Frost and Alan Hirsch explain.

> This assumes that we have a place in our society and that people don't join our churches because, though they want to be Christians, they're unhappy with the product. The missional church recognizes that it does not hold a place of honor in its host community and that its missional imperative compels it to move out from itself into that host community as salt and light.[60]

If Timothy Stanley is right that within modernity "the church forfeited its right to the center of culture when it became part of a system of domination," then the Christendom-mode church is always going to be shackled in its ability to be salt and light to the whole community, especially those most influenced by a rejection of modernist values.[61]

Theological and Biblical Bearings

If the "vast majority of people in churches are not there to be changed but to shore themselves up against the too-rapid changes of a souped-up society," then how will such a transformation to a missional-mode church, with the vast changes it entails, possibly take place?[62] Handling change by changing is a rather counterintuitive act and not easily undertaken. The key conceptual grid explored above needs some theological underpinnings, in order to effect and sustain a missional-mode rather than Christendom-mode of witness. There are three that I will explore briefly.

missio Dei: "It was Karl Barth who in 1932 first proposed that mission should be understood as an activity of God, rather than as a church program."[63] God is on mission—he is a missionary God. It is part of God's intra-trinitarian nature that he is sender and sent, the Father having sent the Son in the power of the Spirit to complete his work, and the Father in turn sending the Spirit through the Son.[64]

> Mission is not primarily an activity of the church, but an attribute of God . . . Mission is thereby seen as a movement from God to the world; the church is

---

60. Ibid., 19.
61. Stanley, "Speaking Credibly?" 29.
62. Wink, quoted in: Drane, "Rebuilding the Household of Faith."
63. Drane, "Looking for Maturity in the Emerging Church," 7.
64. This is my "rough and ready" attempt to compromise between the Eastern and Western Churches on the *filioque* clause of the Nicene Creed. I would argue, of course, that this is not without biblical warrant.

Movement Two—From Shallowness to Dynamic Theological Reflection

> viewed as an instrument for that mission . . . There is church because there is mission, not vice versa.[65]

Thus missional-mode churches assume and expect God to be active in their community and society, before, and even quite apart from, their own church community, events, and programs. "The authentic Christian vision is not focused on programs, but on God, as we discern what God is doing in the world, and then get alongside that."[66]

A "Peculiar People": The second theological pillar of a missional-mode church is to understand and enact the identity of the people of God, who are, and always were, elected for service.

> When the scriptural foundations for Christian self-understanding are properly investigated, it becomes clear that the distinctiveness of the people of God has never been at the expense of the rest of the world. Their proper identity has always been that of being called into a particular relationship with God for the purposes of proclaiming a universal message.[67]

We see this epitomized in Jesus.

> Jesus's own demarcation of his followers from the rest of Israel, let alone from the pagan Gentiles, hardly suggests that he was a modern egalitarian born out of due time. His welcome to all and sundry was balanced by [his] quite sharp exclusivism . . . [68]

This "balance" is enormously difficult in practice, as churches tend to either become sect-like, defining themselves as the people of God over-against the world, or utterly porous and indistinct from the world. "In the world but not of it" was Jesus's vision for his church—indiscretions or excesses in either direction have, of course, done enormous damage to the witness of the church in the world.

How do these first two theological pillars relate? In my view, the second one currently needs to be re-emphasized. If it is mainly the *missio Dei* that provides a framework for being a missional church, the impetus to be a church can easily be lost altogether. David Bosch has detected this danger, because some,

> . . . tended to radicalize the view that the *missio Dei* was larger than the mission of the church, even to the point of suggesting that it excluded the church's involvement . . . it seems the church has become unnecessary for the *missio Dei* . . . [But instead] the church is privileged to participate [in God's mission].[69]

---

65. Bosch, *Transforming Mission*, 390.
66. Drane, "Who Wants to Be a Leader?" 8.
67. Watson, "Salt to the World," 457.
68. Wright, *Jesus and the Victory of God*, 389.
69. Bosch, *Transforming Mission*, 392.

David Watson grapples with this danger too, as after he highlights the churches peculiar calling to service in the world, a calling given by God himself, he nevertheless is attracted to, yet not fully affirming of, the notion that "the function of this particular community among a pluralism of God's saving activities is that of a sign."[70] Yes a *sign*, but surely much more than a sign too.

Likewise, in doing mission in a postmodern world, Michael Amaladoss seems to downplay the particularity of the church in God's purposes.

> We should rather explore the possibilities of a global quest for spirituality, rooted in the experience of the divine or of the Transcendent. . . . People who have a deep experience of their own religion seem able to dialogue with others and to learn from them, because the deeper one's experience of the divine, the more one is aware of the limits of that experience. The greater one's focus on God, the more ready one is to recognize God's presence in others.[71]

The approach of Lesslie Newbigin is likely to be much more fruitful than these other perspectives.[72] The church stands within the tradition of the gospel narrative. This narrative, like most others, including the narrative of postmodernity, makes a claim to truth, meaning, and power. As Andrew Kirk explains,

> Postmodernity . . . is characterized by its "absolute" conviction that any attempt to build a uniform body of knowledge . . . actually hides a sinister design to impose upon all peoples only one right way of looking upon the world.[73]

Lesslie Newbigin explains that within the gospel narrative the church is not a possessor of the story, but a searcher for the meaning of its story. The church is a disciple, someone who trusts that there is more to come, more to be learned, from the one who laid down all power for the sake of others—he is the known center of the story. In this way the church is the "hermeneutic of the gospel" in a pluralist world. It lives out the gospel in suffering holiness and humble, non-coercive proclamation. In doing so it enacts the center of the story, while remaining open to its end point, which is transcultural. "If the church does not find her hearers antecedently inhabiting a narratable world, then the church must herself be that world."[74] This sounds much more like the biblical "election to service" of God's people. This election is a peculiarity that calls the church to recognize and affirm both dimensions of its calling—the church's "face to the world" and its "rootedness in God." "A missionary community is one that understands itself as being both different from and committed to its environment."[75]

---

70. Watson, "Salt to the World," 463.
71. Amaladoss, "Mission in a Post-Modern World," 78.
72. The following synopsis of Newbigin is based largely on Weston, "Lesslie Newbigin."
73. Kirk, "Following Modernity and Postmodernity," 229.
74. Jenson, "How the World Lost Its Story," 22.
75. Bosch, *Transforming Mission*, 83.

Movement Two—From Shallowness to Dynamic Theological Reflection

Integral Discipleship: The third theological pillar to sustain and energize a missional church is found in the glorious breadth of our humanness (this, of course, needs to involve a consideration of the depth of our human problems and possibilities). Humans are created in the "image of God," and as such we can worship God with heart, soul, mind, and strength, which encompasses all of our being and life. Further, Jesus was the incarnate Son of God—he took on human flesh and became one of us. He did not leave that humanity behind as a temporary "necessary evil," for he was raised with his (now glorified) body. This radically affirms God's creation of us in his image, and proves that human life and experience are not alien to the being of God, but, rather, that he knows it from the inside. Jesus is the human *par excellence.* Such profound mysteries should drive a stake into the dualism the western church has inherited from Augustinian Neo-Platonism (which elevates the mind above the body, and which so often leads to a segmented, compartmentalized, and fractured spirituality/godliness/discipleship/embodiment).

Likewise, the depths of our problems need to be constantly realized. For the human *par excellence* "something far deeper was going on . . . head on war with the Satan."[76] Jesus has, in mighty and real ways, triumphed in his life, death, and resurrection. Sin and death are conquered. And yet, as "the church witnesses to the fullness of the promise of God's reign [it also] participates in the ongoing struggle between that reign and the powers of darkness and evil."[77]

Held together, a biblically informed view of humanity and of evil points to an integral discipleship, where becoming "more human" not less is what is required. Mission is the redemption of the world of which we are a part, not redemption from it. Or, in the words of N.T. Wright:

> The great emphasis in the New Testament is that the gospel is not how to escape the world; the gospel is that the crucified and risen Jesus is the Lord of the world. And that his death and Resurrection transform the world, and that transformation can happen to you. You in turn, can be part of the transforming work.[78]

Personal transformation, becoming "more human" in our deeply alienated, postmodern world, is going to entail relational embrace and connection.

> The church needs to be the kind of place where human diversity—racial, gender, socioeconomic, or any other type—can be affirmed. Such a fellowship would challenge the modernist tendency to categorize and segregate distinct types and thereby respond positively to postmoderns.[79]

---

76. Wright, *Jesus and the Victory of God,*
77. Bosch, *Transforming Mission*, 391.
78. NT Wright, interviewed in: Stafford, "Mere Mission," 41.
79. Sellers, "Is Mission Possible in a Postmodern World?" 415.

This is where "integral discipleship" intersects with being a "peculiar people"—that is, theological foundation two and three.

These three theological pillars provide strong structural support for a missional-mode of being for individual Christians and the church. They work together to energize and sustain a life of and for "the other." It starts and ends at the macro-level, the *missio Dei*, which in turn is reflected and embodied at the meso-level, the people of God called for service in God's world, and so in turn at the micro-level, personal "integral discipleship" in the whole of life and human experience.

Practical Considerations

If we understand the *missio Dei* and the fragmented nature of our society fully, we will avoid pre-packaged ecclesiological "solutions." Nevertheless, it is worth making some comments about how these theological ideas are worked out in practice.

There are significant groups within western cultures who are under-represented in the Christian church. This points to the urgent need for radical efforts to reach them. Such mission will only occur effectively in missional-modes of church. According the John Drane, there are,

> . . . seven people groups in the west to whom the church should relate: the desperate poor, hedonists, spiritual searchers, traditionalists, secularists, corporate achievers, and the apathetic . . . to varying degrees, most churches have a surfeit of traditionalists, corporate achievers and the apathetic . . . A way of being church that connects with only certain types of people is not incarnational.[80]

Timothy Stanley suggests that, "If and when the church is able to re-identify itself as a source of freedom for postmodernity, it will regain its right to speak to a culture that still longs for God to speak, heal, and be revealed."[81] This will not be in a Christendom-mode church, but rather one that immerses itself in the life of such distinct portions of society.

The church needs to reach, include, and become largely constituted by the "desperate poor" and the other groups listed by John Drane. One significant question that arises in such a scenario is the validity of targeting homogenous groups. Missiologist David Bosch was particularly scathing of this. He wrote, for example, that, "*Any* form of segregation in the church, whether racial, ethnic, social, or *whatever* is . . . a denial of the gospel."[82]

There are three possible responses to this issue. Firstly, most churches are already "narrow," segregated in many ways—most notably in being biased towards those who

---

80. Drane, "Rebuilding the Household of Faith," 7.
81. Stanley, "Speaking Credibly?" 29.
82. Bosch, *Transforming Mission*, 172.

Movement Two—From Shallowness to Dynamic Theological Reflection

can cope or even thrive in a Christendom-mode of being. "Affirmative action" on behalf of those who have been silenced is to be commended. Secondly, the eventual outcome of missional communities being planted among select peoples and "tribes," will likely be a more inclusive church—if we consider these groups as forming a whole body over the long term. Churches that successfully reach a particular type of people group, if they are truly missional, will in turn become salt and light in their respective communities. They will follow the *missio Dei* as they become a "particular people" within new environs, living as integral-disciples in that "other culture." Thirdly, David Bosch's context of Apartheid South Africa "does much to explain Bosch's later criticisms . . . of Donald McGavran for his 'homogenous unit principle.'"[83] It is fair to say that intransigent polity, deeply affecting a racially segmented church (as well as the ministerial "disaffection" David Bosch personally endured as a result of his misgivings about such segregation),[84] probably affected Bosch's understanding of McGavran's homogenous unit principle (HUP). McGavran's framework of course included nothing of the racial theology or political motivations of Bosch's context. Having said that, Bosch's stance speaks to his outstanding personal integrity. Missiological arguments such as the HUP are generally rooted in an ultimate desire for inclusiveness, not segregation, and are probably better critiqued sociologically rather than theologically.

As I have noted, Lesslie Newbigin asserts that the clearest hermeneutic of the gospel narrative is a congregation of believers. This points to the centrality of worship in postmodern mission. For in worship, we retell the gospel story, over and over in various ways, to God, to ourselves, and to any others who will listen. This worship activity of the "peculiar people" thus edifies God's people and reinforces their role as servants of the world. Such worship should be contextualized for our times and situation, of course, because "the medium is the message"—God has a church for his mission in the world, and God is on mission in *this* world. Some believe that in order for the church to construct and be that story, it "must recover the classic liturgy of the church, in all its dramatic density, sensual actuality, and brutal realism, and make this the one exclusive center of its life."[85] I see this as too restricted to the church's premises or events. However, the story does need to be told and lived out using every conceivable "rhetorical device," for others to hear it well. Such "devices" will draw from all of human life, such that in telling it "integral-discipleship" is fostered.

A missional church will invest enormous effort in its corporate worship, so that in our rapidly changing world God can be the focus of vision (*missio Dei*). Through worshipful mission God's people can be built and energized in service of the world (as a "peculiar people"), in ways that enhance and foster everyday human living in God's world ("integral-discipleship"). Such effort is unlikely to result in "the greatest event

---

83. Yates, "David Bosch's South African Context," 72.

84. Bosch was effectively banned from the pulpit in the Dutch Reformed Church for much of his working life.

85. Jenson, "How the World Lost Its Story," 22.

in the community being held at the church premises," which is a Christendom goal. Rather, it will result in your light shining before others, "that they may see your good works and glorify your Father in heaven."[86]

Individual and Corporate Servantship Practices

- Do a cultural and social exegesis of your street, neighborhood, suburb, council area, and region. What are the most significant patterns and influences where you are?
- Audit your own discourse, both visual and verbal, or even better, have a third-party do it for you. Are there blind spots in what you are communicating, or conflicts in how you are communicating?
- Find analogies and "hooks" to enable yourself and others to be culturally engaged beyond the surface. Are we merely consumers and reflectors of our culture? (For example, as someone who grew up on the mission field, I have at my fingertips a plethora of cross-cultural examples from my childhood to draw on to show how Christians can intersect with their surrounds, both positively and negatively).
- When was the last significant change you made as a response to your changing environment? Are we in a mode of protecting ourselves from change, or changing ourselves for the sake of others?
- Reflect on your church practices, values, and habits. Are we really "doing life" together in a way than enhances our humanity, or is it more like "playing churchianity"?
- Invite neighbors or other communities within your proximity to participate together with you in service-oriented activities. Are you known as a genuine civic contributor?
- Regularly testify corporately to "mission moments." What has God been doing in and to you, or through and by you, and especially around and apart from you this week?

Questions for Reflection and Discussion

- What are the most significant current changes and developments in the society within which you live? Do any of the ones mentioned in this chapter impact particularly on you and your Christian community?
- Critique the three "theological foundations" outlined in this chapter: how do the

---

86. Matthew 5:16.

Movement Two—From Shallowness to Dynamic Theological Reflection

three work together and interrelate. Particularly, is the author right that God's "peculiar people" needs to be emphasized in our current practice?

- How can your corporate worship and relating with others in your Christian community be a hermeneutic of the gospel in the locale where you are? How can your servantship be a hermeneutic of the gospel? Are there particular things to change or intentionally work on?

9

Seeing Mission as Organizing Function

Grae McWhirter

There are many challenges to the church in twenty-first-century Australia. As in many other western cultures, institutional Christianity is on the decline. The rate of change in western cultures has been increasing over recent decades and part of that change has seen people turning away from the church and becoming increasingly disconnected from the gospel. Many believe that this external disconnect is the result of an internal disconnect evident within the church itself. Michael Frost and Alan Hirsch observe that one "of the great problems we face is the prevailing disconnect between God's mission and God's church. This utterly disastrous divorce must be overcome if we are to advance in our day."[1] Consequently, there is a growing awareness of the need to rediscover and recapture an understanding of God's missional heart for his lost world and how this impacts our understanding of the nature and purpose of the church. There is a growing awareness that "mission is not merely an activity of the church. It is the result of God's initiative, rooted in his desire to restore and heal creation."[2]

Therefore, in considering the development of an ecclesiology that has a securely biblical foundation and a contemporary application for western culture, this chapter adopts an approach suggested by Alan Hirsch and Michael Frost in a number of their works. Hirsch describes the approach when he states that "*Christology* determines *missiology*, and *missiology* in turn determines *ecclesiology*."[3] In other words, the person and work of Jesus must inform our mission in the world, and our mission in turn

---

1. Frost and Hirsch, *The Faith of Leap*, 154.
2. Hirsch and Altclass, *The Forgotten Ways Handbook*, Kindle location 1299.
3. Hirsch, *The Forgotten Ways*, Kindle location 1342.

Movement Two—From Shallowness to Dynamic Theological Reflection

must inform the structure and cultural forms of the church.[4] For the purposes of this chapter, I will add a step to the beginning of this process, so that our theology (in this context our understanding of the overall nature, plan, and purposes of God) informs our Christology, which in turn informs our missiology and then ecclesiology. It is worth noting that any such strictly linear progression is somewhat of an oversimplification and that the relationship between theology, Christology, missiology, and ecclesiology is more complex.[5] However, the progression has value and is a helpful paradigm for developing a missional ecclesiology.

Theology: The story of the Bible is the story of the mission and purpose of God to rescue and redeem his creation from the effects and consequences of sin. The mission of God (*missio Dei*) becomes clear initially in the promise to Abraham, where it is seen in the context of its global fulfillment.[6] The creation of the people of Israel by God in the Old Testament was an expression of his mission and the avenue for the promise's fulfillment. Israel was to be the bearer of the promise as reinforced to the patriarchs, declared through the prophets, and recounted through its redemptive history. All of these elements communicated God's saving plan for the whole world. Michael Frost and Alan Hirsch note that the whole biblical narrative is testament to the missional nature of God himself. "God is a missionary God. It is impossible to conceive of the biblical God without seeing God in terms of his mission, which is not merely the activity of God but the revelation of his very character."[7] Mission is rooted in God's purposes to restore and heal his fallen creation. Mission means sending, and it is the "central biblical theme describing the purpose of God's action in human history."[8] Graeme Goldsworthy proposes that the overarching message revealed in the totality of Scripture is one of God's redemptive purposes for his fallen creation, bringing in the kingdom of God through the fulfillment of Jesus.[9] This accurate portrayal of God's mission throughout the Bible leads us from our understanding of the nature and purpose of God to a consideration of the person and work of Christ.

Christology: The coming of the Messiah, then, is an extension and fulfillment of the nature of God and his promise to redeem his creation from slavery to sin. Christ is the purest expression of God's mission. Christ's self-understanding and stated purpose were to "seek and save those who are lost."[10] He demonstrated through his actions and declared through his words the reality of the kingdom of God, calling people to be part of it. Brian McLaren declares, "Missional Christian faith asserts that Jesus did not

4. Ibid.
5. Hill, *Salt, Light, and a City*, 190.
6. Genesis 12:1–3.
7. Frost and Hirsch, *The Faith of Leap*, 172.
8. Gibbs, *Church Next*, 56.
9. Goldsworthy, *Gospel and Kingdom*, 41–42.
10. Luke 19:10.

come to make some people saved and others condemned. Jesus did not come to help some people be right while leaving everyone else to be wrong. Jesus did not come to create another exclusive religion . . . Missional faith asserts that Jesus came to preach the good news of the kingdom of God to everyone, especially the poor. He came to seek and save the lost. He came on behalf of the sick. He came to save the world. His gospel, and therefore the Christian message, is good news for the whole world."[11]

The incarnation as the mode of Christ's coming modeled the means of God's mission to intimately connect with his fallen creation as "Emmanuel, God with us."[12] Alan and Deborah Hirsch note, "The incarnation provided believers with a wonderful and completely definitive understanding of God."[13] They go on to say that the incarnation shapes our discipleship as well as how we engage our world in Jesus's name. That is, the method of mission takes its cue from the incarnation.[14]

The incarnated Christ's purpose to seek and save the lost was achieved in the cross and the empty tomb. The death and resurrection of Jesus stand in the center of the redemptive plans of God as the linchpin of salvation and the only path to the Father.[15] John Stott points out that the death of Christ was for us, that he might bring us to God, forgiving our sin and rescuing us from death. "It is in consequence of his death that he is able to confer upon us the great blessing of salvation."[16] It is that blessing which was promised to Abraham for all nations. It is the focal point of the *missio Dei*. There is no full understanding of the person and work of Christ without a thorough appreciation of his incarnation, life, teaching, death, and resurrection. To understand the mission of God is therefore to understand the mission of Christ, as the Scripture tells us, one is the perfect representation of the other.[17]

It is also worth noting at this point that the development of a missional ecclesiology needs also to be based in trinitarian theology. While here we have begun to lay a foundation of the Father sending the Son, we cannot ignore the sending also of the Spirit. If there were space to develop this further we would see that it is therefore a logical next step to see the Father, Son, and Spirit similarly sending the church.[18]

Missiology: So, a firm grasp of the nature, life, person, and work of Christ, "this enthusiastic proclamation of him as God's Messiah, shapes the church's mission. God's mission in Christ directs the church's energies and vision so that they align with what he has done, is doing, and will do through Jesus the Messiah."[19] With such an

11. McLaren, *A Generous Orthodoxy*, 120.
12. Matthew 1:23.
13. Hirsch and Hirsch, *Untamed*, 234.
14. Ibid.
15. John 14:6.
16. Stott and McGrath, *The Cross of Christ*, 64.
17. Colossians 1:15.
18. Hill, *Salt, Light, and a City*, 153.
19. Ibid., 181.

Movement Two—From Shallowness to Dynamic Theological Reflection

understanding of Jesus, we take the model of mission inherent in his story and nature and develop a missiology. For example, the reality of the incarnation of Christ as an expression of the *missio Dei* informs our understanding of post-Christ mission. Alan Hirsch says that if the incarnation is the most profound way that God engaged the world, then we "must follow in his footsteps—we must become incarnational."[20] The incarnation is an "absolutely fundamental doctrine, not just as an irreducible part of the Christian confession, but also as a theological prism through which we view our entire missional task."[21]

However, the incarnation doesn't stand alone in the formation of our missiology. Jesus's own words to his disciples gave them a missional perspective when he told them that they were salt, the light of the world, and a town on a hill that can't be hidden.[22] When Christ ascended his final words were words of missional command.[23] In this act, the Son passed the baton of the mission of the Father to his newly established church. At Pentecost the Spirit was given to empower the church to fulfill the Commission,[24] thus grounding the ongoing mission of the church in all three persons of the Trinity, and equipping the church to complete the command of Jesus to be witnesses to him throughout the whole world.[25]

The New Testament is replete with instructions to the church designed to rally it to the call of God's ongoing mission. As the Body of Christ we are seen to be his hands and his feet, all members gifted for service with Christ as the head, thus being his presence in this world to continue his work.[26] We are to be Christ's ambassadors charged with the ministry of reconciliation, being consistently prepared to give a reason for our faith.[27]

Michael Frost and Alan Hirsch define mission as "both the announcement of the lordship of Jesus (evangelism, witness) and its demonstration (social concern, service)."[28] Brian McLaren agrees, stating that a proper understanding of mission eliminates old dichotomies such as "evangelism" and "social action," "ministry" and "mission," "missionary" and "mission field," because all those are integrated in an expression of the proclamation and demonstration of Christ's saving love for the world.[29]

---

20. Hirsch and Hirsch, *Untamed*, 234.
21. Frost and Hirsch, *Shaping of Things to Come*, 35.
22. Matthew 5:13–16.
23. See *The Great Commission* in Matthew 28:18–20.
24. Acts 2.
25. Acts 1:8.
26. 1 Corinthians 12; Colossians 1:18.
27. 2 Corinthians 5:19–20; 1 Peter 3:15.
28. Frost and Hirsch, *The Faith of Leap*, 164.
29. McLaren, *A Generous Orthodoxy*, 118–19.

Thus, our missiology has both a proclamation element and a good deeds element, following the model of Jesus who exemplified both of these aspects in his mission on earth.

> Mission is the practical demonstration, whether by speech or by action, of the glorious lordship of Jesus. It is where we get to create little foretastes of the kingdom of Jesus, which has come and is still yet to fully come. If in that kingdom-to-come there will be no unbelief, then the church's mission is to create such a foretaste by commending belief to all. If in the kingdom-to-come there will be no injustice, the church's mission will be to work to eliminate injustice here and now. If in the kingdom-to-come there is no grief, no mourning, no suffering, the church's mission is to overcome such things today.[30]

Ecclesiology: Having understood the nature and purpose of God (theology), the person and work of Christ (Christology), and developed an understanding of the ongoing mission of God the Father, through the Son and the Spirit all sending the church (missiology), then the church has the task of developing an understanding of its existence, nature, purpose, structures, and life (ecclesiology).

It follows, then, that the church should center its life and activity on the redemptive *missio Dei*, which Christ came to enable, and left his disciples to continue. As Graham Hill says, a missional ecclesiology "locates the Messiah, and the church's participation in his messianic mission, at the center of the church's being, organization, and ministries. The messianic mission of Jesus Christ is central to the church's life and being, and the faithful pursuit of this mission is the essential character of the church that is faithfully participating in the redemptive work of the Father."[31]

The notion of a mission-centered ecclesiology, while sounding agreeable to many evangelical Christians, in practice is a significant departure from how the church has understood itself for centuries. In their book, *The Faith of Leap*, Michael Frost and Alan Hirsch use four essential functions of the church (worship, discipleship, community, and mission) to help explain what a missional ecclesiology looks like, compared with how most of the churches in the west look today. They point out that the church has been satisfied to allow worship to act as the organizing principle of the other elements.[32] They note that this is exemplified by the centrality of the Sunday worship service. They trace the historical development of this worship-centered ecclesiology from the Constantinian view of Christ's presence in the Eucharist and the theological perspective of the church as the new expression of the Temple and thus the representation of Christ in the world.[33] Under these circumstances, worship became the organizing principle around which all other functions were centered. This stands at

30. Frost and Hirsch, *The Faith of Leap*, 164.
31. Hill, *Salt, Light, and a City*, 155.
32. Frost and Hirsch, *The Faith of Leap*, 167.
33. Ibid., 172.

Movement Two—From Shallowness to Dynamic Theological Reflection

odds with the ecclesiology of the early church which was a minority movement that understood its primary purpose as continuing the mission of Christ. However, when the empire was Christianized "mission became defunct, and formal worship, maintained by priesthood, effectively trumped the other elements of the ecclesial mix."[34] The fact that community, mission, and discipleship are not mentioned in the "marks of the church" promoted by the Reformers, shows that the accepted ecclesiology of the time was based around the sacraments, maintained by the clergy, and administered at Sunday worship gatherings.[35] Michael Frost and Alan Hirsch contend that mission needs to be placed back as the organizing principle of the church. This is a radical challenge to today's church because mission cannot simply stand as an add-on to existing activities, but rather becomes a guiding principle for all other functions. This reorienting is a "comprehensive recalibration of the church, a rediscovery of mission as its organizing function."[36] It is the wholesale and thorough reorientation of the church around mission,[37] where followers of Christ stop "playing at church" each Sunday and discover that their missional experience *is* their church.[38] The argument is not that mission ought to take *priority* over worship, community, or discipleship; nor that a mission-only church be established. The reality is that all four functions are integral to the purpose of the church and all four are interconnected, reliant upon, and stimulated by each other. It's not about deciding which function to put at the center—that place belongs to Jesus. Nor is it about which function is more important. Rather, it is about which one of them is the best catalyst for the others.[39] The conclusion is that the most biblical approach, based, as demonstrated above, on sound theology, Christology, and missiology, is to have a missional ecclesiology that is manifested as "any church that organizes itself around the mission of God in this world."[40] "When mission guides all these, we get to show the world how to live the love of the Father, through the lordship of the Son, and in the power of the Holy Spirit."[41]

A missional church embraces a missional ecclesiology in its theology, structures, mission, and ministry practices. "It understands its nature as essentially missional—it is from that theological footing that it reflects on and pursues the missional nature of its practices, structures, systems, offices, ministries, and missions."[42] But what will such a church that has adopted a missional ecclesiology, look like? In *The Shaping of Things to Come*, Michael Frost and Alan Hirsch believe every such church would

34. Ibid., 168.
35. Ibid., 169.
36. Ibid., 159.
37. Frost, *The Road to Missional*, 16.
38. Frost, *Exiles*, 131.
39. Frost and Hirsch, *The Faith of Leap*, 166.
40. Ibid., 159.
41. Ibid., 172.
42. Hill, *Salt, Light, and a City*, 165.

look different depending on its individual context. They do, however, suggest some common values. A missional church will place a "high value on communal life, more open servantship structures, and the contribution of all the people of God. It will be radical in its attempts to embrace biblical mandates for the life of locally based faith communities without feeling as though it has to reconstruct the first-century church in every detail. We believe the missional church will be adventurous, playful, and surprising."[43] A church with a missional ecclesiology will not have the importance attached to method or form which churches operating with an ecclesiology tied more to a Constantinian view may posses. A missional ecclesiology, which operates more from an understanding of the incarnation, will reorient a church away from being an introspective community, and free it to participate in intimate relational kingdom growing grounded in the broader community. Alan Hirsch notes "by living incarnationally we . . . create space for mission to take place in organic ways. Mission becomes something that fits seamlessly into the ordinary rhythms of life, friendships, and community. Incarnational ministry essentially means taking the church to people rather than bringing people to church."[44] This will therefore look different in each context as each church connects and incarnates itself in the unique culture of the community in which it exists. Hirsch says that in this way the church will be "formed out of mission and missional action specific to its context. This is what is meant by ecclesiology following mission."[45]

> Mission must be allowed to once again fundamentally reshape our understanding of church . . . Because we believe that somewhere in the nest of paradigms contained in the phrase "missional church" lies nothing less than the future viability of Western Christianity.[46]

Challenges for Missional Ecclesiology in a Western Culture

> "The world is changed. I feel it in the water. I feel it in the earth. I smell it in the air." I have seen this quote used by other church leaders who also feel this is true of our time: the world around us has changed, and that's why emerging generations are disappearing from most churches.[47]

It is no surprise to anyone that the rate of cultural change in the west, indeed around the globe, has increased significantly throughout the twentieth and now in the twenty-first centuries. "In the past cultural change was usually a slow business, as one

---

43. Frost and Hirsch, *Shaping of Things to Come*, 22.
44. Hirsch, *The Forgotten Ways*, Kindle location 1325.
45. Ibid., Kindle location 1352.
46. Frost and Hirsch, *The Faith of Leap*, 154.
47. Kimball, *They Like Jesus but Not the Church*, Kindle location 203.

Movement Two—From Shallowness to Dynamic Theological Reflection

generation succeeded another and made its own minor adjustments to social habits and ways of thinking. But now change is neither subtle nor gradual: it is traumatic and immediate."[48] Tom Sine points to 9/11 as an example of this traumatic change. He says the "reality is that our world will never be the same again. We are now living in a world in which ongoing acts of terrorism make life more uncertain for all of us and the worst may still be ahead of us."[49]

Mike Riddell lists a number of western cultural distinctives which represent some of the changes in influences and values that have taken place in our society. He names such things as postmodernity, urbanization, pluralism, technology, relativism, and others.[50] Tom Sine adds, for example, globalization to the list and says that we are now living in a "global economic order in which distance is dying, borders are melting, and we are being permanently linked to one another in ways we never have been before."[51] We could also add multiculturalism, new atheism, increasing materialism, and more.

Dan Kimball observes, "In our increasingly post-Christian culture, the influences and values shaping emerging generations are no longer aligned with Christianity. Emerging generations don't have a basic understanding of the story of the Bible, and they don't have one God as the predominant God to worship. Rather, they are open to all types of faiths, including new mixtures of religions."[52] He notes that in the west today, the people who need to hear the gospel most likely aren't going to be in a church to hear it. They are going to be sleeping in, shopping, or going out for breakfast. Good preaching or great music isn't what these people are looking for.[53] A far more comprehensive renewal of church life than new music or revised liturgies is needed.[54]

Throughout Europe, Canada, Australia, and New Zealand, church influence and attendance have been declining for decades across all denominations and theological persuasions.[55] Church attendance in the United Kingdom in 1851 was about the same as the current figure for the United States, at 39 percent. Since the First World War there has been an ever-increasing rate of decline. By 1979 attendance stood at just under 12 percent, falling to 7.5 percent by 1998. Eddie Gibbs remarks that these statistics are alarming, not just because they are declining, but because the rate of decline is increasing.[56] Many people during the past few decades who have turned to the Christian churches seeking truth and meaning have left empty-handed, confused

---

48. Drane, "Cultural Change and Biblical Faith," 1.
49. Sine, *The New Conspirators*, 59.
50. Riddell, *Threshold of the Future*, 101–15.
51. Sine, *The New Conspirators*, 59.
52. Kimball, *They Like Jesus but Not the Church*, Kindle location 208.
53. Ibid., Kindle location 3425.
54. Drane, *Mcdonaldization*, 88.
55. Ibid., 2.
56. Gibbs, *Church Next*, 17–18.

by the inability of Christians to implement the principles they profess. "Churches, for the most part, have failed to address the nagging anxieties and deep-seated fears of the people, focusing instead upon outdated or secondary issues and proposing tired or trite solutions."[57] It has been observed, for example, that in the United States, the majority of church effort is spent reaching a diminishing 40 percent of the population, and leaving the majority unreached. The reason for this omission, it is surmised, is that the church in the west has forgotten its call to be "sent."[58]

It hasn't just been those raised outside the churches who are not finding meaning from the church. Many young adults raised within the church have left, laying the blame squarely at the church's feet.[59] Those under thirty-five in particular are being born and raised with a different set of values, a changing world view, and an evolving belief system largely disconnected from Christianity.[60] John Drane suggests that Christianity is linked with a history that has driven culture to its current series of crises. He suggests that the prevailing view may well be that Christianity is part of the problem so it cannot also be part of the solution.[61] Consequently, the places people look for spiritual guidance become other cultures and world views, or within ourselves "and both of these are playing a significant part in the rising culture."[62] Mike Riddell's diagnosis is that the church in the west is suffering from internal confusion, cultural isolation, spiritual aridity, and a failure in mission.[63] It may be that the therapeutic flavor and self-help focus of the type of Christianity being promoted by the church at large is contributing to the church's failure. Brian McLaren observes that much contemporary faith appears self-centered and individualistic.

> My largest concern is me, my soul, my personal destiny in heaven, my maturity, and my rewards . . . Is it any surprise that people 'won to Christ' by self-interest come to church asking 'What's in it for me?' Is it any surprise that with this understanding of salvation, churches tend to become gatherings of self-interested people who gather for mutual self-interest—constantly treating the church as a purveyor of religious goods and services, constantly shopping and 'trading up' for churches that can 'meet my needs' better? Is it any surprise that it's stinking hard to convince churches that they have a mission to the world?[64]

While much of the research and many of the comments about the church of the west focus on the United States and the United Kingdom, the general trends are

57. Ibid., 20.
58. Hirsch and Ferguson, *On the Verge*, 250–51.
59. Kinnaman and Hawkins, *You Lost Me*, 11.
60. Kimball, *Emerging Worship*, Kindle location, 181.
61. Drane, "Cultural Change and Biblical Faith," 9.
62. Ibid., 10.
63. Riddell, *Threshold of the Future*, 1–13.
64. McLaren, *A Generous Orthodoxy*, 117–18.

Movement Two—From Shallowness to Dynamic Theological Reflection

not inapplicable to Australia, although our spiritual history is different from other western nations. Tom Frame's insightful assessment of Australian spirituality entitled *Losing My Religion* is a helpful affirmation of the uniquely Australian version of the western trends regarding the Christian church. It seems from the outset of the European establishment of the penal colony of New South Wales, Australia became the first truly post-Christian society (in contrast to the American colonies). The founders of New South Wales "came from a society where religion was in decline and disarray, eroded by skepticism and indifference. The climate this established was that of indifference to religion."[65] This was an indifference toward religion which has permeated Australian society ever since and increased along with the declining trends of religious attitudes evident in all western cultures. Frame cites the Bertlesman Foundation which reported in July 2008 that of twenty-one countries surveyed, only four showed less interest in (organized) religion than did Australia: the United Kingdom, Russia, France, and Germany.[66]

So how can a church that adopts a missional ecclesiology engage with these cultural and ecclesial challenges? Dan Kimball suggests that the church needs to view our current culture as a missionary would. We are the foreigners in a post-Christian world, more akin to the early church than the Constantinian church of Christendom.[67] In this context, "a well-developed missional theology of the church, its nature, structures, and mission, is crucial for the health of churches, for faithfulness to the gospel, and for mission in the contemporary cultural context."[68] This may well mean that the church will need to be "turned inside out in order to bring those outside in."[69]

Tom Sine suggests that effective leaders in missional churches are interested in the intersection of faith and contemporary culture. He says that we should "look at the ways in which this new global economy not only magnifies the values of modern and postmodern culture, but also seeks to increasingly define for people everywhere what is important and what is of value. Let's take a closer look at the better future we are being invited to come home to."[70] This is just an example of the type of engagement missional churches need to have with culture. Rather than adopting a position against culture, missional churches need to adopt an incarnational position within culture. This does not mean acquiescing to its values, which may be contrary to the values of Scripture or the gospel. But with the freedom from old methods and forms which missional ecclesiology can bring, new contextualized methods can be uniquely applied incarnationally, so that the unchanging gospel of Christ can bring light, hope, and grace to a lost world. There is no formula which can be applied at this point to

---

65. Frame, *Losing My Religion*, Kindle location 885.
66. Ibid., Kindle location 1536.
67. Kimball, *They Like Jesus but Not the Church*, Kindle location 405.
68. Hill, *Salt, Light, and a City*, 150.
69. Gibbs, *Church Next*, 228.
70. Sine, *The New Conspirators*, 69–70.

describe the precise steps that a missional church must take, as if there were a pre-packaged program or "one size fits all" missional kit. Having a missional ecclesiology is not so easily generically packaged. While there are many examples of Christian communities who are attempting to apply a missional ecclesiology to their context in creative and effective ways, each one is uniquely geared to its local cultural context and consequently not able to be copied. For example, one faith community's engagement with multiculturalism may reflect the local Sudanese refugee community while another will be shaped differently as it engages with the local Chinese business community. Neither will approach these missional challenges in the same way, but neither will refuse to engage with their local multicultural issues if they claim to be missional.

Whatever the individual community's cultural context or unique challenges, it will no longer suffice simply to invite the seeker to come to us to hear the gospel on our turf. "Instead, the church will have to be the church in the world—gathering for worship in order to go out in mission. Its programs must be geared to equip and support the people of God in the strategic locations where the Lord has already placed them to serve as his representatives."[71]

In the end, the challenge to the missional community, the call to live an "incarnational life, to serve as Christ did, and to lead others into the risky vocation of following the *missio Dei*, is not a simple or easy task. It is a lifelong calling to service, sacrifice, selflessness, and effort. It will be worked out in neighborhoods and people groups around the world, and fuelled and led by the least likely saints."[72]

Individual and Corporate Servantship Practices

- Engage your church in some critical self-reflection:
    a. Set aside a group of gifted servant leaders to facilitate your church in discovering what it holds as the core purpose of its existence.
    b. This could be done through surveys, focus groups, National Church Life Survey or other data, etc.
    c. Reflect on which of the four elements of church life (worship, community, discipleship, and mission) is the main catalyst for church life.
- Engage your church in some biblical teaching on the nature of the church:
    a. Design a series of three or four messages which are aimed at discovering the biblical purpose of the church by addressing: (1) Biblical theology (God's heart and mission); (2) Christology (Jesus's living out God's heart and mission); (3) Missiology (Christian participation in God's heart and mission); and (4) Ecclesiology (the shape of a church which is centered around God's heart and mission).

---

71. Gibbs, *Church Next*, 228.
72. Frost, *The Road to Missional*, 21.

Movement Two—From Shallowness to Dynamic Theological Reflection

      b. Follow these messages up with small group discussion questions to allow group reflection on the application of this teaching.
- Engage your church in a process to reorient practices, culture, or ministries as a result:
    a. Use small groups or special focus groups to dream about what a missional church and its servantship may look like.
    b. Formulate a new statement that encapsulates your church's desire to have mission as its organizing function, and servantship as its ministry orientation.
    c. Encourage your church to look to the unique needs of the community in which your church lives and ask how your church can demonstrate and proclaim the Lordship of Christ in that context.
    d. Challenge the current servant leaders of ministries to examine their practices, goals, and culture in the light of outwardly focused servantship and missional theology.

Questions for Reflection and Discussion

- What do you believe is your church's organizing function—worship, community, discipleship, or mission? What leads you to that conclusion?
- What would be the potential impact on your church if it adopted mission as its organizing function?
- How would this impact its servantship practices?
- What would be the impact on your community if your church adopted mission as its organizing function and servantship as its ministry practice?

10

Recalibrating Church in Post-Christendom

Peter Ong

A changing western world that is rapidly becoming more secular sounds the warning bells for the church. It calls the church to reflect theologically about its mission and to engage with the world. This chapter seeks to outline a missional ecclesiology for a changing western culture, and then to practically engage with the ecclesial and missional challenges for the church in the context of post-Christendom. While much has been written in the area of practical missional engagement, Graham Hill rightly observes that the "proverbial elephant in the room" in the whole missional conversation is the "lack of systematic or intentional ecclesiology . . . or lack of theology for that matter" guiding it.[1] Practical missional engagement must be underpinned by a biblical missional ecclesiology.

Theological Foundations for a Missional Ecclesiology

The development of a missional ecclesiology[2] will need to be informed and shaped by other key disciplines, such as biblical theology, systematic theology, church history, and missiology.[3] Biblical and systematic theologies provide the scriptural framework for an understanding of the church and its mission, while church history provides lessons on how the church has engaged (or not engaged) in mission. Missiology provides

---

1. Hill, *Salt, Light, and a City*, xvii.
2. I am assuming that missional ecclesiology itself is a theological discipline.
3. Due to word limitations, this section of the chapter will mainly focus on biblical and systematic theologies and not so much on church history—despite the importance of church history in providing the context and shaping of the two theological disciplines. Missiology will be touched upon in the second part of this chapter when we discuss practical missional engagement.

Movement Two—From Shallowness to Dynamic Theological Reflection

the framework and methodology to integrate all these key disciplines; and will assist in the praxis of the missional ecclesiology. These key disciplines are deeply intertwined.

> Missional ecclesiology is a movement of thought, rather than an organized movement, which is concerned with all cultures as missional fields, the missional nature and expressions of the church, the missional nature of God and Scripture, and the missional presence of God in the world.[4]

The definition above highlights that missional ecclesiology is "concerned with all cultures," and while we are only dealing with the western context in this chapter, Graham Hill rightly points out that "any missional ecclesiology which ignores the ecclesiological insights of the Majority World thinkers will be deficient, impoverished, and found sorely wanting."[5]

Missional ecclesiology, as a theology of the church and its mission, draws from both systematic and biblical theologies. The late missiologist Paul Hiebert argues that systematic theology too often has "a weak sense of mission"; for the central question that systematic theology seeks to answer is: "What are the unchanging universals of reality?"[6] Biblical theology, on the other hand, examines the narrative nature of Scripture and sees the whole of Scripture as one big, unfolding, cosmic story. Hiebert asserts that biblical theology is important because it gives meaning to life by helping us "to see the cosmic story in which the human story and our biographies are embedded." God speaks to us through Scripture in the context of "concrete settings of place and personal history," and as such the church's story is part of that cosmic story.[7] Christopher Wright points out that our theology of the church's mission must be grounded in biblical theology, in that "we need to pay attention to the whole story of the Bible and see our mission in the light of all of it."[8] Therefore, missional ecclesiology is underpinned by these two key foundational theological disciplines.

Simply put, missional ecclesiology is "the study of the church through the lens of mission."[9] Richard Bliese suggests that "mission needs to drive our understanding of ecclesiology." However, Bliese notes that the challenge has been to define mission in relationship to other doctrinal categories in order to gain enough clarity and precision to perform this "driving" role. Mission, as a theological concept, does not stand well alone. Its strength lies in the fact that "it has the unique ability to bring together in a

---

4. Hill, *Salt, Light, and a City*, xvi.

5. Ibid. While this is outside the scope of this chapter, it nevertheless should be highlighted that the church in the west is but part of a global church. Voices from the global church will greatly contribute to the development of a missional ecclesiology that will help the western church engage in mission in a post-Christendom context.

6. Hiebert, *The Gospel in Human Contexts*, 39–41.

7. Ibid.

8. Wright, *The Mission of God's People*, 39.

9. Quote by Graham Hill, postgraduate class lecture called "Theology, Culture, and the Mission of the Church," 2012.

coherent way multiple aspects of the biblical witness."[10] I would suggest that missional ecclesiology brings together the biblical theology of mission, the *missio Dei*, the grand narrative of God's mission in the world, and key systematic theologies, such as Christology, ecclesiology, and eschatology.[11] However, I would also echo Darrell Guder's warning that the theology of *missio Dei* is difficult to translate into "the deeply rooted and long since defined classical patterns of western theology."[12] Therefore, there is no one neat theological system to hang a missional ecclesiology on. The theologies that shape a missional ecclesiology are intricate and interdependent.

Firstly, in developing a missional ecclesiology, we must define mission. One can suggest that mission begins with God, and that he has a purpose and goal for his whole creation, which is to bring all things under the reign of Christ.[13] It is "a vast, comprehensive project of cosmic salvation."[14] And as part of that divine project, God has called into existence a people to participate with him in the accomplishment of that mission. All our mission flows from the "prior mission of God," and, as Christopher Wright puts it,

> It is not so much the case that God has a mission for his church in the world, as that God has a church for his mission in the world. Mission was not made for the church; the church was made for mission—God's mission.[15]

Christopher Wright helpfully frames our understanding of the church in terms of "the people of God," and the theology of the church's mission in terms of "who the people of God are and what they have been called to do." He poses this as the big question he is seeking to answer in his book, *The Mission of God's People*: "Who are we and what are we here for?"[16] Wright answers this by suggesting that the church is God's people: (1) who know the story that they are part of; (2) who care for creation; (3) who are a blessing to the nations; (4) who walk in God's way; (5) who are redeemed for redemptive living; (6) who represent God to the world; (7) who attract others to God; (8) who know the one living God and Savior; (9) who bear witness to the living God; (10) who proclaim the gospel of Christ; (11) who send and are sent; (12) who live and work in the public square; and (13) who praise and pray.[17]

The motif of the "people of God on mission" runs constantly through the Bible. In the Old Testament, God had chosen Israel to be his people, to be a light to the other nations. As reflected in one of her missional psalms, they were to "declare his glory

---

10. Bliese, "The Mission Matrix," 239.
11. There are others that we will not have time or the space to include in this chapter.
12. Guder, "Missional Theology for a Missionary Church," 5.
13. Acts 20:27; Ephesians 1:9–10; Philippians 2:9–11; Colossians 1:15–20.
14. Wright, *The Mission of God's People*, 46.
15. Ibid., 24.
16. Ibid., 17.
17. Ibid., 8–13.

among the nations" and "say among the nations, 'The Lord reigns.'"[18] In the New Testament, the apostle Peter also picks up on this motif when he writes to the scattered people of God who were facing persecution, and reminds them that as a "people belonging to God who have been called out of darkness and into his wonderful light," they are to "declare his praises."[19] David Bosch states that mission is "alerting people to the universal reign of God."[20]

The *church* and *mission* are intrinsically linked notions. David Bosch argues that mission refers to a "permanent and intrinsic dimension of the church's life," such that it is impossible to talk about church without at the same time talking about mission. Because God is a missionary God, God's people are missionary people. The church's mission is not secondary to its being; the church exists in being sent and in building up itself for mission.[21] Darrell Guder goes further to say that:

> The church does not do mission, it is mission. By its very calling and nature, it exists as God's 'sent' people (*missio* = sending). Its worship, its proclamation, its life as a distinctive community, and its concrete demonstration of God's love in acts of prophetic and sacrificial service are all witness to the good news whose sign and foretaste it is to be.[22]

To sum up, we conclude that missional ecclesiology is grounded in the biblical theology of the *missio Dei* and the participation of God's people in it, and that these two notions are intrinsically linked. Neil Cole sums it up well:

> The church is not sent on a mission by God; rather, God is on a mission and the church is called to join Him. The mission is not the church's; it is the *missio Dei*, or "mission of God," that we are called to be part of.[23]

Having looked at biblical theology, we will now briefly outline some of the key systematic theologies that are foundational to the shaping of a missional ecclesiology. The first of these is *Christology*. Graham Hill captures the link between the *missio Dei* and Christology well:

> A missional ecclesiology defines itself through the mission of God and the person and work of Jesus Christ. It locates the Messiah, and the church's participation in his messianic mission, at the center of the church's being, organization, and ministries.[24]

---

18. Psalm 96:3 and 10.
19. 1 Peter 2:9.
20. Bosch, *Believing in the Future*, 33.
21. Ibid., 32.
22. Guder, "Missional Theology for a Missionary Church," 5.
23. Cole, *Church 3.0*, 47.
24. Hill, *Salt, Light, and a City*, 155.

Alan Hirsch argues that, "Christian mission always starts with Jesus" and is defined by him, and that he is our "constant reference point—we always begin and end with him." It is Jesus who determines the church's mission in the world, and therefore our sense of purpose and mission comes from being sent by him into the world.[25] Furthermore, Hirsch argues that for the church to engage in mission in a post-Christian culture, "Christology determines missiology, and missiology determines ecclesiology."[26] A right understanding of Jesus—his deity, humanity, ministry, death, resurrection, and kingly glory—should shape our understanding of the church and its mission.

The second systematic theology that shapes a missional ecclesiology is *ecclesiology* itself. Alan Hirsch points out that in his reading of Scripture, "ecclesiology is the most fluid of the doctrines" for the "church is a dynamic cultural expression of the people of God in any given place," since "church must follow mission."[27] In the missionary endeavors of the Apostle Paul we see that wherever he went to preach the gospel people come to faith and become the "church" in that place. Their expression of church and faith was shaped around and within their culture.

There are many systematic formulations of ecclesiology, but for the purposes of this chapter I will refer to Paul Minear's study of the church in the New Testament.[28] This study by Minear identifies ninety-six images used by New Testament writers to describe and define the purpose and functioning of the church. Minear's argument is that the Bible relies on word pictures and metaphors to convey to us what the church is and what the church is to do, rather than giving us systematic dogmatic formulations.[29] John Driver further develops this examination of biblical word pictures, from a missiological perspective, when he classifies these into four groups: (1) pilgrimage (the way, sojourners, the poor); (2) new-order (the kingdom of God, new creation, new humanity); (3) peoplehood (the people of God, the family of God, the shepherd, and the flock); and (4) transformation (salt and light, a city, a spiritual house, a witnessing community).[30] Wilbert Shenk says that these images, when taken together, describe the church as "a covenant community of missionary witness and transformation that moves throughout the world—God's people among the peoples."[31]

Finding inspiration from John Driver's work, Graham Hill's book, *Salt, Light, and a City*, captures the missional purpose of the church:

> The church in mission is the salt of the earth, the light of the world, and a city set on a hill. As salt, light, and a city set on a hill, the church in mission is to

25. Hirsch, *The Forgotten Ways*, 142.
26. Ibid.
27. Ibid., 143.
28. Minear, *Images of the Church in the New Testament*.
29. Shenk, "New Wineskins for New Wine," 74.
30. Driver, *Images of the Church in Mission*.
31. Shenk, "New Wineskins for New Wine," 74.

Movement Two—From Shallowness to Dynamic Theological Reflection

let its "light shine before people, that they may see your good deeds and praise your Father in heaven." The purpose of the church's missional nature is the glorification and worship of the Father.[32]

The third systematic theology that undergirds a missional ecclesiology is *eschatology*. Eschatology provides the hope and the end point for the church in mission. The biblical movement from *creation* to *new creation* provides the backdrop for God's people on mission. Miroslav Volf helpfully points out that:

> The all-embracing framework for an appropriate understanding of the church is God's eschatological new creation. The eschatological character of the church demands that systematic ecclesiological reflection begin not immediately with the church itself, but rather with God's new creation in relation to God's people.[33]

God is on a mission to bring the whole cosmos under the reign of Christ in the new creation. Darrell Guder suggests that "the missionary church lives out her vocation in the dynamic tension between what God has begun and will certainly complete 'in the day of Jesus Christ,'" and argues that "crucial to the church's missional renewal is the rediscovery of biblical eschatology."[34]

Missional Churches in a Rapidly Changing Culture

The main challenge that post-Christendom presents to the western church is "cultural captivity." The western church has become blind to its cultural captivity. Darrell Guder suggests that as we missionally assess the history of the western church, "We realize that we need to be evangelized by our Christian brothers and sisters from other, non-western cultures, whose vision of God's gospel is not shaped by our cultural captivity."[35] Michael Frost adds that the western church is in cultural captivity to the paradigm of corporate capitalism, and that the church's very understanding of its purpose and mission is shaped more by the free market than the teaching of Jesus.[36] Out of these dynamics are born consumer-orientated churches characterized by personal gain, where Christians ask, "What does this church have to offer me?" instead of being mission-orientated churches.[37] John Drane, in his book, *The McDonaldization of the Church*, argues that church in postmodernity is "a secular church in a spiritual society."[38] And because of the ineffective and compromised witness of

32. Hill, *Salt, Light, and a City*, xiii.
33. Volf, *After Our Likeness*, 128.
34. Guder, "Missional Theology for a Missionary Church."
35. Ibid., 7.
36. Frost, *The Road to Missional*, 76.
37. Kimball, *Emerging Church*, 95.
38. Drane, *The McDonaldization of the Church*, 54.

the church, David Bosch further warns that "the greatest danger for our missionary ministry appears to be that it will be sovereignly ignored" by those the church is seeking to reach.[39] Darrell Guder says that the problem is that the *missio Dei* theology has not translated into the structures of churches, which are "still shaped by the mindset of Christendom, and which have not come to terms with the paradigm shift that surrounds them."[40] Wilbert Shenk argues, "With the collapse of historical Christendom, the church today is a minority in most countries," and that "to be viable the church must assume a missionary relationship to every culture."[41]

Alan Hirsch warns that the church today lives in a significant time in which our actions will bear directly on the church of the future. Christians in the west must "recalibrate at the most basic level, their approaches to Christology, ecclesiology, and mission." These recalibrations, however, do not involve trendy fads or innovative techniques, but rather require the "reactivation of the dormant missional potentials of the church that Jesus built." To activate this "dormant ethos," Hirsch suggests that we need at least four recalibrations, which are: (1) recovery of the centrality of Jesus in his own movement; (2) recovery of discipleship as our core task; (3) recovery of the ethos/structure of apostolic movements; (4) recovery of a missional-incarnational impulse. Coming back to Christology, Hirsch argues, "We must constantly recalibrate back to him [Christ] in order to legitimize ourselves as his people."[42]

In light of this, we now turn our discussion to what a missional church is. Alan Hirsch suggests that a proper understanding of missional begins with recovering a missionary understanding of God himself. By his very nature God is a "sent one" who takes the initiative to redeem his creation. Because we are the "sent" people of God, the church is "the instrument of God's mission in the world."[43] Therefore, key to Hirsch's thinking is that "every disciple is to be an agent of the kingdom of God, and every disciple is to carry the mission of God into every sphere of life." The people of God must see themselves as "missionaries sent into a non-Christian culture."[44] Darrell Guder goes further to argue that, like the early church, we need to understand ourselves as "missionary communities, sent where we are for God's mission." He believes that "the Scriptures function for us as they did for the first Christian communities: they evangelize, edify, correct, shape, and send us as the continuation of the apostolic mission in our particular contexts today."[45]

Michael Frost asserts that a core question for all missional Christians is, "What does the reign of God through Christ look like in my neighborhood? If the kingdom

---

39. Bosch, *Believing in the Future*, 61.
40. Guder, "Missional Theology for a Missionary Church," 5.
41. Shenk, "New Wineskins for New Wine," 77.
42. Hirsch, "Reawakening a Potent Missional Ethos," 7.
43. Hirsch, "Defining Missional," 22.
44. Ibid.
45. Guder, "Missional Theology for a Missionary Church," 6.

Movement Two—From Shallowness to Dynamic Theological Reflection

of God has come and is overlapping with the broken world in which I live, how can I alert people to it? What does it look like? Where do I see the evidence of it?"[46] Frost says that the missional church is to be absorbed into the *missio Dei*, and not believe that its activity alone is the mission; also the church needs to recover an eschatology that recognizes that "our political or religious activity cannot establish the kingdom of God." We need "a belief that the coming reign of God is the framework for all missionary practice."[47]

Michael Frost developed a series of missional indicators in his book, *The Road to Missional*, which are worthy of reflection. He asserts, "A mission-shaped church both announces and demonstrates the reign of God through Christ, both locally and globally, in the way of Jesus." The missional indicators are developed under the three categories of *announcement, demonstration,* and *the way of Jesus*.[48]

We now turn our discussion to the marks or features of a missional church. While the praxis of a missional ecclesiology can vary from context to context, Graham Hill helpfully provides four *notae missionis* that a missional church should display. They are: (1) *missional foundations*—an unswerving commitment to the gospel of Jesus Christ and to the reliability of the Scriptures; (2) *missional ecclesiology*—the missional church embraces a thoroughgoing missional ecclesiology in its theology, structures, mission, and ministry practices; (3) *missional contrast*—the missional church engages specific cultures as a contrast society; (4) *missional outlook*—the missional church views all cultures as mission fields.[49] The strength of Graham Hill's *notae missionis* is that it keeps the gospel and the Scriptures central to the missional discussion. It also emphasizes the importance of good theology underpinning missional praxis.

Wilbert Shenk suggests a similar list of characteristics of a missional church: (1) It is intensely aware that its priority is to witness to the kingdom of God, so that people are being liberated from the oppressive power of idols; and that the church is consciously discerning and naming the idols; (2) It is deeply committed to the world but is not controlled by the world, and the absence of this tension indicates that the church has made its peace with the world; (3) Its mission is patterned after the example of Jesus the Messiah—whereby the cross is central, and mission is cruciform; (4) It has a keen awareness of the eschaton—the kingdom has been inaugurated but awaiting its final consummation; and (5) Its structures will serve and support its mission to the world—the church must stay abreast of its changing cultural context, which will require the dismantling of archaic forms that impede missionary witness and the devising of new structures that support the mission.[50] Wilbert Shenk's list is helpful in reminding us of the cruciform nature of mission, which is countercultural

---

46. Frost, *The Road to Missional*, 28.
47. Ibid., 37.
48. Ibid., 60–61.
49. Hill, *Salt, Light, and a City*, 164–65.
50. Shenk, "New Wineskins for New Wine," 78.

to a consumer-orientated church, and the importance of Christology and eschatology in shaping the church on mission; as well as his emphasis on the need to engage with the world missionally but not be polluted by it.

In terms of some of the practices of a missional church, Graham Hill also provides some features of a church practicing and shaped by the mission of God: (1) *cultivating missional perspectives*—where the missional church intentionally defines itself by the *missio Dei*; (2) *cultivating missional postures*—where the church follows the messianic mission of Christ and the pattern of the *missio Dei* by being both contextual and inculturational; (3) *cultivating mission practices*—such as, (a) engaging in acts of hospitality and generosity for the sake of others; (b) being the missional church in community, where missional ethics are lived out and modeled; (c) helping people become disciples of Jesus in their unique and cultural settings; and (d) always seeking genuine reform in order to be missional, in light of the gospel.[51]

Stuart Murray, in an attempt to define a missional church, appeals to Paul Hiebert's *center-set model*. Murray suggests that this model resonates with a postmodern culture where the notion of boundaries is "uncongenial," and appeals to churches wanting to encourage "belonging" before "believing."[52] He further suggests that the centered-set churches have distinctive features such as: (1) a definite center comprising non-negotiable core convictions rooted ultimately in Jesus; (2) the center is the focal point, around which members of the community gather enthusiastically; (3) core convictions shape the church and separate it from other communities in a plural and contested culture; (4) the church expends its energy on maintaining the core rather than patrolling the boundaries; (5) confidence in the core convictions frees the church to be inclusive, hospitable, and open to others; (6) those who "belong" are moving towards the center, however near or far away they currently are in terms of "belief" and "behavior"; and (7) this is a dynamic rather than a static model, suitable for communities living towards a vision, and missional churches that anticipate constant interaction with others.[53] These distinctive features resonate with some of the aforementioned marks and practice of a missional church and, in combination with them, provide a dynamic model of what it means to be a missional church without being too prescriptive.

While the identification of the need to cultivate a missional posture is important, where the church seeks to be inculturational or incarnational, the missional church requires the tools to effectively understand the culture to which it is sent. This is where the discipline of *missiology* is helpful. David Bosch argues that the church in a postmodern age will require a missiology of western culture.[54] He characterizes

---

51. Hill, *Salt, Light, and a City*, 167–79.
52. Murray, *Church after Christendom*, 27.
53. Ibid., 29–30.
54. Interestingly, Bosch says that African and Asian theology and missiology have become indistinguishable. Partly due to the dynamics of Christendom, the nature of theology in the west is rarely missional.

Movement Two—From Shallowness to Dynamic Theological Reflection

the five ingredients of a missiology of western culture as: (1) including an ecological dimension; (2) countercultural; (3) ecumenical (as opposed to denominational); (4) contextual; and (5) primarily a ministry of the laity—a missiology of western culture must flow out of a local worshiping community.[55] He sounds a warning for the church in the west saying:

> . . . unless we develop a missionary theology, not just a theology of mission, we will not achieve more than merely patch up the church. We are in need of a missiological agenda for theology, not just a theological agenda for mission.[56]

The ability to undertake missional theology for a specific cultural context is crucial for the effectiveness of the church in mission. The members of a missional church must see themselves as a "missionary" to the culture to which the church is sent. Missionaries, by the very nature of their task, must become theologians.[57] Paul Hiebert argues that "theology began as an accompanying manifestation of Christian missions, and not a luxury of the world-dominating church."[58] It was a necessity as the gospel transformed people's lives within the culture it reached, and believers were required to think theologically about their former behaviors and practices in light of the gospel. The apostle Paul demonstrated this reality as he planted churches on his missionary travels. In all his letters to these churches, Paul would theologize about specific issues that the believers in those towns/cities faced, in order to help the believers grow in their understanding of what the gospel meant for them in their culture. Darrell Guder suggests that "the theological reflection of the early church accompanied its mission and grappled with its challenges as a missionary church," and that "the purpose of that theological labor was to equip and support the church in its missionary vocation."[59]

According to Paul Hiebert, to communicate the gospel in a culture, a third way of doing theology is required (in addition to systematic and biblical theologies). This third theology is referred to as *missional theology*—"a way of thinking biblically about God's universal mission in the context of the world here and now, with all its particularities, paradoxes, and confusions." The central question it asks is: "What is God's word to humans in their particular situation?" In other words, missional theology seeks to build the bridge between biblical revelation and human contexts. It seeks to remove the gap between "orthodoxy and orthopraxy, between truth, love, and holiness."[60] A missional church must be able to undertake missional theology in order to understand the culture to which it is sent in order to be effectively communicating the gospel in word and deed.

---

55. Bosch, *Believing in the Future*, 55–59.
56. Ibid., 32.
57. Hiebert, *The Gospel in Human Contexts*, 44.
58. Ibid.
59. Guder, "Missional Theology for a Missionary Church," 7.
60. Hiebert, *The Gospel in Human Contexts*, 44–45.

In conclusion, this chapter has outlined a missional ecclesiology for a changing western culture by arguing that its development is greatly informed and shaped by the biblical theology of the *missio Dei*, and the systematic theologies of Christology, eschatology, and ecclesiology. The second part of this chapter sought to practically engage with the ecclesial and missional challenges for the church in the context of post-Christendom, and argues that the main challenge facing the western church is cultural captivity. The western church must recalibrate itself to the gospel and realign itself to the *missio Dei* in order to become the missional church, shown by its characteristics and practices. In order to recalibrate, and to be salt and light in the cultures to which it is sent, the church must engage in serious, in-depth, localized, missional theology.

Individual and Corporate Servantship Practices

- Study the whole of Scripture through the lens of biblical theology, and keep a journal of how this informs your understanding of God's mission in the world and your role in this mission today.

- Design a preaching and/or Bible study series that helps your congregation or group understand the Bible as one big unfolding cosmic story about God bringing all things under Christ, and how your church fits into this story.

- Read Paul's letters and examine how he exegetes both culture and Scripture in order to help the believers in their understanding of the gospel and servantship in their own culture.

- Read the newspaper regularly and identify the key cultural issues facing you and your church in your own context. Pray about these issues, and equip your people to deal with them in light of Scripture.

- Identify the "people groups" or community to which your church has been sent. Undertake a cultural study of them, and explore ways of communicating the gospel to them in word and deed.

- Explore with your servantship team: "What would the reign of God in Christ look like in the neighborhood that we are seeking to reach with the gospel? How can our church be God's agency in this transformation?"

- Evaluate all your current corporate church practices. What do you observe about them in terms of: (1) Whom they are directed at? (2) Frequency of practice? (3) How are they practiced? How do they help advance the gospel and the mission of God to the people to whom your church has been sent?

Movement Two—From Shallowness to Dynamic Theological Reflection

Questions for Reflection and Discussion

- What are the challenges facing the church in mission and servantship in the contemporary postmodern context?

- In what ways do you see the church in the West trapped in "cultural captivity"? How have these impacted the church's mission in the world? What areas of your church's corporate life, practices, or servantship need recalibration in the light of the gospel and God's mission?

- What are the essential characteristics and practices of a church that is intentionally and missionally engaging the postmodern world?

11

Considering Emerging Innovations

JIM COLLINS

This chapter attempts to construct a provisional ecclesiology for the emerging church movement. To do so, Gibbs and Bolger's recent definition of the emerging church is utilized. A seven-point presentation of the main ecclesial beliefs of the emerging movement is then presented. The emerging church is found to be Jesus-centered, praxis-focused, missional, community-oriented, and adopts a holistic approach to spirituality across all spheres of life that is expressed in a culturally relevant manner.

Although the impact of the emerging church movement on the wider church and the world-at-large is yet to be determined, it shows both positive reasons why we should welcome it, and some negative aspects that are to be guarded against. Its courageous responses to the many challenges of doing church in our postmodern, twenty-first-century culture are to be admired—particularly its desire to reclaim our biblical and traditional heritage of Jesus-following. However, any compromises on the accepted, evangelical essentials of the Christian faith to accommodate unorthodox beliefs are highlighted and are to be graciously rejected.

The End of One Age and the Beginning of Another

> *You and I happen to be born at an "edge," at a time of high "tectonic" activity in history—the end of one age and the beginning of another. It is a time of shaking. Yesterday's maps are outdated, and today's soon will be too.* —Brian McLaren[1]

The western church in the twenty-first century lives in tumultuous times. The old certainties of modernity are passing away, and along with it "Christendom" is fast

---

1. McLaren is quoted in Stoddard and Cuthbert, *Church on the Edge*.

Movement Two—From Shallowness to Dynamic Theological Reflection

disappearing. Traditional modes and models of church are under threat from a culture that is postmodern and post-Christian: marked by rampant secularization and rapidly declining church attendance. Yet, in the midst of this gloomy setting, a movement of "fresh expressions of church" is emerging. Evangelical opinion is strongly divided over this *"emerging church"*: seen as a breath of fresh air for the stifling institutionalized church; or as the moves of confused Christians, dangerously steering the church towards heresy. Either way, the question of how to contextualize the gospel to today's shifting culture remains a crucial topic requiring urgent action.[2]

This chapter poses three key questions: *What, exactly, is the emerging church? What does it believe about church?* and, *Should we welcome it as friend or foe?* To answer these questions adequately, we will first need to provide an overview of the movement and a working definition of the emerging church. We will then turn to look at the ecclesiological emphases of the movement: seeking to understand both their *theological* foundations and how their *practices* compare against traditional ecclesial forms. Finally, an assessment of the potential impact of the emerging church is given, including its positive and negative characteristics.

What is the "Emerging Church Movement"?

There is no such thing as the emerging "church."—Scot McKnight[3]

Ironically, given there has been so much talk on the "emerging church" over the past few years, finding a definitive view of the term is still surprisingly difficult. This is due to the "fluid" nature of the movement, confusion over who or what represents the emerging church, and some knee-jerk efforts to categorize the emerging church.

Initial attempts by evangelicals to understand this movement have tended to focus on the postmodernist *epistemology* (philosophy of knowledge) that underpins the prominent voices in the emerging church "conversation." Don Carson's *Becoming Conversant with the Emerging Church* is the prime example of this: narrowing his analysis to the USA Emergent Village's[4] "spokesman" Brian McLaren's apparent denial of absolute truth, then widening his conclusions to the whole emerging church.[5]

---

2. Ibid., 3, offers a quick reminder that the word *"culture"* means "the way we do things around here." They note that since "how we do things is changing," we would be wise to at least acknowledge that, even if we don't know what to do about it.

3. McKnight, "What Is the Emerging Church?"

4. More usually referred to as "Emergent."

5. Don Carson's conclusions have been largely (although graciously) rejected by the emerging church as a misrepresentation, due to his lack of investigation and interaction with the movement's key figures. Scot McKnight (2006) sees Carson's inaccurate representations of the emerging church—through concentrating on a *certain part* of more liberal thinkers in Emergent—as "sloppy work." Unfortunately many evangelicals have adopted Carson's stereotype of the emerging church, and dismiss it unquestioningly. However, as you would expect of someone of Carson's caliber, he did identify some

Brian McLaren and others prefer to loosely define the emerging church movement as a "conversation amongst friends": consciously avoiding any institutionalism, or rigid doctrinal statements. Jared Siebert accepts that, whilst this may be "irritatingly vague," when discussing the emerging church and its culture "one must adopt the stance of a poet or a jazz musician rather than that of a chess player or accountant."[6] Scot McKnight agrees that forcing the emerging church "into a *theological definition* is to do violence to it—it isn't a theological movement and so can't be defined that way."[7] However, Eddie Gibbs and Ryan Bolger's explanation, below, captures the *essence* of the movement; their research producing the best definition to-date:[8]

> Emerging churches are communities that *practice* the way of Jesus within postmodern cultures. This definition encompasses nine practices. Emerging churches (1) identify with the life of Jesus, (2) transform the secular realm, and (3) live highly communal lives. Because of these three activities, they (4) welcome the stranger, (5) serve with generosity, (6) participate as producers, (7) create as created beings, (8) lead as a body, and (9) take part in spiritual activities.[9]

Emerging Church Movement: Ecclesiological Emphases

Even with Eddie Gibbs and Ryan Bolger's useful definition, producing a coherent *ecclesiology* that comprises all the divergent ideas in this "conversation" is difficult. Nevertheless, a tentative attempt to identify the foundational beliefs that underlie the above "practices" follows.

---

relevant and helpful insights into the movement (as we will see later).

6. Siebert, "The Ecclesiology of the Emerging Church."

7. Italics added for emphasis. Scot McKnight helpfully clarifies this statement: "By saying that the emerging movement (EM) is not a 'theological' movement, I have something specific in mind. The EM is not known by its innovative doctrinal statement or by its confessional stances. Now, to be sure, every movement is 'theological' in one way or another, and that means the EM is a theological movement. But, what we need to keep in mind is that it is not a 'Reformed' movement with a new twist, or an Anabaptist movement with new leaders (though I think it is more Anabaptist than anything else), and it is not a Wesleyan movement centuries later. It is instead, best to see it as a *conversation* about theology, with all kinds of theologies represented, with a core adhering to the classical creeds in a new key." McKnight, "What Is the Emerging Church?" There has, of course, been some significant controversy over Rob Bell's latest book: Bell, *Love Wins*.

8. Gibbs and Bolger have also faced criticism from some circles due to their perceived bias toward the emerging church. Their defense, quite rightly, is that the book's purpose was to "listen to the concerns of emerging church leaders and to appreciate their insights," rather than to critique the movement (Gibbs and Bolger, *Emerging Churches*, 11). In this way, their comprehensive study of the US and UK emerging church scene is a great basis from which to understand the background and current thrust of the emerging conversation.

9. Ibid., 45 (italics added for emphasis).

Movement Two—From Shallowness to Dynamic Theological Reflection

A Return to Jesus-centered Christianity

As the emerging churches questioned the effectiveness of existing church models for today's culture they began to focus on the life of Jesus as a reference point, re-exploring the Gospels. As Joe Boyd reports: "Nothing I was doing on Sunday was what I thought Jesus would be doing if he were here."[10] Inspired by the works of N. T. Wright, Dallas Willard, John Howard Yoder, and others, emerging churches embrace Jesus's gospel of the kingdom of God (Mark 1:15). They see the gospel as embracing a *new way of living*, as a participant in the kingdom of God; not merely restricted to an individual's assurance of eternal life-after-death.

This focus has produced what Eddie Gibbs and Ryan Bolger see as a new ecclesiology—a return to an ancient ecclesiology in which God's ongoing *missio Dei* is integral to the church.[11] Alan Hirsch describes how this results in a theological "formula" for post-Christian culture engagement: "*Christology determines missiology, and missiology determines ecclesiology.*"[12] Christian mission always starts with Jesus and is defined by him.[13] Jesus is seen as the perfect embodiment of God and the exemplar "model" for all disciples (Heb 1:1–3; Heb 12:1–2; 1 John 2:6). Their vision is "*Jesus—obsessively, dangerously, undeniably Jesus.*"[14] Those associated with the emerging church like to refer to themselves as "Jesus-followers," as opposed to mere "Jesus-admirers." The church is understood to be a community of Christ followers seeking to imitate Jesus's actions of love in all the circumstances of their daily lives.

The Importance of Orthopraxy over Orthodoxy

The contention here is that *how a person lives* is more important than *what he or she believes.*[15] Emerging churches understand that Jesus presented a welcoming yet challenging message which invited his followers to *live distinctively* in the world. Alan Hirsch notes that whilst evangelical thinking has claimed Christianity is an all-of-life phenomenon, it is our lifestyle *practices* which have constantly let us down in this manner, often tarnishing Jesus's reputation.[16] The emerging church reflects a concern

---

10. Ibid., 47.

11. Ibid., 91.

12. Hirsch, *The Forgotten Ways*, 142–43.

13. Perhaps this is why the emerging church's ecclesiology is so hard to pin down: it is expected to *evolve*, as Jesus's mission demands it. It may need to be "permanently provisional." Siebert, "The Ecclesiology of the Emerging Church."

14. This is an extract from Pete Greig's (founder of the 24/7 Prayer movement) popular and inspiring poem *The Vision*, which captured the imagination of many in the emerging church as it was emailed around the world. The story of this poem can be read in: Greig and Roberts, *Red Moon Rising*.

15. McKnight argues that what most characterizes the emerging movement is *praxis*—how the faith is lived out. McKnight, "What Is the Emerging Church?" 14.

16. Hirsch, *The Forgotten Ways*, 113.

to bridge this gap between theory and practice: attempting to distance itself from a hypocritical "church-as-religion," and preferring to measure a person's life by their true fruit, not profession of belief.[17] John Burke argues that if our theology does *not* lead us to become more like Jesus, "we must reassess our theological priorities and perspectives."[18]

The Church Is on a Mission from God

David Bosch, whose seminal missiological works influenced many of the emerging church leaders, said: "Christians find their true identity when they are involved in mission."[19] The church is God's chosen instrument to enact his ongoing redemptive mission at this stage in salvific history. The emerging church considers its job description as *Jesus's body in the world*.

With the numbers of unchurched adults[20] growing exponentially each generation, "it is both naïve and unkind" to assume that spiritual seekers will *go to church*. Jesus's *incarnational* mission (John 1:14; 20:21) instructs us to "go" to those who need God's redemption. Alan Hirsch says that a *missional* reading of the Bible requires that "we see Jesus's strategy is to get a whole lot of little versions of him infiltrating every nook and cranny of society by reproducing himself in and through his people in every place throughout the world."[21] This forces churches to train their members as *missionaries* to serve their surrounding communities.

Church Is a Loving, Open, and Hospitable Community

The emerging church movement abhors the idea of church as a meeting, a building, or a set of religious routines. Church is seen as a people, a rhythm, and a way of life, alongside other Jesus-followers in organic, "liquid" community. Reacting against the rigid clergy/laity divide that developed during the Christendom era, emerging churches tend to have very relational structures, characterized by relatively flat servantship models that cultivate participation of all members. This reflects the Apostle

---

17. Rob Bell presents a well argued, amusing parody of this hard-nosed, judgmental Christianity, which he calls "brickianity," in Bell, *Velvet Elvis*, 26–28. As with most emerging church leaders, Rob Bell's approach to following Jesus has been significantly affected by his own negative experiences of over-religious, fundamentalist Christianity (growing up in an arch-Reformed church in West Michigan). As Bono reportedly said: "Christians are hard to tolerate; I don't know how Jesus does it!"

18. Webber et al., *Listening to the Beliefs of Emerging Churches*, 65 and 109.

19. Bosch, *Transforming Mission*, 83.

20. Stoddard and Cuthbert report that in the United Kingdom, 40 percent of the population has never set foot in a church building. Similar percentages would be reported in other western settings. Stoddard and Cuthbert, *Church on the Edge*, 30.

21. Hirsch, *The Forgotten Ways*, 113.

Movement Two—From Shallowness to Dynamic Theological Reflection

Paul's insistence that each individual member of the church body is uniquely gifted and indispensable to effective, God-glorifying community (1 Cor 12; Rom 12:3–8).

Over and against the "in-versus-out" mentality of many traditional churches towards spiritual seekers, emerging church communities make a conscious effort to welcome the stranger, without belief barriers. As Michael Frost states, following Jesus "means *engaging* meaningfully with the lives of others."[22] The maxim "*belong-believe-behave*" is adopted to encourage people of differing religions and sexual orientation to experience a journey of faith, and discover Jesus's love in community. By being so open to all, emerging churches make themselves vulnerable, but these "participant communities consider it a risk worth taking."[23] Karen Ward explains: "We truly believe that following Jesus calls for a reordering of our lives and because of this, we provide time and space for seekers to explore and discern what entering into such a life will mean."[24]

Christians Should Pursue a Holistic, Life-Embracing Spirituality

The basis for emerging church life is not found in organizational patterns or buildings, but in people's *spiritual activity*. Robert Webber states that in the latter days of evangelicalism Christianity became mired in an excessively narcissistic, selfish focus.[25] This is exacerbated when tied to a "Sunday-church" mentality, and misses a true holistic, biblical spirituality. Emerging church communities reject the notion of a sacred-secular divide. They have sought to recover the idea of living like Jesus in *every sphere* of society and daily life (1 Cor 10:31). In line with the idea of a priesthood of all believers, this is an important concept: where I live, work, and socialize becomes my mission field.

Emerging church ecclesiology has given rise to a wave of "new monastic communities." A desire to recapture *biblical discipleship* has also grown: age-old spiritual disciplines, previously the province of Catholicism, have seen a great resurgent interest.[26] Exploration of alternative forms of worship has led emerging churches to be creative, sensory, and experiential in their worship gatherings. In what is termed an *ancient-future* faith, church services may include creeds and liturgy together with modern music and audio-visuals. The emerging movement also comprises the "house

---

22. Frost, *Exiles*, 141 (italics added for emphasis).
23. Gibbs and Bolger, *Emerging Churches*, 172.
24. Webber et al., *Listening to the Beliefs of Emerging Churches*, 171.
25. Ibid., 15.
26. Dallas Willard, Richard Foster, and others reignited an interest in Christian spiritual practices (again based on Jesus's way of life). The emerging movement has also embraced the writings of classical spirituality (e.g. Teresa of Avila, Brother Lawrence, and Ignatius of Loyola), and even the use of icons, liturgies, and devotional readings such as *lectio divina*.

church" and "simple church"[27] movements, along with churches that may not even have a worship service. Embracing traditions from across the church spectrum is also a conscious effort to foster harmony amongst the wider church: a generous orthodoxy and post-denominational unity.

The Kingdom Gospel Includes Social Justice, Compassion, and Mercy

The gospel of emerging churches is not confined to personal salvation; it extends to a "social transformation arising from the presence and permeation of the reign of Christ."[28] Scot McKnight notes, "The emerging movement thinks love defines Christian existence."[29] Such an understanding of our redemptive mission encapsulates commitment to the care of creation, a desire to see beauty in urban spaces, engaging social justice issues, championing the poor and marginalized, and addressing people's physical and emotional needs. Based upon Jesus's own messianic manifesto (Luke 4:18–19; cf. Acts 26:20; James 1:27), this approach includes ministry in *word*, *deed*, and *power*,[30] necessitating a different approach to church. Many emerging church leaders consider their role comprises Christian *activism*, as opposed to solely pastoral, intra-church activities.

The Church Is to Be Counter-Cultural yet Culturally-Relevant

The emerging church aims to be a prophetic movement amidst our secular and materialistic world, challenging the world's value systems. Robert Webber states, we are called to be "authentically transformed people, conforming to the image of Christ, conducting ourselves as salt and light in the political, economic, educational, institutional, and family life of our neighborhood, the state, the nation, and the world."[31] As ever Jesus's instruction to be "in the world, but not of the world" requires a careful balance: to contextualize the gospel without falling foul of syncretism. As Paul Quicke rightly warns, the church's values can easily derive uncritically from culture without being tested by biblical standards.[32]

---

27. Both these movements are founded on the idea that a truer biblical expression of church is practiced in cell-group style communities that meet in homes, or other small venues, and aim to multiply and grow rapidly. They are highly relational and unstructured.

28. Gibbs and Bolger, *Emerging Churches*, 63.

29. McKnight, "What Is the Emerging Church?" 23.

30. The emerging movement sees no distinction between evangelism and social action. Ministry comprises an integrated love and appreciation for the whole person. In many branches of the emerging church (particularly in the United Kingdom) this is evidenced in "post-charismatic," low-key healing ministry, avoiding the excesses of earlier charismatic expressions of church.

31. Webber et al., *Listening to the Beliefs of Emerging Churches*, 215.

32. Quicke, *360-Degree Leadership*, 41.

Movement Two—From Shallowness to Dynamic Theological Reflection

Scot McKnight explains three distinct methods which have developed in the emerging church: ministering *to* postmoderns; ministering *with* postmoderns; and ministering *as* postmoderns.[33] It is this third category of emergents that attracts all the attention. They embrace the idea that we cannot know absolute truth, or at least, that we can't know truth absolutely; and frequently express nervousness about the presentation of Christianity as propositional truths. Understandably, this controversial line of the emerging conversation has caused a great deal of disquiet in the evangelical community.

Having established our emerging ecclesiology, we now turn to assess its implications for the future of the church.

Emerging Church Movement: Positive or Negative Impact?

So far only faint harbingers of the new era are discernable. —Harvey Cox[34]

There is no doubt that our world is undergoing a major culture shift. The emerging church is rightly asking us to get ready for this new world.[35] Don Carson's study identified five *strength* elements of the emerging church: "reading the times; pushing for authenticity; recognizing our own social location; evangelizing outsiders; and probing links with tradition."[36] Indeed, we can readily affirm that all seven of the emphases of the emerging church ecclesiology as set out above are aimed at *recovering biblical emphases*, deeply rooted in the New Testament. However, their spectrum of beliefs, mindsets, and methodologies are disparate and varied, and as Carson and others warn, the movement contains a "number of worrying weaknesses."[37]

---

33. McKnight explains the first two categories describe most emerging Christians, trying to rescue "folks *from* postmodernity or *walking alongside* such folk in order to lead them to paradise." McKnight, "What Is the Emerging Church?" 11–14.

34. Cox is quoted from his 2004 lecture "Is New Zealand's future churchless?" in Stoddard and Cuthbert, *Church on the Edge*, 18. Cox goes on to say, "Church leaders could do worse than take the philosophy of Mao Tse Tung's cultural revolution in China and seek to "let a thousand flowers bloom." Some will wither and die very quickly, some will doubtless become non-orthodox or heretical, but among those that thrive are likely to be found new social groupings needed to contextualize our faith into the new world of post Christian, postmodern, and post secular New Zealand." His comments probably reflect the future outlook for most western church environments.

35. Webber's excellent assessment of emerging theology notes the insight his five contributors share stems from their "modern" seminary educations failing to prepare them for the new cultural horizons and issues, Webber et al., *Listening to the Beliefs of Emerging Churches*, 195–201. That, coupled with a reaction against self-focused, mega-church style experiences, has driven them to explore new ecclesiological forms for the emerging culture.

36. Siebert, "The Ecclesiology of the Emerging Church."

37. Carson's conclusions on emerging theology include a warning that "because of its 'porous borders,' people are not sure what the emerging church is, what it stands for, or how to think about it." (Webber et al., *Listening to the Beliefs of Emerging Churches*, 195). While pro-emergents say we should keep in mind the movement is yet too young to have produced a full-orbed theology, Webber

Consequently, there is a clear need for us to discern truth from error as we assess how this new movement might develop. Of course this is not the first time the church has faced this need. The Reformer Philip Melanchthon left us a biblical-theological grid to filter out any unorthodox beliefs, comprising *unity* around the essentials of the faith, *liberty* for the non-essentials, and in all things *love*.[38] In a recent journal Mark Driscoll provided a classification for emergents based upon such principles. In his analysis, Driscoll isolates that part of the emerging church (primarily those involved with Emergent) that would seek to *revise* evangelical doctrine as aberrant.[39] He accepts the methods by which truth is articulated and practiced must be culturally appropriate, and constantly translated: a "living orthodoxy" (1 Cor 9:22–23). But he emphatically argues that "the truths of Christianity are constant, unchanging, and meant for all people, times, and places" (Jude 3).

Chief of Mark Driscoll's concerns is the *centrality of Jesus's work on the cross*. Apart from the cross, he says, the church has "nothing unique to offer the world that they couldn't get from a psychologist or self-help seminar with principles for community and self-esteem."[40] John Hammett suggests that, at times, Brian McLaren has been "disturbingly vague, cavalier or flippant about questions that are serious and vitally important, such as the *ultimate fate of those in other religions*."[41] Scot McKnight also weighs into this controversy, acknowledging the emerging church has not been well known for its evangelistic endeavor to date. As he rightly declares, "unless you

---

concedes that the language of emerging writers "does not have the clarity most desire." Some consider this lack of theological clarity to be exemplified in Bell's *Love Wins*.

38. His list has five *essential* central tenets of the gospel—the Bible as the inspired word of God; the existence of one true God (in Trinity); salvation by faith in Jesus Christ's deity and substitutionary atonement; Christ's bodily resurrection; and his physical return (Malphurs, *A New Kind of Church*, 50–55). Malphurs identifies some possible *nonessentials* (that aren't as clear biblically): church government; mode of baptism; the Lord's Supper; role of women in church; spiritual gifts; when the church meets; and church practices. In the case of differences in these areas, the key word is *liberty*: there is room to flex. The final filter is, no matter what differences exist, to always treat others in *love* (without condoning their beliefs and behavior). This seems to be a very sound approach to assessing emerging beliefs.

39. Driscoll provides three categories: *Relevants* are characterized as updating church styles and structures, with little change to doctrine; *Reconstructionists* propose more informal, incarnational, and organic church forms; *Revisionists* are "theologically liberal and question key evangelical doctrines, critiquing their appropriateness for the emerging postmodern world." With this perspective, revisionists prefer an "evolving theology." Driscoll, *Confessions of a Reformission Rev.*, 89–90.

Driscoll's insight is uniquely valuable as he was involved with the beginning of the emerging church journey in the United States, but later publicly distanced himself from those in the Emergent camp (Brian McLaren, Doug Pagitt, etc.) who were pushing a theological agenda that worried Driscoll. In his trademark, reactive, blunt style, Driscoll provides these examples: "referring to God as a chick, questioning God's sovereignty over (and knowledge of) the future, denial of the substitutionary atonement at the cross, a low view of Scripture, and denial of hell—which is one hell of a mistake" (sourced from: TheResurgence.com/?q=node/5).

40. Webber et al., *Listening to the Beliefs of Emerging Churches*, 185.

41. Hammett, "An Ecclesiological Assessment of the Emerging Church Movement," 9.

Movement Two—From Shallowness to Dynamic Theological Reflection

proclaim the good news of Jesus Christ, there is no good news at all; if there is no good news, there is no Christianity."[42]

John Burke also shares concerns over how the movement may err: "one fear I have for the emerging church is that we will cut loose from the anchor of the *authority of the Scriptures* in hopes of relating to our relativistic culture."[43] Despite the fact that key leaders of the emerging movement announced that they "love, have confidence in, seek to obey, and strive accurately to teach the sacred Scriptures,"[44] the "revisionist" end of the emerging spectrum does indeed seem to be somewhat "rubbery" on their view of scriptural authority, hesitating to affirm the infallibility or inerrancy of God's word. Burke accepts this may be reaction against past abuses of Scripture, but urges the emerging church not to "lose sight of the primary source of our knowledge of God."[45]

So, what can we say about the overall impact of the emerging church's ecclesiological emphases? Perhaps, as Mark Driscoll says, we should find the "entire conversation encouraging, stimulating, and frightening."[46] *Encouraging* in that the emerging movement's desire to reorient church around the person, life, and work of Jesus may well be an exciting, corrective guidance of the Holy Spirit to the church as a whole. *Stimulating* in that the focus on a missional, dynamic, praxis-oriented, communal approach to church is refreshing and may well ensure our faith-life regains its relevancy and vitality in the world. *Frightening* in that the reticence to proclaim core tenets of the Christian faith may lead to an erosion of Scripture as our bedrock of truth, knowledge, and praxis. Perhaps only time will tell.

Concluding Thoughts

> *As an evangelical, I've had my concerns, but overall I think what emerging Christians bring to the table is vital for the overall health of the church.*
> —Scot McKnight[47]

---

42. McKnight, "What Is the Emerging Church?" 26 (italics added for emphasis).

43. Webber et al., *Listening to the Beliefs of Emerging Churches*, 61 (italics added for emphasis).

44. Jones et al., *Our Response to Critics of Emergent* (emergentus.typepad.com/emergentus/2005/06/official-respon.html).

45. Webber et al., *Listening to the Beliefs of Emerging Churches*, 150. Siebert notes the emerging church demonstrates a similar model of knowing and theological reflection to Wesley's "quadrilateral": valuing Scripture, tradition, experience, and reason (Siebert, "The Ecclesiology of the Emerging Church."). Although this is true, across the spectrum of the emerging movement the *relative* standing of these four elements varies.

46. Driscoll, *Confessions of a Reformission Rev.*, 92.

47. McKnight, "What Is the Emerging Church?"

As we have seen above, the emerging church movement describes a broad spectrum of those who have noticed our culture is rapidly changing and are willing to undergo ecclesiological thinking and experimentation together for the gospel of Jesus.

This rethink covers everything: servantship, church structure, the role of a pastor, spiritual formation, how communities live out our mission, etc. It is not just about tinkering with a worship service. In its search for missional solutions to today's post-Christian context, the emerging church is urging a repatriation of biblical discipleship, community-focus, and a holistic approach to our spiritual life based on kingdom principles. Whilst the lack of a definitive church theology prevents a comprehensive analysis of the underlying beliefs of the emerging church, its dynamic energy and flexibility remain perhaps the movement's greatest strength. Only with relatively "fluid," dynamic expressions can the church hope to keep abreast of cultural change. At its best the emerging church movement is a corrective of the Holy Spirit, to be welcomed and embraced. As such it may spark a revival of biblical Christianity amongst the western nations. At its worst, the glimmers of erroneous theology we have highlighted could grow into divisive heresies if left unchecked by the wider, established church. Either way, without clear, Jesus-centered Bible teaching, the emerging church will drift on a sea of uncertainty.

Finally, Philip Melanchthon's wise words sum up the church's best response to the movement: "*In the essentials we purse unity and in the nonessentials liberty; in all things love.*"[48]

Individual and Corporate Servantship Practices

- Set aside some time as a servantship group. Read the Gospel of Mark together—in one sitting. List the central themes of Jesus's ministry. How do these compare to your current church themes?

- Consider the goals of your church. How could your church goals be reshaped to focus more on Jesus's servantship?

- Do you consider your church to be mission-oriented? What percentage of your church activities do you consider to be community focused (i.e. serving the benefit of others, not just church members)? Discuss three practical steps you could introduce to increase your outreach locally.

- Read Micah 6:8, James 1:27, and Romans 12:1–2 as a servantship team. These verses emphasize a practical Christianity. How do they make you feel—burdened or buoyed? Why do you think that is? Spend some time praying about God's desires for your church, and your motivations.

- Jesus-followers are called to serve as transforming agents, who are "in the world

---

48. Malphurs, *A New Kind of Church*, 138.

Movement Two—From Shallowness to Dynamic Theological Reflection

but not of the world." As a church, are there areas where you too closely conform to culture? Are things of the world polluting you? How are you practically equipping your congregation in the renewing of their minds?

- Study *The Life You've Always Wanted* by John Ortberg.[49] Plan to help your church members and small groups spend a season focusing on what it would mean to recover the idea of living like Jesus in every sphere of society and daily life.

- What are the most pressing needs in your community? Choose one. How could your church creatively make a difference in this area, in partnership with your community?

Questions for Reflection and Discussion

- Assessing our church practices and behaviors is a key part of ensuring we remain *both* faithful to biblical principles, and responsive to our changing cultural context. Discuss your church's core practices. Are they helping people grow in embracing the gospel as a new way of living?

- Is it fair to assess Christianity by how a person lives? How do you think your community perceives the impact and influence of Jesus in your life and that of your church?

- Central to much of the missional church is a desire to show God's love in action. What does a biblical picture of God's love really look like? How is presenting God's truth an act of love?

- How has the missional church movement impacted your view of church and its servantship?

---

49. Ortberg, *The Life You've Always Wanted*.

12

Rediscovering Community

Steven Rodda

The uniqueness of the twenty-first century is not so much the fact that society is changing, but that it is changing so fast. Where once there were decades, if not centuries, between technological advancements and societal revolutions, "now change is neither subtle nor gradual: it is traumatic and immediate."[1]

Additionally, with such a rapid pace of change comes the progress of such change. We have moved from one place to another without time to process the meaning behind such a change, leaving the western church in a state of confusion and bewilderment. Nigel Wright sums it up, "The fact is that none of us has ever been this way before."[2]

The days of the church at the center of civic pride and confidence have evaporated. Instead, it now finds itself on the margins of a culture which sees the church as antiquated and irrelevant, or quaint and benign. Mike Riddell is a little more blunt when he declares, "the Christian church is dying in the West."[3] The decline of the western church is a statistical reality, as well as being apparent in popular mindsets.[4] Riddell goes on to say, "The frightening reality is the extent to which Christianity in the West has already been disposed of in the popular mind as an archaic and oppressive system."[5]

This chapter describes some key changes in twenty-first-century western society and examines how the twenty-first-century church may rediscover its ever timely

---

1. Drane, "Cultural Change and Biblical Faith," 1.
2. Nigel Wright, from "Foreword" in Murray, *Post-Christendom*, xiv.
3. Riddell, *Threshold of the Future*, 1.
4. Gibbs, *Church Next*, 17–22.
5. Riddell, *Threshold of the Future*, 8.

Movement Two—From Shallowness to Dynamic Theological Reflection

biblical identity and engage with some of the missional challenges of a rapidly changing culture.

New Challenges in the Twenty-first Century

The church of the twenty-first century finds itself facing a multitude of changes which affect not only the mission of the church in western society, but also the lives of individual members of the church. The most difficult aspect of twenty-first-century culture is its lack of predictability because of its "discontinuous rather than incremental" nature.[6] This discontinuous change is experienced in lifestyle change, philosophical change (postmodernity), and cultural change (post-Christendom).

Lifestyle Changes

Time

The evaporation of available time has greatly affected Christians, for "with discretional time at a premium for many people, church attendance has become one option among many."[7] The demands of many workplaces and schools have a draining effect on people, who are less inclined to engage actively in regular gathered worship or service activities. Leisure activities have become increasingly important in a time-pressured culture. With ever increasing options there is no end of activities, many of them fun and exciting, to occupy a person's time. Families in particular find it hard: "some families feel there is more to be gained by supporting their children's sporting events or even going together to the shopping mall, than by enforcing attendance at church."[8]

Less Volunteerism

Having less time means having less involvement from non-employed members of the church. As Reggie McNeal observes, "Church ministry . . . is an add-on activity to an already crowded life."[9] What has traditionally been a volunteer-powered organization is being rocked by the lack of available people. Mike Riddell suggests, "The mainstay of this approach has been spouses not in employment."[10]

---

6. Gibbs, *Church Next*, 36.
7. Riddell, *Threshold of the Future*, 4.
8. Ibid.
9. McNeal, *The Present Future*, 48.
10. Riddell, *Threshold of the Future*, 5.

Fragmentation

The media today involves fast cutting of scenes, fragmented storylines, sound bites and tweets, channel surfing, shorter and shorter magazine articles and Internet stories. Much of the world's video is now seen in clips on YouTube instead of coherent programs. This inevitably affects how generations of this postmodern trend respond. As Steve Taylor points out, "When you're used to surfing from image to image, three-point sermons start to sound like archaic King James English."[11]

Furthermore, it isn't just the presentation of culture that is fragmented, but the culture itself.[12] People's thinking and behavior have been influenced in such a way that many people now communicate in sound bites and clips via multimedia enabled devices such as mobile phones and webcams, through chat rooms, messaging, and "tweeting," rather than face-to-face conversation.

Individual Pick'n'mix Lifestyles

Such fragmentation eventually requires some attempt at piecing together a coherent understanding of life. Some have found the answer to this in adopting a pluralistic mosaic of different world views and values.[13] This provides an immense challenge to a church which now has to contend not just with traditional world views and religions, but a multiplicity of combined "pick'n'mix" montages.

Consumerism

In an era where the global economy is the headline story in the media, it is not surprising to see that consumerism has trumped all other "isms" at the beginning of the twenty-first century. Sociologist Steve Bruce notes, "Consumption has become more important than production. How we spend our money says far more about us than how we earn it."[14] Gordon Lynch highlights the pervasiveness of consumerism in its extension from the economic sphere to an individual's and communities' very identity: "Consumption can be seen as an important way in which people express their personal and social identities, as well as their broader understanding of what it means to live a good and fulfilled life."[15]

---

11. Taylor, *Out of Bounds Church*, 21.
12. Ibid., 22.
13. Ibid., 24.
14. Bruce, *God Is Dead*, 231.
15. Lynch, *Understanding Theology and Popular Culture*, 60.

Movement Two—From Shallowness to Dynamic Theological Reflection

Technology

Our ability to consume has been ably assisted by the quantum changes in technology in the last two decades. However, technological advances have not produced the time savings they were expected to bring, but instead opened up a new world of opportunities for consumption. Moreover, they have engulfed Christ-following professionals with ethical dilemmas where complex decisions need to be made in the areas of personnel management, business practices, ethical investing, medical ethics, marginal legalities, etc.[16]

Community to Society

Finally, the contours of human interaction and relationship have moved from people living in community, which focused on shared relationship, to people living in society, which focuses on shared property (be it intellectual, ideological, or commodities). Steve Bruce asserts, "Religion has its source in, and draws its strength from, the community. As the society rather than the community has increasingly become the locus of the individual's life, so religion has been shorn of its functions."[17]

This is expressed no more powerfully than in the increase in relationship breakdowns which have progressed from alienation of extended families, to fracturing of nuclear families. There are no simple answers to this breakdown, and no simple categories for the typical family. Relational breakdown produces stresses and strains, as well as a real or perceived sense of alienation from their faith community.[18]

A New Paradigm: Postmodernism

Accompanying such lifestyle changes, and certainly influencing them, is a paradigm-shift from the latter part of the twenty-first century, known as postmodernism. Postmodernism is a critique of modernity, and as such offers no real alternative of its own. As Mike Riddell explains, "It says simply that the previous cultural and philosophic synthesis, 'modernism', is at an end, and something else is emerging to take its place."[19]

It has four basic identifying factors.

---

16. Riddell, *Threshold of the Future*, 7.
17. Bruce, *God Is Dead*, 13.
18. Riddell, *Threshold of the Future*, 5.
19. Ibid., 101.

Pursuit of Spirituality

The postmodern mindset is suspicious of the Enlightenment era approach which claimed science and rationalism as "the exclusive standard of worthwhile knowledge."[20] Alternatively, it reasserts the need to connect with spiritual aspects of life that contain notions such as wholeness and healing in reaching our full potential as human beings.[21] However, this is a spirituality in which the church is seen as unnecessary.

David Hay records numerous stories told by people who have found the church to be either lacking in some important aspect of spirituality, or simply regard it as unnecessary.[22] Hay outlines several reasons why many of the spiritually active people in his study mistrusted the religious institutions: religious institutions foster ignorance, are rigid and authoritarian, are narrow-minded, are hypocritical, and religious institutions damage people.[23]

Suspicion of Metanarratives

Because of their institutional heritage, postmodernity regards traditional metanarratives (overarching explanations and truth claims) as oppressive. This does not mean that there are no narratives. Rather, postmodern thinking values the sharing of individual stories rather than institutional ones. John Drane clarifies, "The very thing that makes New Age so popular is not that it has no metanarrative, but that it offers a different one than that which the West has traditionally embraced."[24] In this setting, the good of community becomes subservient to my needs when I establish my own identity.

Pursuit of Authentic, Connected Humanity

"The Truth" has been replaced by truths, which are to be discovered in relationship and experience. Connectedness has replaced conformity in identification with social groups. The ability to be "true to one's self" while still remaining connected to others is seen as an ultimate form of individual authenticity.[25]

---

20. Bruce, *God Is Dead*, 229.

21. Drane, *Do Christians Know How to Be Spiritual?*, 10.

22. This is particularly illustrated in four detailed accounts from individuals who are at the fringe of Christian communities, or have rejected them altogether. Hay, *Something There*, 74–75.

23. Ibid., 212–18.

24. Drane, *McDonaldization*, 134.

25. Gibbs, *Church Next*, 34.

Movement Two—From Shallowness to Dynamic Theological Reflection

Delight in Paradox and Playfulness

Coherent systems and consistency give way to relativism, pessimism, and skepticism.[26] In such a relativistic framework, paradox is accepted as a sign of the spiritual and unpredictable aspects of life. In the midst of such pessimism and skepticism, there is also a celebration of irony, spontaneity, and playfulness.[27]

Steve Bruce is reluctant to give the "post modern turn" the sociological credit that some do. He sees many postmodern aspects as far less potent than many assume. He also regards the changes described as being exaggerated, mistaking surface appearance for reality. He also claims that postmodernity is "too blunt an instrument."[28]

In a postmodern era it is only in how the church reflects modernity, in its identity and its mission, that it is besieged by postmodernism. When a biblical examination is made of the church and its mission, what is eventually seen is that Christianity is something all of its own, sharing qualities with pre-modernity, modernity, and post-modernity, but being defined by none. It is a completely unique world view, just as the gospel of Jesus Christ is unique.

However, it is not against the backdrop of postmodernism that the future church will be defined, but by its ability to find new ways to live and serve in a post-Christendom era.

A New Cultural Era: Christendom to Post-Christendom

While postmodernism has reacted to the Enlightenment era, another more significant cultural shift has been taking place. Stuart Murray asserts that, "The shift from Christendom to post-Christendom is at least as significant for church and society."[29] The institutional church, which is the figurehead for Christendom, no longer holds sway as a major influence on western culture in any country except the United States of America. Christendom has gone, he claims, and the church no longer finds itself in the center, but on the margins of society.[30]

Stuart Murray claims that the end of the Christendom epoch is only a generation away as the institutionally churched generation dies off. This dramatically shifts the place of the church in western society. Murray defines post-Christendom as "The culture that emerges as the Christian faith loses coherence within a society that has been definitively shaped by the Christian story and as the institutions that have been developed to express Christian convictions decline in influence."[31]

---

26. Murray, *Post-Christendom*, 13.
27. Bruce, *God Is Dead*, 229.
28. Ibid., 229–32.
29. Murray, *Post-Christendom*, xvi.
30. Frost and Hirsch, *Shaping of Things to Come*, 9.
31. Murray, *Post-Christendom*, 19.

For some, post-Christendom means post-churched, as Alan Jamieson describes, "The church is seen as overwhelmingly boring, irrelevant, abusive, and passé."[32] However, post-Christendom *does not* necessarily mean post-Christian. Stuart Murray concludes, "Whether post-Christendom is post-Christian will depend on whether we can re-imagine Christianity in a world we no longer control. Christendom is dying, but a new and dynamic Christianity could arise from its ashes."[33]

A Biblical View of the Church and Its Mission in a Rapidly Changing World

In order for the community of Christ to effectively minister in the current climate, a biblical view of the church and its mission is needed which enables Christ-followers to fruitfully engage with the culture we are now living in. While modern, postmodern, and post-Christendom cultures will come and go, understanding the biblical gospel and mission of Jesus Christ is the primary way that his followers develop a redemptive culture rather than a culture that merely reflects the prevailing forces of its day.

Be a Missional Community

Since the beginning of the industrial era, churches have become more and more focused on the efficiency of a well-oiled machine. Erwin McManus observes, "We have embraced the conveniences of the assembly line, the efficient, and the standardized and have grown in disdain for the chaotic, the unpredictable, and the disorganized."[34] But as McManus elaborates, the postmodern heart yearns for a church that beats with an unprocessed, unsystematic, organic, life-imitating pulse. Olive Drane similarly observes, "We have been encouraged to adopt a very mechanistic approach to life . . . This meant emphasizing and valuing reason over and above intuition, a way of being which has eventually left us spiritually dehydrated at the start of the twenty-first century."[35]

It has become apparent that the church has become machine-like, rather than mission-like. As Mike Riddell notes, "Our churches are structured for preservation and continuity, not for mission."[36] The purpose of the church is not bringing people in to process, but sending people out to proclaim.[37] The church has found the hope

---

32. Jamieson et al., *Five Years On*, 107.
33. Murray, *Post-Christendom*, 8.
34. McManus, *Unstoppable Force*, 13.
35. Drane, *Spirituality to Go*, 3.
36. Riddell, *Threshold of the Future*, 12.
37. Matthew 28:19–20.

of the world, that is, Jesus Christ and him alone.[38] And thus, the goal of the church is the mission of bringing Jesus to the world.

Much of church ministry has been focused on getting people into the church building. This has meant an emphasis on marketing strategies that increase the appeal of the church in order to attract people. However, postmoderns are not so much interested in something that works in church, they want something that works in life, right where they are.

Michael Frost and Alan Hirsh identify the ministry shift needed here as a move from being an attractional community to an incarnational one. A missional church is a sent church; "the existing church, which is invariably static . . . needs to recover its *sent-ness* in order to become the missional church."[39] Much of the attractional model has been built on the appeal of the early church community in Acts 2:47.

However, a reading of the book of Acts as a whole reveals the Holy Spirit continually moving Christ's followers farther and farther into the world in order to fulfill Jesus's missional description of his community in Acts 1:8. The activity of the book of Acts is seen in incursion into the world, rather than a concentration in an isolated place. The missional church community is to follow the example of the missional Christ who was not only attractive, but also incarnate.[40] Thus the goal of ministry among the members of the church community is not to shape people to live in the church culture, but to send and equip them to live like Christ and proclaim Christ in the world where they live.

Be a Bible-shaped Community

The Enlightened modern mindset saw a preference for education as the goal of spiritual formation. Principles, precepts, and propositions were communicated so that Christians would know how to live. The increasing problem, however, is that knowing intellectually is not the same as knowing experientially, and the postmodern generation, "finds the religious in personal experience."[41] Knowledge without experience leads to dormancy.[42] In a postmodern age, where experience is key, we must move from seeking to transmit concepts in an already information-saturated society, and focus on Bible-shaped transformation of character as the goal.[43]

In his study of the human spirit, David Hay notes that many who describe themselves as believing in God but not belonging to a church, rarely mention that they

---

38. 1 Peter 1:13.
39. Frost and Hirsch, *Shaping of Things to Come*, 12.
40. Acts 6:7, 8:1–4; John 1:14; John 20:21; Luke 4:42–43.
41. Beaudoin, *Virtual Faith*, 74.
42. James 2:26.
43. Romans 12:2; 2 Peter 1:5–8.

have personally read the Bible.[44] He goes on to say, "Their comments hardly strayed beyond the sentimental view that the Bible contained some 'nice stories.'"[45] The Bible had become something the church used, not something they used.

The gospel message is not one of intellectual awareness of the kingdom of God, but holistic experience of it. Closer examination of the context of Scripture shows that the knowledge spoken of is the knowledge of experience and encounter which conveys intimacy and proximity, not distant observation. When Paul and Barnabas exhort the Christ-followers of Asia Minor by saying, "We must go through many hardships to enter the kingdom of God," they were not talking about academic rigor or memorizing four spiritual laws.[46] They were in fact speaking of the life experience of living out the gospel in their behavior and choices, not just their statements of belief.

Postmodernity more closely reflects the holistic message of Scripture, which it is not just what-you-know that counts (belief alone), but who-you-are (belief *and* behavior). As Stanley Grenz explains, "The gospel we proclaim must speak to human beings in their entirety."[47] The holistic approach of postmodernity encourages seeing one's spiritual life in less dualistic terms, rejecting the Hellenistic/Enlightenment view of compartmentalized existence. Doug Pagitt describes holistic spiritual formation this way: "we forget about working on a part of a person's life, and instead work with people as if there is no distinction between the spiritual, emotional, physical, social, professional, and private aspects of life."[48]

Much of the Bible's transforming power has been lost because people have been taught to *use it*, instead of allowing it to *exert itself* upon us. Chris Seay contends, "As postmodern missionaries, we must push beyond our logical Western boundaries into a new place of mystery and wonder. Much of the 'turn off' of modern Christianity has been its lack of the mystical."[49] Christ-followers must once again assert that they are not only "people of the book," but also people of the mysterious new birth of the Spirit, that "blows where it chooses, and you hear the sound of it, but you do not know where it comes from or where it goes."[50]

Be a Storytelling Community

The original context of theology was story. As Jesus walked the countryside of Judea and Galilee he taught about the kingdom of God in stories. People came to comprehend God's nature through the experience of the lost son, or the parable of the

---

44. Hay, *Something There*, 221.
45. Ibid.
46. Acts 14:22.
47. Grenz, *Primer on Postmodernism*, 172.
48. Pagitt, *Reimagining Spiritual Formation*, 22.
49. Seay, "East Meets West," 28.
50. John 3:8.

vineyard workers, or the two sons.[51] Storytelling was the preferred method of delivery for God's prophets for centuries, as God says through Hosea, "I spoke to the prophets, gave them many visions and told parables through them."[52]

This prompts Scott Crowdell to claim that were the church "to rediscover itself as a story-formed community, many features of the apostolic paradigm would re-emerge."[53] Story provides the necessary context for an apostolic (or sent) community to communicate the gospel. Not only does being equipped with the gospel story empower and release the Christ community to share at an accessible level with people, it also encourages Christ-followers to be more willing to listen to the story of those they seek to reach. This would produce "a Christianity confidently grounded in its story but open to the world of which it is a part," enabling connection through shared story.[54] One of the reasons for the church's existence is to provide a place of participation, where a person can share their own story—a place where they might participate in community and have their lives changed by the experience.

This does not mean that we abandon preaching. Instead it means that we further refine and develop our preaching ability, informed by a "more varied and integrated approach."[55] Working on our medium for sharing the message helps us avoid the "Bible-bashing" stereotype. As John Drane elucidates, "'The medium is the message,' and the way Christians have communicated their message has often betrayed the good news they claim to have."[56]

Thus we must be a storytelling community that tells not just our story, but God's story—the story of Jesus, of God's love, of sin and redemption, and of the way of the cross and the resurrection. While we do well to be wary of too much systematization, we must also consider the danger of replacing theology with therapy. We must speak of the themes of sin and hell and consequences.[57] Gene Veith warns that we must resist the dangers of a *megashift* in ministry, that substitutes postmodern ideology for biblical theology.[58] The questions of postmodernity should be heard, and the answers re-phrased accordingly and informed by compassion and context, but we must always tell the biblical story, not the story that "itching ears" long to hear.[59]

---

51. Luke 15:11–32; Matthew 20:1–16; 21:28–32.
52. Hosea 12:10.
53. Crowdell, "The Postmodern Church," 18.
54. Ibid., 20.
55. Murray, *Post-Christendom*, 266.
56. Drane, "Cultural Change and Biblical Faith," 12.
57. Veith, *Postmodern Times*, 213; Gibbs, *Church Next*, 66.
58. Veith, *Postmodern Times*, 214.
59. 2 Timothy 4:3.

Be a Spiritual Community

The reality of postmodern times is a spiritual one, not a rational one.[60] John Drane asserts that being spiritual is not an exclusively Christian activity—it is a human activity.[61] David Hay, after his extensive study of the biology of the human spirit, contends, "Spiritual awareness is a constant in our biological makeup."[62] Consequently, Chris Seay suggests, "If the truth of the gospel is to be experienced, the church must embody it. In a postmodern culture, the effort to know Christ must fully engage the head and the heart."[63]

Spirituality must be reclaimed as the domain of the Christ-follower, not esotericism, but this Christian spirituality is a spiritual groundedness in the reality of citizenship in a spiritual kingdom that affects our ordinary, everyday lives.[64] Otherwise, "the people we refer to as 'the lost' may be more spiritual than most of us pastors."[65]

The Bible speaks of the spiritual work of the Holy Spirit as re-creation.[66] What the hands of humans do means nothing compared to the work of the Holy Spirit—"Neither circumcision nor uncircumcision means anything; what counts is a new creation."[67]

In emphasizing incarnational relationships and community, we must be careful not to overcompensate for the modernist focus on results. As Angie Ward comments, this has sometimes resulted "in a lot of motion but little movement."[68] When the church takes on the role of remodeling people, it gets in the way of the Holy Spirit, whose role it is to recreate human beings.[69] Thus another way has to be found in spiritual formation, away from conformity and pragmatism, and toward wonder, creativity, and connection

The move needed is toward transformation.[70] To settle for substituting modern culture with postmodern culture would be fatal to the church. What is always needed, and what is always called for within the Christ-community, is an expectation of holistic life change and growth; a true "renovation of the heart" that remembers that we must always be "born from above."[71]

---

60. Ecclesiastes 3:11.
61. Drane, *Do Christians Know How to Be Spiritual?*, 77.
62. Hay, *Something There*, 205.
63. Seay, "East Meets West," 28.
64. Philippians 3:20; Colossians 3:2.
65. Seay, "East Meets West."
66. 2 Corinthians 5:7.
67. Galatians 6:15.
68. Ward, "Looking for Leaders," 22.
69. Ezekiel 36:26; John 3:6.
70. Romans 12:2.
71. John 3:3; Willard, *Renovation of the Heart*, 42.

Movement Two—From Shallowness to Dynamic Theological Reflection

Be a Connecting Community

For too long the modern church saw its job as *conveying a message* instead of *connecting with their community*. A connecting community finds out where people "are at." On the whole, we can't earn an opportunity to be taken seriously when talking about Jesus or God until we have connected with people on issues they are already interested in. We have to earn the right to be heard. Instead of reasonable arguments, postmodern people are far more affected by the revelation of God seen in the community of faith, which lives out God's revealed word, particularly in love.[72] Once again, it is the incarnation of God's revelation through a missional body of followers, "known by their love," and patterning their life together after the ultimate Incarnation, that conveys a faith which is as tangible as James envisaged (especially at an experiential and relational level).[73]

A community of Christ-followers who genuinely do care for each other, their neighbor, and even their enemy, speaks so loudly that those nearby are encouraged to *open the door* to observe what is going on.[74]

For too long people have been getting the message that if they behave the way God wants, then God will want them. But Jesus tells us that God wants both the wayward and the well behaved.[75]

The primary task of a witnessing community is to present Christ, not to present morals. As Tim Keller says, "Pushing moral behaviors before we lift up Christ is religion."[76] The witness of the Christ-community is a witness of grace. It is a witness to the grace of God in the person, work, death, and resurrection of Jesus Christ. It is a witness to the changes the grace of God brings within a person, changing them so that they may be a demonstration of the gift of grace.[77]

Moreover, it is not only the community outside the church that is in need of connection, but also the community within. Large numbers are leaving the western church of the twenty-first century.[78] Alan Jamieson, in his initial study of church leavers, notes that evangelical churches "have a wide open back door through which the disgruntled, disillusioned, and disaffiliated leave. In the wake of rising pluralism and growing societal skepticism towards the Christian faith such leave-taking appears to be increasing."[79]

---

72. 1 Corinthians 13:3.
73. John 13:35; James 2:17.
74. Romans 12:10; James 2:8; Matthew 5:43.
75. Luke 15:11–32.
76. Keller, "Religion-Less Spirituality," 26.
77. Ephesians 2:8–9.
78. Jamieson et al., *Five Years On*, 12.
79. Jamieson, *A Churchless Faith*, 16.

As Alan Jamieson notes, in an attractional church model, "we seem to expend huge amounts of energy, expense, and prayer to bring people into the churches through the front door while ignoring the seepage of previously committed people out the back door."[80] A connecting church, however, makes efforts not just to see people *converted*, but *continuing* in their relationship with Christ and his community.[81]

Be a Journeying Community

One way of maintaining connection with others is to endeavor to be a journeying community. The journeying metaphor resonates with the Old Testament exilic community, the New Testament diaspora, and now the twenty-first-century post-Christendom church.[82] Eddie Gibbs stresses, "The response of a Christian witness to a person enmeshed in postmodern categories must be that of the fellow-traveller."[83]

The industrialized church of the modern era appears to have embraced the ideal and the end goal of producing successful Christians and churches. But as Eddie Gibbs observes, "The gospel is more concerned with people's holiness, than their happiness."[84] The modern church has often become so concerned with the end product that it too easily loses sight of the real end game, which is not mastery of life and circumstances, but remaining *mastered* by the radical Lord Jesus in the midst of life's circumstances. The Apostle Paul speaks of this *being-mastered* in terms of contentment—the multifaceted aspects of journeying with Christ are characterized by genuine contentment.[85]

This contentment referred to by Paul speaks against the sense of immediate fulfillment which is so hungrily sought by the modern church. Personal fulfillment is ultimately eschatological and will only be partially known in this life.[86] To pursue it now is to ignore the "now-and-not-yet" story of Scripture that reminds us,

> When the perishable has been clothed with the imperishable, and the mortal with immortality, *then* the saying that is written will come true: "Death has been swallowed up in victory."[87]

Biblical contentment has more to do with seeking the sufferings of Christ than the success of the modern church.[88] Yet too easily, "We have chosen comfort and

---

80. Ibid., 154.
81. Hebrews 10:23–25.
82. Ezekiel 11:17; Isaiah 60; 1 Peter 2:11–12; Frost, *Exiles*, 26.
83. Gibbs, *Church Next*, 35.
84. Ibid., 53.
85. Philippians 4:12–13.
86. Gibbs, *Church Next*.
87. 1 Corinthians 15:54 *emphasis mine*.
88. Philippians 3:10.

convenience over servanthood and sacrifice. But in the end, what we have chosen is organization over life, and this, perhaps, is the fundamental dilemma we face—that at best the church is seen as a healthy organization."[89] In a postmodern age we must recover the vitality that comes from dying to self and living for Christ, and "doing nothing out of self-conceit, but considering others better than ourselves."[90] We must lead with humility and service, and confront oppressive power structures in the church and the world. "Following him [Jesus] in a postmodern situation calls for a discipleship of suffering with and for others."[91]

It is this recognition of suffering, as well as a transparency about doubts, that enables Christ-followers to connect with those who do not yet know Christ in their own journey. David Smith writes, "Christians cannot approach such conversations as people of massive strength and untroubled confidence, but rather as those who are also wounded and have their own unresolved dilemmas. When this is admitted then there is an opportunity for true companionship, replicating something like the experience of the Emmaus two . . ."[92]

John Drane rightly describes the church's path to life: "The church will only live insofar as it is prepared to die in order to experience afresh the resurrection power of the Holy Spirit."[93] In an over-achieving western world that is starving to death on success, the suffering, serving church will shine like a city on a hill, and provide a stream of life through its self-giving.

Only a church that endeavors to build innovative communities of disciples, rather than static institutions of tradition, will meet the challenges of rapid and discontinuous change in the twenty-first century. Openness, spirituality, storytelling, and vulnerability will enable the contemporary church to speak a language postmoderns understand. A missional identity shaped by the Scriptures rather than modern methodology, and a willingness to embrace approaches which are relevant and which emerge from the margins of society, will gain greater ground than a Christendom model. Ultimately, the church needs to learn the way of the cross-cultural missionary in our own setting. Perhaps then the Christian story may be heard again. Our culture is rapidly changing, and we are called to be a particular kind of community that witnesses to the redemptive and transforming person and gospel of Jesus Christ.

Individual and Corporate Servantship Practices

- Identify the most pressing lifestyle challenges in your community.

---

89. McManus, *Unstoppable Force*, 14.
90. Philippians 2:4.
91. Pagitt, *Reimagining Spiritual Formation*, 132.
92. Smith, "Moving Towards Emmaus," 17.
93. John 12:24; Drane, *McDonaldization*, 155.

- Recognize the critique postmodernism brings to Christian culture.
- Come to terms with the reality of living in a post-Christendom era.
- Allocate resources to determining not just "what works in church," but also, "what works in life."
- Shift the discipleship paradigm from how to live in church culture to how to live like Christ in the world.
- Examine how much we have taught people to "use" the Bible to get what they want instead of allowing God to use it to transform us.
- Promote participation in, instead of observation of, God's story.
- Evaluate whether your church seeks spiritual transformation or programmed self-improvement.
- Look for ways to be connected to the surrounding community.
- Be transparent about the sufferings of Christ as seen in your individual and corporate journey.

Questions for Reflection and Discussion

- Which of the challenges of the twenty-first century do you see as most influential in your community? What would you add to the list?
- What is the role of the Bible in your church? Describe how people think it affects them.
- Consider the following aspects of community: missional, Bible-shaped, storytelling, spiritual, connecting, journeying. Which aspect most reflects, and least reflects, your church community?

Movement Three

From Theories to Courageous Practices

Servantship is the cultivation of *courageous missional, ecclesial, and servantship practices.* Dynamic theological reflection and courageous ministry practices are interweaved in servantship. Theological thought, then, is located in the context of spirituality, biblical reflection, and the authentic, courageous practices present in the ordinary life of the faith community. Helmut Thielicke asserts the same when he writes, "How all-important it is that a vigorous spiritual life, in close association with the Holy Scriptures, and in the midst of the Christian community, be maintained as a background for theological work . . . insofar as we are determined to be true theologians, we think within the community of God's people, and for that community, and in the name of that community—how shall I say?—we think as a part of the community itself . . ."[1]

I wrote in my book *Salt, Light, and a City* that,

> [m]inistry practice operates, too often, without an adequate or reflective theology of the church, or a theology of mission. Theological reflection on the mission of God and the nature of the church is separated, in many instances, from concrete ministry practices. Although ecclesiology, missiology, worship, and ministry practice are deeply connected, Christian leaders and congregations can lose their enthusiasm for conducting a life-giving conversation between theological reflection and missional or ministerial practices. Fragmented ministry practices, personal conflict and dissatisfaction, retreat from difficult questions about programs and purposes, and unquestioning adoption of offshore solutions, are some of the results.[2]

For these reasons, and more, a well-developed missional theology of the church, its nature, structures, mission, and servantship is crucial for the health of churches, for

---

1. Thielicke, *A Little Exercise*, 4–5, 37.
2. Hill, *Salt, Light, and a City*, 149–50.

faithfulness to the gospel, for mission in the contemporary cultural context, and for servantship in the Spirit of Jesus Christ. This missional theology of the church and its servantship is also important for the longevity, integrity, and theological and personal conviction of Christian leaders and congregations. As Helmut Thielicke reminds us, such theological reflection, if it is to be life-giving, must be characterized by spiritual discipline and vitality, submission to the truth of Scripture, and participation in authentic Christian community.

In other words, a vigorous theology of servantship needs to develop within the context of risky and innovative local practices. Such courageous practices are the third movement in radical servantship. Chapters 13 through to 20 provide space for eight Christian leaders to tell provocative stories—stories which illustrate how they are moving from mere theory to courageous servantship practice in their own settings. These servant-disciples talk about their efforts to cultivate the concrete practices of Christ-imitating, radical servantship in their settings.

13

Shaping Missional Churches and Associations

Graham Hill

Missional church writings have proliferated in the last twenty years. Many pastors, theologians, and denominational leaders are asking questions about what it means for local churches to be authentically missional. At the same time, various people are seriously questioning the role of denominations, denominational servantship, and denominational affiliation in a (so-called) postmodern and post-denominational context. While denominations remain with us, and, as I suggest in this chapter, they have an important role to play in their relationship with local churches, their worth is accentuated if vitality, mission, and servantship characterize their structures and ministries. It seems to me that the shaping of local missional communities goes hand in hand with the formation of missional networks, associations, and paralocal organizations.[1]

It seems that numerous Christians are willing to overlook (or tolerate) a variety of denominational labels in their quest to find a church which suits their needs, theological commitments, and particular tastes. Nigel Wright observes, "It is this new freedom, or it could be an indifference, regarding specifically denominational values, which can be described as post-denominationalism."[2] It is worth exploring what missional ecclesiology and perspectives have to say to denominational servantship and affiliation in this environment. It is imperative that we explore this in relationship to the missional mandate of the local congregation, however, since missional churches and missional associations must be cultivated concurrently if they are to be fostered at all.

---

1. This chapter was first published in Cohen and Parsons, *Beyond 400*.
2. Wright, "Post-Denominationalism and the Renewal of a Denominational Witness," 1.

Movement Three—From Theories to Courageous Practices

The *missional church movement* can be traced back through the Gospel and Our Culture Network in the United States of America and the United Kingdom, through to such theologians as the British and South African missiologists Lesslie Newbigin and David Bosch. The perspectives of such theologians as Lesslie Newbigin and David Bosch captivated the imaginations of a group of missional ecclesiologists, including George Hunsberger, Darrell Guder, and Alan Roxburgh, who in turn inspired an emerging generation of missional thinkers and practitioners such as Brian McLaren, Dan Kimball, Michael Frost, Erwin McManus, and other missional authors and practitioners. All of these authors mentioned in this paragraph have become an influential part of the missional conversation or movement, whether they self-identify with this movement or not. Although it is a movement of *thought*, rather than an organized movement, its missiological nature, ecclesiological concerns, and most influential authors and writings, are identifiable and examinable.

It is worth providing a brief definition of the core characteristics of the *missional church movement* here. The missional church movement emphasizes emerging, contextualized, and culturally appropriate forms of community and worship. It is dedicated to refocusing churches on mission, western society as mission field, and to mission being sourced in the *missio Dei*. Its theology of the church combines the notions of the church as a contrast society, the development of ecclesial forms to facilitate mission, and the embrace of an essentially *missional* ecclesiology. It enfolds a growing body of literature, practitioners, communities, and theologians in the west—networked less by definitions than by a similar assessment of the missional challenges and possibilities of contemporary and post-Christendom western culture. It must be recognized, however, that the diversity of the group and its perspectives makes it a very loose, young, evolving, and complex *movement* or *conversation*. Whether we call it a *movement* or a *conversation*, it is clearly growing in influence and recognition, especially in western settings.[3]

The influence of missional ecclesiology on the shape of the contemporary church, therefore, cannot be ignored. Here I briefly examine the primary concerns and perspectives of missional ecclesiology, which are summarized under the headings "a missional theology of the church," "grounding missional ecclesiology in local, worshipping communities," and "missional experimentation and church planting." From there I suggest some preliminary implications for denominational servantship and affiliation. The central perspectives of emerging missional ecclesiology are described in the following few sections of this chapter, not to provide a definitive treatment of that topic, but to lay a foundation for considering the future of both missional

---

3. In an introduction to their book on missional churches, Gibbs and Bolger write, "This study of missional churches represents a determined attempt to identify the key practices of this disparate movement, which is so diverse and fragmented that some observers and insiders do not like to think of it as a movement at all. For insiders, it is more of a conversation . . . Although the communities they lead may be small in number, the numbers are growing rapidly as their influence spreads through websites, blogs, chat rooms, and conference interactions." Gibbs and Bolger, *Emerging Churches*, 29.

congregations and missional associations in a postmodern and post-denominational setting.[4] In doing so, I am seeking to catalyze a conversation around the relationship between genuinely missional churches, revitalized missional associations and denominations, and an emerging, biblical, missional theology of the church.

A Missional Theology of the Church

The development of a robust, biblical, and systematic missional ecclesiology is long overdue and, thankfully, is beginning to gain momentum.[5] My book *Salt, Light, and a City: Introducing Missional Ecclesiology* is an attempt to address constructively the lack of a systematic ecclesiology in the missional church conversation.[6] I am utterly convinced that there must be a concrete outworking of missional ecclesiology in the local congregation. According to the North American Gospel and Our Culture Network, Michael Frost of the Baptist theological seminary, Morling College, and Alan Hirsch of the Forge Mission Network, churches that embrace a missional ecclesiology will demonstrate the following *indicators*. Michael Frost and Alan Hirsch propose that the first three provide "energy and direction" for the remaining twelve, and they go on to shape their book chapters around these first three themes or indicators.

For each of these fifteen indicators I begin with quoting the indicator verbatim, and then briefly elaborate on each one, adding insights on missional ecclesiology from other missional church movement writings as appropriate.

The North American Gospel and Our Culture Network outline their twelve key *indicators of a missional church* and describe what each one looks like in practice, as well as providing concrete examples of churches who are genuinely attempting to apply a missional ecclesiology in their local contexts in these ways.

It is possible for pastors and denominational leaders to go through this following list and ask probing questions about our present practices and models of pastoral and denominational servantship. The question worth asking is, "How faithful to these indicators are our approaches to pastoral ministry and denominational servantship?"[7]

---

4. Summarizing some of my findings in my PhD thesis: Hill, "Examination of Emerging-Missional."

5. See, for instance, the passionate advocating of missional ecclesiology, missiological alertness among churches and leaders, theologizing missionally, forming a missiological hermeneutic and approach to apologetics, and forming concrete missional communities, in: Moynagh, *Emergingchurch. Intro*, 30–31, and 146; Drane, *The McDonaldization of the Church*, 9–10 and 171–82; Sweet, *Church*, 251; McLaren, *Church on Other Side*, 36 and 141–42; McManus, *Unstoppable Force*, 23 and 169; Kimball, *Emerging Church*, 17, 68–70, and 93–95; Murray, *Post-Christendom*, 251–53, 302–6, 321–22, and 337–38; Hunsberger and Van Gelder, *Church between Gospel*, 14–15, 45–48, and 362–69.

6. For a fuller examination of the key theological perspectives of a missional ecclesiology, in conversation with twelve leading Catholic, Orthodox, Protestant, and Free Church thinkers, see my book: Hill, *Salt, Light, and a City*.

7. Barrett, *Treasure in Clay Jars*, 159–72, and Frost and Hirsch, *Shaping of Things to Come*, 11–12.

Movement Three—From Theories to Courageous Practices

1. "The missional church is *incarnational*, not attractional, in its ecclesiology."[8] It incarnates the gospel in contemporary culture, rather than attracts people to sacred or contemporized sanctuaries. Leaders who embrace a missional ecclesiology are sensitive to the current post-Christendom and postmodern contexts, and are shaping their ministries and evangelistic approaches accordingly.[9]

2. "The missional church is *messianic*, not dualistic, in its spirituality." Frost and Hirsch allege that, like Jesus, the missional church has a world view which is "holistic and integrated," rather than dualistic. For instance, it seeks to promote the discipleship of the whole person, not just their mind.

3. "The missional church adopts an *apostolic*, rather than a hierarchical, mode of servantship." The fivefold gifts of Ephesians 6 are all equally recognized, and a flat rather than hierarchical servantship approach is maintained.

4. "The missional church proclaims the gospel."[10] A faithful, creative, and contextually sensitive presentation of the gospel narrative is used.

5. "The missional church is a community where all members are involved in learning to become disciples of Jesus."[11] Discipleship and learning to live in God's reign are valued, expected, and sought after. Mentoring, training, and nurturing are intentionally shaped so that "the skills and habits of Christian discipleship" are ingrained in individuals and the community.[12]

6. "The Bible is normative in this church's life."[13] Knowledge of the Scriptures is complemented by a passion to obey them, processes for hearing and following them communally, and a desire to put them into conversation with the community's context.

7. "The church understands itself as different from the world because of its participation in the life, death, and resurrection of its Lord."[14] Therefore, there is an evidenced longing to conform to Christ instead of the plethora of cultures surrounding them, and a willingness to be different, to take risks, to embody Christ's love, and to suffer.

8. "The church seeks to discern God's specific missional vocation for the entire community and for all its members."[15] Missional life is embraced by the

---

8. Again, for clarification, the first sentence of each of 1–3 is taken from Ibid., 12.
9. Roxburgh, *Missionary Congregation*, especially chapter 5, "Toward a Missionary Ecclesiology," 57–66.
10. Barrett, *Treasure in Clay Jars*, 162.
11. Ibid., 163–64.
12. Ibid., 163.
13. Ibid., 164.
14. Ibid., 165.
15. Ibid., 165–67.

whole community and is its clear priority, the community's faithfulness to its particular missional vocation is pursued and recognized by all, and giftings in the community are identified, developed, and released.

9. "A missional community is indicated by how Christians behave toward one another."[16] The world knows who their Lord is by their love, generosity, self-sacrifice, and the fruit of the Spirit.

10. "It is a community that practices reconciliation."[17] A heterogeneous community intentionally evolves as barriers are removed, conflicts are constructively resolved, difference is valued, and peacemaking and reconciliation are honored.

11. "People within the community hold themselves accountable to one another in love."[18] They covenant with each other in this regard, evaluating the quality of their structures, relationships, and community, and seeking honest and transparent unity of spirit.

12. "The church practices hospitality."[19] Welcoming strangers into the love and care of the community is pivotal to their missional life and communal values.

13. "Worship is the central act by which the community celebrates with joy and thanksgiving both God's presence and God's promised future."[20] Communal worship is culturally sensitive, but also transformational, communally unifying, and eschatologically oriented.

14. "This community has a vital public witness."[21] Its public witness demonstrably influences the church's immediate surroundings and social contexts, as it seeks practical justice, peace, transformed lives, and the like.

15. "There is recognition that the church itself is an incomplete expression of the reign of God."[22] There is an eschatological and providential vision undergirding the life of the church and this vision is of the reign of God, and the church's frailties are viewed in the light of the broader realities of the kingdom of God.[23]

Such perspectives, whether we agree with them unreservedly or not, have very real implications for our understanding of the nature of the church and, by implication, for our appreciation of the very nature of our ministries (including those ministries' concrete forms and practices). The question emerges, "Do our denominational and

---

16. Ibid., 167.
17. Ibid., 167–68.
18. Ibid., 168–69.
19. Ibid., 169–70.
20. Ibid., 170.
21. Ibid., 171.
22. Ibid., 171–72.
23. Ward, *Liquid Church*, 8–10.

Movement Three—From Theories to Courageous Practices

pastoral servantship practices and forms facilitate these fifteen indicators, in concrete and practical ways?"

Grounding Missional Ecclesiology in Local, Worshipping Communities

Local, worshiping communities and ministries are the natural place in which missional ecclesiology is grounded, in which the witness of the Christian church is made credible, and in which Christians are discipled into a radical engagement with people in their culture.

When missional ecclesiology is grounded in such faith communities and pastoral servantship contexts, these communities have the following features—in addition to the fifteen indicators previously mentioned in this chapter. These features may seem idealistic given the inadequacies and failings of actual Christian communities, yet they are expressed, even if only embryonically, in ministries which embrace and pursue genuine missional vitality:

1. They are churches and ministries which facilitate transformation within cultures, through their constitution as alternative communities. Christian communities in general, and ministries in particular, need to be bonded together as alternative, distinct, and visible communities. These are churches "offering an alternative form of life," "rediscovering the tradition as a reservoir for transformation," and experiencing "the intersubjectivity of persons formed by a new center, Jesus Christ as the head of the *communitas*."[24] In this authentic *koinonia*, they may also stand in contrast to the disintegration of community life and social cohesion in modern consumerist cultures.[25]

2. They are ministries which are given definition and direction by the four dimensions of worship, community, mission, and relationship to the wider body of Christ. Therefore, their experimentation and missional life are grounded in a holistic expression and understanding of church.[26]

3. Stuart Murray maintains that they will be simpler than we have known some ecclesiality in the past to be, "recovering friendship . . . as our relational paradigm . . . (which is) non-hierarchical, holistic, relaxed, and dynamic . . ."[27] They also enjoy the rich benefits of being community around meals and laughter. He invites his readers to "imagine" communities (and ministries) that are enriched

---

24. Roxburgh, *Missionary Congregation*, 49–56. This view of the missional church as an alternative community is found in such works as Webber, *Younger Evangelicals*, 118–20 and Shenk, *Write the Vision*, 16.

25. Hall, *End of Christendom*, 59–61. Cf. Webber, *Younger Evangelicals*, 51–52, and 101–6.

26. Moynagh, *Emergingchurch.Intro*, 148–49, 155–56, and 166–67.

27. Murray, *Post-Christendom*, 275.

by apostolic and prophetic poets and storytellers, and that are characterized by mission, social action, and spiritual contemplation. These will be safe places to pioneer, experiment, and take risks.[28]

4. Based on his analysis of the works of Lesslie Newbigin, George Hunsberger, and the Gospel and Our Culture Network in North America, Pete Hendrick notes the following about the characteristics of missional congregations and ministries:[29]
   a. They understand that they exist in a cross-cultural situation;
   b. They enter into dialogue with their context and culture;
   c. They provide opportunities for their members to reflect on culture from a biblical view;
   d. They pray for and seek their own transformation;
   e. They accept the marginal position in which they find themselves;
   f. They bear witness in their social and cultural situation.

5. George Hunsberger adds to this list by including some practical shifts congregations and their ministries need to make in order to move from religious vendor to mission:[30]
   a. A shift from program to embodiment;
   b. A shift from committee to team;
   c. A shift from being clergy dominated to being laity oriented;
   d. A shift from recruitment to mission;
   e. A shift from (the leader as) entrepreneur to missionary.

These, then, are some of the features of local, worshipping, Christian communities who are grounded in a missional theology of the church.

Missional Experimentation and Church Planting

Experimentation, creativity, and innovation are deeply embedded in the theology and practices of a missional church and association. Missional church authors often cite such innovative communities and experiments as examples of missional ecclesiology in practice, and as evidence of fresh and creative ways of being missional church.[31]

Gibbs and Bolger in their book *Emerging Churches* have gathered the stories of numerous missional leaders and pastors planting innovative missional communities.[32] Stuart Murray, attempting to classify the missional church movement, has

---

28. Ibid., 77–282. For other writings with similar perspectives cf. Drane, *The McDonaldization of the Church*, 28; Riddell et al., *Prodigal Project*, 132; and Gibbs, *Church Next*, 168–69 and 213.

29. Hunsberger and Van Gelder, *Church between Gospel*, 302–7.

30. Ibid., 344–45.

31. See, for example: Frost and Hirsch, *Shaping of Things to Come*, 182–200; Moynagh, *Emergingchurch.Intro*, 13–14; and Gibbs and Bolger, *Emerging Churches*, 239–328.

32. Ibid., 239–328.

demonstrated the vast range of missional and ecclesiological experimentation that they are undertaking in western culture. He includes such things as contextualized cell churches and churches in cafés, workplaces, pubs, club-culture, cyberspace, various specific subcultures, youth settings, indigenous neighborhoods, and marginalized contexts. He also notes the emergence of midweek church, 7-day-a-week church, post-Alpha-course church, "organic" church, contextual liturgy, multi-congregational church, menu church, multicultural church, new forms of monasticism and monastic orders, "common-purse" communities, and "boiler rooms" (that is, contemporary communities formed around imaginative prayer). What Stuart Murray and others are demonstrating is the extent of the missional ecclesiological experimentation and church planting that is developing alongside the missional church movement literature.[33] They are demonstrating that a missional theology of the church gives birth to local missional innovation and broader missional associations. At times these associations are denominations, but often they are missionally like-minded networks, relationships, and associations of missional leaders, innovators, and churches.

The planting of new missional opportunities is vital if the church in the western world is going to be relevant to postmodern cultures. Established churches and ministries are often well placed to experiment with missional initiatives, and should be encouraged to plant missional communities and projects for reaching particular subcultures. Gerard Kelly asserts, "somewhere in the genesis and genius of these diverse groups is hidden the future of western Christianity. To dismiss them is to throw away the seeds of our survival."[34]

Some Implications for the Future of Associations and Paralocal Organizations

Having described some of the key perspectives of missional ecclesiology, this chapter will now suggest some preliminary implications for paralocal servantship and denominational affiliation in a postmodern and post-denominational setting.[35]

Perspectives on denominationalism, ecumenism, catholicity, and unity are evident in the missional church material, but not usually in a systematized or structured way. The texts *Missional Church* and *Church Next* are exceptions to this, when it comes to the question of the missional role of denominations. *Missional Church* dedicates a chapter to the historic development of denominations, biblical-theological, historical, sociological, and organizational perspectives on denominations, and proposals for the purposes of such paralocal and parachurch organizations.[36] The authors conclude

---

33. Murray, *Church after Christendom*, 67–98.
34. Kelly, *Retrofuture*, 185. Also quoted in Frost and Hirsch, *Shaping of Things to Come*, x.
35. There is some discussion these days about whether *postmodernity* is, in fact, better understood as *late-modernity* or *hyper-modernity*.
36. Guder, *Missional Church*, 46–76.

that "a missional ecclesiology takes seriously the organizational life of the church both in its expressions of local missional congregations and in paralocal missional structures." They go on to call for a "careful evaluation" of these systems through the lens of missional ecclesiology, and our understandings of the unity, catholicity, and apostolicity of the church.[37]

Some in the missional church movement claim that even though we are in an age of post-denominationalism, and even though much ecumenical and denominational activity "can seem life-emptying, dull, and bureaucratic,"[38] paralocal organizations and broader-church-gatherings are useful—as long as they serve particular functions. These functions include practical accountability, the encouragement that is present in broader-church participation (such as regional gatherings and worship events), genuine support and resourcing, and encouragement and care, especially in difficult times. Appropriate paralocal functions also include networking of pioneers and missional initiatives, and coaching and mentoring. While funding emerging initiatives and serving as permission-givers, denominations and paralocal organizations can also fund approaches to selecting and training pioneers, partner with missional churches in planting, advocate for missional churches and their leaders, research fresh approaches to church and distribute their findings, facilitate learning networks, create space for theological and ecclesiological reflection, and actively sustain these innovative churches.[39]

Churches seeking to engage missionally with their communities, therefore, will often be looking for denominational and paralocal affiliations which are relational and missionally productive, and for denominational servantship which serves the missionary activities and nature of the local churches. Such denominational affiliation and paralocal servantship will help local churches navigate the post-Christendom and postmodern contexts while these local communities go about shaping appropriate ministries and evangelistic strategies. Paralocal organizations will provide resources for shaping missional disciples, and will encourage servantship structures that catalyze ministry and mission (rather than inhibit mission through their forms and presumptions). Churches and pastors will often be looking for denominational and inter-church relationships (the operative words being "relationship" and "association")—especially associations which offer resources, coaching and help in the complex challenges confronting them as they experiment with approaches to discipling believers in contemporary western culture. Constructive paralocal associations will

---

37. "The church's nature as both one *and* catholic means that these structures must exist in a symbiotic relationship with local congregations and their denominational structures. The apostolic character of the church implies a variety of ways in which its mission is carried out, and thus a variety of structures that a missional ecclesiology must address." Ibid., 75.

38. Moynagh, *Emergingchurch.Intro*, 158.

39. Ibid., 158–65 and 210–42; Williams, *Mission-Shaped Church*, 125–49.

Movement Three—From Theories to Courageous Practices

help churches navigate the tension between contextual relevance and counter-cultural faithfulness in their life together and in their missionary endeavors.

The fifteen indicators mentioned in the first section of this chapter are not easy to implement, and, moreover, how they might be applied in one context might be quite different from another. Therefore, such churches will be looking to their denominational and paralocal connections for guidance and support. Many of these connections will inevitably be grounded in like-mindedness, in geographic proximity, and in similarity of church culture, rather than in denominational affiliation. Instead of being threatened by this, denominational servantship will be honored and respected by pastors if they appreciate and broker such missional connections. Such paralocal support will need to help churches shape practices of hospitality and community engagement, and design worship experiences that are meaningful and eschatologically oriented. It will facilitate the discovery of forms of public witness which testify to the values of the kingdom of God, and build communities which evidence centripetal force through their attractive love, community, and discipleship. Such support will help churches explore centrifugal mission in their local settings, around the dynamic missional life of a particular faith community. This kind of multilayered support is beyond the scope of most denominational bodies—hence the need for these communities to connect with support groups at denominational, geographical, cultural, parachurch, paralocal, and other relational levels. The role of denomination as broker of relationships is central. The key perspective maintained by such denominations is one of service of the local faith community, along with the recognition that genuine mission is grounded in local, worshipping communities (these, of course, do not exist in isolation, but are connected to the broader Christian community in concrete ways through denominational, geographic, and other relational ties and associations).

In *Church Next*, Eddie Gibbs calls this the movement "from bureaucratic hierarchies to apostolic networks." Beginning with the institutional and cultural problems of mainline denominations in the West, the shift in western Protestantism toward "superchurches" and "new apostolic networks," and the emergence of "dynamic churches in the majority world," Gibbs goes on to propose implications for local churches, regional networks of churches, and denominational and ecumenical institutions. His implications and proposals revolve around notions of relationality, flattened organizational structures, permission giving, resourcing and equipping, diversification and decentralization, healthy accountability, and the potential of networks.[40] Such dynamic networks, whether they be formal denominational links or not, facilitate missional experimentation of the kind described earlier in this chapter. They also facilitate innovative church planting, and the healthy dialogue that must exist between established churches, denominations, and missional plants. These three exist in a symbiotic relationship. Not all symbiotic relationships are comfortable or always and in every way mutually beneficial. Nonetheless, the particular symbiotic relationship here is far too

40. Gibbs, *Church Next*, 69–92.

often antagonistic, masking the lateral thinking, innovation, mutual enrichment, and advancement of the kingdom of God that is possible. Each party gains from the other two, and antagonism must be replaced by cooperation and grace.

Ecumenical cooperation is critical to missional effectiveness in postmodern culture, from a missional church movement perspective. Globalization, multiculturalism, intellectual pluralism, and the burgeoning dialogue between evangelicals, mainline churches, Catholicism, and Eastern Orthodoxy have facilitated such ecumenical openness in the missional church movement and among younger evangelicals.[41] However, missional ecclesiology demands that both denominational and ecumenical structures be examined for their "cultural captivity," so that authentic "structures of connectedness" are developed which facilitate the church's mission.[42]

In some forms of evangelicalism and the ecclesiology of Reformed churches, the unity of the church is primarily of an internal, spiritual character, rather than an external one. This unity is through being joined in the mystical body of Christ. Whether or not there is visible fruit to such unity, and without denying the visible existence of the catholic and local church, this unity is an invisible bond that is forged by the Spirit of Christ and our common profession of his death, resurrection, saving and sanctifying work, and Lordship.

In missional ecclesiology, however, there is an emphasis on the visible and concrete expressions of unity and catholicity. All such unity and catholicity must manifest itself in the local community of believers, and any unity of the church universal is outworked in the unity of both the local church and the broader paralocal organizations. Similarly, catholicity includes communities of faith joining in a shared mission, understanding themselves as part of a broader mission and movement. This identification with a broader movement, which is expressed both concretely and particularly in their specific local congregation, is one of the key theological and practical functions of denominational and paralocal organizations.[43]

Robert Webber notes the wide range of sources for this "recovered" emphasis on the visible unity and catholicity of the church, including the communication revolution, the worship movement, post liberalism, and missional ecclesiology. There is a recognizable intentionality about ecumenical, inter-church, and denominational cooperation and networking, even between diverse and differing communities of the Christian faith. This intentionality reflects a genuine desire for practical expressions of catholicity and unity.[44]

41. Webber, *Younger Evangelicals*, 37–38 and 110–12.
42. Guder, *Missional Church*, 248–68.
43. For evidence of these perspectives see Berkhof, *Systematic Theology*, 572.
44. Webber, *Younger Evangelicals*, 107–23. Webber's full list of sources includes: secularism, pluralism, globalization, the communication revolution, inter-Christian dialogue, charismaticism, the demise of denominationalism, the worship movement, the interest in ecumenical spirituality and theology, and Vatican II. He also suggests that missional, Radical Reformation, and Postliberal ecclesiologies have played their part in focusing younger evangelicals on the visible church.

Movement Three—From Theories to Courageous Practices

This does not mean, however, that denominational distinctives have no place in the current cultural or ecclesial contexts, or that those who embrace a missional ecclesiology are unconcerned for such theological distinctives. It should not escape our attention that missional church movement authors come from a wide range of theological positions and denominational standpoints and, without relinquishing those distinctives, strive together for a re-missionalization of denominational, ecclesial, and local church structures and practices. Their theological distinctives add texture to the burgeoning literature on missional ecclesiology, and they lose nothing by embracing their distinctives and their common passion for mission. Nigel Wright has argued persuasively, for instance, for the attractiveness and contribution of Baptist tradition and theological distinctives in the current cultural context.[45] Many of the values and ecclesiological perspectives espoused by Baptists strike a chord with the missional literature—liberty of conscience, the separation of church and state, regenerate church membership, the priesthood of all believers, the autonomy of the local church, the Lordship of Christ, the supremacy of Scripture, and congregational forms of church government, for instance. However, if Baptists and other theological traditions are to revitalize their theologies, structures, and associations, they must embrace a missional theology of the church, and in doing so reclaim, retell, and reimagine their life together through the paradigm of the *missio Dei*.

Only by making the mission of God their organizing principle can paralocal associations become missional and support the missional dynamism at local level. Only be shaping their life around the *missio Dei* can local churches, fresh expressions, and Christian denominations become authentically missional, and be given new life among a younger generation of believers. The same principles are true, I have argued, for local churches as for denominational servantship and associations. It is my contention in this chapter that missional ecclesiology contributes much to this fresh discovery of local and paralocal dynamism, mission, and connection.

Individual and Corporate Servantship Practices

- As a ministry team, work through the list of fifteen indicators of a missional church. Ask probing questions about your present practices and models of pastoral (or denominational) servantship. Ask how faithful your approaches to pastoral ministry and denominational servantship are to these indicators.

- Bring your church together for a day to discuss how you might facilitate transformation within your cultural setting. Prayerfully discuss what it means for your church's practices, theology, and servantship to:[46]

---

45. Wright, "Post-Denominationalism and the Renewal of a Denominational Witness," 6–11.
46. Hunsberger and Van Gelder, *Church between Gospel*, 302–7.

a. Understand that they exist in a cross-cultural situation;
  b. Enter into dialogue with their context and culture;
  c. Provide opportunities for their members to reflect on culture from a biblical view;
  d. Pray for and seek their own transformation;
  e. Accept the marginal position in which they find themselves;
  f. Bear witness in their social and cultural situation.
- Spend time considering the implications for your church of the practical shifts congregations and their ministries need to make in order to move from religious vendor to mission:[47]
  a. A shift from program to embodiment;
  b. A shift from committee to team;
  c. A shift from being clergy dominated to being laity oriented;
  d. A shift from recruitment to mission;
  e. A shift from (the leader as) entrepreneur to missionary.
- Cultivate authentic relationships with paralocal organizations, seeking ways to partner with them in the mission of God (denominations, mission agencies, youth work groups, etc.).
- Ask God for the grace to help your church and its paralocal affiliations move "from bureaucratic hierarchies to apostolic networks."

Questions for Reflection and Discussion

- Do your denominational and pastoral servantship practices and forms facilitate the fifteen indicators of a missional church, in concrete and practical ways?
- How can your church develop deeper and more authentic relational networks?
- What associations and networks are needed for your church and its servantship to more fully participate in the mission of Jesus Christ?
- What resources and support do you need from denominational and paralocal organizations? How will you give back to these paralocal organizations and associations, for the sake of the glory and mission of God?
- How does a theology of servantship affect your relationship to these networks and associations?

---

47. Ibid., 344–45.

14

Deepening Discipleship

Graeme Anderson

This chapter examines the practical outworking of the *trinitarian missional ecclesiology* developed in my earlier chapter. Initially, the reality of the current church is looked at. The differences in having worship, mission, or discipleship as the organizational centers of church communities are then discussed. The focus of this reflection is to ponder what it might look like to have discipleship as the organizational center of a church. The chapter then briefly outlines four case studies spanning four centuries of missionary activity, pointing out the importance of discipleship as the foundation of all missional expression. Dallas Willard's model of transformation is then utilized to outline this expression of a missional church. Finally, the issue of sexuality will be examined through the lens that has been constructed throughout this chapter.

Considering Jesus's Poignant Question

It is interesting to note how often the term "outsider" is used to describe those who are not churched. Perhaps the use of this term reveals the heart of a people clinging to the sense of safety on the "inside"—hiding behind a barrier created around our refuges of "rightness."

What could it look like to move outside these self-absorbed boundaries built on the foundation of shallow theology, lazy teaching, and lukewarm spiritual practice?—stopping to consider carefully Jesus's poignant question, "Which of these was a neighbor to the man who fell . . . ?"[1] instead of hastily continuing on our way inside in a

---

1. Luke 10:36.

mission to form a new committee discussing how to more effectively connect the outside with us . . .

(In the assumption that our "job" is to tell our neighbors who we are and which service might be better, we have forgotten that our privilege is to find out who our neighbors are and how we might be of better service.)

. . . perhaps our neighbors are quietly grateful that we've stayed inside for this long.

"Church is for discipleship. Discipleship is for the world."

> The aim of God in history is the creation of an all-inclusive community of loving persons with God himself at the very center of this community as its prime Sustainer and most glorious Inhabitant.[2]

It seems evident that it is not enough for churches to merely exist within the local area in the hope that through a kind of spiritual osmosis, new "converts" will cross the threshold and begin to live transformed lives. As a result, there has been a shift over the last decade or two towards a church community which lives and operates in a different way to the traditional norm. Through this shift, the trinitarian God is at work forming communities of Jesus's disciples.

What does this shift look like and where will it take us into the future? It seems, often, that this shift is based on protest of the past and the present; a reaction to teaching, theology, and practice that has, perhaps, led Christians away from their primary calling to "go into all the world making disciples . . ."[3]

Communities have become distracted and caught up in small picture movements[4] and first world issues.[5] Church servantship has been spending more and more time indulging in academic issues of doctrine and governance. It is clear that these areas are highly important, but it seems they have become the de facto vision of the church. Communities are defining themselves on what they do not believe and which groups they do not agree with. This is no wonder. For generations, ecclesial institutions have been defining themselves based on governance, hierarchical structure, and (perhaps worse) specific approaches to doctrine that set them apart from other institutions.

The result is a church in the western world that has rapidly lost its voice, influence, and potency; a church that is longing to return to the days of modernism when it last had some sort of respected voice in the wider community. This longing is evident in the style and make-up of many contemporary models of "evangelism." It is assumed

---

2. Foster, *The Life with God Bible*, 1.
3. Matthew 28:20.
4. For example, the way songs are written or sung.
5. For example, who has the money and how the church going to get it.

that if people can be convinced of the historicity of the Gospels, they will submit their lives to Christ. They can. They don't.

Rather than looking to the past and worrying about the present, this shift must be founded in a vision which embraces the present and looks to the future;[6] founded in an awareness of what God is doing now—creating an all-inclusive community of loving persons—and why God is doing this—because he himself is the "center of this community as its prime Sustainer and most glorious Inhabitant."

It is generally agreed that there are four key foci within a church. These are the areas of community, worship, mission, and discipleship. It has traditionally been accepted that worship is the organizational center of each of the other areas.[7] From this perspective, the purpose of discipleship is to worship, the purpose of community is to worship together, and the purpose of mission is to bring people to worship God. The church here is a reflection of the *Agnus Dei*.

More recently, there has been a movement toward a missional expression of church. In this context, mission is the organizational center of the church. The implications of this are equally interesting. Mission is an expression of worship, mission is what disciples do (in order for there to be more disciples), and mission is what sent communities are called to do. The church here is a reflection of the *missio Dei*.

This chapter reflects on what it might look like for the focus of Christian community to be on discipleship to Jesus. The implications of this do not (and should not) detract from the importance of the above two models. The primary place for disciple making is community. Disciples grow together in living lives worshipping Creator God. Disciples take on the sending nature of Christ and learn to be present within the communities to which they have been called on mission. The church in this context is a reflection of the *Imago Dei*.

During a postgraduate class at Morling College, Sydney, Dan Kimball said the following, "The world doesn't understand the gospel and the cross, but the world understands acts of compassion and justice. If we don't make disciples, there will be less people to perform acts of compassion and justice. We need to make more disciples as Christians." However, the entire content of what followed was how to be involved in acts of compassion and justice. There was no conversation or content which involved what it looked like to *make disciples*. I sense this approach is responding to the danger of merely talking of action without involvement. However, there is a danger in this response heading towards involvement and forgetting why.

Through discipleship the church will be a distinct presence in society and therefore help to bring genuine transformation to the lives of individuals and communities. Through discipleship communities of faith are formed and grow, reflecting the

---

6. "Embrace" in this context refers to an accepting acknowledgment rather than an unquestioning integration.

7. It was only three years ago, for example, that I gave a series of sermons entitled, "Discipleship, Community, and Mission."

mission of God in the world. As Dallas Willard states, "Church is for discipleship. Discipleship is for the world."[8]

A Common Foundation of Discipleship

It is worth spending some time reflecting on what that statement has looked like in history. This will be done in four brief case studies. These illustrations will each look at discipleship as the foundation of mission.

Madame Guyon lived from 1648 to 1717. She was a French mystic, who was at one point jailed for a brief book she wrote on discipleship titled, *A Short and Easy Method of Prayer*. This book has since been released under the title, *Experiencing the Depths of Jesus Christ*. This book outlines the importance of discipleship. It also uncovers the simplicity of authentic discipleship. In this book, she comments on the foundation of mission,

> The way to reach the lost is to reach them by the *heart*. If a new convert were introduced to *real prayer* and to a *true inward experience of Christ* as soon as he became converted, you would see countless numbers of converts go on to become true disciples.[9]

She goes further from this to comment on evangelistic endeavors focused merely on the outward person rather than the heart. This is a reality that is often found in contemporary church communities, a fixation on modifying behavior rather than learning how to live as a disciple of Jesus.

> ... the present way of dealing with only the external matters in the life of the new convert brings little fruit. Burdening the new Christian with countless rules and all sorts of standards does not help him grow in Christ ... The new Christian should be led to God.[10]

William Carey lived from 1761 to 1834. He was an English Baptist minister and missionary. Through his mission endeavors into India, and his approach to mission, he became known as the "Father of modern mission." Our aim is not to mimic his technique or method of mission. That is best left in the eighteenth and nineteenth centuries. However, it is interesting to note his foundation and approach to mission.

He states, "One of the first, and most important of those duties which are incumbent upon us, is *fervent and united prayer* . . ."[11] This is the action of a disciple of Jesus—acknowledging and resting in the Reason for the mission. This prayer leads

---

8. Willard, "The Gentle Art of Making Disciples."
9. Guyon, *Experiencing the Depths of Jesus Christ*, 117.
10. Ibid., 117.
11. Carey, "An Enquiry into the Obligation of Christians to Use Means for the Conversion of the Heathens," 298.

Movement Three—From Theories to Courageous Practices

the disciple towards the vision that is being prayed for. "We must not be contented however with praying, without *exerting ourselves in the use of means* for the obtaining of those things we pray for."[12] William Carey, as well, saw the importance of being involved in the vision of the kingdom of God for the work of mission. The life of discipleship leads the individual and community into kingdom living. The outcome of this is worth noting in full.

> As our blessed Lord has required us to pray that his kingdom may come, and his will be done on earth as it is in heaven . . . we are the subject of grace, and partakers of that spirit of universal benevolence and genuine philanthropy, which appear so eminent in the character of God himself.[13]

Hudson Taylor lived from 1832 to 1905. He was an English Protestant missionary to China. Hudson could potentially be termed the "Father of the modern missional movement." This is due to the fact that he was one of the first missionaries to listen to and be present within the culture to which he was sent. This approach led him to be ridiculed by and shunned from other expressions of mission. The experience that formed the foundation of Taylor's approach to mission is particularly striking. He writes,

> Not many months after my conversion, having a leisure afternoon, I retired to my own chamber to spend it largely in communion with God. Well do I remember that occasion. How in the gladness of my heart I poured out my soul before God; and again and again confessing my grateful love to Him who had done everything for me . . . I besought Him to give me some work to do for Him, as an outlet for love and gratitude; some self-denying service, no matter what it might be . . .[14]

Hudson Taylor then experienced the presence of God and rested within this presence for the afternoon. At the end of this time, he knew that he had been called towards the service of God.

> For what service I was accepted I knew not; but a deep consciousness that I was no longer my own took possession of me, which has never since been effaced.[15]

Hudson Taylor was sixteen when this took place. This was clearly a deeply formative event for him that became the foundation of both his action and approach to God throughout his life

Frank Laubach lived from 1884 to 1970. He was a Christian missionary and mystic. He spent his formative missionary years on a small island off the coast of the

12. Ibid., 299.
13. Ibid., 294.
14. Taylor, "The Call to Service," 300.
15. Ibid., 301.

Philippines. While on the island, building relationship with the people group he believed he had been called to, he was confronted with his own discipleship. "Although I have been a minister and a missionary for fifteen years, I have not lived the entire day of every day in minute-by-minute effort to follow the will of God."[16] He acknowledged the effect this would have on the mission he was involved in. "What right then have I or any other person to come here and change the name of these people from Muslim to Christian, unless I lead them to a life fuller of God than they have now?"[17] His conclusion was this,

> My part is to live this hour in continuous inner conversation with God and in perfect responsiveness to his will, to make this hour gloriously rich.[18]

His approach to others came out of this foundation,[19]

> Pray inwardly for everybody one meets . . . This simple practice requires only a gentle pressure of the will, not more than a person can exert easily. It grows easier as the habit becomes fixed . . . *Yet it transforms life into heaven.*[20]

I am not advocating that missional expressions be mirror images of the above case studies, and I am certainly not implying that missional endeavors mean being called out of one's context and country. What is being observed above is the common foundation of discipleship each of these individuals had during four different centuries. The expression of mission in the current century will be different. The foundation of mission and missional activity, however, must remain the same. The person of Jesus Christ and what it means and looks like to follow him throughout each day.

Discipleship in Contemporary Settings

I have reflected on discipleship being the foundation of a missional community. I have then looked at some people who have either taught this or lived this (or both). Now, I need to look practically at how this can take place in current expressions of Christian community. This will create a foundational lens through which it will be possible to discuss a current issue that missional communities will need to address.

Missional living can be approached through Dallas Willard's model of transformation. This is the VIM model (*Vision, Intention, Means*). As Willard states, "If we are to be spiritually formed in Christ, we must have the appropriate vision, intention

---

16. Laubach, *Letters by a Modern Mystic*, 3.
17. Ibid., 13.
18. Ibid., 8.
19. Through Frank Laubach's work he devised a literacy model that has since been used to teach over sixty million people to read in their own language. He became known as the "Apostle to the illiterates."
20. Laubach, *Letters by a Modern Mystic*, 75 (italics added).

Movement Three—From Theories to Courageous Practices

and means."[21] Should a missional community dwell on vision alone, their direction will be circular and the vision itself will become a kind of idol. Their existence will become more about their vision (often based on protest) than their God. On the other hand, should a missional community focus too much on the means (what is done), they will quickly become paralyzed and stifled. "Nothing is so deadening to the divine as an habitual dealing with the outsides of holy things."[22] These actions will become legalistic and lead to superstition.[23] Their existence will become more about their appearance than their God.

What will the primary *vision* of a missional community of disciples be? "A vision of God's kingdom is a place to start . . . This vision . . . makes it possible for us to intend to live it."[24] This will mean that teaching, communication, and direction will all be founded on the present reality as well as the future and full realization of God's kingdom. The smaller and context-driven visions of each separate community must grow from a firm vision of God's kingdom.

The primary *intention* of a missional community is to live within the present reality of the kingdom of God. As Dallas Willard states, ". . . the simplicity of spiritual formation lies in its intention. Its aim is to bring every element in our being, inside and out, into harmony with the will of God and the kingdom of God."[25] This may look different depending on who is in the wider community and the culture in which the community is situated. This intention must come from vision rather than means.

An intention to live in a certain way based on action will always lead to guilt and condemnation. Intention flowing from the kingdom of God, however, will lead to freedom. Aiden W. Tozer states that a growing hunger after God himself, ". . . is the only harbinger of revival which I have been able to detect anywhere on the religious horizon."[26] Lesslie Newbigin also comments on this knowledge of God, ". . . the ultimate secret of knowing is in following Jesus."[27]

What are the *means* through which this intention will work? It is important at this point to steer clear of focusing on behavior or simply moralizing. For example, David Putman and Ed Stetzer give the definition of what it looks like to be a follower of Jesus, ". . . to live as Jesus lived, to love as Jesus loved, and to leave what Jesus left behind."[28] This is a good start. What follows, however, is an entire book focused on techniques and ideas which only address the exterior of living as a disciple.

21. Willard, *Renovation of the Heart*, 59.
22. Macdonald, *Thomas Wingfold, Curate*, 27.
23. For example, "If I don't attend to a habit or rhythm, I'll have a bad day, or the mission will be jeopardized."
24. Willard, *Renovation of the Heart*, 60.
25. Ibid., 60.
26. Tozer, *The Pursuit of God*, 7.
27. Newbigin, *Discovering Truth in a Changing World*, 19.
28. Putman and Stetzer, *Breaking the Discipleship Code*, 22.

Spiritual disciplines create space in the life of the disciple for the Spirit of God to act. These disciplines are not righteous in and of themselves,[29] they simply place the individual or community before God so that he can transform.[30] These habits, without a kingdom-focused vision and an authentic intention to live within the kingdom of God, will quickly become burdening and legalistic. When the disciple can see that he or she is simply orienting their whole person and whole community towards Christ, the actions make sense and maintain the simplicity they need.

The outworking of this is a community of disciples who are learning how to be truly present within their context. Aiden W. Tozer well notes this outcome, "Let every man abide in the calling wherein he is called and his work will be as sacred as the work of the ministry. It is not what a man does that determines whether his work is sacred or secular, it is *why* he does it."[31]

Disciples of Jesus are also learning how to be truly present with each other. As Jürgen Moltmann notes,

> . . . we do not at all seek the other but only ourselves in the other. We leave the other alone and remain alone ourselves. A further reason can be found in the fact that we accept and treat each other only in terms of reciprocity . . .[32] The suffering of his love has changed everything, and the more we go outside of ourselves, the more we will discover and experience this change ourselves.[33]

There are a number of contemporary issues missional communities need to address. These issues need to be addressed gently, graciously, with robust theology, and an adherence to Christian doctrine. An issue that I would like to spend some time examining here is the issue of sexuality. This issue forms the backdrop to the current public debate of same-sex marriage. It also provides a context through which to view same-sex attraction, sexual expression outside of marriage, and even some parts of marriage itself. I do not aim to address all of these issues. I would like rather to discuss the big picture of sexuality and how a missional community (based on a trinitarian missional ecclesiology) might be able to approach such a loaded area.

It seems that the Christian community carries a *vision* that has become quite confused in this area. The church, generally, seems willing to follow contemporary culture in seeing sexuality synonymous with the act of sex (and more specifically, genital sex). All that is stated and discussed in this area, then, becomes focused on sex.

The *intention* within this vision is to keep the biblical commands towards sexual purity. That is, sexuality can only be expressed within the boundaries of marriage. As

---

29. Willard, *The Spirit of the Disciplines*, 138.
30. Foster, *Celebration of Discipline*, 7.
31. Tozer, *The Pursuit of God*, 127.
32. Moltmann, *The Open Church*, 29.
33. Ibid., 32.

Movement Three—From Theories to Courageous Practices

a popular Christian book on the sexuality of young men states, "You are sexually pure when no sexual gratification comes from anyone or anything but your wife."[34]

The outcome of this is that the *means* of sexual expression is the act of penetrative sexual intercourse. The context of this expression is necessarily marriage and marriage alone. Christopher Ash, in a recent and very popular theology of marriage, gives his definition of marriage that also seems to focus on the act of sex, "Marriage is the voluntary sexual and public social union; of one man and one woman; from two different families... Intrinsic in this union is God's calling to lifelong exclusive sexual faithfulness."[35]

The outcome of this can be seen clearly in a book on marriage recently released by Mark Driscoll and his wife Grace. In this book, marriage and the act of genital sex seem to sit on equal ground. As a result, the necessity of a pure sexuality before and during marriage is repeatedly emphasized. Early in the book, Mark Driscoll ponders the present reality of some sexual sin Grace indulged in before they were married.[36] "Had I known about this sin, I would not have married her. But God told me to marry Grace, I loved her, I had married her as a Christian, we were pregnant, and I was a pastor with a church plant filled with young people who were depending on me."[37] As a result of this and other factors, it is unsurprising that the Driscolls were not enjoying the act of sex within their marriage. Driscoll laments, "I had a church filled with single young women who were asking me how they could stop being sexually ravenous and wait for a Christian husband, then I'd go home to a wife whom I was not sexually enjoying."[38]

Missional communities will back themselves into a corner if they blindly allow the discussion of sexuality to remain solely focused on the act of sex. This approach will close the door on any fruitful relating with a culture that is desperately seeking a meaningful way to express sexuality. As Richard Foster states, "The problem with the topless bars and the pornographic literature of our day is not that they emphasize sexuality too much but that they do not emphasize it enough. They totally eliminate relationship and restrain sexuality to the narrow confines of the genital. They have made sex trivial."[39]

> Despite the fact that incarnation and embodiment play a central role in our faith, the church as a whole has not been of great help, especially recently. We rarely, if ever, talk about our bodies or about touch. When we do, it is often in the context of purity, safety or abstinence... the church as a whole has shaped

---

34. Arterburn, *Every Man's Battle*, 106.
35. Ash, *Marriage*, 211. This definition has a complete lack of covenantal language and merely describes the boundaries of marriage.
36. It's interesting that he does not account for his own sexual sin before they were married.
37. Driscoll, *Real Marriage*, 11–12.
38. Ibid.
39. Foster, *Money, Sex, and Power*, 92.

our relationship to touch and to sexuality in the negative, focusing on how we should control and repress our bodies.[40]

We need a renewed *vision* of sexuality within the kingdom of God. Here, sexuality, as distinct from the act of sex, is the offering of one's self as a gift to another. Sexuality within this vision is a reflection of the relationship between the persons of the triune God. This act of sexuality is devoid of manipulation or control in that it is inherently free and non-coercive. "Our human sexuality, our maleness and femaleness, is not just an accidental arrangement of the human species, not just a convenient way to keep the human race going . . . it is intimately related to our creation in the image of God."[41]

Genesis 2 paints a vivid picture where authentic and healthy sexuality is integrated into the entire lives of the man and the woman. There was no shame present because there was wholeness.[42] Michael Frost writes, "By 'sexuality', I mean that essential, all-pervasive complementarity between persons and, in a certain sense, between all living things."[43]

The *intention* within this vision is no longer focused on how, when, and with whom one can engage in the act of genital sex. The intention is also no longer centered on denial, suppression, or control. We are sexual persons. We must never try to deny or reject that in any way.[44] Rather, the intention here is to learn how to healthily express one's sexuality while being authentically present within one's context and community. We have a choice, as Tara Owens points out, "We can choose to embrace the reality that God wants to redeem our sexuality and begin to release it to God to see what he might do. Or we can choose the path that feels safer and more predictable—the path of rules and regulations, the life of the Law."[45]

Sexuality, within this vision, is not focused on self.[46] Sexuality, within this vision, can be deeply vulnerable. It involves being fully present in order to bless others. This offering may be unappreciated, unseen, and even rejected. Within this vision, those who are single, those who are attracted to the same sex, and those who are carrying scars from the misuse of and abuse by sex are able to move towards a healthy expression of sexuality.

The intention within this vision is to learn from Jesus how to express one's sexuality. The fact is, Jesus himself was fully human, therefore, he was able to express his sexuality in a healthy and holy way—as a single man living in community.[47]

40. Owens, "Longing Bodies, Aching Souls," 37.
41. Foster, *Money, Sex, and Power*, 92.
42. Ibid., 93.
43. Frost, *Longing for Love*, 30–31.
44. Foster, *Money, Sex, and Power*, 115.
45. Owens, "Longing Bodies, Aching Souls," 40.
46. Self-gratification is a detached and therefore reduced or hollow expression of sexuality.
47. "Jesus had longings and felt desires just as we did, just as we do. Even more scandalous is

Movement Three—From Theories to Courageous Practices

By what *means* can one express their sexuality? Primarily through learning how to be present with others and engaged within community. This community may be as exclusive as husband and wife. On the other hand, it may be as wide as a city.

As a single man[48] I quickly and repeatedly discovered that the more I endeavored to "control" my sexuality, the more it "crept out" in unexpected and increasingly compromising ways. I began to discover that the practice of hospitality was a healthy and effective way of expressing my sexuality.

Richard Foster states, "The single person's sexuality is expressed in his or her capacity to love and be loved."[49] He also states, ". . . to chat over coffee, to discuss a great book, to view a sunset together—this is sexuality at its best . . . human sexuality is a far larger reality than merely coitus."[50]

We are able to see Jesus expressing sexuality as he washes the feet of the disciples in the upper room; as he overflows with gut-wrenching compassion for the crowds surrounding him; as he engages with the woman at the well . . . the woman washing his feet . . . the woman thrown naked at his feet . . . the women at the foot of the cross.

The outcome of this approach is that there is a new context in which to discuss same-sex attraction and marriage. There is a new context in which to discuss singleness and dating. There is a new context in which to share a vision of the kingdom of God and what it looks like to live in this kingdom as a disciple of Jesus.

My hope is to be a part of a community of disciples intending to live day-by-day within the present reality of the kingdom of God. Dallas Willard states clearly how a pastor is to lead disciples in this context: "You ravish them with a vision of the beauty of Jesus and of life with him in his kingdom."[51]

Individual and Corporate Servantship Practices

- Lead a small group through James Bryan Smith's *The Good and Beautiful God* study series.[52]
- Develop a VIM model for your formation in Christ.
- Consider the focus of your community and assess whether its expression of mission is leaning more towards *vision* or *means*.

---

that Jesus went about his life being a human being fully alive to his sexuality. He didn't shuck it off as irrelevant. He didn't live without the touch of others to keep himself more pure and holy. He was fully God and fully human, and he welcomed touches that the world around him thought thoroughly improper." Owens, "Longing Bodies, Aching Souls," 38.

48. I married at the age of 33.
49. Foster, *Money, Sex, and Power*, 115.
50. Ibid., 92.
51. Willard, "The Gentle Art of Making Disciples."
52. Smith, *The Good and Beautiful God*.

- Read part three of Richard Foster's *Celebration of Discipline*.[53]
- Develop space for the corporate disciplines to be expressed and experienced within your missional community.
- Research and engage with fasting (as appropriate for your context).
- Reflect in a small group as to how fasting gives space for the Holy Spirit to reshape your response to desires.

Questions for Reflection and Discussion

- What is the *organizational center* of your church (discipleship, community, worship, or mission)? How does this shape your church's expression of mission?
- In what ways might it be true that it is primarily through discipleship that the church will learn to be present within communities?
- How might a trinitarian missional ecclesiology of sexuality change your community's engagement with current culture?

---

53. Foster, *Celebration of Discipline*.

15

Nurturing Missional Modes of Servantship

Christine Redwood

The Christendom model, where there is no distinction between church and state, has collapsed, and a new post-Christendom society is emerging. Christian leaders need to appropriately respond to this shift. This chapter critically assesses how this cultural shift has caused shifts in mission, church, and servantship. Overall these fresh theological perspectives are promising. Mission has rightly been identified once more as originating in God, Jesus is the one who ushers in the kingdom of God, and the church is called to join in fulfilling God's purposes. Thus our missiology shapes our ecclesiology. Churches are, hopefully, becoming missional churches. Churches are to be incarnational, serving in their communities in relational ways. Not surprisingly this requires a new type of servantship. It is a servantship formed in teams with different people bringing a range of gifts together in order to equip the whole church to be missional. As a younger and upcoming leader, I am intentionally seeking to develop a missional mode of servantship. I outline the journey I've been on, and where I am transitioning to in the next twelve months.

Some Theological and Cultural Reflections

There has been a major cultural shift, particularly in western societies, which have moved from a Christendom culture to a post-Christendom society. A new theological paradigm is required for the church to address this trend. Other shifts have occurred as a result of this transition. Reflection on mission has returned to focusing on God—it is God who initiates mission, and supremely in the person, work, and message of Jesus we learn what the kingdom of God entails. Thus the church is called to follow Jesus, it is to be missional. For inherited churches this will require a reorientation in how things are done. A new type of servantship is needed, one that can address these changes, releasing missional churches which connect with the post-Christendom society.

The cultural shift which the church undertook in the third century, known as Christendom, had massive implications for the Christian faith. This shift lasted for roughly a thousand years impacting the Christian's understanding of mission, church, and servantship. It was a cultural shift whereby Christianity became so intertwined with the state that "the church was the entire society and the entire society was the church."[1] Thus Christians moved from being a "marginalized, subversive, and persecuted movement" to a powerful religion that dominated society and culture, particularly the geographical region of Europe.[2] This cultural shift over time allowed Christians to "be at home in society" because it was believed that the culture was Christian.[3] This, however, is no longer the case, and Christian leaders must recognize that the culture is changing if the church is to continue to be a faithful witness to Jesus.

Western culture in particular is transitioning to what is referred to as a post-Christendom society. Post-Christendom is defined as the "culture that emerges as the Christian faith loses coherence within a society."[4] Many churches are in crisis not knowing how to cope with this massive change. As I noted in my earlier chapter in this book, I minister within the Baptist Churches of New South Wales and the Australian Capital Territory (Australia). These churches have, in the last ten years, "experienced zero aggregate numerical growth, and aged significantly."[5] It is vital as western Christians that we grapple with the cultural shifts which are happening all around us. Many are grieving the loss of power and privilege.[6] Others deny that any change has taken place, and keep going on the same.[7] Still others celebrate the demise of Christendom and the opportunity it presents for the church to be once more faithful Christians.[8] I have grown up very aware that Christianity is a minority faith in the secular Australian society in which I live. When reading about Christendom my response was to cringe and to dismiss it as not being authentic Christianity. Yet as Stuart Murray warns, it is dangerous to dismiss Christendom without first learning the full depths of it, because if we do not reflect on Christendom we will be "ill-prepared for challenges

---

1. Hanciles, *Beyond Christendom*, 84.
2. Frost and Hirsch, *The Shaping of Things to Come*, 8.
3. Kreider, "Beyond Bosch," 63.
4. Murray, *Post-Christendom*, 19.
5. Pratt, "Awake O Sleeper," 6.
6. Frost, *Exiles*, 6.
7. Murray, *Post-Christendom*, 206.
8. Hauerwas and Willimon, *Resident Aliens*, 18.

ahead."[9] We still live in the "shadow of Christendom," and this legacy will continue to impact the way we engage mission, church, and servantship in the future.[10]

Therefore, one of the primary servantship challenges for the church today is acknowledging and understanding the cultural shift that is taking place, and equipping our local congregations to recognize it as well. Christians too often seem to be operating within a Christendom mindset, oblivious to the changing cultural context; this is detrimental to the spread of the gospel.[11] We need a fresh theological perspective that can speak into the shift. I connect personally with Walter Brueggemann's metaphor of *exile*. Christianity and the culture around the church are "no longer [in a] sustainable alliance," and many Christians feel like exiles living in a foreign land.[12] This is a situation the Jewish exiles had to work through, so our Scriptures provide great theological resources for equipping people to live as God's exiles.[13] Similarly, the metaphor of *resident aliens* has been used to express what it is like to be a Christian.[14] The church is called by God to be a new people aligning with Christ and his mission. Properly understood, this idea involves a seismic shift for the church and its theological, ecclesial, and missional imagination.[15] Leaders, through preaching and teaching in their local congregations, can begin to process this change. Space needs to be given for grieving the loss of the old way of doing things, the loss of a Christendom theological mindset, and also to filling people with hope by giving them a new vision for the church in this post-Christendom context.

This process requires a shift in how the church thinks about and does mission. Mission in the Christendom era was strongly connected to the State; thus the gospel went hand in hand with "territorial expansion and political domination."[16] It was assumed that there were places that were Christian and those that were not, thus Christian mission was foreign mission, going to new places and setting up a Christian society there. The assumption was that to be Christian was to be a European.[17] Incentives were given to attract people into the church.[18] The Christendom shift elevated the church to a place of power, meaning that great concentration and effort were spent in maintaining that position. This took precedence over mission in many cases.[19] It also gave the church a close association with violence. Often coercion was used to

9. Murray, *Post-Christendom*, 208.
10. Kreider, *The Change of Conversion and the Origin of Christendom*, 99.
11. Frost and Hirsch, *The Shaping of Things to Come*, 9.
12. Brueggemann, *Cadences of Home*, 2–3.
13. Ibid.
14. Hauerwas and Willimon, *Resident Aliens*, 24.
15. Ibid.
16. Hanciles, *Beyond Christendom*, 19.
17. Ibid., 101.
18. Kreider, "Beyond Bosch," 62.
19. Murray, *Post-Christendom*, 129.

force people to convert to Christianity, or they faced death.[20] Mission became one of many programs for the church to do. Sometimes mission was separate from the church altogether, as boards and para-church organizations were set up either focusing on foreign missions, or, later, home missions as well.[21] This model of mission has been greatly challenged within the post-Christendom shift.

Mission has had a theological renaissance in recent decades. *Missio Dei*, the mission of God, was coined in the twentieth century in order to stress that mission is "grounded in an intratrinitarian movement of God himself."[22] Mission begins in God, thus shifting the Christendom "ecclesiocentric understanding of mission" to, instead, recognizing mission first from a theocentric perspective. This means mission is not an activity of the church, but, as stated in John 20:21, the church is sent by God in order to fulfill his purposes to redeem creation.[23] A missional church understands this, and seeks in its own local context to be God's sent people proclaiming and living out the gospel where it is located.[24]

For the leaders of local churches, particularly the established ones which I am involved in, the challenge is to shift a congregation so that it understands itself as being part of God's mission. This will need to be expressed "and nurtured in their corporate life"[25]—for instance, through regular preaching, but also more broadly through and in corporate prayers, Bible studies, church budgets, and a willingness to affirm and hear different Christians from the congregation share how they are part of God's mission. This theological shift in our understanding of the church is crucial. The church is part of God's mission, and this is particularly known in light of Jesus and his proclamation concerning the kingdom of God.

The kingdom of God is a phrase often used by Jesus to describe his message and ministry. Jesus begins his public life by declaring, "the time has come . . . the kingdom of God has come near. Repent and believe the good news."[26] Jesus both "taught and embodied" this kingdom and, as his followers, we are called to do the same.[27] Tom Sine speaks about how, through Jesus, "God's new order has actually broken into our troubled world," and every Christian is invited to live this new order in their ordinary lives.[28] Healing and a concern for the weak and the poor characterize this kingdom—it is a kingdom marked by love, justice, hope, and mercy. The church, as the people of God and citizens of this kingdom in their local setting, is to be a community where

20. Ibid., 130.
21. Guder and Barrett, *Missional Church*, 6.
22. Wright, *The Mission of God*, 62.
23. Guder and Barrett, *Missional Church*, 4.
24. Gibbs et al., *Church Next*, 55.
25. Murray, *Church after Christendom*, 137.
26. Mark 1:15.
27. Nessan, *Beyond Maintenance to Mission*, 26.
28. Sine, *The New Conspirators*, 120.

this kingdom takes on a "visible, practical form."[29] God ultimately fulfills the kingdom of God, so the church is never to be static; it is always on a journey moving towards the kingdom.[30] This understanding releases all Christians to be part of God's purposes. Missional leaders guide and equip people to live out this vision by immersing them in God's story, and inviting them to imagine themselves as part of the kingdom of God.[31] They help people listen and identify where God is at work in their local community, so that they might experiment and join in. In both word and deed the church is to be an active presence partaking in God's purposes for their community.

Incarnational mission is one way to be witnesses to Christ in this post-Christendom context. Taking Jesus as the model for the way his followers are to do mission, incarnational mission notes how God fully entered into the human experience. Likewise, those who follow Jesus must make him their model and be people that live in close proximity with those they seek to witness to.[32] To live incarnationally is to "demonstrate Christlikeness . . . close enough to people that our lives rub up against their lives" so they see something different in how we live, while at the same expressing such difference in "cultural forms that make sense and convey impact."[33] This requires careful reflection, as too often we swing from one extreme to another, either withdrawing from the world, or conforming totally to the world in order to be seen as relevant. To be incarnational is to know the people we are working with, and to share the gospel in a way that will connect with them.[34] David Bjork, reflecting on his missional experience in post-Christendom France, realized he had to shift from a church paradigm to a kingdom of God paradigm, especially in terms of ministry methods, and that this meant employing a more relational stance.[35] Again, the emphasis is on "life-to-life," in the everyday building of relationships, rather than "establishing a Christian institution."[36]

Crucially, this kind of missional engagement means that leaders need to become servants, giving up "ecclesiastical rights and privileges."[37] When our missiology is the driving vision, this in turn shifts our ecclesiology—the church thus begins to become a missional church and the servant-leader a missional leader.

My church has developed from the inherited church model, coming from the Christendom tradition. Yet my church also recognizes the world has changed, and is open to asking questions about what that means for this church. Around us new forms

---

29. Hauerwas and Willimon, *Resident Aliens*, 87.
30. Ibid., 51.
31. Roxburgh et al., *The Missional Leader*, 76.
32. Frost, *Exiles*, 54.
33. Ibid., 55.
34. Drane, *After McDonaldization*, 87.
35. Bjork, "A Model for Analysis of Incarnational Ministry," 280.
36 Ibid., 288.
37. Ibid.

of church are emerging which are offering fresh perspectives. They embody "diversity, flexibility, and cultural sensitivity," which Stuart Murray argues are what "post-Christendom churches need."[38] There is much that can be learned from these churches. These new experiments on the fringes, can, if allowed, renew the more mainstream church. These emerging churches contain the "germ of cultural regeneration" with their "freshness and vitality that come from the deeper communion of mission."[39] I am pleased to note that in my setting, the Baptist Union of Australia is encouraging the growth of such churches.

For inherited and established churches this is a major shift, as there is still much baggage these churches carry. Slowly changes are happening even in the inherited church. One of the features of the missional church is its emphasis on authentically living as a community of God's people. Inherited churches are thinking through such things as communion, worship, servantship, and communication, and, for instance, regularly eating together in order that they might shape their community to be a people that are generous and thankful.[40] As individuals, there needs to be "regular and intentional participation" in the church we belong to. There needs to be a commitment, so that collectively, as we participate in the ecclesial practices, we are shaped to be God's people sent into the world as witnesses to Jesus.[41] Some inherited churches are cutting back on programs and simplifying practices. They are re-centering on a holistic approach that seeks to create a body of people who embody the alien values of the gospel.[42] As a leader I have the responsibility to do more than just preach this new vision of church. I must begin to model it. I need to embody this message in my life if I expect people to follow my example.[43]

Nurturing Missional Modes of Servantship

Just as there are inherited ways of doing church, there are also inherited forms of leadership. Christendom produced leadership that was hierarchical and performance-based.[44] It tended to emphasize the role of the pastor as someone functioning as a shepherd, particularly through teaching and pastoral care.[45] Yet this too needs to be re-assessed in the post-Christendom shift. Christian leaders can be in danger of becoming institutionalized. Leaders become dependent on the institution, finding safety, security, and prestige there, and, in turn, their congregations become depen-

---

38. Murray, *Post-Christendom*, 256.
39. Frost, *Exiles*, 129.
40. Guder and Barrett, *Missional Church*, 181.
41. Ibid., 180.
42. Gibbs et al., *Church Next*, 224.
43. Frost and Hirsch, *The Shaping of Things to Come*, 156.
44. Murray, *Post-Christendom*, 261.
45. Frost and Hirsch, *The Shaping of Things to Come*, 168.

dent on the leader to do all the missional and pastoral work.[46] In too many churches distinctions are made between the professional clergy who give ministry and the laity, those who receive this ministry.[47] This is not a biblical concept. In the New Testament there is only one people. Leaders are to equip the people so that all will be involved in ministry and mission.[48]

The new model of *servantship* is sometimes referred to as *apostolic leadership* (we'll call it *apostolic servantship*). This is servantship that recognizes the changing culture and responds "by shaping a church movement that more resembles the world of Acts." In other words, they are living out God's mission in their very lives.[49] Apostolic servantship recognizes a wide range of gifts and persons, and emphasizes the importance of diversity. Ephesians 4 informs biblical servantship by suggesting there are five foundational servantship functions needed for missional churches—there is the traditional pastoral and teacher roles, but also the more neglected apostolic, prophetic, and evangelistic roles that churches need to recapture.[50] Missional servantship is team servantship. Stevens argues that this team servantship derives from the Bible—there are multiple elders, deacons, apostles, and prophets found in the early churches.[51] Leaders are there to serve the mission of Christ and his people, as servant leaders, equipping the "saints for the work of the ministry."[52] Forming such leaders means recognizing the different gifts that people bring to servantship, and selecting a wide range of people who together can transform a church to be missional. Mentoring is one of the key tools used to develop missional leaders.[53] Being a leader in a post-Christendom context means that we are able to listen and relate to people, helping them discern where God is in their lives.[54] There are great challenges ahead for leaders, so careful thought needs to be given to developing into this new servantship model.

My Missional Plan

Over the next twelve months I am planning on intentionally moving to a more missional mode of servantship. This is a journey that has already begun both personally and in ministry, and it is the path on which I wish to keep walking. I was the student pastor at Hornsby Baptist church in Sydney between 2008 and 2010, and in late 2010

46. Cole, *Organic Leadership*, 40.
47. Stevens, *The Other Six Days*, 26.
48. Ibid.
49. McNeal, *The Present Future*, 126.
50. Frost and Hirsch, *The Shaping of Things to Come*, 169.
51. Stevens, *The Other Six Days*, 147.
52. Ephesians 4:11–12.
53. Cole, *Organic Leadership*, 233.
54. Roxburgh et al., *The Missional Leader*, 31.

I began to assess where I should go next. As a student pastor I had thrown myself into all different ministries and had grown and stretched myself. Yet I sensed I needed to be more intentional in my next step. As I prayed, I became convicted that I need to get back to my initial calling.

The metaphor which best describes my servantship is that of a storyteller. As a leader I seek to be one of God's storytellers, "poets charged with the task of keeping and imparting the stories" of God.[55] My passion is to communicate the gospel in such a way that people are invited to participate and join in God's story. "Communicate" is a broad term. I mean preaching, but I also mean through Bible studies, dramas, stories, articles, and opening up space for hands-on missional and ministry experiences. In 2011 I am devoting myself to developing the gift of preaching, understanding that servantship can be exercised through preaching.[56] I was accepted into an evangelistic preaching internship with the Baptist Union. As was noted previously, congregations need preachers prepared to speak into the post-Christendom context, that is, people who can name the cultural shift that has taken place and lead others through a time of grieving, as well as articulating a new vision for the future. The first signs of this are happening in my church. For instance, at the beginning of this year we did a preaching series through the book of Daniel, focusing on the motif of *exile*. We were seeking to learn from Daniel how we too could be witnesses to God in a foreign land.

Paul Quicke speaks about preacher-leaders as being of vital importance in the local church as change agents, transforming their congregations by walking with the people of their church and faithfully speaking God's Word into their lives.[57] It has been such a blessing to have mentors who are committed to preaching, and prepared to work through a sermon from beginning to end with me. It has given me the chance to experiment with different ways of communicating—for instance, interacting with the congregation and opening up room for discussion and questions. Preaching too needs to shift: Walter Brueggemann speaks about preaching needing to be "a poetic construal of an alternative world."[58] I plan to continue to read widely, especially about the cultures around me, so I might better be able to speak into and critique it. I need to soak myself in studying the Scriptures, so I might hold the vision of God close. Finally, I need to continue to immerse myself for the rest of this year in the art of speaking; creatively proclaiming the gospel so that lives might be transformed.

Travelling to different churches as a preaching intern during the last few months of 2011 has reminded me of the urgency of the task at hand. There are so many lovely people inside these churches, but there is a lack of vision and will to want to connect with the community. I see dying churches. I see so many people who do not know Jesus, and we do not seem to have any idea about how to connect. This deeply troubles

---

55. Arthur, *The God-Hungry Imagination*, 31.
56. Quicke, *360-Degree Leadership*, 17.
57. Ibid., 89.
58. Brueggemann, *Finally Comes the Poet*, 6.

Movement Three—From Theories to Courageous Practices

me. But there is something in my church which gives me hope: a core group of young adults who want to change the way we worship together. In our corporate life there is a growing awareness that we are on a mission. Whenever I have the chance to lead an evening service my emphasis is on praying for this world, inviting others to pray, finding people who are willing to share how God is at work in their lives, and praying for them. I focus on calling the church to missional challenges and commitments—for example, supporting Christian campaigns such as Micah Challenge, who are fighting to reduce global poverty. We have begun to be a community who fellowships together. At the beginning of this year I organized a dinner that provided space for us to connect and to share together. Now it has become a regular pattern, eating together once a term and sharing our food.

My Bible study group is also working through a series on what it means to be missional in our culture. This includes sharing who it is we are connecting with, and praying for them. This accountability means we have all become more intentional about spending time with non-Christians and doing life with them. From 2012 onward I have the opportunity to create and implement more missional initiatives. In the next twelve months I would like to visit people from my church in their lunch breaks, making video clips showing ordinary people in our church seeking God and sharing Christ in their daily lives. I am committed to forming worship services which celebrate in real and tangible ways that the kingdom of God is near.

During the next twelve months I need to find ways to connect with people outside the church. I've been in Bible College too long, and I've grown comfortable. The best place for me is not full-time pastoral ministry, particularly if I am encouraging others to be more missional. I need to become more missional so I can model it to others. I have a few ideas about how it could work out bi-vocationally; perhaps I will get a second job working in a missional role as high school Scripture teacher or school chaplain. Or perhaps I will work in a part-time job in my local community, or develop my writing skills and pursue that as a second job. Alongside these two jobs (one in the church and one outside the church), I am also passionate about serving the community through volunteering. I will explore joining one of the council programs and visit lonely people, joining the musical society, being a mentor at a local school, or starting a book club. I have tried all these things over the last three years but when I get busy I let them go. This will continue to be a challenge. Right now I imagine I will have more time if I am studying less, but life can quickly fill up, and so I will need great wisdom in determining how all these different pieces will fit together.

To this end nurturing my personal spiritual life is vital. I begin and end each day by contemplatively reading a portion of Scripture, and allowing my prayers to be shaped by the Scripture as I commit my day to the Lord. I would like to continue to develop this discipline. I need times to be renewed, and this is best done by creating spaces to be alone, dreaming, praying, and studying the Bible.[59] Also, having a good

---

59. Sine, *The New Conspirators*, 219.

network of people is important; people who can hold me accountable and inspire me to continue along this path. Currently I have a mentor. Mentoring picks up on the pattern we see with Jesus and his disciples. It provides a relationship where a leader can grow; the relationship is focused giving both "personal support and accountability."[60] In turn, I am learning how to be a mentor to others, and this year I have taken on a mentoring role with one of the students at theological college.

The early church teaches us the importance of team servantship. John Stott argues from Acts 20:17–28 that pastoral servantship is to be plural, not the "so-called one-man [sic] band."[61] Being part of a team is very important to me. I would like to work with other leaders who have a similar missional vision and who are open to new possibilities and women serving with them. In such a team I would want to be held accountable to the role I had been given. I most connect with the prophetic/teaching/evangelistic functions, and as a result would like to continue to explore these functions further. I am excited about the possibilities that this post-Christendom shift brings, and I continue to dedicate my life to God and ask that his Spirit would transform me to be the right leader for this time.

Individual and Corporate Servantship Practices

- Work through a preaching series which addresses the cultural shifts taking place.

- Preach on one of the exilic or post-exilic prophets to equip the church in how they might respond to this shift.

- Provide more in-depth training on what it means to be a missional church through small groups. Encourage people to read a book from the missional church literature together and discuss what this might mean for the group.

- Be a permission-giving church which allows people the opportunity to experiment and try new ways of doing and being church. Come alongside people with ideas and mentor them, helping them to critically reflect as they experiment.

- Find a mentor for yourself who can help you keep developing as a preacher, and give them permission to encourage and critique you.

- Read! Read theological books, secular books, fiction, non-fiction, and the Bible, to understand what is happening in the world around you.

- Regularly invite people up the front in a church service to share how they are part of God's mission in their everyday lives. Make it a time to celebrate and affirm them. Commission them through prayer to continue to live in light of God's mission.

---

60. Lewis, *Mentoring Matters*, 93.
61. Stott, *The Living Church*, 81.

Movement Three—From Theories to Courageous Practices

- Spend time praying for the local community. Encourage people to take prayer walks around their neighborhood.

Questions for Reflection and Discussion

- How can we provide space for people to respond to the cultural changes around them?
- How can leaders model this missional vision in their lives? How can they genuinely embrace servantship?
- What type of leader (disciple/servant) might be neglected in your church's servantship team?

16

Exploring Servantship and Cultural Shifts

Jamie Freeman

Since the fourth century, western societies have been deeply connected with the religious establishment and culture of the Christian church. This has become known as *Christendom*. Laying privilege at the hand of the Emperor Constantine, and at subsequent rulers of various states, Christendom "was the cultural phenomenon that resulted when Christianity was established as the official imperial religion."[1] As a result, the once persecuted and marginalized movement found itself increasingly at the heart of state, empire, and civilization. Stuart Murray suggests that due to this, the Christian followers experienced "massive church growth, wonderful new buildings, changes in laws and customs, [and] church leaders taking on political and social roles."[2] Subsequently, this position of the church in society was further expanded and solidified throughout the following centuries.

However, as cracks in this relationship between church and state have emerged, and western culture is increasingly removed from its Christendom roots, a paradigm shift has occurred. Alan Roxburgh comments, "The fourth and twentieth centuries form bookends marking transition points in the history of the church. Just as the fourth century's adoption of Christianity by Constantine forced the church to struggle with its self-understanding as the new center of the culture, twentieth-century Christians must now struggle to understand the meaning of their social location in a

---

1. Frost, *Exiles*, 4.
2. Murray, "Christendom and Post-Christendom," 1–2.

decentered world."³ The church has moved from the center to the margins and this is known as *post-Christendom*.⁴ Stuart Murray⁵ defines post-Christendom as:

> The culture that emerges as the Christian faith loses coherence within a society that has been definitively shaped by the Christian story and as the institutions that have been developed to express Christian convictions decline in influence.

Tim Keller is quick to point out that despite this cultural shift "certain churches with supposedly obsolete beliefs in an infallible Bible and miracles are growing," and "despite the secularism of most universities and colleges, religious faith is growing in some corners of academia."⁶ This seems to suggest that the decline in influence may not be as significant, swift, comprehensive, and evidenced by certain inevitable characteristics, as some have argued.

Influence, Authenticity, and Mission

This highlights the need to define the use of the term *influence*. For the purpose of this chapter, influence is the ability to affect, alter, or sway an individual's or culture's thoughts, beliefs, or actions. Therefore, it is important to note that the influence of the Christian church should not be tied to, and limited by, its identity as a centralized institution within western society. Influence is something which can shape and inform beyond the confines of institutional delegated and legislative authority.

Tim Keller's conclusion is that "the world is polarizing over religion," a place that is equally "more religious and less religious at the same time."⁷ However, he does emphasize the need for "evangelical churches ensconced in the declining, remaining enclaves of Christendom" to become missional in order to survive.⁸ To see this happen it is necessary for the church in the west to embrace a complete paradigm shift, and reorient itself to engage with the increasingly "non-Christian society around it."⁹

According to Michael Frost this Christendom mindset is prevalent within the Christian church today. He states that, "although the Christendom story no longer defines western culture in general, it remains the primary definer of the church's self-understanding in almost every western nation." ¹⁰ Stuart Murray agrees, and argues

---

3. Roxburgh, *Missionary Congregation*, 7–8.
4. Murray, "The End of Christendom."
5. Murray, *Post-Christendom*, 19.
6. Keller, *The Reason for God*, x.
7. Ibid.
8. Keller, "The Missional Church," 1.
9. Ibid.
10. Frost, *Exiles*, 5.

that this is both significant and problematic for the way we "interpret the Bible, the way we engage in mission, and the way we do church."[11]

There are those who suggest that what will naturally emerge, as a consequence of embracing this paradigm shift and rejecting Christendom, is a more authentic expression of the Christian faith and ecclesiology.[12] However, to receive this without any qualification is naïve and possibly dangerous. "In abandoning all that is signified by Christendom, might we be in danger both of mitigating the claim of Christ and of misconstruing our own true identity as the church in relation to the world?"[13]

Coinciding with this cultural shift has been a change in the understanding of *mission*. Throughout Christendom mission was primarily seen as a program or activity of the church and thus formed part of its ecclesiology. As a result it was often left to the responsibility of specialists, which created a divide between the individual Christians who made up a church congregation and the concept of mission.[14] Furthermore, mission was often associated with imperial expansion or military conquest to "heathen nations," and assumptions were made that once whole cultures were Christianized there was no longer any need for mission.[15] To combat this, the Latin word *missio Dei* emerged and was used to challenge this Christendom perspective of mission. Consequently, mission became understood "not primarily [as] an activity of the church, but an attribute of God. God is a missionary God."[16]

Fundamental to the doctrine of *missio Dei* is the incarnation—God the Father sending the Son incarnated into culture. This again highlights the sending nature of the missionary God. God the Father and the Son send the Spirit and all three send the church into the world. As Alan Hirsch and Michael Frost conclude, "the church is therefore defined by its mission and not the other way around . . . the church doesn't *have* a missional strategy; it *is* the missional strategy."[17]

The *incarnation* has therefore become a model for mission in this new paradigm. However, there are those who suggest that this is not very helpful in describing the authentic missionary task of the Christian church.[18] Eckhard Schnabel argues that the incarnation of Jesus into the world is "unique, unrepeatable, and incomparable" and Jesus's missionary commission to his disciples in John 20:21 does not command their incarnation but rather their "obedience, unconditional commitment, and robust activity in the service of God and in the power of the Holy Spirit." Andreas Kostenberger

---

11. Murray, "Christendom and Post-Christendom," 4–5.
12. Hirsch and Altclass, *The Forgotten Ways Handbook*, 26–27.
13. Cowell, "In Defence of Christendom."
14. Murray, *Church after Christendom*, 135.
15. Murray, "Christendom and Post-Christendom," 3.
16. Bosch, *Transforming Mission*, 389–90.
17. Frost and Hirsch, *The Faith of Leap*, 21.
18. Schnabel, *Early Christian Mission*, 1574–75.

suggests that a more appropriate term, which captures the essence of the mandate for mission set forth in John's gospel, is *representational*.[19]

Tim Chester, who also rejects the use of the term *incarnational mission*, proposes that 1 Corinthians 9:22 presents "the locus classicus of missional contextualization"— *I have become all things to all men so that by all possible means I might save some.*"[20] Chester's grievance is not necessarily with what people "affirm through the phrase 'incarnational mission,' but that this is the wrong theological category to use."[21] Regardless, the phrase *incarnational mission* has helped the church emerging out of Christendom to rediscover the importance of engaging with the surrounding culture.

Responding to Cultural and Servantship Shifts

Despite these debates around terminology and theology, it is important that God's mission post-Christendom is seen in the way the church orients and responds to the surrounding culture. Mission in this context will require a greater emphasis on contextualization and holistic Christ-like living, which encompasses not only whole believers and faith communities but, also, all of the faith movement.

So what implications does this change in culture and understanding of mission have on the church post-Christendom? One variation which has begun to emerge is the understanding of the church as a movement or organism rather than an institution. Frank Viola attributes this to the *living entities* imagery which is used in the New Testament to describe the church, for example, a *body*.[22] He concludes, "Each image teaches us that the church is a living organism rather than an institutional organization." Stuart Murray suggests that in order for the church to reinvent itself as a missional movement it will involve a far greater shift than just individual congregations being genuinely missional, but, rather, whole denominations adopting this mindset and approach.[23]

With the current emphasis on being a missional movement, and the tide seemingly out on the role of the institutional organization, Tim Keller provides a helpful warning about drawing too hard a line between the two forms, opting that "a strong movement, then, occupies the difficult space between being a free-wheeling organism and a disciplined organization."[24]

The idea of simplicity therefore becomes a key concept for the church to embrace as it comes to terms with this current change in climate. Alan Hirsch's use of the term "simplexity" provides a useful framework for the church as a post-Christendom

19. Taylor, "5 Questions with Andreas Köstenberger on Excellence."
20. Chester, "Why I Don't Believe in Incarnational Mission," 1.
21. Chester, "Questioning the Incarnation as a Model for Mission," 1.
22. Viola, *Reimagining Church*, 32.
23. Murray, *Church after Christendom*, 139.
24. Keller, "Ministry Movements."

movement.²⁵ This phrase brings together "two key ideas that are critical to organic systems—namely, simplicity and complexity." He goes on to highlight the crucial importance for movements to refine their message, arriving at a simple and concise explanation, without losing the defining characteristics which make it a movement. This not only applies to its core message but also to its frameworks, structures, and practices. Tim Keel observes the difficulty in simplifying complex cultural and theological observations within our contexts, and therefore the role of servantship in this new paradigm is to "imagine structures and ways of understanding and organizing ourselves" to effectively respond to the new paradigm.²⁶

As a result, it is important for servantship in a missional context to have a judicious approach to structures and activities. This involves the ability to discern where energies are placed, what structures can be removed or simplified, and, subsequently, what frameworks are still needed. Alongside this, what is required is a "clear, unifying vision for the future together with a strong set of values or beliefs."²⁷ The significance and power of simplicity as a model for a missional movement is that you end up doing fewer things well.

The Externally Focused, Centrifugal Church

Stuart Murray suggests that the church as a movement will also have to contend with a shift from the maintenance mindset of Christendom—"maintaining a supposedly Christian status quo," to an emphasis on mission "within a contested environment."²⁸ This involves a complete re-orientation of thoughts, values, and practices.

Central to this idea is the church as externally focused, or *centrifugal*. There are some who would argue that this approach neglects the body or community, and who therefore opt for a "simultaneously centripetal and centrifugal" approach to mission in the post-Christendom era.²⁹ However, Rick Rusaw and Eric Swanson note that despite being orientated outwardly "externally focused churches are internally strong."³⁰ Some of the distinguishing characteristics of these missional movements include the focus of their budget, community engagement and involvement, and ultimately how they measure their effectiveness—all these are focused outwardly. As a result "nearly everything that is done inside the church should prepare and equip people not only for personal growth but also for personal impact."³¹

---

25. Hirsch and Altclass, *The Forgotten Ways Handbook*, 158.
26. Keel, *Intuitive Leadership*, 189.
27. Keller, "Ministry Movements."
28. Murray, "Post-Christendom, Post-Constantinian."
29. De La Hoyde, "The End of Christendom and Mission in the Local Church."
30. Rusaw and Swanson, *The Externally Focused Church*, 17.
31. Ibid., 17–18.

Throughout Christendom the church functioned primary in a *centripetal* fashion and this was the case due to the position that it held at the center of western culture.[32] This model for mission is inwardly orientated and involves "getting people into the church and generating activity there."[33] As a consequence, the church in post-Christendom is faced with a significant dilemma—to maintain or to adapt? In the current transitional period, churches which developed under the outlook of "come to us," will need to embrace a more external orientation. However, it is not one or the other. The church in post-Christendom will need to engage in both *centrifugal* and *centripetal* forms of mission, with the main thrust to *go* accompanied by the *attractive nature* of a Christ-centered "counter-cultural and counter-intuitive" community.[34]

Mark Driscoll states, "Churches must both bring people in and send people out, and must therefore structure themselves to achieve both objectives."[35] He argues that both are seen in the life of Jesus. For example, Jesus's ministry includes many centripetal moments, where crowds (both large and small) are drawn to his teaching (e.g., Luke 9:10–17), miracles (e.g., Mark 2:1–12), and hope for a restored life (e.g., Luke 19:1–10).

Changes in Servantship

To coincide with the shift in culture, mission, and church, there is increasingly an evolution in the way servantship is perceived and practiced. As David Bosch asserts,

> The movement away from ministry as the monopoly of ordained men to ministry as the responsibility of the whole people of God, ordained as well as non-ordained, is one of the most dramatic shifts taking place in the church today.[36]

In order to understand this shift in servantship, it is important to trace from what it is emerging. The inherited leadership model has its roots deep within a Christendom and institutional framework. With the impact of Constantinian reforms, church leaders began to hold significant leadership positions within government and secular society.[37] As time progressed, leadership became more about status rather than function and was therefore a key motivator in a civilization dominated by hierarchical structures. What emerged in the Christendom era was a clear distinction between professionals and amateurs—an increasing divide between the clergy and the laity.

Frank Viola notes the negative consequences of this position in his chapter *Reimagining Leadership* in which he highlights that the clergy/laity divide "has allowed

---

32. Murray, *Church after Christendom*, 22.
33. Rusaw and Swanson, *The Externally Focused Church*, 16.
34. Keller, "The Missional Church."
35. Driscoll, *Confessions of a Reformission Rev.*, 26–7.
36. Bosch, *Transforming Mission*, 467.
37. Pamphilius and Schaff, "Nicene and Post-Nicene Fathers Series 11."

the body of Christ to lapse into an audience due to its heavy reliance on a single leader."[38] The effects of this are unhealthy and damaging to both the leaders and the churches they lead.[39]

In the current climate there are a plethora of leadership models appearing—each claiming to be more effective or biblically based. One example which has emerged is the corporate or organizational model. Perhaps the most well known church to take its cue from the secular corporate world is Willow Creek. At their Global Leadership Summit held each year, Willow Creek has expert presenters from the secular world, such as Jim Collins and Colin Powell, addressing their audience on matters of leadership and management.[40]

There are criticisms to this approach of leadership and organizational structure, with claims that, "successful churches are reaching deep into business theory to feed their habit" (in regards to achieving rapid growth).[41] The *Economist* asserts, "the merger between business and religion has been fabulously successful in America"—it now has the rest of the world in its sights.

However, the worrying trend of secular bureaucracies led to the 2003 documentary, *The Corporation*, in which a psychological profile is performed on the modern-day corporation, with the profile revealing the corporation as "psychopathic." Drawing from the ideas of German sociologist, Max Weber, the *Economist* summarizes his position,

> Bureaucracies have flourished because their efficient and rational division and application of labor is powerful. But a cost attends this power. As cogs in a larger, purposeful machine, people become alienated from the traditional morals that guide human relationships as they pursue the goal of the collective organization.[42]

This should serve as a caution for the church as it gleans from secular leadership and management. With churches "dubbing their senior functionaries CEOs and COOs" it is worth highlighting that the embrace of titles, office, and status over function is characteristic of the institutional and bureaucratic mindset, but runs contrary to that of a movement, which implies function and fluidity.[43]

In opposition to and rejection of this corporate model, some have opted for the decentralized, almost *leaderless* approach to church leadership and governance. Mark Sayers suggests that this reaction in some circles is similar to the decentralized nature of movements such as Al Qaeda: "It seemed to herald the arrival of a new fluid,

---

38. Viola, *Reimagining Church*, 160 (see 153–65).
39. Murray, *Church after Christendom*, 188.
40. Chu, "How Willow Creek Is Leading Evangelicals by Learning from the Business World."
41. *Economist*, "Church as Businesses."
42. *Economist*, "The Lunatic You Work For."
43. *Economist*, "Church as Businesses."

organic style of organization which would come to dominate the world."[44] However, certain commentators have recently suggested that Al Qaeda was most effective as a top-down, hierarchical organization. As Malcolm Gladwell states, "Al Qaeda was most dangerous when it was a unified hierarchy. Now that it has dissipated into a network, it has proved far less effective."[45] Proponents of this position often argue that a move away from the role of the professional clergy is necessary because it has oppressive tendencies and becomes a "quest for power," restricting a congregation's spiritual growth, rendering it "lame." [46] However, as Stuart Murray suggests, these "attempts by some emerging churches to abolish leadership structures have been discouraging" because there are many references to leadership in the New Testament.[47]

This highlights one of the difficulties in deciphering a biblical structure of church government and servantship. There has been a move to recover some of the neglected ministries, which include the apostolic, prophetic, and evangelistic gifts. Specific attention has been given to understanding the apostolic task, which is seen as a reference point for the other ministries.[48]

Frost and Hirsch use the term APEPT to describe the fivefold ministry model found in Ephesians 4.[49] They argue that,

> Only when all five roles are operating within the leadership of a local congregation, and the congregation as a whole has embraced the five functions within its corporate life, can one say that an APEPT version of leadership is occurring. We believe such a matrix is the antidote to the triangular or hierarchical model that empowers certain leaders and disempowers the majority of Christians.[50]

However, the biblical picture of servantship and church governance is a little more ambiguous due to the "lack of didactic material" and the fact that there is "no unitary pattern."[51] Millard Erickson suggests that there are no specific teaching texts or commands for churches to "adopt a particular form of church order" (e.g. APEPT). And the passages in 1 Tim 3:1–13 and Titus 1:5–9 only provide a list of basic qualifications for positions which previously existed. Stuart Murray also suggests that the focal point of Ephesians 4 is not on church leadership but rather on a "harmonious church."[52] Furthermore, in the descriptive texts one sees multiple models emerge.

---

44. Sayers, "The Weakness of Social Networking Vs Discipleship and Depth."
45. Gladwell, "Small Change."
46. Viola, *Reimagining Church*, 161.
47. Murray, *Church after Christendom*, 188.
48. Hirsch and Altclass, *The Forgotten Ways Handbook*, 115.
49. Frost and Hirsch, *Shaping of Things to Come*, 165–81.
50. Ibid., 225.
51. Erickson, *Christian Theology*, 1094.
52. Murray, *Church after Christendom*, 189.

Some seem to highlight a more democratic form, while others have strong "monarchical elements."[53] In conclusion, Erickson suggests that the evidence from the New Testament is inconclusive.

What is seen is that "each church adopted a pattern that fit its individual situation" and it was likely that servantship and governance structures could have taken on a variety of forms depending on the specific context (e.g. Jewish, Greek, etc.). Therefore, as the church discerns the implications of servantship in the new paradigm, it is important that, in the pursuit of God's mission in his world, his church is judicious and wise in its approach to servantship and governance. The embrace of neglected ministries such as the apostle, prophet, and evangelist is helpful as it validates certain characteristics and gifts which have been suppressed throughout Christendom. Discovering how to best utilize, empower, and release these gifts (as well as all ministries) within the church and wider community is crucial. However, the servantship emphasis in post-Christendom should be less on developing a specific model and more on empowering churches to adopt a "pattern to fit its individual situation."[54] Each situation is contextually shaped, taking into account the gift make-up of the faith community and the type of servantship required. It is also important for the focus to remain on function rather than title or office.

What is encouraging and equally important is that the church continues to ask questions regarding the roles, forms, and structures of servantship in the new paradigm—both how the church can be more biblical and how it can be more effective in making disciples and preparing God's people for works of service.[55] As Stuart Murray summarizes, the role of the leader is to "empower rather than perform, to develop processes to sustain the community and equip those who really are on the front line."[56]

Exploring the shifts in culture, mission, church, and servantship impact on the climate in which the church today is situated. The movement from Christendom to post-Christendom challenges the way the church thinks and operates. It needs to redefine servantship based on context and develop leaders accordingly. In this, the divide between the clergy and the laity must wane, encouraging participation and a multi-voice approach. Alongside this it is necessary for the church to maintain a healthy tension between sending people out and bringing people in.

Individual and Corporate Servantship Practices

- Rediscover the journey in Acts of a marginal and persecuted church flourishing.
- Do a Bible study/personal study of the way the Bible explores the relationship

---

53. Erickson, *Christian Theology*, 1094–95.
54. Ibid.
55. Matthew 28:19–20 and Ephesians 4:12.
56. Murray, *Church after Christendom*, 191.

Movement Three—From Theories to Courageous Practices

- between the "believer" and the world (e.g., John 17).
- Develop networks with local government and community organizations.
- Take time to understand the needs and particular demographics of your community.
- Participate in events within the local community.
- Consider your church's governance and management practices (i.e., budgets and outcomes) regularly to ensure there is a balanced focus between the internal and external.
- Regularly (from the platform and in small groups) talk about the wide variety of spiritual gifts in Scripture and present these in your church.
- Celebrate and share stories of people being empowered to use their gifts.

Question for Reflection and Discussion

- What does it look like for your church to reorientate itself to engage with the increasingly non-Christian society around it?
- Does the church need to be at the center of culture in order to influence it? How can you influence society from the margins?
- How does the Christendom mindset affect the way the church practices and understands worship, discipleship, community, and mission?
- What type of servantship structures have you experienced within the church? How might this be made more contextual?
- Does your church represent the 80/20 rule—20 percent of the people do 80 percent of the work? What would it look like for this to shift?

17

Welcoming Multiculturalism

Christine McGowan

This chapter reflects on the vision and multicultural ministry of West Ryde Baptist Church community. It considers their vision and the practical and social implications of missional changes and strategies which they have implemented in their desire to be a multi-ethnic community reflecting both the diversity around them and the kingdom of God. Examples are given which reveal what it has meant for them to contextualize the gospel and be missional in a rapidly changing multicultural society.

These strategies, changes, and examples are considered alongside biblical principles and theological insights, together with the opinion and experience of relevant contemporary writers and practitioners. From these it becomes clear that the biblical model for the church is one of unity and equality within the body of Christ; that followers of Jesus are called to follow his example of extending grace, love, and acceptance to *all* people, regardless of age, gender, or culture.

A Visible Sign, Witness, and Foretaste of the Kingdom

West Ryde Baptist Church is a community which seeks to be a multicultural church reflecting the diversity in the community around them in their servantship, membership, and witness. Their desire is to be a visible sign, witness, and foretaste in their community of the kingdom of God, where together people from every nation and tribe worship God together.

West Ryde Baptist Church (WRBC) is situated in the northern suburbs of Sydney, Australia. It originated as a church plant in 1924 from a neighboring Baptist church in

Movement Three—From Theories to Courageous Practices

Eastwood. Church membership currently stands at seventy-nine,[1] although regular attendance at Sunday's service would be closer to one hundred and ten. This church is part of a local community which has undergone significant change in recent years, shifting from a predominantly white Caucasian population to one that is now culturally diverse.

According to the 2006 National Census, West Ryde had 19,073 residents, made up of numerous ethnic groups including Australian[2] (53 percent), Chinese [plus Hong Kong] (8.5 percent), Korean (4 percent), Indian (3.4 percent), and British (2.2 percent).[3] There are many church denominations in the West Ryde area including Anglican, Baptist (Australian and Chinese Baptist), Catholic, Christadelphian, Korean, Lutheran, Presbyterian, Uniting Church, and a number of independent charismatic churches.[4]

As the demographics of the local community changed, so too the realization that our understanding and practice of doing mission and evangelism also had to change. Jesus's command in Matthew 28:19–20 took on new significance as we reflected on the reality that "all nations" had now come to West Ryde. Being a missionary no longer referred solely to overseas mission, as our local community was now a mission-field and we its missionaries.[5] Missiologist Lesslie Newbigin affirms this finding saying, "The greatest challenge to Christian mission [is] now within the very nations that had once sent missionaries out around the world."[6]

This realization resulted in many changes for our church, including an intentional new direction and focus. This led to a redefining of our vision in 2007 to one that reflected our desire to live out the words of Revelation 7:9–10: "After this I looked and there before me was a great multitude that no one could count from every nation, tribe, people, and language, standing before the throne and in front of the Lamb." The vision of WRBC is now, "To inspire everyone to follow God in his plan for every people of every culture to worship him together."

A re-evaluation of current values was another change that came with this new thinking. We recognized that being missionary in a multicultural society meant mission needed to become a core value of the church's character and life. As such we changed our values statement to one that reflected a commitment to value our

---

1. As of 16th October 2012—according to the church secretary. Members who are currently actively involved in church life would be approximately fifty-six and non-members about twenty (not including children).

2. The terms Australian and western used in this chapter refer to "Australians of Anglo-European origin" and are used interchangeably. Indigenous Australians are not a visible minority in West Ryde.

3. The census results also include religious affiliation—Catholic (30.1 percent), No Religion (16.6 percent), Anglican (12.9 percent), Hindu (4.0 percent), and Presbyterian and Reformed (4.0 percent). Statistics, "2006 Census Quickstats."

4. TrueLocal, "West Ryde."

5. Kimball, *Emerging Church*, 69.

6. Newbigin cited in Roxburgh, *What Is Missional Church?*, 3.

differences, and embrace a willingness to learn and change. It also included our desire to connect with the wider community as we "reach out beyond ourselves with the message of Jesus Christ." The congregation was encouraged to intentionally seek opportunities to be a blessing to all peoples regardless of culture or beliefs, demonstrating Christ through their words and actions—an idea David Boyd discusses in detail in his book *You Don't Have to Cross the Ocean to Reach the World*.[7]

Changing the vision and values of the church was not easy and not everyone was keen to come on board. Leaders learnt early on that we could not be too idealistic or expect everyone to embrace the vision as this only led to frustration, discouragement, and disappointment.[8] Bringing in these changes was a slow and challenging process that included many hours of individual and communal prayer. Extensive teaching was provided to help people as they wrestled with what these changes actually meant for the church; teaching on the biblical foundation, on the how and why we were now moving to intentionally become a multi-ethnic church.

There was also a growing recognition that we could no longer expect people to come to us or rely on using an attractional model for ministry. We instead needed to change our approach to one that was missional; that reached out seeking connections and building relationships with people in the community. This meant learning to better understand our local context and think cross-culturally as traditional missionaries have done in the past. It meant continually asking questions about what God was doing in the world and seeking ways to join him in his mission.[9]

Alan Roxburgh and Scott Boren refer to "the called-out community of God in the midst of the specificity of a culture."[10] By this they mean that we need to contextualize the gospel into our unique cultural context, and be a presence in that neighborhood. Michael Frost and Alan Hirsch call this contextualization: "Understanding the language, longings, lifestyle patterns, and worldview of the host community and adjusting our practices accordingly without compromising the gospel."[11] For WRBC to be what Paul calls "all things to all people" we realized we would need to know, understand, and accept our cultural differences.[12]

Whilst there are many different and valid ways a church community can express the kingdom of God, we chose to commit ourselves to contextualizing the gospel in a multicultural context, rather than selecting a culture and contextualizing to it. We decided the best way to carry out the *missio Dei* or mission of God in the context of our culturally diverse community was to embrace *all* people and so provide a glimpse of

---

7. Boyd, *You Don't Have to Cross the Ocean*, 42.
8. Deymaz and Li, *Ethnic Blends*, 131.
9. Van Gelder cited in Roxburgh, *What Is Missional Church?*, 7.
10. Ibid.
11. Frost and Hirsch, *Shaping of Things to Come*, 85.
12. 1 Corinthians 9:19–23.

the unity we can have in Christ.[13] Welcoming and accepting *all* people demonstrates that the traditional and social distinctions of the wider society no longer have a place, thus removing their power and laying a basis for social change.[14]

As such we have resisted the easier option of having separate congregations of different ethnic groups meeting separately in the same building, even with shared servantship. Our desire to be a multi-ethnic, multi-generational church led to our having just one inclusive service which feels more like a gathering than a meeting. This service is intentionally kept short, only allowing time for essentials such as worship in song, prayer, communion, Bible reading, and teaching, usually in the form of a sermon. It is strategically designed to bring people together, allowing more time for building relationships within the context of cross-cultural differences, and providing greater opportunity for participation, conversation, and interactivity.

Reflecting the Diversity of Our Surrounding Community

WRBC is now a church which intentionally reflects the gender, generational, and cultural diversity of the surrounding community. There is an almost equal ratio of males to females within this church, and ages are reasonably spread from small children to the elderly.[15] Different cultural groups are also represented, with the most populous cultures being Australian (58 percent), Korean (22 percent), Chinese [Hong Kong and Mainland China] (9 percent), and Filipino (5 percent).[16]

However, we recognize that there is still a long way to go if we are to be truly reflective of our local community. This becomes clear when you consider that some ethnic groups are absent from the church body yet are represented in the local community, such as the Indian community. As such we are continually seeking new ways and opportunities to reach after our vision. One new possibility currently being trialed is missional satellites. This involves small groups choosing and being committed to a particular missional focus, such as specific ethnic groups. Members are encouraged to get to know this culture, praying and thinking strategically about how they can reach this group with the gospel.

Living as part of a postmodern global community, diverse in culture, religion, and ideology, has meant people in western cultures now share life with people of different beliefs and values. To better understand those with differing beliefs and values to us, WRBC held seminars with speakers invited to come and share about

---

13. Grenz, *The Baptist Congregation*, 87.

14. Edgar, "Multiculturalism Is an Essential Part of the Gospel," 3; McKnight, *Galatians*, 201.

15. The figures for congregational size are an approximation taken from a review of the 2011 church directory.

16. The majority of Koreans at WRBC are, however, part of "mission homes" set up as a ministry of a Korean pastor who also attends this church. Their numbers continually vary, as most are students and generally in Australia for only one year before returning home to Korea.

the lifestyle, beliefs, and values of their particular ethnic group and religion. These evenings proved popular with people from the local community as well as building bridges between us. These evenings revealed areas of similarity shared by cultures, which created opportunities for further dialogue.[17] They also gave people a starting point for sharing their faith with those outside the church, much like Paul did in Acts 17.[18]

The seminars also reminded us that being part of a religiously diverse society means we need to be considerate of other people's beliefs. There are many people in our community who are skeptical and struggle to believe in absolute truth. When we declare Christ to be the only way to God we are declaring their religious beliefs to be untrue.[19] This calls for us to show grace and sensitivity so as not to be perceived as arrogant and intolerant.

Because of this we seek to demonstrate tolerance by showing the inclusive and unconditional love of Christ. This is not about accepting other beliefs as truth, but accepting the people who hold them. It is about not being dogmatic or condescending of people or their views but showing respect by listening to what they have to say.[20] Through playgroups, English as a Second Language, and English conversation classes, WRBC offers both a service to the local community and an opportunity for church members to build relationships with those outside the church. These non-threatening contexts provide opportunities for questions to be asked and stories shared.

In our attempt to emphasize community engagement we encourage church members to intentionally reach out into the community like Jesus did, meeting people where they are at, addressing their needs and desires in culturally relevant ways. This means spending time with neighbors, work colleagues, and local shop workers—for example, being friendly and welcoming, talking, listening, and getting to know them.

Whilst most church members would acknowledge our equal value to God and the priesthood of *all* believers, Dan Sheffield argues we need to go further and ensure people *feel* like they have a "valid voice" and are "equal in value and worth to the community as a whole."[21] This attitude leaves no room for any one group or culture to dominate another. It reminds us that the gospel demands "the powerful to give up power and the powerless to endure and be faithful," as all are called to follow the example of Christ who voluntarily gave up power and privilege for the sake of the kingdom.[22]

---

17. Similarities include many moral and ethical truths such as honesty, charity, and good works; a common desire for social justice issues, caring for the marginalized, feeding the poor, and freeing the oppressed; our belief in a higher power, such as God or gods, and acknowledgement of the failure of humanity, and resulting in their separation from God.

18. Gnanakan, *Proclaiming Christ in a Pluralistic Context*, 106.

19. Dickson, *If I Were God*, 205.

20. Muck, *Those Other Religions in Your Neighborhood*, 101.

21. Sheffield, "Leading a Multi-Cultural Congregation," 6.

22. Law, *The Wolf Shall Dwell with the Lamb*, 42.

Movement Three—From Theories to Courageous Practices

To this end WRBC encourages people from different cultural backgrounds to participate in all areas of church community life, worship, and congregational decision-making.[23] Our commitment to every-member ministry, actively and intentionally seeks to equip, empower, and release *all* people to minister out of their gifts, abilities, passions, and life experience.[24] Evidence of *all* people being encouraged to serve and participate is reflected in the cultural diversity of those involved in worship leading, prayer, Bible reading, and the make-up of the servantship and pastoral teams. The danger of tokenism, or making a perfunctory gesture toward the inclusion of minority group members, is, however, a concern that requires continual reflection by the church's servantship.

One of the difficulties of having this cultural diversity is determining which culture the community will operate under, as it is impossible to be culture-free. The existence of two dominant cultures at WRBC, a particular Asian group and Anglo-Celtic Australians, has made this task more difficult and has resulted in the need for ongoing vigilance to ensure we do not become a bi-cultural rather than multicultural church. It was decided that as the church was part of a contemporary Australian context this would be the preferred culture to operate under, and English would be the language emphasized and used in WRBC's gathering times.

Whilst all agreed with this decision in theory, its practical application has not been easy. Discussion and disagreement have ensued between church leaders and one of our Asian pastors who wanted to create a second service to cater specifically for the needs of Asian students whose English is poor (i.e., students of one particular ethnicity). However, this was strongly discouraged for a number of reasons: (1) it is not only Asian students of this particular ethnicity who struggle with English; (2) it increases the risk of the church becoming two distinct communities; and (3) to have a separate service works against the strategy WRBC has adopted for pursuing its vision of all people worshipping God together.

To help this situation a number of ideas were suggested. People were encouraged to pray and worship in their own language and style if they so desired. Full sermon notes were provided each week to help meet the needs of those who struggle to follow or understand the sermon. Homogenous small groups were also encouraged as we recognized the desire of some ethnic groups to continue to speak in their own language, practice some of their own traditions, and worship God in their own heart language. These groups provide a place for people to pray, learn, and build relationships with people from their own cultural background.

All parties have worked through this difference of opinion and vision with grace, understanding, and love. Different views are to be expected in a multicultural church—when we deal with this difference with genuine love we display the values of the kingdom of God to the world.

23. Grenz, *The Baptist Congregation*, 82; 1 Peter 2:9.
24. Romans 12; 1 Corinthians 12; Ephesians 4.

Overcoming Difference—Transforming into a Multicultural Church

Over the past five years there have been a number of significant changes at WRBC which reflect our commitment to being inclusive and to connecting with the local community. West Ryde is filled with people from diverse backgrounds who have no extended family and speak little English. Many are isolated in small crowded units with few friends and are seeking community and a place to belong. As a people who belong to God, WRBC understands it is called to continue the *missio Dei* by partnering with God to "build a community where all people belong."[25] As such we seek to reflect God's love for *all* people by providing a place that welcomes *all* people, offering them acceptance and love.[26]

This building of unity is encouraged through various church community activities which promote acceptance and inclusivity. One such activity is our joining together each Sunday after the service to share in a lunch hosted by the Koreans in our congregation. This shared lunch is particularly important to those from Asian backgrounds who see Sunday as a day set aside for time with church family.[27] Many miss this aspect of their culture and struggle to understand how westerners can go to a church service and then go home.

Other activities include social events such as picnics, fellowship occasions, and small groups which can be general or specific to a particular age, gender, culture, or interest. The small group Bible study for young mothers, with its mixture of ethnicities—Korean, Irish, Filipino, Sri Lankan, and Australian—is an example of different cultures growing in community. They put aside differences and share life together.

For those outside the church community there are ESL classes, the homework club, friendship club, conversational English classes, the annual international dinner, and the Christmas concert. These last two events have been particularly successful in the past at building connections with people from the local community who come and share stories, singing, and dancing from the traditions of their particular country.

WRBC's multicultural vision has been a key factor for many people being drawn to this church—particularly those from Asian backgrounds who want to be part of an English-speaking congregation and community. This has at times proven difficult for one of our Asian pastors who sees himself as a missionary to his ethnicity in Australia, and tends to single out and take responsibility for any people of that ethnicity who visit the church. Unfortunately this has resulted in some choosing not to stay, leading to discord between this pastor and the church servantship. Recognizing that much

---

25. Richmond, "Struggles in Multicultural and Cross-Cultural Ministry."
26. James 2:1–4.
27. Anderson and Cabellon, *Multicultural Ministry Handbook*, 95.

of the tension is due to language and cultural differences has meant solving this difference of opinion with humility, persistence, patience, understanding, grace, prayer, and love.

Conflict is to be expected, however, as we live with two realities: the fractured, divided society we live in and the kingdom reality of Galatians 3:28 where, "There is neither Jew nor Greek, slave nor free, male nor female, for you are all one in Christ Jesus." Division created by our cultural differences is in many ways an expression of the curse of the Fall, which has been lifted through the life, death, and resurrection of Jesus Christ.

In Revelation 5:9 and 7:8–12 we see the reversal of this curse with "all tribes and people and languages" worshipping God together. David Boyd writes, "The New Testament teaches that our ethnicity is not a reason for creating division. Rather, the gathering together of many races within the church is an incredible declaration of the redemptive plan of God and is the greatest visible expression of unity the world can see."[28]

One of the difficulties WRBC has faced in becoming a multicultural church in a post-modern society is the wide gap between our two primary cultures, an Asian ethnicity and Anglo-Celtic Australian. Whilst the Australian culture becomes increasingly more secular and individualistic, this particular Asian group continues to remain more traditional, Christianized, and communal. This Asian community tends to think in terms of "us and we," and Australians in "I and my." This Asian culture is hierarchical and status is ascribed, meaning pastors are automatically recognized as the absolute authority deserving of respect and obedience—unlike western culture where trust and respect are earned over time.[29]

These differences are also evident in the expectations of obedience between the senior pastor (Anglo-Celtic Australian) and a pastor of one of our Asian groups. The majority of Australian members struggle to attend one Bible study each week or meet for prayer once a month, whilst the students of this Asian group meet as directed for prayer each morning at 5.30am and on Friday evenings; attend Bible studies three evenings a week and on Sunday afternoons, and are involved in evangelism at Strathfield on Saturday nights. Some within this Asian group have expressed their view that Australians are lacking in commitment and respect—while some Australians perceive these Asian students to be legalistically obedient.

Cultural differences expressed in both verbal and non-verbal communication through posture, eye contact, facial expressions, and touch have also lead to tension and misunderstanding. A recent example of this was a phone call that began with "What can I do for you?" The Asian receiver interpreted this as the caller thinking they always want something. The tendency of some cultures not to look a person in the eye has been interpreted by others as being rude, aloof, or disinterested, rather

---

28. Boyd, *You Don't Have to Cross the Ocean*, 140.
29. Law, *The Wolf Shall Dwell with the Lamb*.

than submissive or respectful as intended.[30] These differences make unity and building relationships more complex than in a homogenous church.

Yet the example of the early church shows that the gospel is big enough to prevail over our differences. Love and grace triumph over difference and misunderstanding. Throughout the New Testament we see churches confronted by and overcoming the difficulties associated with cultural diversity. Acts 6, 11, and 15 tell of situations which threatened to divide the church, and Paul's letter to the Ephesians explains and promotes the unity of the local church for the sake of the gospel.[31] This unity does not mean uniformity; being *one* people does not mean individuals have to lose their culture, i.e., stop being Filipino, Chinese, or Korean. It means our differences no longer represent barriers to fellowship; believers now "belong to each other in a way that distinctions which formerly divided them lose significance."[32]

Our equality in Christ transcends our differences as together we are a new creation, the body of Christ.[33] WRBC seeks to recognize that all cultures are valid, encouraging people to retain their culture whilst seeking to create a new culture which reflects the kingdom of God. We encourage interaction between people from different cultural backgrounds, seeing this as a way to broaden our understanding and experience of biblical truth and helping them see the limitations and strengths of their own.

In *Crossing Borders*, Helen Richmond and Myong Duk Yang comment that the "greatest hindrance to becoming a multicultural church is the attachment to our own cultures."[34] This has been the reality at WRBC for many who through arrogance or ignorance believe "*our* way is the best, right, or only way." People's biases have surfaced as changes have been made to meals, music, singing styles, and prayer. Some have struggled to accept the value of doing things in a way foreign to their cultural background and traditions, especially those who have been at the church for a long time. Yet one church member recently commented, "some of us would prefer to keep things as they are, but we realize that change is necessary if we are to continue to be relevant in the community in the future." There is also the fear of losing identity and being taken over, which again comes mostly from the older church members who remember the "good old days" and seek to have things as they used to be.

There is, however, congregational agreement that to remain relevant and be effective for Christ we must continue to "move from an ethnocentric worldview to one that embraces both the stranger and the citizen."[35] Though not easy, most recognize this calls for a commitment which involves sacrifice, tolerance, patience, love, and

---

30. Thew, "My Neighbour Is Korean."
31. Hawthorne et al., *Dictionary of Paul and His Letters*, 464.
32. Gaebelein et al., *Expositor's Bible Commentary*, 468; John 17:21–23; Ephesians 4:2–6.
33. Romans 12; 1 Corinthians 12; Ephesians 2:11–19.
34. Richmond and Yang, *Crossing Borders Shaping Faith*, 316.
35. Boyd, *You Don't Have to Cross the Ocean*, 127.

Movement Three—From Theories to Courageous Practices

respect.[36] For many it means changes in attitude and practice. To help the congregation become more inclusive and desiring to be multicultural, the leaders keep the church's vision at the forefront of their teaching and practice, educating and modeling this to the church community. The *missio Dei* and the role believers play are kept before the congregation. There have been intentional changes in vocabulary, moving from an "us and them" terminology to a "we and our."[37]

Healthy, strong, cross-cultural relationships are essential in multi-ethnic churches where it is so easy to misinterpret another's actions or words. A recent example of this was a conversation I had with one of our Asian pastors. Our conversation seemed straightforward to me, but due to the sensitive nature of the issue we were discussing I sent him an email to clarify that I had understood him correctly. The next day I received an email from him and a call from his wife both distressed at my representation of our conversation. Thankfully we both valued our relationship enough to pursue the matter and seek a resolution, which involved discussing the issue through further emails and obtaining the help of a third party. This highlights the importance of honest, open dialogue and the need for issues of conflict to be acknowledged and managed appropriately, as Jesus instructs in Matthew 18:15–20.[38]

It is clear from Scripture that followers of Jesus Christ are called to follow his example of extending grace, love, and acceptance to all people, regardless of age, gender, or culture. West Ryde Baptist Church seeks to do this by being a multicultural church which reflects the diversity in the community around us in both our servantship and membership. We seek to be a visible sign, witness, and foretaste in the community of the kingdom of God where together people from every nation and tribe worship our amazing God together.

Individual and Corporate Servantship Practices

- Be intentional about being a multicultural church community—unity in diversity does not come by accident.

- Get to know your local context and think cross-culturally. Spend time in the community. Learn about the different ethnic groups. Intentionally engage people in conversation and build relationships by frequenting the same shop or café and getting involved in community activities. Prayerfully discern where God is already at work and how you can partner with him.

- Establish a biblical and theological foundation for becoming a multicultural church. Provide teaching and training on what it means to be a multicultural church. Invite speakers in from churches already practicing this ministry.

36. Philippians 2:1–4; Ephesians 2:14–25.
37. Thew, "My Neighbour Is Korean."
38. Deymaz and Li, *Ethnic Blends*, 47.

- As a church, establish values and develop a vision statement which reflects your desire for unity in diversity. Continue to remind and educate the congregation as to why you are seeking to be multicultural, ensuring they are on side.

- Build multicultural servantship and ministry teams which send the message "all are welcome and have a voice here." Develop cultural diversity in your service leaders, music teams, welcomers, preachers, and other up-front roles such as prayer and Bible reading.

- Create an inclusive church service which reflects the cultural diversity of your congregation and community. Be open to different styles of worship and encourage people of different ethnicities to express worship in their own heart language.

- Be mindful of those from non-English-speaking (or English-as-second-language) backgrounds. Consider providing full sermon notes, using simple PowerPoint slides and other visual aids. Ensure preachers don't speak too fast, use slang, or jargon.

- Have a welcome sign out the front in different languages.

- Build relationships which cross the cultural boundaries. Share meals, socialize together, and encourage small groups and conversation.

- Enjoy and celebrate your diversity. Create opportunities for people to share things from their own cultural background, e.g., food, dance, dress, story, etc. Hold an international dinner and invite people from the community.

Questions for Reflection and Discussion

- How would you describe a healthy multicultural church? Is this your church? If not, what intentional steps could you take to change this and become a more welcoming, inclusive church community?

- Consider the structure, programs, practices, and decision-making in your church—do they reflect the cultural diversity present in your church community?

- What do you learn from Galatians 3:26–29 about living and ministering in a culturally diverse society today?

18

Cultivating Narrative and Storytelling

Christine Redwood

I work as an associate part-time pastor in an established church. This church is situated in the middle-class suburb of Hornsby in Sydney. I oversee the evening congregation. My focus is how to make disciples committed to Jesus, particularly among the younger generation. This is an important missional question, since the majority of young adults in Australia are not connected to the Christian faith, and show no interest in wanting to engage. Understanding contemporary culture is vital in making the changes necessary to reach this emerging generation. The aspect of contemporary culture relevant to my ministry situation is postmodernity. This is a transitional label which tries to capture the shift happening in western culture. Postmodernity will be studied with regard to how this shift has affected communication. One of the theological insights discovered is the value of stories. There is a shift back to the Scriptures as a narrative calling people to be disciples with their whole lives. Storytelling is one way to connect with postmodern young adults.

My Ministry Situation

I am a pastor who serves at Hornsby Baptist Church. I direct the evening congregation which meets together at 6pm every Sunday. The congregation predominantly consists of young adults and youth. In the wider community a large percentage of people hold some form of formal qualification, like a diploma or degree.[1] Most of the young adults in the church are also involved in pursuing further education. My attention is with the young adults, teaching them about the mission of God, and equipping them

---

1. Statistics, "What Are Our Qualifications?"

so they might reach other young adults in the Hornsby Shire of Sydney. I want to be part of the movement in this church to embodying a more missional ecclesiology. Missional churches understand that the church came into existence as the kingdom of God was established through Christ and the Spirit, and that the church is called "to participate in God's mission in the world."[2]

Making disciples with this missional focus among young adults is vital, as they are both the present and future church. This age group can be categorized as part of Generation Y, those born in the years between 1981 and 1995.[3] As wider research shows, right across Australia "attendance at religious services [is] quite low" among Generation Y, even among those who profess faith in Christ.[4] Forty-eight percent of young people do not identify "with any religion or denomination," and out of that number 20 percent had been raised as Christians but had rejected faith and Christian religious identification as young adults.[5] These are sobering statistics which emphasize the urgency for mission amongst this age group. Furthermore, with regard to my church, in the 2009 National Christian Life Survey, those between the ages of nineteen and twenty-five, when asked if they had a high level of satisfaction with Hornsby Baptist Church, revealed that thirty-eight were satisfied, twenty-three were neutral, and thirty-one were dissatisfied.[6] Serious theological reflection is needed in understanding contemporary Generation Y culture, and then forming new missional strategies, worship environments, interpersonal connections, and church practices.

Contemporary Culture: Postmodernity

Contemporary culture can be examined from many angles. People researching the generational characteristics and changes of Generation Y noticed that something bigger was changing—western culture was transitioning. Not only was there a generational shift, but also "a philosophical disconnect with the wider culture" was occurring with the church.[7] This cultural shift is often described as a move away from modernity to postmodernity. How the church engages with this change will have massive implications for the nature of the church and its mission in the twenty-first century.[8] I want to examine this change in contemporary culture in light of what it might mean for how the western church communicates the gospel to people today.

Postmodernity questions modern assumptions and has brought helpful correctives. In modernity it was common for communication to be seen as transmitting

2. Van Gelder, "From Corporate Church to Missional Church," 446.
3. Mason, *The Spirit of Generation Y*, 228.
4. Ibid., 124.
5. Ibid., 78.
6. Research, "Young Adult Retention," 20.
7. Gibbs and Bolger, *Emerging Churches*, 32.
8. Long, *Emerging Hope*, 20–21.

knowledge from the sender to the receiver. Knowledge was driven by logic and linear ways of thinking, and this influenced the way sermons were crafted and delivered.[9] For many modern churches the Bible is still approached as an object to be examined. The predominant way the gospel is proclaimed is through expositional preaching.[10] The danger with this preaching style is the tendency to reduce the gospel so that it becomes "entirely cerebral" as people assent to the right doctrines without any transforming moment with God.[11] There is also a tendency for preachers to come across as arrogant, as the only ones with God's knowledge, imparting such information to the passive congregation.[12] Young adults no longer put their trust in a preacher or their assertions simply because of their role, and authority figures are regarded with suspicion.[13] In a postmodern culture there is a shift away from these practices, to "symbolic communication" which allows people more freedom to engage.[14] Indeed, the very notions of truth and knowledge have come under great scrutiny.

The word "truth" has become a contested word in our culture. The modern world view was driven by the discovery of objective truth. As it stripped away pre-modern myths and pursued scientific rational analysis it believed it could understand the world and thus be better able to pursue a brighter future.[15] Emergent theologians often critique the church for buying too much into this modern framework. Brian McLaren describes Christians as making God into "our image" so that the gospel is likewise communicated as objective, something that could be grasped through "logical argument . . . absolute principles, propositions, formulae, like any good scientist."[16] Now postmodern thinkers have begun to question whether objective truth is even possible, and they have illustrated how people work in a context with "particular narratives."[17] The dominant modern metanarrative described the world as "steadily moving towards . . . a new era of blessing for all." That narrative has collapsed under the weight of twentieth-century history, which was marked by war, oppression, and the growing gap between the rich and the poor.[18] As a result, metanarratives are now often viewed with suspicion. Postmodern thinkers stress how often the powerful used these stories to dominate and force a certain perspective on the world.[19] This challenge to metanarratives has resulted in "all the reigning master narratives los[ing]

---

9. Webber, *Ancient-Future Faith*, 24.
10. Riddell, *Threshold of the Future*, 53–54.
11. Ibid., 54.
12. Willimon, "Postmodern Preaching," 34.
13. Middleton and Walsh, *Truth Is Stranger Than It Used to Be*, 29.
14. Webber, *Ancient-Future Faith*, 24.
15. Grenz, *A Primer on Postmodernism*, 44.
16. McLaren, *More Ready Than You Realize*, 53.
17. Liederbach and Reid, *The Convergent Church*, 60.
18. Wright, *The Challenge of Jesus*, 115.
19. Grenz, *A Primer on Postmodernism*, 45.

their credibility," indeed the idea of metanarratives "is itself no longer credible."[20] This trend influences young people, who, when given a logical answer to a question, will respond with "whatever." Objective truth is not always as important to young adults as it is to the community of which they are a part. This will often determine the world view they take up.[21] Christians are theologically wrestling with this aspect of contemporary culture, with a variety of responses emerging.

There is a range of theological approaches on offer when it comes to communicating the truth of the gospel in contemporary culture. The foundation for Christians has to be the Bible, which declares itself to be God's word and thus true.[22] Yet one approach by Brian McLaren wants to avoid such "arguments that pit absolutism versus relativism." He sees these arguments as distracting and ineffective when it comes to witnessing in a postmodern, pluralistic culture.[23] Instead of discussing absolute truth claims, McLaren argues that the missional focus should be on living a life of love, and calling people to be transformed by Jesus.[24] Another approach proposed by William Willimon suggests that Christians need to distance themselves from abstract propositions which modernists deal with, and, instead, maintain that knowledge and truth for a Christian come through a relationship with Jesus Christ.[25] Jesus says, "I am the way, the truth, and the life."[26] For Christians "all truth is relative" to Christ.[27]

Don Carson's approach challenges postmodernist arguments. For Carson, this is a serious epistemological issue which needs to be addressed. He critiques the hard postmodern perspective which sets up an impossible standard—either human beings have to be able to know everything completely, or we are incapable of knowing anything at all.[28] In other words, it demands "that we be God . . . or else forever condemned to knowing nothing objective for sure."[29] Proposing a new way, Carson calls for "critical realists" who can hold that meanings "can be adequately determined," while aware of the difficulties.[30] N. T. Wright takes a similar line, drawing together modern and postmodern thought. He argues one has to acknowledge the "reality of the thing known, as something other than the knower," that is there is objective reality, and yet we only know this reality through dialogue between "the knower and the thing

---

20. Ibid.
21. Long, *Emerging Hope*, 82.
22. 2 Chronicles 6:17; Psalm 33:4; Jeremiah 10:10; John 7:28; 1 John 5:20; Revelation 19:9.
23. Crouch, "Emergent Evangelicalism," 43.
24. Ibid., 42.
25. Willimon, "Postmodern Preaching," 35.
26. John 14:6.
27. Willimon, "Postmodern Preaching," 35.
28. Carson, *Becoming Conversant with Emergent*, 104–5.
29. Ibid.
30. Ibid., 110.

known."[31] That means being aware of what narrative you are working in.[32] People live in narratives; it is how we make sense of the world.[33] Once you are aware of what story you are operating in you can critically engage in the world with the story always open to been modified.[34] The church must dwell in the story of Jesus.

Theological Engagement: The Biblical Narrative

Communicating through story is very powerful in contemporary culture. John Drane reflects on the contradiction which exists in postmodernity—even though postmodern philosophers reject metanarratives, he argues that people are still searching for "a story that will give meaning to life."[35] The evidence of movies, songs, books, and television, shows the power of stories, and perhaps for many in popular culture there is still a search for a story bigger than themselves.[36] This is to be expected, concludes John Drane, since western culture is rapidly changing and many feel uncertainty. Stories are capable of articulating the emotional angst, and giving release and purpose.[37] Stories have the ability not just to reach the head but "engage the heart and indeed the whole person." They draw people in gently and reorient their imaginations.[38] Part of what it means to be a missional church is "through inculturation and contextualization" to bring the gospel to bear on culture.[39] Those who seek to communicate the gospel have to know the "landscape of the heart" of those in their community. They need to immerse themselves in the "stories, symbols, values, and rituals" of the people they are with, if the gospel is to have any power.[40] The church also needs to know and love the biblical narrative.

There is a great missional opportunity here as Christians turn to the narrative of the Scriptures. Christians are rediscovering Scripture as an overarching narrative concerning God's kingdom. The goal of communication for Christians is not simply to tell people about Jesus, but to see people becoming disciples of Jesus and being transformed as they enter the church community.[41] A postmodern understanding, rather than standing outside the biblical story, encourages people to "indwell the story . . . so that it becomes our story." It's about forming a relationship with God in the

---

31. Wright, *The New Testament and the People of God*, 35.
32. Ibid., 37.
33. MacIntyre, *After Virtue*, 212.
34. Wright, *The New Testament and the People of God*, 44.
35. Drane, *The McDonaldization of the Church*, 133.
36. Ibid.
37. Ibid., 136.
38. Bausch, *Storytelling*, 27.
39. Hill, *Salt, Light, and a City*, 172.
40. Troeger, *Preaching while the Church Is under Reconstruction*, 140.
41. Long, *Emerging Hope*, 181.

context you are in.[42] The biblical narrative takes precedence over systematic theology, and it is the biblical narrative the church must continue to return to.[43] The Christian story that is revealed in the Bible speaks about how God engages and reveals himself to people. Christians have to ultimately reject the postmodern belief that there are no metanarratives, as Christians have a center and it is the "story of Jesus of Nazareth" that we proclaim.[44] N. T. Wright suggests we offer the story of Jesus knowing that it is a "story of healing and self-giving love." Such a story in the power of the Spirit has the ability to put back together postmodern people who have deconstructed everything, including themselves.[45] The church must learn to communicate this narrative in meaningful ways to this new culture.

Communicating the gospel is not merely about imparting knowledge. Instead, it is through relationships that together we learn to live the gospel story in our lives. Young Christians tend to observe as well as listen to what Christian teachers say—"modeling is becoming crucial" as learning becomes relational.[46] The whole worship gathering needs more attention, with multiple voices given the opportunity to contribute.[47] For young adults engaged in university education, the "emphasis is on mixed-modes and flexible learning. Churches need to employ similar teaching methods."[48] For instance, worship gatherings need to be intentional as they encourage a "high level of participation," allowing all people to reflect and share their own stories as they see God at work in their lives.[49] Stuart Murray sees great value in what he terms "multi-voiced worship," which gives space for questioning and interactive learning. This often resonates with people in a pluralistic culture.[50] There is a real challenge for established churches to move congregations away from expressions of worship that require little of them, and many resist because it demands more. However, it is very worthwhile if it means that more people are able to become disciples of Jesus and integrate their beliefs with every aspect of their lives.[51] Churches which have God's mission at their heart will be seeking to use all they have to enable people to become "devoted disciples of Jesus Christ" in their "unique cultural and personal setting."[52] Thus the goal of communication is more "an invitation" to be part of "an alien people" formed around Jesus Christ. This, Hauerwas argues, is where the real shift occurred in the world—when

---

42. Middleton and Walsh, *Truth Is Stranger Than It Used to Be*, 174.
43. Bausch, *Storytelling*, 196.
44. Grenz, *A Primer on Postmodernism*, 164.
45. Wright, *The Challenge of Jesus*, 129.
46. Long, *Emerging Hope*, 84.
47. Ibid., 190.
48. Mason, *The Spirit of Generation Y*, 337.
49. Gibbs and Bolger, *Emerging Churches*, 172.
50. Murray, *Post-Christendom*, 267.
51. Gibbs and Bolger, *Emerging Churches*, 160.
52. Hill, *Salt, Light, and a City*, 177.

Movement Three—From Theories to Courageous Practices

God formed a new people.[53] The church is called to reflect and embody "a way of life together." This communication needs to be "experiential, personal, engaging," and relational.[54] This mindset changes the way worship gatherings function.

Worship gatherings are a time for the whole congregation to enact out the gospel narrative. Living in a culture that is influenced by postmodernity can have an impact on how worship gatherings are shaped. For instance, a church service need not always be linear, but could become a more fluid and organic gathering that gives space for people to encounter God.[55] Robert Webber draws on ancient church practices and notes how every facet of worship from the music, to the prayers, to the sacraments told the story of "God's saving work in history."[56] Dan Kimball points to the Bible to argue that worship should involve all our senses. Smell was engaged through incense, Christians laid hands on one another as they prayed, and they tasted the bread and the wine of the Lord's Supper. They heard music and Scripture readings, and saw the beauty of the place in which they worshipped.[57] This is particularly relevant for young people who live in a world where they are "constantly immersed in an intermingling and layering of the popular arts."[58] We can borrow from popular culture by blending images and words together to provide "rich interpretations."[59] However, Sarah Arthur cautions against getting too caught up in trying to tell every story experientially. God's word has the power to stand by itself, and sometimes simply telling the story evokes the imagination in powerful ways.[60] The worship services provide a space for people to immerse themselves each week in the story of Jesus, and thus be empowered to go out with the mission of God in their hearts and minds.

As for preaching, there is still a role, but it too needs to change to be appropriate in this emerging culture. Preaching, like the whole of the worship gathering, needs to wrestle with people's imaginations. Walter Brueggemann proposes that preaching "is an event of transformed imagination." He argues preachers need to become poets and storytellers as they present the good news concerning the kingdom of God breaking into this world; there is a new and alternative society which the church is called to participate in.[61] To reach people with this good news, and especially among the deep places of resistance, it will not be through more instruction but through stories.[62] One of the changes noted in the postmodern culture is a transition from being left-brain

---

53. Hauerwas and Willimon, *Resident Aliens*, 24.
54. Ibid., 105.
55. Kimball, *The Emerging Church*, 121.
56. Webber, *Ancient-Future Faith*, 104.
57. Exodus 25:6; Acts 6:6; 1 Corinthians 11:23–26; Psalm 150; 1 Kings 6:29–30.
58. Savage, *Making Sense of Generation Y*, 125.
59. Ibid.
60. Arthur, *The God-Hungry Imagination*, 151.
61. Brueggemann, *Finally Comes the Poet*, 109–10.
62. Ibid.

to right-brain thinkers (if that is a valid way to speak of the shifts in approaches to thought). In other words, this is a shift to a more experiential, non-linear, and creative culture.[63] The Bible is ripe with resources to draw from which evoke the imagination. What's more, a preacher's role (especially among young people saturated with the dominant stories of their culture) is to awaken a "sense of holy dissatisfaction." It is to help them question the other metanarratives on offer, and stir a desire to seek for the truth that is found in Christ.[64] Richard Jensen argues that preachers need to be conscious that they are preaching in a post-literate society.[65] This is a culture dominated by technology and visual stories, so Jensen maintains that preachers need to think in stories rather than ideas when forming their sermons (as this will better connect with the new culture).[66] Preachers need to become storytellers.

My Ministry Situation

Bringing this back to my own ministry situation, I have realized that working in an established church requires patience, since changing a church's culture takes time. Tom Sine advises to start small, experimenting and discerning where God is at work.[67] I suspect that there are both modern and postmodern cultural dynamics among Sydney's youth and young adults, and so wisdom and prayer are needed about what is right for this context. Small changes are happening. For the last few years we have grown a preaching team, so there are multiple people who preach, both women and men. These bring their stories and personalities to the text. Attempts have been made to include more participation, for example, breaking into small groups to pray, asking questions and allowing people to talk amongst themselves, and reading liturgies together. There have been both resistance and excitement regarding these changes. Yet church leaders are called to faithful improvisation. This means, at times, taking risks for the sake of God's mission. Churches engage in this not simply with their own creative efforts, but always in the strength of the Holy Spirit who "reminds us of the story and sheds light on our path."[68]

This year I have also experimented with changing the whole worship service. One night we had a creative service. There was no sermon, and instead there was an emphasis on singing and art. We set up different areas for people to worship in, based on the book of Revelation, which was the book we were working through in our preaching series. People painted scenes from Revelation, others formed discussion groups, incense was lit in conjunction with the offering, and people wrote prayers to

63. Frost and Hirsch, *The Shaping of Things to Come*, 184.
64. Ibid., 192.
65. Jensen, *Thinking in Story*, 55.
66. Ibid., 61.
67. Sine, *The New Conspirators*, 277.
68. Middleton and Walsh, *Truth Is Stranger Than It Used to Be*, 195.

God. Many responded and found it meaningful. The other experimental service held this year was a discussion night on the topic "Is there life after death?" Small groups formed around tables. People presented different perspectives, answering this question from an Atheistic, Hindu, Buddhist, Islamic, and then Christian viewpoint. After each world view was presented, questions were asked and the small groups discussed that world view. This was received well, and particularly by two new people who are spiritually seekers. One of them, who had never been to a church before, was amazed and excited to see a church prepared to discuss other viewpoints. Given this feedback these types of worship gatherings will continue to grow.

My view on preaching has shifted over the last eighteen months. I see myself primarily as one of God's storytellers. Thus I seek to tell and dwell in the story of Scripture, even occasionally constructing narrative sermons. I have, for instance, told the whole story of Esther as a first-person narrative. I believe preaching is an oral event and so try not to rely on notes when I speak. I seek to be honest and passionate about the stories of the Bible, of discipleship, and of the church. The aim in preaching and the worship services is to see people becoming disciples of Jesus, transforming their imaginations and lives. This is what Dan Kimball asserts—that we must make changes and analyze our culture (coming up with fresh ways to communicate the gospel), but this must be measured by what these practices produce. The aim is to see the people of God become mature, wholehearted, fully committed disciples who are involved in God's mission in their communities.[69]

The church needs a fresh approach as it seeks to bring the gospel to bear on a new generation. My ministry responsibilities entail nurturing and communicating the gospel to the young adults in the evening church, who are in turn to go and make disciples of other young adults. To do this one needs to understand contemporary culture. An important aspect of contemporary culture is the shift to postmodernity. Postmodern thinking critiques how modern communication was often driven by logic and a metanarrative which has failed. Postmodern thinkers regard all metanarratives with suspicion. Christians must challenge the notion that all metanarratives are dead, and instead offer the story of Christ in a humble way. Stories are powerful in contemporary culture. The Bible is being rediscovered as a relational story that calls people to join. Christians can engage through storytelling which involves the imagination, senses, emotions, and participation. If Christians hear the stories of those they seek to reach, and in turn share the story of Christ, this strategy could resonate with many people in western culture today. These insights are very relevant for my ministry situation, and there are already things happening in my church as new disciples are taking the step to join God's mission.

---

69. Kimball, *The Emerging Church*, 15.

Individual and Corporate Servantship Practices

- Have a go at preaching a narrative-driven sermon.

- Give people room to participate in a church gathering;, allow them to respond during a sermon; ask them questions; encourage them to discuss amongst themselves; break up into small groups and pray; move people around the room.

- Learn about other world views; allow opposing voices to be heard and give people the opportunity to discuss them in light of Christianity.

- Start a church magazine which allows people to write articles expressing these things, celebrating what is happening in the life of the church, and allowing the different missional stories to be heard.

- Get creative: for instance, hold a photo exhibition that invites people to take photos of their community in an effort to help them identify where God is at work in their suburb.

- Spend time during a service to eat together as a form of worship. Take communion together; share food together while speaking about how we can be living this out in our everyday life.

- Leave space after a sermon for people to respond; if possible try to get them to do something physical—write down their response, take a stone and drop it in the water.

- Go in-depth: we spent one service wrestling through discussion of Deuteronomy 7 where God commands the Israelites to kill the Canaanites. Tackle the tricky issues.

- Find ways to communicate the gospel that immerse all the senses. One service during a parables series we set up the parables so that people could both hear the message, and then have the chance to interact, plant a seed, dig for treasure, and smell bread cooking.

Questions for Reflection and Discussion

- How can your worship gatherings be spaces and times when people are immersed and invited to participate in the story of God?

- How can people's imaginations shaped by the Bible?

- What are the alternative stories being told in our culture today? How does Christianity respond to these stories?

19

Disturbing the Present and the Status Quo

Lynette Edge

Over two hundred years ago the founding matriarch of The Salvation Army, Catherine Booth, preached a series of sermons in which she was discussing the state of the church at that time. She said, "Now, as in the individual, there is such a tendency to rest in form, so in the church collectively . . . evidently it would be madness to go on as we are. That will mend nothing! Somebody must strike and do something worthy of the emergency. *There is no improving the future, without disturbing the present,* and the difficulty is to get people to be willing to be disturbed!"[1]

With the inspiration of Catherine Booth's words ringing in my ears, I set out on the task of reflecting on my current ministry context in light of my reading, ministry experiences, and reflection upon theology, culture, and the mission of the church.

I will begin by presenting a description of my current ministry context, before offering some reflections concerning this church. It is the intention of this chapter to raise issues that, in Catherine Booth's words, might help to improve the future, even if it means disturbing the present and the status quo.

My Current Ministry Context

My husband and I currently minister at a Salvation Army church situated in the heart of the Sydney central business district. It is the oldest Salvation Army church in the Australian eastern territory, being established in 1882. It was also one of, if not the largest, Salvation Army church in the Australian state of New South Wales for much of

---

1. Booth, *Papers on Aggressive Christianity*, 18 (italics added for emphasis).

the twentieth century. As its slogan, the church has often used the phrase, "the church in the city with the city at heart."

Whilst being seen as the flagship church for a traditional expression of Salvation Army worship and practice for most of its existence, it would no longer lay claim to such a role, as the numerical and musical strengths of the church have been in decline for many years.

The strengths of this church include its wealth of physical resources, including a six-hundred-seat auditorium and three-hundred-place function center. There is still a wealth of people resources too, despite the numerical decline, with a Sunday morning congregation of about two hundred people and evening service of about ninety. Its city location and proximity to transport are strengths as well. Not only is public transport easily accessible, this location is also critical for connection to the inner city social and community services with which we are linked. Throughout its history, our church has supported many social and community work innovations, including establishing one of the first hostels for the homeless, commencing a phone counseling service, and being instrumental in the foundation of the youth service which has developed into the Oasis Youth Support Network.[2] Often these innovations were the brainchild of individuals in the church who then offered the financial backing to all their development. Today the sense of connection with the housing and addiction rehabilitation programs of The Salvation Army in the city remains strong.

Among the weaknesses or challenges we face is that the core members live in the suburbs of Sydney, rather than in the inner city where the church is located, and commute to church on Sundays. This not only makes mid-week engagement difficult, it also reinforces the belief that church equals Sunday worship alone—as this is the only time most of our people connect with each other. Our church is situated in the same building as The Salvation Army's head office, which is essentially a city office block, and therefore there is no "shop front" to the church.

Within this context there are still some very real opportunities. It is possible to network with other Salvation Army social and community centers in meaningful ways which open many doors to relationships and new ministries. There is also the fact that the traditions of the past are no longer dominant. This in turn has led the church to look for new vision and direction into the future.

Amongst the threats which face our church is that of the declining numbers of committed attendees over the past twenty-one years, leading to fewer people in servantship and active ministries than would have been the case in the past. This is also the case as people are less prepared to commute into the city and dedicate a full day to activities than they would have been in the past. This leads to the questioning of the culture of the church, as the "way we do things around here" needs to be questioned. Every city Salvation Army church in Australia (and possibly the western world) is facing the same issue in this regard. Another threat to our congregation is that being

2. For the inner-city youth work of Oasis, see http://salvos.org.au/oasis/

a high profile church in the denomination means that many people, from both within and outside the church, have strong opinions about who we are and what we should be doing.

In light of this brief analysis of my church's current situation, I propose to explore some key theological and missiological challenges which face our church today.

The Christian faith is intrinsically incarnational; therefore, unless the church chooses to remain a foreign entity, it will always enter into the context in which it happens to find itself.[3] With the words of David Bosch ringing in our ears, let us turn our attention to mission and ministry at our church in light of the current challenges.

Ecclesiology and Missiology

I would imagine that ecclesiology has rarely been explicitly placed on the agenda at this church, and yet I believe it is a critical question for our church to explore at this time. Its relationship to missiology is also vital at this time in our journey.

This church has been a large, Sunday-focused, commuter church for most, if not all, of its existence. The Sunday activities, and especially the two worship services, have been the center of the church, and the numbers at those services have been the way the church measures its success. Music has been a major focus for this church and excellence in this area of worship has formed a key part of their identity.

The lack of shop-front to the church further symbolizes this focus, as the only day the church is "open" is a Sunday—on all other days an employee of the office building in which we are situated staffs the foyer.

The Salvation Army city church has, in many ways, followed the "build it and they will come" approach to ministry. This metaphor for ministry comes from the movie *Field of Dreams* where a disembodied voice tells Kevin Costner to build a baseball field for past greats of the game, and he is assured that "if he builds it, they will come."[4]

In missional circles this approach has also been called the *attractional* model of mission. This model assumes that people would come to our churches and in fact to faith in Christ, if only we would get the product we are offering, especially the Sunday worship services, right.

The problem is that this approach to ministry has put the proverbial cart before the horse. Deciding on a form of church, an activity, or a program, and then advertising and trying to get people to come to it is, as Andrew Hamilton says, "mission in reverse." He goes on to suggest that "pagan Aussies don't want to come to church, and simply making the Sunday event more attractive is not the answer to the problem."[5]

---

3. Bosch, *Transforming Mission*, 190.
4. And in the movie, of course, they did.
5. Hamilton, "How Not to Pick a Fight," 90.

In a post-Christian context, the nature of the mission should determine the shape of the church as the body of Christ incarnated in the culture. We must therefore engage with our missional theology and let that shape both our mission and our ecclesiology.

Stuart Murray says that too many churches have seen mission as a program or added extra which is bolted onto the church rather than being integral and foundational to its very nature. He says that "missiology must precede ecclesiology and missional theology must precede both."[6]

Michael Frost and Alan Hirsch claim that an ecclesiology which takes a *Come-To-Us* stance is unbiblical. "It is not found in the Gospels or the Epistles. Jesus, Paul, the disciples, and the early church leaders, all had a *Go-To-Them* mentality."[7]

This is not to say that we shouldn't be attractive to people outside the church. The New Testament church was obviously very attractive to many who joined them in following Jesus. Rather, a *Come-To-Us* stance should not be our missional model or paradigm—that place should be taken by the *Go-To-Them* approach. The challenge for our church here is that the Sunday service has long been the major focus of our life and ministry together and it is a radical challenge to re-imagine the focus elsewhere.

An alternative ecclesiological and missional model is the *incarnational* model of mission. "The missional church recognizes that it does not hold a place of honor in its host community and that its missional imperative compels it to move out from itself into that host community as salt and light."[8]

John Olley, the former Principal of the Baptist Theological College of Western Australia, says that the way of Christ is "not the Constantinian model of imposition, nor the model of withdrawal, since light is to shine in darkness and salt is to be spread around, but a pattern of incarnation, a model of participation, living different values with sacrificial service despite opposition, being like Christ."[9]

These are metaphors Jesus used which help us understand our incarnational missional calling. In Matthew 5:13–16 he told his followers,

> You are the salt of the earth. But if the salt loses its saltiness, how can it be made salty again? It is no longer good for anything, except to be thrown out and trampled underfoot. You are the light of the world. A city on a hill cannot be hidden. Neither do people light a lamp and put it under a bowl. Instead they put it on its stand, and it gives light to everyone in the house. In the same way, let your light shine before others, that they may see your good deeds and glorify your Father in heaven.

---

6. Murray, *Church after Christendom*, 132.
7. Frost and Hirsch, *Shaping of Things to Come*, 19.
8. Ibid.
9. Olley, "Light and Salt."

This brings us to consider another challenge for a commuter-based city church. If the community in which we are called to have direct ministry is not one in which the members of the church live, then we have to ask about the nature of the ministry of the church.

Salt and light are biblical metaphors which call us to direct, meaningful, and constant contact and engagement with the society and culture in which we live. For members of the congregation this means re-thinking the Sunday service as the centerpiece of our life together. It means learning to value the ways in which members are engaged with their local communities, friendships, and networks.

Andrew Hamilton says that if our missional theology drives our ecclesiology then the outcome will be refreshingly simple. "It requires us to live amongst the people in our communities, to love them, to share the good news of the kingdom both in action and in speech with them, and then as they become followers of Christ, to invite them into our communities of faith . . . In incarnational mission [the Sunday] gathering exists to support the believers as they move out in mission rather than being seen as the place to bring people to . . . an incarnational approach to mission takes both the gospel and the context seriously and sends Christians out as missionaries rather than calling pagans to come and attend church."[10]

As we respond to the call of incarnational ministry our gatherings will stop being the prime focus of our church, and our ministry in the communities in which we live and work will be our focus.

This ecclesiological engagement will also compel us to re-consider what we consider "real church." Is the Sunday service the only valid worshipping community and should the goal of every missional event be to get people to the Sunday service? Could other groups held outside our building, and not held on a Sunday, be church? And what would it mean for us to empower and equip such a decentralized model of church at this city church?

Emerging from this exploration of ecclesiology and missiology comes a further engagement with the question of community in the church today.

Community and Connection

We are told that in the early church,

> All the believers were together and had everything in common. They sold property and possessions to give to anyone who had need. Every day they continued to meet together in the temple courts. They broke bread in their homes and ate together with glad and sincere hearts, praising God and enjoying the

---

10. Hamilton, "How Not to Pick a Fight."

favor of all the people. And the Lord added to their number daily those who were being saved.[11]

This is a snapshot of community that demonstrates mutual care, shared life, worship, and deep fellowship. Throughout the centuries, church life was often linked to communities of people who lived in close proximity and who shared many aspects of their common life together, as it seemed for the community in Acts. Since that time, corporate worship often reflected the life of the community, the patterns of worship reflected a context in which people already knew each other, and, therefore, the idea of developing relationships with each other and focusing on community building at church was not on the agenda—since the Sunday worship event was a gathering of people who already knew each other.

This creates a challenge in the twenty-first century, when churches are gatherings of otherwise disconnected people who meet only once a week at the Sunday worship event. The creation of community is a real challenge for a city church today, in a way that previous generations and maybe rural communities today do not face. This is even more real in a city commuter where people often live more than an hour's commute from the church and also from each other.

To this challenge, Pete Ward offers an important insight when he says that the church in the future will be liquid, rather than solid. "We need to shift from seeing church as a gathering of people meeting in one place at one time, that is, a congregation, to a notion of church as a series of relationships and communications. This image implies something like a network or a web rather than an assembly of people."[12]

Eleanor Todd suggests that this transformation proposed by Pete Ward is already taking place in the way that the "noun *church* is becoming more of an action, a description or a phenomenon, *going to church* is giving way to *being church*."[13] This may be a challenging transition for our church, but one that may prove ultimately important to grasp.

> The church is primarily a people, not simply a place to meet. It is a movement and not an institution . . . church is a seven day a week identification, not a once a week, 90 minute respite from the real world. The church lives as a committed community in this world, which desperately needs redemption.[14]

The search for authentic community, and the longing for meaningful relationships, friendships, and community are prevalent today. This is an opportunity for the church, and we have the possibility of offering these things to our culture. One of the challenges is to focus on the community building and friendship networks which exist *outside* the Sunday gathering. By strengthening and validating the web of relationships

---

11. Acts 2:44–47.
12. Ward, *Liquid Church*, 2.
13. Todd, "Book of the Month," 376.
14. Gibbs and Bolger, *Emerging Churches*, 38.

in which our church attenders live, we will increasingly cultivate church as a verb and not only a noun.

Embracing this way of understanding ourselves could release our church from the limitations of a Sunday-centric way of being and encourage non-centralized connections and ministries. It has been suggested that, "the first reformation was about freeing the church. The new reformation is about freeing God's people from the church. The original reformation decentralized the church. The new reformation decentralizes ministry."[15]

We might also be challenged to consider that Australia has one of the highest levels of home internet connection in the world and Australians are amongst the greatest users of social networking sites. The Sunday-centric life of our church has great potential to be broadened through embracing and harnessing these technologies. Not only may relationships within the church network be strengthened, but also new technologies may be used to further engage in missional connections. The church website and other social networking tools might become a place for spiritual seekers as well as a tool of community connection and interaction.

Spiritual Seekers

The *Sydney Morning Herald* recently ran a front-page piece underlining a point that missiologists have been making for some time. Spirituality is not dead in western cultures, and "certainly not in Australia." We were told that "God is not dead in Australia" and the "rumours of his failing powers are exaggerated"; furthermore, the "default setting of this country is faith."[16]

This is certainly consistent with a view expressed by Eddie Gibbs when he says that in the west today there is a "hunger in people's hearts for the transcendent dimension of life."[17] If this is the context in which we live, then there will be implications not only for our ministry, but, in fact, also for our personal expressions of faith as well. John Drane has authored a book with a provocative, yet self-explanatory title, *Do Christians Know How to be Spiritual?*[18] The very title alone leads us to believe that Christians during the period of modernity have not necessarily been good at connecting with our own spirituality. Shirley McLaine articulated this opinion, when she said in her popular autobiographical work *Out on a Limb* that "your religions teach religion, not spirituality."[19]

There is a challenge before Christians today to recover a Christian spirituality in which "personal encounters with God lead us to a sense of the meaning of life and

---

15. McNeal, *The Present Future*, 43.
16. Marr, "Our Faith Today."
17. Gibbs, *Church Next*, 169.
18. Drane, *Do Christians Know How to Be Spiritual?*
19. MacLaine, *Out on a Limb*, 198.

the fulfillment of our own true personal potential to be the best that we can be and in doing so, to make the world a better place."[20]

Whilst not everyone could be described as "spiritual seekers," and not everyone reads Shirley McLaine, this group still clearly presents an important area of mission and ministry today. Therefore "the missional task of the church today involves respecting the magnetic urge toward God that is intrinsic in us all, and finding ways to help tune the settings of those in the midst of spiritual searching so they are pointed toward God. In doing so we must remember that we are not initiators of faith, but partners both with people and with God."[21]

It has been suggested that evangelism has fallen into disrepute due to various imperialistic and arrogant approaches which have been used in its name. Stuart Murray suggests that an incarnational and explanational evangelism supersede an exhortational and invitational model. He concludes that "unpretentious long-term witness is our best hope."[22]

Ann Morisy suggests that one way forward in engaging spiritual seekers is to re-imagine vocation and discipleship as a journey that all people are on, not just a path for Christians. Once we see all people as fellow travelers on a spiritual journey we can "encourage and enable people to express discipleship regardless of whether they are Christian." This "overthrows the usual 'belong, believe, behave' formula and presumes that the expression of venturesome love can be a route to faith and not just an expression of faith."[23]

She also suggests that many seek personal transformation in their lives today and "given that the church and associated agencies are the original dealers in transformations, it would be irresponsible to ignore a market that is rampantly seeking transformational experience."[24]

Our church is in a unique place to encounter those who are spiritually searching and desirous of transformation—especially through our engagement with a local rehabilitation program. This program is a spiritually based recovery program based on the Alcoholics Anonymous twelve steps. As such, participants are invited to consider a holistic journey to recovery in which faith in a higher power is central and personal transformation possible.

In this context, and in light of the above discussion about engaging with spiritual seekers, we may be able to facilitate mentoring relationships between people at our church and participants in the recovery program. This may provide a model which

---

20. Drane, "Rebuilding the House of Faith."
21. Taylor, *Out of Bounds Church*, 82.
22. Murray, *Church after Christendom*, 231.
23. Morisy, *Journeying Out*, 221.
24. Ibid.

removes the power dynamic of traditional evangelistic approaches and invites Christians to become fellow strugglers on the spiritual journey.[25]

Our engagement with spiritual seekers may also open another door which is vital for mission and ministry today—that of social action.

Social Action as Essential Expression of the Gospel

Some years ago, The Salvation Army took part in the National Church Life Survey. This survey gave our denomination the feedback that one of the weakest points in our denominational life was that of "service." This was a surprise for us. It means that the average attendee at The Salvation Army's Sunday worship is not personally involved in service to others or in helping the needy.

I believe that this dimension of our life as followers of Christ is essential, not only because of our Salvation Army identity, but in response to the gospel itself. It is even more so in the twenty-first century where social engagement has gained new credence.

During the period of Christendom the churches' message focused on issues of guilt and life *after* death, where forgiveness and the promise of heaven were central. In this period of post-Christendom, there is a need to reclaim the focus on the message of the gospel as it speaks to us about life *before* death. This is a call to reconnect evangelism with social justice.[26] Ray Anderson suggests that we need to redefine mission so that it is about seeking justice and not only about "saving souls."[27] Stuart Murray goes so far as to suggest that in this post-Christendom era we will need to deliberately blur the boundaries between evangelism and social action.[28]

Some time ago I heard Tim Costello, now CEO of World Vision Australia, reflect on his own discipleship. He said he spent the first part of his Christian life concentrating only on the first half of Jesus's command given in Matthew 22:36–40. Tim Costello had focused on loving God, evangelizing so that people would get into heaven, saving souls, praying, and studying the Bible.

Then when he was at university he was confronted with the second part of Jesus's command—which was that love for God is equally yoked to love of one's neighbor. He acknowledged that, according to Jesus's words recorded in Luke 10:25, our neighbors are the people whom others pass by, the people others find hard to love, those who are forgotten and overlooked, and that he had neglected this dimension of the great command. Tim Costello came to realize that his commitment to social justice and compassionate action was as vital to his faith as were his efforts in loving God and

---

25. Murray, *Post-Christendom*, 159.
26. Ibid., 162.
27. Anderson, *An Emergent Theology for Emerging Churches*, 195.
28. Murray, *Post-Christendom*, 157.

proclaiming the gospel. Tim suggested at this meeting that love for God and love for those in need are two partners in Christian discipleship that each Christian needs to take seriously.

At our church we have a remarkable opportunity to engage individual Christians in social action as we partner with ministries to the homeless and those addicted in our community. We have a strong history of supporting those who are doing these ministries, but not such a strong tradition of individual members becoming personally involved in ways other than financially. As we foster the social engagement of individuals, not only will we respond to the biblical call to love our neighbors, but also our own path of discipleship will be strengthened.

In his exploration of healthy churches in the United Kingdom, Robert Warren discovered that one of the striking characteristics of healthy churches was "the extent to which they have looked out beyond themselves and engaged with the whole of life and with the wider community. They are not ghetto churches, hiding from life. Rather, church is not the be-all and end-all of their existence. It is God's love for all creation and for all that is that motivated them—in the whole of their living. The starting point for these churches is the world around and the whole of life. They demonstrate in their life the truth that no group is happy or healthy unless it has a task to fulfill beyond itself."[29]

As we encourage and promote social action as evangelism, I believe we will respond to the biblical and cultural imperative to bring in God's kingdom today.

Through this chapter I have sought to integrate my understanding of theology, culture, ecclesiology, and the mission of God and the church. All these things inform my ministry at The Salvation Army city church. I have raised issues of missiology and ecclesiology and how they shape our life together. Further issues of community connections, social action, and responding to spiritual seekers have also been explored.

Ours is a congregation which was established only two years after Catherine Booth preached the sermon quoted at the outset of this chapter.

Her words, therefore, come with fresh challenge to us today, when she declared, "It would be madness to go on as we are. That will mend nothing! Somebody must strike and do something worthy of the emergency. There is no improving the future, without disturbing the present."[30]

Individual and Corporate Servantship Practices

- Undertake an analysis of your faith community looking for strengths, weaknesses, opportunities, and threats. Where do you hear God speaking to you in these reflections?

29. Warren, *Healthy Churches' Handbook*, 22.
30. Booth, *Papers on Aggressive Christianity*, 18.

Movement Three—From Theories to Courageous Practices

- Consider the various networks and groups associated with your faith community. How might Pete Ward's notion of liquid church shed light on these networks and groups?

- Reggie McNeal has suggested that the so-called "second reformation" is about freeing God's people from the church. What are the implications of this insight for your faith community?

- Experiment with blogging. Maybe ask a few people from your church or faith community to blog each week on how that makes connections from their spiritual journey and their working life. Try asking diverse people from your congregation to blog on their reflections of how their Sunday worship impacts their midweek life and activities.

- Ask who are the spiritual seekers in your local community. Reflect on how those in your faith community could share the journey of spiritual seeking with them.

- Identify a social action which would enrich your community and with which members of your faith community could be involved. Maybe start with a one-day or one-week project and then spend time reflecting on the experience together.

Questions for Reflection and Discussion

- What do you think about the dichotomy of the "come to us" and the "go to them" missional stances? Which do you find yourself most engaged with and why?

- Andrew Hamilton says that when our "missional theology drives our ecclesiology the outcome will be refreshingly simple." Do you agree or disagree? Why or why not?

- If it is true that church is about a network of relationships in Christ, then how might you work to strengthen those relationships today?

20

Challenging Cyber-spaces

Paul Winch

I am a "digital immigrant," ministering among a people who are "digital natives." Students at the University of Technology, Sydney, were predominantly born in the 1990s, and have grown up using email, web-based applications, and even mobile phones. Not only are the vast majority totally used to such technologies, but their enrolment at a technical university also generally confirms an intense interest, or at least comfort, in such matters. I, however, grew up in the 1970s when no such technology existed. On top of that, I was also brought up in a missionary family living in remote areas of tropical Indonesia, and so memory of childhood television or even landline telephones is very limited. Hence, use of the contemporary technology so readily available usually comes late for me. For example, students signed me up to email in the late 1990s so that they could contact me that way. Likewise, as a result of their frustration during organization of a university campus mission in 2003, student leaders gave me a mobile phone so that they could call me in the tumult of running a large-scale event. And as part of my action-reflection for a Master of Arts in Theology unit, I finally signed up to the social networking site *Facebook*, after years of repeated begging from ministry colleagues. It is safe to say that I struggle to be "incarnate" amongst the tribe in which I minister—where people "see media [not] in an instrumental way [but] rather as integrally related to culture."[1] To them such things are not extras, incidentals, or accessories, but part of the very fabric of what they do and who they are. Another way of existing is not usually a considered alternative.

This chapter seeks to apply a missional ecclesiology within such a context. What servantship practices should the church adopt if it is to be missionally effective in this cultural setting?

1. Horsfield and Teusner, "A Mediated Religion," 280.

Movement Three—From Theories to Courageous Practices

How the Internet Shapes Community

Ecclesiology is about community—a community founded in Christ. Nevertheless, it is simply not true that "whether we're high-tech or low-tech followers of Jesus, it's still the message, not the medium, that matters."[2] The medium matters a lot, since the medium influences a community profoundly. It is futile to attempt to dehistoricize and universalize Christian discipleship, or to try to conceptualize Christian community apart from the actual and concrete expressions of its ecclesiology.

> Every expression of Christianity, every experience of spirituality, every Christian idea, is a mediated phenomenon. It is mediated in its generation, in its construction, and in its dissemination.[3]

This is no less true of technology. Automobile travel, for example, has had a profound influence not just on social mobility, but also therefore on the way Christian faith has been expressed, since "village style" Christianity and church life have largely disappeared over the last century. People now live in urban settings, with lifestyles changing as a result.[4]

> Technology does not appear in a vacuum but is embedded in culture and society, thus having particular values and biases that must be considered, particularly in light of Christian responsibility to honor and glorify God.[5]

In the cultural context of the university in which I minister, there is a heavy use of Internet technologies and applications. Every student is issued with an email account and expected to use it for their enrolment, academic management of their degree, and much more. Many course-related activities require the use of online resources. Wireless access to the Internet is available across the campus, most lecture rooms have multimedia facilities (including Internet), and computer labs and Internet kiosks are in all buildings. These kiosks are usually in very common space areas, such as foyers, lobbies, and atriums. In other words, Internet technology is prevalent if not ubiquitous in the culture, making a Christian evaluation even more pressing.

Steven VanderLeest provides a helpful starting point for such an evaluation.

> It is true that technology has no agency—it cannot make an ethical choice . . . [However] Technology expands one's choices and increases the scope of one's agency . . . [Therefore] Technological products are never neutral. At the very

---

2. Daniel, "Church Netiquette," 28.
3. Horsfield and Teusner, "A Mediated Religion," 279.
4. Single causality of social change is of course far too simplistic, and I do not mean to attribute the car with such status in this example. It is but one of many factors in the historical development of the last century, which should make it clear that technology contributes significantly to what Horsfield and Teusner call the "mediated phenomenon" of Christian experience.
5. VanderLeest, "Teaching Justice by Emphasizing the Non-Neutrality of Technology," 115.

least, the engineer designs them to perform their intended tasks, and therefore biases them toward that use.[6]

What then are the biases (intended design functions) of the Internet, and in particular Web 2.0?[7] I narrow the focus to Web 2.0 because,

> Web 1.0 is used in ways that are simply an extension or amplification of what was already going on in the pre-electronic world, be it in the business, academic or social spheres. However, in the past few years, new technologies have been developed that allow the Internet to be used in distinctly new ways. *These ways are in turn shaping new behaviors*, rather than simply being new ways of doing old things.[8]

There tends to be more egalitarianism built into Web 2.0 applications. "Web 2.0 is all about the power of collaboration and the rise of the amateur."[9] Wikis rely on group (usually volunteer) participation and contribution in authoring and editing articles. Blogs are highly interactive, with others making comments or referring others to the blog through hyperlinks. YouTube allows and solicits feedback and rating surveys from users. Anyone can post on these sites, and anyone can create a blog and publish content. This is a radical change from Web 1.0 where websites were still largely owned and run by institutions and other bodies who had the resources to host them, and their function was largely information dissemination and client relations.

Peter Horsfield and Paul Teusner draw some similarities between the "democratization of the internet" and the paradigm shift that happened during the rise of the printing press.

> In the same way that the facility of printing and the widespread implementation of printing within the wider culture changed the cultural construction of Christianity, the same may be expected of the Internet.[10]

The way the printing press began to shift intellectual power away from the elite, due to people being able to accumulate home libraries, is magnified multiple times over with the Internet, especially Web 2.0.[11] It was no accident that the Reformers used the vernacular in their writings, since due to the printing press their message could be easily disseminated, and in widely understood language. This changed the shape of Christian expression irreversibly. The Roman Catholic Church, for instance, now encourages the use of indigenous language in church liturgy.

6. Ibid., 116–17.

7. Web 2.0 is not so much new technology as a new way of using the Internet. Applications such as Facebook, MySpace, Wikipedia, blogs, and YouTube are all considered to be "Web 2.0."

8. Van den Heever, "Web 2.0," 92 (emphasis added).

9. Ibid., 97.

10. Ibid., 291.

11. Access to the Internet is now at such levels that it has likely surpassed access levels to physical books.

Similar effects could be expected over time with the spread of Internet technology. This is a period of democratization of knowledge. But more than that, due to the international/global nature of the Internet, the approach people take to such knowledge is also likely to be shaped. This has been called *glocalization*—a global perspective on local issues. "There is a new holism now emerging as a consequence of the digital age."[12]

With somewhere between 30 to 40 percent of Australians using *Facebook*, could it be that Web 2.0 has become a primary way of society knowing itself?[13] It certainly acts as football and movies do in the Australian environment, or food in an Asian context, providing commonality across diverse and often humdrum lives—a talking and connecting point around shared experience. More profoundly, however, it is also the medium of the dialogue. In this way it undoubtedly shapes community. However, one must ask whether this is any reason to blindly use such technology? Many Christians in my ministry situation would never question using it, although I have occasionally come across people who have decided to stop using *Facebook* (even if only for a short period of time).

Surface Warnings from Popular Critiques

There are a few common attacks on living within the framework of an integrated "online" and "offline" life. It is often said that such a lifestyle reduces productivity and interferes with "real" relationships.

It is true that many workplaces ban the use of some Internet applications such as *Facebook* during work hours, since many employees find it hard to resist its interference with work tasks and responsibilities. A number of students I know routinely deactivate their *Facebook* accounts during exam periods.

Yet the critique put forward runs deeper than a work interference issue. It relates to issues of human attention span, creativity, and the like. "Multitasking, which is often held up as a prized skill, has caused us to fragment our focus at the cost of our ability to fully engage in an activity."[14]

It is worth considering, however, if such analysis would make sense for those who are indigenous to such a culture. Tex Sample has argued that those bought up with new sounds, new technology, and so forth usually integrate such experiences into their ways of thinking and self-expression.[15] Multitasking may therefore come more naturally to those brought up in an integrated online/offline environment, because, to use the language of Sample, it has been "wired into their souls." The result is dif-

---

12. Shane Hipps in an interview with Mark Galli in "From the Printing Press to the Iphone," 64.
13. Facebook registers over eight million users in Australia.
14. Wilson, "Please, Not Another E-Mail!" 18.
15. See: Sample, *The Spectacle of Worship in a Wired World*.

ferent skills and ways of thinking. Far from being something so fracturing to human psychology that it cannot be utilized with discipline and fruitfulness at work and in life generally, it is much more likely that, for those indigenous to the culture, it will function like any other new technology—such as when the telephone was integrated seamlessly into culture decades ago. Used well it can actually enhance such things as productivity. Abused or used badly, and functionality will decline markedly.

Perhaps of more immediate concern in a ministry environment is a second common critique, which is that *Facebook* (for example) interferes with "authentic relationships." This is expressed well by Lenora Rand,

> Like many good things . . . [*Facebook*] can become addictive. Of greater concern is that they can become a substitute for face-to-face, in the flesh contact . . . If we are finding a way to reflect and confess, care for one another and experience community without ever walking through the doors of a church building, what do we need the 'real' church for?[16]

However, there are studies which actually show the opposite—a supplemental and strengthening effect, rather than a replacement effect. For this reason, many scholars acknowledge the potential of Web 2.0 applications to enhance church life and relationships. "Online forms of religious community serve more as a complement than as a replacement to religious expression and communion in the offline world."[17]

Likewise, Andrea Useem suggests,

> The Internet's success springs from a powerful longing for community—the very same force that drives congregations . . . Congregational life and online life are not competing in a zero-sum game . . . Overall, online religious activity leads people to become more involved in their local faith communities.[18]

The Internet has helped the rise of what has been called the "new spiritualities." People of different backgrounds and minority beliefs can find each other and relate much easier over the Internet than they often can physically, especially in mass urbanized societies. Networked together they can advocate and promote their views, and appear more significant than they really are.

Thus, if we were to utilize an action-reflection approach to this phenomenon, I suspect that most Christians would quickly realize that, since the Internet technology is all around us, it is no use ignoring or merely decrying it. It is also not helpful to move toward blind acceptance, but, rather, it is important to understand it and shape our responses to it in constructive and positive ways.

---

16. Rand, "The Church on Facebook," 25; See Crouch, "Rekindling Old Fires."
17. Horsfield and Teusner, "A Mediated Religion," 291.
18. Useem, "The New Connectivity," 24. See Rice, *The Church of Facebook*.

Deeper Issues

Of more significant concern, and therefore necessary analysis, are questions around the technology's *structure* rather than *function*. Function relates to user intentions—why and how will people use Web 2.0 applications? In a sense, these are the concerns raised immediately above—the critiques regarding productivity and authentic relationships are concerns which could be leveled at almost any human use of technology. However, structure relates to the deeper issue of design intention.

> The primary message of any medium is to be found in its structure, in the way it particularly engages our senses, and in its influence upon patterns of human interaction, and remains critically important in gaining any insight into the fundamental influence of the mass media.[19]

Web 2.0 applications such as *Facebook* are particularly well suited to a late-modern/postmodern culture. However, they also advance or promote such culture. Many media theorists have noted this two-way influence, with examples from television, movies, and now the Internet. Theologian Tex Sample puts it this way,

> [There has been] a leap in the entertainment industry, in motion pictures, recording and playback equipment, and later in computer, digitalization, and virtual reality. While popular culture and entertainment are a 'result' of these shifts, they are also a major stimulus to these changes because they so markedly enhance consumption. They do not simply mirror the transformations but play a basic role in them.[20]

The way in which Web 2.0 applications participate in this cultural milieu is manifold (both as mirror to it and amplifier of it). Perhaps, most strikingly, there is little or no personal commitment required in using such applications. Participants choose simply to view or engage as they wish, and engagement in social networking sites can be a powerful self-expression, but, often, with little accompanying cost. This is known as *ambient intimacy*—being subjected to (or even being the subject of) knowledge of significant personal details from the trivial to the profound, yet with little interpersonal consequence or responsibility. Interaction from others can be ignored at whim if so desired. In *Facebook*, this facility is extended to removing or hiding unwanted posts from your "wall" and delisting "friends" from your account. The web of interpersonal relationships, as expressed on *Facebook*, can be incredibly malleable. To a degree, this is an example of *humble design* that is to be applauded, since it provides a protective mechanism against abuse. It can, however, easily amplify the human propensity to avoid interpersonal face-to-face conflict, while at the same time providing an enhanced means to escalate it. Such discord may be the result of

---

19. Tatarnic, "The Mass Media and Faith," 452.
20. Sample, *The Spectacle of Worship in a Wired World*, 43.

simple misunderstandings between people due to the virtual nature of the communication that takes place, or, on the other extreme, cyber-bullying. Much conflict on the Internet, in blogs, *Facebook*, and so forth, is somewhere in-between these extremes, resulting, for example, from the disclosure of information about others in a very public forum (a disclosure that was both public and private/personal/subjective at the same time).

This level of free choice and personal expression, stripped from an embodied interaction with others, easily turns personal communication into a commodity—something to be traded in and engaged with, or not, at one's personal discretion.

> The Internet presumes cultural facility with the practices of anonymous urban populations and mass markets . . . [It] is dependent on people understanding the literacies and practices of the autonomous individual consumer as the mechanisms for making decisions in the modern segmented marketplace serviced by product and brand advertising. This dynamic of consumerism taken up textually in intellectual theories of reader-reception and autonomous meaning making are fundamental operating assumptions of a medium such as the Internet.[21]

Humble and ethical hermeneutics are often not applied by Web 2.0 users. The writer/publisher is often out of the field of reference to the reader, and engagement with a "speech-act" is subverted into simulacra via extreme hermeneutical suspicion. How many blogs turn nasty? How many of the new spiritualities are actually a mix-and-match approach to religions which are marketed or promoted on the Internet as a means of psychosomatic wholeness, and yet bear little historical weight?

Thus we see a correlation between the structure of Web 2.0, and wider worldview questions—a reinforcing, iterative process. Web 2.0 particularly fits well with a postmodern understanding of and relation to authority. The Enlightenment metanarrative of (1) progress via autonomous individualism, (2) objective rationalism, (3) scientific positivism, and (4) technological pragmatism, has been severely questioned or abandoned within a postmodern world.[22] Now, no external authority has primacy.[23] In effect, any truth claim is as valid or invalid as any other. People can ignore any authority or attack any perceived threatening authority on the same basis. "Postmodernism admits no possibility of an absolute truth in theory; in practice this means that all types of authority can no longer be derived from external sources."[24]

---

21. Horsfield and Teusner, "A Mediated Religion," 284.

22. These four categories are slight variations on those proposed by Engen, "Mission Theology in the Light of Postmodern Critique."

23. For good introductions to these postmodern worldview questions and answers, see: Stanley, "Speaking Credibly?"; Drane, "Contemporary Culture and the Reinvention of Sacramental Spirituality"; Jenson, "How the World Lost Its Story."

24. Van den Heever, "Web 2.0," 100.

Martha Tatarnic observes this exact phenomenon in relation to religion, within the mass media of television.

> These two messages—religion as culturally irrelevant and religion as culturally important—may appear to conflict with one another, and yet their inconsistencies actually seem to coexist quite comfortably. In fact, these two messages are the same; that is to say, they stem from the same primary message as delivered to us through the structure, the nature, and the use of our electronic media.[25]

Within such a system it is hard to see how the demands of the gospel can be propagated. To be heard, rather than reacted against, Christianity often needs to be seen as appealing, as helpful, as beneficial—all without actually promoting itself that way, lest it be considered a threat. "Authentic knowledge" is so often experienced in our electronic, mass media era as mediated by the glamorous and the successful. The new spiritualities often have a successful or glamorous spokesperson: Tom Cruse, Madonna, and so forth.

> Postmodernity is oft expressed as the consumer quest for emancipation from intrinsic authority . . . Religion is consumed in ever-new special effects of our own making that conform to our insatiable quest for "shock and awe."[26]

Yet sating individual desire and acquiescing to the pursuit of immediate happiness do not sit comfortably with the "take up your cross and follow me" demands of discipleship to Jesus Christ. As Shane Hipps put it,

> This culture is on an extraordinary pace towards needing things to be more efficient. But that is a value that is ultimately antithetical to the gospel. I've never heard of efficient wisdom, efficient love, efficient suffering, efficient compassion. So what does it mean that we inhabit a world that is so dominated by this ideology?[27]

Potential Ways Forward

A missional ecclesiology, and theology of Christian servantship, as applied to this integrated online/offline feature of contemporary society, will need to grapple intentionally with these deeper critiques as to the *structure* of Web 2.0 applications.

I have argued in my earlier chapter that three interrelated theological pillars are foundational to a missional ecclesiology in postmodern societies:

---

25. Tatarnic, "The Mass Media and Faith," 450.
26. Stanley, "Speaking Credibly?" 26–27.
27. Galli, "From the Printing Press to the iPhone," 64.

Missio Dei—The Macro Level: Mission is essential to God's character, and mission is his ongoing work in the world, including within a postmodern society.

A "Peculiar People"—The Meso Level: The *missio Dei* is seen particularly in God establishing a people belonging to him, in and through Jesus Christ, and yet who are called to face the world in love and service in the power of the Spirit. There is church because there is mission.

Integral Discipleship—The Micro Level: God's people face the world in love and service by following Jesus, the incarnate son of God and the human *par excellence*, in all aspects of life, mission, and community. God's mission is to redeem the world in Christ, not to rescue us out of the world. The *missio Dei* aims for us to become more human, not less, which, because of our human nature, requires relational embrace, that is, profound connection with other "Peculiar People."

As we engage this theological task we need to be attentive to hermeneutical questions.

> The hermeneutical cycle now so beloved of practical theologians has at its heart the integration of personal experience with wider historical and biblical awareness. In sorting out matters of personal identity and meaning, most people intuitively start with their own experiences of life, and then ask questions of the wider tradition. Most clergy, on the other hand, are still trained to start with the tradition and then to apply it to the circumstances of real life.[28]

It seems to me that the integration of an online/offline lifestyle is so basic to human experience, at least in my ministry context, that it would be impossible to observe and analyze the phenomenon in any other way than from the "inside." However, is this just another way of saying that we should start with the micro-level of my above framework? Integral discipleship, of course, extends to our use of Web 2.0.

Anyone who has had the misfortune of being misunderstood on a blog post or *Facebook* status update, anyone who has utilized online technology for rapacious vengeance or slander, and anyone who has experienced virtual stalking or cyber-bullying, will quickly realize the potentially dehumanizing affects/dimensions. Like all technology, Web 2.0 needs to be approached with caution and works best when used with safe-care. Relationships need to be protected and nurtured—commodification of interpersonal communication can be resisted. It helps to remember that the design intent of *Facebook* appears to be for supplementing existing friendships, and personal experience testifies that it is very good for reunion with old friends, and for "light touch" keeping up with current acquaintances.

> Some thinkers believe that the culture industries of capitalism use media to dupe people into the fantasy world of commodified life. It would be foolish

---

28. Drane and Drane, "Worship and Preaching," 16.

Movement Three—From Theories to Courageous Practices

to deny that a good deal of such influence takes place through media. The tendency of capitalism to commodify whatever it touches is basic to its faults . . . The problem, however . . . is that they depict people as cultural dopes who have no capacity to resist cultural captivity or to make alternative or even opposing uses of the offerings of the media industries.[29]

Secondly, then, some tactics on Web 2.0 applications can be used to subvert its biases towards a consumerist nirvana. One such alternative use of Web 2.0 applications would be in the area of justice education and action, which of course fits directly into the arena of "integral discipleship" too. While I am skeptical of much of what passes as social action on *Facebook*, for example, it does seem that significant things can happen. A few Internet-based promotional or awareness-raising campaigns have been effective, such as the Save Darfur coalition, which has gained some traction in politics. A number of Christian courses on justice issues are being offered online.[30]

One way that such a pursuit of "integral discipleship" in the area of justice and the Internet interconnects with being a "peculiar people" is in the way Christians are banding together for the sake of providing equity in the area of Internet technology. For example, increasingly, access to employment opportunities, government programs, local council initiatives, health care information, and so forth is becoming available principally online. For those without the technological skills or wherewithal to make use of this resource, this is an obvious equity issue. There are a number of initiatives and remedial efforts which are seeking to address this issue. Christian Community Computing Centers (C4s) are spreading rapidly around the world, generally in poorer neighborhoods, ethnic minority areas, and developing nations. They take the form of Internet cafes in the Philippines, computer clubs in Zambia, and electronic learning centers in Eastern Europe. According to Sas Conradie, there will be "over 5,000 identified Christian community technology centers by 2010" in the United States of America alone.[31] The aim in all this is for Christians to provide free education and help in online and computer literacy among needy communities, as well as access to computer and Internet resources. Such centers, therefore, provide avenues for job creation, job skilling, and access to employment opportunities—all within an environment that seeks to bear witness to Christ. This is what Michael Frost and Alan Hirsch call "proximity spaces" by means of which "in journeying together, and in doing things together, [people] will be invited into an on-going conversation about God, meaning, and so on."[32] In other words, people get caught up in the *missio Dei* through interaction with the "peculiar people."

---

29. Sample, *The Spectacle of Worship in a Wired World*, 28.

30. Blier, "Webbing the Common Good"; Ebertz, "Technology for Ministry"; VanderLeest, "Teaching Justice by Emphasizing the Non-Neutrality of Technology."

31. Conradie, "Christian Community Computer Centers (C4s)," 15.

32. Frost and Hirsch, *Shaping of Things to Come*.

Most of the students amongst whom I minister could easily contribute to such schemes. I could imagine that many of them would find it invigorating to their discipleship, and a way of practically expressing their involvement with the *missio Dei* as the "peculiar people" of God. They would certainly have their eyes opened to the power imbalance that Internet illiteracy and inequity create.

In conclusion, postmodernity appears to have rejected the techno-secular world view of the Enlightenment, but seems complicit in the consumerist world of freedom and choice which late modernity promised. In fact, Web 2.0 applications appear to many postmoderns as an ideal way to cultivate the identity and meaning they long for—they have rejected (some of) the values provided by the metanarrative of modernity and are looking for alternatives. The potentialities of self-expression and individual choice enhanced by Web 2.0 provide a medium for that construction to take place. Unfortunately, for some this construction is not much more than a simulacrum (an unsatisfactory imitation, substitution, or vague semblance).

Nevertheless, Web 2.0 can still become "sacred space" for Christians. It can enhance and maintain offline relationships, supplement the ministry of local churches, and even, on occasions, can substitute for face-to-face encounters and engagement. In addition, the story of the gospel can be told through the hermeneutic of a believing online community, although with difficulty. In fact, many Christians probably have far more to do with non-Christians through their *Facebook* friendships than otherwise. The potential drawbacks associated with disembodied but public communication will need to be handled with great care, and in contemporary culture this provides one of the key contexts in which concrete discipleship is learnt. The biases of Web 2.0 applications, which tend towards reinforcing consumerist values—including the deeper structural issues of communication commodification with little accompanying commitment—will need to be subverted. Pursuing justice and equity ideals through Web 2.0 media is one avenue for the "peculiar people" of God to participate in the *missio Dei*, where standing against the prevailing system is so often necessary.

I cannot think of a more worthy summary than these words by Alan Padgett:

> The Christian God is not a "god of the gaps," because the Creator is at work in all reality, including technological creativity. The good news about Jesus Christ comes deep into this world, with all of its problems and earthiness . . . But the work and word of Christ come from God, who is also beyond anything finite and created.[33]

Therefore, with regard to a missional ecclesiology as it applies to Web 2.0, let it be said that we have a much greater hope than a consumerist world can offer, and a much better future than a techno-secular world view envisions. The people of God can offer an enfleshed, viable, Web 2.0-complementary, alternative community, through which people can taste and see that the Lord is good.

33. Padgett, "God Versus Technology?" 580.

Movement Three—From Theories to Courageous Practices

Individual and Corporate Servantship Practices

- Categorize and count the diversity of your social media connections (follows on twitter, friends on *Facebook*, etc.). What does this "mirror" tell you?
- Work hard on your communication. How are gospel priorities such as forgiveness, justice, love, patience, grace, and repentance possibly expressed within the limited medium of Web 2.0 applications?
- Participate thoughtfully: How often have you entered an argument or debate (or similar) in a blog or other online site in a manner that perhaps you wouldn't in a face-to-face situation?
- Reflect self-critically: Is your time using social media appropriate? Justified? Helpful?
- Mix it up by complementing your avenues of communication: For example, follow-up an online interaction with a phone call; when misunderstandings occur take things off-line and turn to face to face.

Questions for Reflection and Discussion

- Do the potential uses of social media toward self-aggrandizement and image management tempt you from seeking life in him who is truly "living water"? Why or why not?
- In what ways do you find that social media both enhances and complicates your relationships? How best can relationships be fostered and nurtured in an integrated "online" and "offline" lifestyle?
- How does a theology of servantship shape our approach to social media?
- Discuss: "The mission of God that results in daily cross-carrying in following Jesus is somewhat juxtaposed in a technological medium like Web 2.0 that is often used for endless playfulness, fulfilling consumer choice, and self-expression rather than relational commitment and love."

Movement Four

From Forgetfulness to Transforming Memory

Servantship is the cultivation of *transforming memory*. In an age which easily forgets, we remember our spiritual and servantship heritage, and we remember Jesus Christ—crucified, resurrected, glorified, and reigning. This transformed memory cultivates personal and corporate renewal as we engage in transformational contemplation on the person, work, and mission of our Servant Lord. Such contemplation, if it is to be truly converting, is accompanied by whole-of-life discipleship to Jesus, and passionate participation in his extraordinary mission and purposes. Such transforming memory is the fourth movement in radical servantship.

It is important that Christian leaders experiment with new and anomalous ways of being, doing, and becoming church. We settle too often for the safe, acceptable, and mundane. In doing so we often relinquish our missional effectiveness, diminish our pastoral passion, and forgo our radical call as God's chosen, peculiar people.

We also tend to assume, from time to time, that we are the first to experiment, to embrace risky practices, to lead provocatively, and to behave with radical missional passion. Nothing could be further from the truth. Generations have gone before who have provided us with humbling, provocative, astonishing, self-sacrificial examples.

One such pastoral leader and evangelist was my great-grandfather, John McKittrick. Born on 17 March 1903, he came to faith in Jesus Christ in 1924, while on a ship bound for Australia. From 1933 to 1982 he gave himself completely to serving the mission of Jesus Christ in Australia, among the addicted, the vulnerable, the despised, the violent, the abused, and the forgotten. The following chapter is his story, in his own words. In the Preface to John McKittrick's autobiography, Dennis Ang and Stan Reeve offer the following reflection.

> Those who knew John McKittrick loved him. He was a man who had found real joy in his Saviour, Jesus Christ, and whose whole aim in life was to share that joy with those who were lost.

Movement Four—From Forgetfulness to Transforming Memory

In this he was completely selfless—an untiring, uncomplaining worker for his Lord. The number of people he aided in one way or another, whether by providing for someone's physical wants, or by pointing another to Christ, or by lending spiritual strength and encouragement to a brother in need, can never really be known while we are here on earth. Only a very few of the instances are recorded in this book.

They should be enough, however, for the reader to readily see that John McKittrick was a man in whom Christ lived, and in whom and through whom Christ was glorified![1]

---

1. McKittrick, *Just One of God's Servants*, v.

21

Caring for the Broken and the Vulnerable

John McKittrick

A New Life, a New Creation

As I begin to write some of my experiences, I feel, in a measure, presumptuous, for there are so many dear servants of God all over the world who no doubt have had perhaps more wonderful experiences than I have had, but we do not hear about them. So many people have said to me, "You must write your life story—people should hear about the experiences in your life, that it may help some." I can assure you that's my only desire!

I thank God I was brought up in a Christian home. In Deuteronomy 6:5–7 God says, "Thou shalt love the Lord thy God with all thy heart and with all thy soul, and with all thy might, and these words which I command you this day shall be in your heart and you shall teach them diligently unto your children and shall talk of them when you sit in your house and when you walk by the way and when you lie down and when you wake up." My parents were godly people and tried to fulfill this and all other Scriptures. My dad's religion began in his own life, then in the life of his family. Because of this his ministry outside was God-honoring and blessed by God. He was a well-received lay preacher, preaching in mission halls and open-air meetings in Glasgow. The highlight of the open-air meetings was the backcourt meetings. He went into the back court of tenement buildings with other workers and sang and preached the gospel, reaching people as they went about their daily tasks.

When he was called up to go to the army, Pastor D.J. Findlay of St George's Tabernacle said it would take three men to fill his place in Christian service! His dear wife faithfully backed him up, my godly mother, who spent hours each day in prayer.

Movement Four—From Forgetfulness to Transforming Memory

You would think that having been brought up in such an atmosphere of Christian love the family would all become Christians, but brother Bob and I were not converted till after teenage days, and the other three in early life. Samuel is now in the Baptist ministry, and Elizabeth and Joseph are in glory. Bob was called by God from being an engine driver to be a city missionary, and what a great ministry he had! He, too, has since gone to glory—he was knocked down by a speeding car and killed as he was escorting an old couple across the road.

Bob and I were mates all through our teenage lives. One thing which stands out about those days is how, when we brothers went camping every weekend in the summer with two or three other mates, we invariably arrived home on Sunday night to find our parents and several other godly souls praying to God for our salvation. I know now that this was one of the great factors in keeping us from many evils. I was deeply conscious of this on many occasions. Bob and I stopped going to church on Sunday, being mainly interested in sport.

I decided I would leave home and go to Australia. Before going I married Mary Larmour, a lady I had met whilst holidaying in Northern Ireland. I did not want to lose this little Irish colleen. Her grandparents brought up Mary and I had to go to Granddad to ask for her hand. He was totally blind and was sitting in his garden when we talked. He said, "John, turn round, face the church, and promise before God you will always love and care for her." I did so and I have sought always to do this. By the way, the marriage was not consummated till she arrived in Australia about ten months later with my parents and family.

She and my parents prayed much for me as I set off for the new land, and I believe it was in answer to their prayers and those of many others that I was converted. On the ship deep conviction of sin came upon me. I didn't like the company of the kind of fellows I had always associated with. Their language was not always the nicest and they would often tell dirty stories. Instead of listening to them I sneaked down to my bunk and began to read the little Bible my mother had given me, and which I had promised to read every day, but had had no intention of doing so.

I attended a service one Sunday night in the dining saloon and there I accepted Christ as my own personal Savior. I could not tell you anything the preacher said, but I knew I was a sinner and that Christ the Son of God died for my sins on the cross, and I accepted him as my Savior. I knew all this from home and Sunday School, but had never done anything about it till that day.

On the ship I met a dear old Scottish gentleman who offered me a job at the Newcastle Steel Works. This, I believe, was an answer to prayer, as were many other things, because I arrived at Newcastle almost stony broke. I did not come out by assisted passage and the fare was much for a young fellow. The lady who owned the boarding house where I went to live took me in on condition I paid on payday.

Another real answer to prayer was that on the Lord's Day I went looking for a church to worship in and was led to the Newcastle Baptist Tabernacle. The minister,

Rev. B. Gawthrop and his dear wife and the young people made me feel so welcome, and I settled in with these dear ones and was baptized. Although just a young Christian I knew I should be doing service for and with my Lord. I asked could I teach in Sunday School and was given a class of seven eleven-year-old girls. One lass had not been to Sunday School for weeks. I went to visit her and found she was a very sick girl. I went several times to see her and had the joy of leading her to Christ. Her dear mother died not long afterwards—I had the joy of leading her to Christ as well.

Could I put in a little bit of humor here? Later I went to board at the same place as another young fellow from the church. Harry and I were not pleased with the porridge—it was too thin. So we decided that on Sunday morning Harry would make the breakfast, but Harry made the mistake of making the porridge too thick—we had to nearly cut it with a knife! The dear landlady was not too pleased, but she got the message.

I worked hard and saved, and prepared a home for my wife, parents, and family who joined me ten months later. My conversion brought such joy to my parents it completely changed everything. The first thing I did after my decision was to write home and tell them. Mother was in the community washhouse in the backyard. Father got the letter, opened the window, and called out, "Mother come up, good news!" She rushed up the three-story stairs, drying her hands as she went. Dad said, "John is converted!" They threw themselves into each other's arms and wept with joy.

Dad soon found ways of witnessing for his Lord in the new country. One of these ways was to join the Northern District Open Air Campaigners, and he took his two eldest boys with him. It was out in the open-air I learned to preach, and from this began preaching in churches.

Called to Fulltime Service: The Sydney City Mission

It was six years after my conversion that God called me into the Sydney City Mission. I relate about the call so that it might help some young Christians. I was happy in my Christian service with no thought of full-time service, when there came a letter from a fellow Christian who was a city missionary, saying there was a vacancy for a missionary and he felt I was the man for the job. He said to write immediately as the vacancy had been open for a while. He also stated that in my application I should tell the committee all about my capabilities. This was a big decision to make—we had three children and one about to be born, I had a steady job, and we were happy in our house. Mary and I took it to God in prayer and got my parents and other Christian friends to pray. About a fortnight later I made application, very briefly enclosing a reference from Rev. F. Rayward who was then the Superintendent of the Newcastle Central Mission. I had worked with Mr Rayward in the open-air meetings. By the way, when I went to see Mr Rayward about the reference he said, "Jock, what salaries will you receive, you have a wife and little family to keep?" I replied, "I haven't even enquired about that. If God wants me in this work he will provide our needs."

At this time I began to feel that this must be God's plan for me, because of certain happenings. I thought that if the Mission Council were to invite me for an interview it would be good if I were working on night shift, as I could go to Sydney after work and be back for the next shift. To work this shift it meant I would have to do a job I had never done before: this was to start the finished kiln. I was not surprised when the foreman said on the Friday, "Jock, could you come in on Sunday night and start the finished kiln?" Of course I said, "Yes!" By this time I was waiting for the prepaid telegram that arrived inviting me to meet the committee on the Wednesday.

When I arrived at Sydney on the Wednesday it was the busy peak hour, and when I saw all the crowds of people I was scared, I felt like getting the train back home again. I said, "Lord if you want me here I'll come," and peace came to me. When I got to SCM Headquarters, Rev. S. A. McDonald, the General Secretary, was engaged, and I was shown into the hall. It was the night of the Annual Meeting and on all the seats were copies of the Annual Report. I picked one up and read of something that was involved in serving in the Sydney City Mission, and again I wanted to run home! Again I said, "Lord I'll come," and again came peace.

Mr McDonald took me to another building where members of the Council interviewed me. It was some weeks before word came that I was accepted. I believe in the meantime Mr McDonald went to Newcastle and heard me preach in the open-air and at a special children's meeting in Mayfield Baptist Church.

After the appointment was made I was still very nervous and felt so inadequate. In my readings God led me to Genesis 18 where God said Sarah would bear a son and she laughed for all the laws of nature said it was impossible. God was displeased and said, "Is anything too hard for God?" The other word from God was from Exodus 4:10 and 11, where Moses, being commissioned to go and lead the people of Israel out of Egypt, said to God, "I am not eloquent," and God said, "Who made your mouth?" I went to the Mission knowing there was nothing too hard for God and that he who made my mouth would speak through me in his own wonderful way.

It was hard to leave my little family and my dear wife who was expecting another child at any moment. We often laugh about that: Mary had mumps and she was expecting. Mother and father lived nearby, so she had help if needed. John was born about three weeks later.

Early Days in the Mission: Woolloomooloo and Millers Point

My first fortnight in the Mission was spent in the district of Woolloomooloo with a dear old missionary who was filling in because of staff shortages. He had labored in this district of the red light for many years and everybody in this district knew him.

One day he took me round the place where these women operated and it was moving to see how even these poor fallen women respected him. He talked with one woman and she wept as he talked. Afterwards he told me her story. She had become pregnant as a young teenager and her father cast her out of the home. He told me she would always say it could have been so different if dad had not been so hard.

I said everybody knew him; we had a dear mother at Paddington who was influenced to Christ through this dear old man. She tells how while she was bathing her baby and the next little girl was crying her heart out, there was a knock at the door and a voice saying, "I'm coming in." In walked the missionary, picked up the little girl, and nursed her till mum was finished, had a word and left, putting a pound note in her hand. One night there was a meeting in a house and the old man kept on his overcoat till finally he had to take it off—and, underneath, no jacket—he had given it away! He was very unorthodox in his conduct of meetings and in all of his work, but this dear man of God had a great witness for his Lord and Master of whom we read, "He went about doing good and the poor heard him gladly."

Before long I was settled in as missionary at the Millers Point Branch of the Mission. A new work had been added to this branch: the hall was to be open every night so men could come in from the street, play table games, have a cup of tea and biscuits, and have a little message from the Bible. At this hall a men's free breakfast was conducted on the Sunday morning, and over a hundred men attended and heard the gospel preached. For the first time I saw men under the influence of methylated spirits (metho). One man who was heckling had a big red face and a white tongue.

Millers Point was a small district and I went round from door to door visiting three times in nine months. We had a good ministry in this district; one outstanding conversion was a man who came one morning to the hall without shoes, in his stockinged feet. He had slept in the Domain and someone had stolen his shoes, and he felt that it was the end. He was on his way up to the bridge to commit suicide when he saw the mission hall, came in, and came to Christ. He was gloriously changed and came out to the open-air meetings, giving his testimony to what Christ his Savior had done for him. We had a ministry to the young people, especially the boys. It was in a depression time and I used to cut their hair and do other things to help them. I went up one day to see our Superintendent and to ask him if I could do some hospital visiting, and he said, "We have something else for you"—it was the district of Paddington. We were sorry to leave the workers and people of Millers Point and dear sister Edgar. One worker said, "We resented your coming, but we are sorry you are going."

"His Will Be Done": Paddington

The shift from Millers Point meant we had to leave the house we lived in, in Lower High Street, and seek a house in Paddington. I had decided we must live in our district and my wife was right with me. We found a double-storied place not far from the hall. We had a really distressing experience in relation to this. One night we woke up with John, the baby, crying and discovered bugs crawling all over him. The old lady who lived in the house before us had not been able to keep it clean. It was not a very nice experience for us who had never seen a bug before, but we accepted it as part of the new life and got in and cleaned it up.

The Paddington ministry was a great one with dear sister Pite and a great crowd of lovely workers, and we were six-and-a-half years in this district. At the close the Municipal Council sent us a note of thanks with an accompanying letter to our Mission Council. This was, of course, because of the help given to the needy through soup kitchens and in many other ways. We had a ministry to unemployed men. A little weatherboard cottage became vacant close to our back door, so I rushed to the landlord and took it; the rent was ten pound per week. I rang Mr McDonald and he said, "You will have to put it to the Mission Council." I said, "I will lose the cottage." He said, "All right, Mr Cowley and I will come and see it." I rushed round to the landlord and told him not to say I had already paid the first week's rent. They saw the cottage and I told them I would do a work amongst unemployed men. Mr Cowley said "Fine, my boy, go ahead. Here is the first week's rent."

In this work God raised up a dear man who said, "John McKittrick, help people who are in real need and I will foot the bill at the end of each month." I presented to him a list of all helped and he paid the bill. One time he was looking over the list and he saw a tube of toothpaste listed. He said, "John McKittrick, you are a bit extravagant, I use ordinary soap to clean my teeth." Here was a dear man giving hundreds of pounds to help needy people and washing his teeth with soap! I had taken the tube of toothpaste to a man in jail; I thought it would be good to take the little practical gift as well as telling him of our wonderful Savior.

The most important part of the ministry was that we saw young and old come to know Christ as Lord and Savior. On Friday night we had a Bible study; up to twenty young people came; then we went out for an open-air meeting. One night it was very cold and windy, and we nearly did not go to the open-air meeting, but then decided to go to Elizabeth Place; it had houses on three sides, with only one opening.

A young man came and sat down on the footpath, attracted by Ben Ewing's singing. We showed him the way of salvation and on the Sunday night he came to the service and announced he had accepted the Lord Jesus as his Savior. Ernie became one of our teachers and is now an Anglican minister. I believe what contributed to Ernie's conversion was that that night our open-air meeting was followed by a night of prayer at the hall. Several young people stopped for some hours and others till Saturday morning when it was time to go to a meeting that they conducted themselves at Bronte Beach.

We had many and varied experiences as we sought to help the needy and bring the gospel of Christ to them. The Mission directed those who came to Christ into the church of their choice, and because of that we had no service on the Sunday mornings. I well remember some young men going with me to Burton Street Baptist Church—at least two were new converts—and on the way home praying and praising God as we walked. Another time I took a new convert to the Lord's Table at Burton Street and, as we sat in meditation, thinking of Calvary and all that our blessed Redeemer suffered for us, this dear man who had been redeemed from much let out such a loud sob it was heard all over the church—what a moving occasion! Another morning, hurrying to Burton, I saw I could not make it in time so, with my three children, slipped into the Salvation Army meeting. It was a visiting officer who said to his congregation, "Have freedom to express your Christian joy in your own way." There was a dear old man who took out his handkerchief and began throwing it in the air and walking up and down the aisle, occasionally shouting, "Hallelujah!" It was a bright, happy service, at least the children thought so—they wanted to go to the Salvation Army every Sunday morning!

A big night at this branch was the Annual Meeting when over two hundred people came, people who had had many happy associations with Paddington Mission, many who had found Christ. Our local Member of Parliament, Mr M. O'Sullivan, MLA, never missed, and he always brought a word of real appreciation and encouragement.

It was while at Paddington that our lovely lass Mary, our eldest daughter of ten, was taken to be with the Lord. She was a lovely girl, and how we missed her, but I will leave my wife Mary to tell you that from a copy of a paper she gave at a young people's meeting in another district:

> I take this opportunity just to testify what Jesus means in a mother's life. Having brought nine children into the world and being the grandmother of ten you will surely grant that I must know something of what I am talking about. My first little baby only lived three weeks, having been born prematurely. This was a big blow to me, but in this big sorrow the Lord Jesus was very real. Only a mother will know about those days, weeks, and months of waiting and glad anticipation, then disappointment and awful loss. Our third child was taken also, when she was a lovely lass of ten years. I went into Paddington Women's Hospital to have my seventh child, leaving this very capable lovely girl assisting her father to look after the four others. Whilst in hospital complications set in and I was kept in longer than usual. Whilst there, Mary, who was a big strong girl, was suddenly taken ill. The doctor diagnosed it as meningitis and she was rushed to the Children's Hospital. She was there three days when I was discharged from hospital.
>
> I had just arrived home and was having a cup of tea with my husband and a dear friend from Melbourne when the doorbell rang sharply. The door was opened, I heard the boy say, "You are wanted at once at the hospital." My husband then told me Mary was critically ill. He rushed off to the hospital just in time to see her pass home to be with Jesus. This was

Movement Four—From Forgetfulness to Transforming Memory

a big blow to us. Dad and I cried together night after night but through it all we proved the power of our wonderful Savior the Lord Jesus Christ. Here is a copy of a letter we sent to more than a hundred sympathizers who expressed their sympathy by wreath, letter, or card. "Our dear friends, thanking you for your sympathy we want you to know we have been so conscious of the sustaining power of God; truly his grace is sufficient for every need. As we watched our girlie grow we rejoiced because she was not only growing a big girl physically but mentally and above all spiritually. Having accepted Christ as her Savior at the age of six we saw the fruits of God's Spirit in the young life and this is sufficient indication of the help she was in the Mission and in the home. In four days she was taken off with meningitis. What a loss to us, but our loss is heaven's gain, and we do not grudge Mary to our dear Lord. She was a sweet little bud down here; she is now blooming in the garden above. She was able to play and sing the beautiful hymns of Zion; today she is singing in the heavenly choir. We were training her for service here but God said, 'Your place is up here.' We miss her so much but we have sweet peace in our hearts. We know that our Heavenly Father doeth all things well. 'The Lord hath given and the Lord hath taken away, blessed be the Name of the Lord.' Thanking you for your expressions of sympathy and love at this time."

I could go on telling you of the wonderful way God undertook through our whole lives. It was not always easy to make ends meet on a missionary's salary—seven little lives need a lot of care and understanding, but I can say from a heart full of praise and thanksgiving: "God always undertook." When we were struggling to pay off our home, more than once my husband went in to the solicitor to be greeted by, "John McKittrick, a friend of yours rang up to say take fifty off John McKittrick's mortgage and charge it to me." I think of the time we were on holidays at Katoomba and the Mission Accountant promised to send our salary. Somehow it was overlooked and there was the daily trip to the Katoomba Post Office, whilst the cupboard was becoming more and more bare, but it still came just in time. The wife of one of our missionaries could vouch for this because she was a girl in our district at the time and she was spending the holidays with us. She used to call it black Friday. God never once let us down. I would say to you dear young people that the secret of real living, not only for mothers, but also for all, is to take the Lord Jesus into your life and let him have control. He will never let you down. It is we who fail him.

God holds the key
Leave all things in the Father's hands
He holds the key
He will unravel every knot
Wait patiently

His promises will stand each test
His love bestows the very best
Oh, do not fear—pray, trust and rest
God holds the key.

When Bill Clack and I arrived at the hospital, our little girl Mary was nearly home. We gathered with the nurses round the cot and committed our dear one to our great heavenly Father. On the way down the ward Bill pulled out his New Testament and said, "John, the promise is here." I said, "Bill, when Mary took sick I committed her to God's keeping and his will be done." God gave me the strength to stand beside a little white coffin in Kinsella's parlors and tell my people we were proving all that we had told them of God's power for every circumstance of life.

We were appointed to Balmain and again found it so hard to part with the dear workers and many friends.

Tents and Tennis: Balmain

What a challenge the district of Balmain presented! One of the highlights was the Tent Missions. I could see what a great opportunity to reach people this could be. All through the district there were single blocks of land not built on; with a tent we could get to the people's very door, and then the unusual way of presenting the gospel would appeal to the people. I went to an auction of army gear and picked up a second-hand tent that would seat about two hundred people. The men of the district were a fine bunch; some of them were young in the faith but they got right behind the effort. Missions were held all through the district, people came into the tent and were gloriously saved. One of the missions went for continuous days, seven days at four different places. You might ask how we managed to do that. The workers came each Saturday morning early, dismantled the tent, carted it to the new site, and set it up again ready for the night meeting; it was a colossal task. I remember one dear brother saying to me, "My muscles are all sore!" No wonder, they all loved it!

Eventually the tent was blown down and ripped to pieces in a storm. We continued the mission in a church hall, but it was not the same. One man whose wife was a young Christian (converted one night in the missionary's home) said to his grown-up family at the breakfast table, "We must do something about another tent, I'll give one pound," and that morning he got ten pounds. I used this in an appeal for a new tent. The money was given, so I went and bought another good second-hand tent. The mission was continued in the tent and the first man to be converted was this same man. He and his wife have borne a great witness for Christ through all the years. We built a mission hall by volunteer labor on one of the sites where we had the tent at this time; God used Birchgrove Branch over the years to the salvation of precious souls.

Movement Four—From Forgetfulness to Transforming Memory

We lived in Birchgrove and the first fruits of the Balmain ministry were our next-door neighbor. Mary and Mrs Emblem had morning tea together and little chats about eternal things. This dear lady is now a member of a church at the Lakes District; her two young people were converted too, and have set up Christian homes. A granddaughter is a missionary in Brazil.

Another great witnessing ministry was in the open-air. I had a box on a three-wheeled bike that carried a record player and an amplifier. I could pull into a street, play a good record, and then speak the message. Every Saturday morning I went to Woolworths' busy corner in Rozelle, sometimes joined by some of our young people, and heralded out the glad message of God's love in Jesus our wonderful Savior. On Tuesdays I went to Palmolive at lunch time, Levers on Wednesdays, the Dock on Thursdays, and spent Sunday nights after service on the main street outside the Post Office, at which meeting we were often joined by people from other churches and always a good number of our own people.

We had many different receptions but mostly were well received. Mr McDonald came to the Dock meeting one day and was moving around amongst the men when one man said, "I don't believe in what you are telling us, but I believe in him." I had had the privilege on one occasion of showing this man some practical Christianity.

One Sunday morning I was preaching at the Balmain Baptist Church when a big man, who had just enough drink to make him want to fight everybody, made his way, after a while, up to the pulpit to fight the preacher. He tripped on the little platform in front of the pulpit and, as he fell, he struck a big heavy oak flower stand and lay on the floor. As the deacons were taking him out he said, "He got me a beauty, didn't he?" My own young people never forgot this incident; in fact, it was one of them who reminded me about it.

In the midst of this busy round of preaching activities I did not neglect visiting the people. I went through every part of the district from door to door more than once. I had the privilege of ministering to a dear spastic young man for over ten years. In the morning I would run over and get him out of bed, and wash and dress him. Barry was almost completely helpless, everything had to be done for him; may I pay tribute to a dear mother who just lived for him. Barry is a bright lovely Christian. In the dining room of the house he had a big, heavy oak music stand and on the stand a big Bible; he had a pencil with a rubber on the end and with the pencil in his mouth he turned the pages. He loved God's word, and loved to be taken in his chair to services.

At our golden wedding celebration a young woman told of her poor crippled father who was visited sometimes twice a day by the missionary who helped her mother to get him out to the side of the bed and prop him up with pillows to give a little measure of ease, then helped get him back to bed at night. She told of how her mother got a poisoned leg, and how no one could be found to look after the family whilst she was in hospital. The missionary brought a single mattress from home and slept on the floor beside her father, and cared for him and the two little girls. This dear man used to cry with pain, as we would shift him to try to ease him. One day he said, "What have I done to deserve this?" I replied, "I cannot explain it, but one thing I do know, there will be no pain in heaven." He is there now; he came to know Christ as his Savior.

I must mention a part of this ministry that I believe God blessed, and that was the sports program. We had teams in the Churches Soccer Association for men and boys, and some of our Christian young men used this to touch the lives of young people outside the church.

We built a tennis court just behind the mission hall. I went to see the owner of this block of ground to ask if we could rent it from her. She was a very gracious lady, and said we could have it on the one condition that if she sold we would immediately vacate. The block was used very often by people to dump rubbish, but our men and young people spent many hours clearing and preparing it. The many redback spiders were one of the hazards! I went to see a cartage contractor five doors up the street about ashes for the foundation. This man had the contract for taking the ashes from Lever Bros to the dump and he was happy to help. I said, "How much per load?" He said, "If you like you can give the carter something." He was a fine old man—I coveted him for Christ. His backyard adjoined a portion of the tennis court ground and he sought to save us a lot of work by tipping loads of ashes and making a ramp so that the lorries could drive into the court and save us barrowing all over, but the plan had to be abandoned—the first load sank down in the ashes, and, worse still, the petrol poured out of the motor and it was rationed in those days! This dear old man just ran and got a container and tried to catch some of the spilling petrol. He set an example that many Christians could well follow.

The tennis court proved a great boon. On Saturdays and during the week, especially on Ladies' Day, it was going from early morning. On Saturdays as many as thirty would be enjoying the fellowship and the fun. Dick Low would be trying to give everyone a game; we had to have four-game sets. One day I played a set with one of our young men, and as we both came off the court he said, "Many games like this and you will convert me to tennis"—Dan was a keen cricketer. I replied, "I know what I would like to convert you to." Later he did come to our Lord Jesus and became an active worker in his church and the Christian Police Fellowship.

During the war days our mission halls became Civilian Aid Centers. They were prepared to help people if their homes were bombed and destroyed. We had about fifty palliasses stacked up and lots of emergency food stored in cupboards. We had trained personnel, people who had at least the St John Ambulance Certificate. We missionaries and Sisters had to sit for the examination. I was on holiday at the time of the final examination and on my way to the place of examination I was checking up on my paper on burns. Whilst waiting to start, there was a suggestion to have some prayer. Sister Bladon prayed, "Lord, you know how busy John McKittrick has been, help him." The examiner took us in groups of three. One of the questions asked at our group was, "If you got a fishing hook in your arm, what would you do?" I was able to

Movement Four—From Forgetfulness to Transforming Memory

answer because one of my boys got a fishing hook in his arm whilst on holiday and I rushed with him to the doctor who cut it out. When I came back an old fisherman said, "What you should have done was to take the hook through and not pull it back." The other question was on burns. I got my certificate although it was not necessary for me to have it; I had a good number of trained workers. When the siren went on the night the Japanese were in Sydney Harbour, we were all prepared for what might happen.

A real prayer ministry followed all this up and that is why God blessed. One Sunday School picnic a man said to our Sunday School Superintendent, "Where do you get all the children from?" He said, "Half an hour's prayer before Sunday School." We started the Lord's Day with a prayer meeting at 7am. We also had a prayer meeting each Wednesday night and before all other meetings. We had people who knew how to pray. There was the young woman who prayed, "Lord, may the City Night Refuge be a rescue shop within a yard of hell," and the dear old lady of eighty who would cry, "Lord save Beattie Street!" and "Lord, save my husband!" God answered her prayers—her husband was converted before he died and people were converted in Beattie Street.

We were buying our own home; an uncle of mine in the homeland had willed us about two hundred and fifty pounds. I went to the local agent and told him to let me know if he had anything that would suit our family. I was riding along one morning when I saw the "For Sale" board on a house. When I went in to the agent to see about it, he said it would be the very thing for us, but had not thought of it before. Mr Cowley, our treasurer, bid for it and terms were arranged for paying it off. It was an old two-story place. With the help of the family we painted inside and outside, and we were very happy in Terry Street.

Then came the challenge of the City Night Refuge, such an entirely different ministry! What an uprooting, and what a sad parting—after thirteen-and-a-half years we had become part of the district!

Before we leave this district may I be permitted to put in two cuttings from Balmain papers?

> Workers come in all shapes and sizes. One of the smaller and least assuming varieties is young John McKittrick, Superintendent of the Sydney City Mission in Beattie Street. I'd hate to have to compete with him on a piecework job. Have you seen his spare-time job of the last few weeks, the new tennis court in Beattie Street! John McKittrick has put in some terrific toil there, all work so that those who help him to help others can play. That bike of his is a worker too: I've seen him transporting bags of cement on it, bags of sand, and even a wheelbarrow. "Mac" breaks every union rule ever made, works about an eighty-hour week, probably doesn't know what he gets paid for it, definitely doesn't care whether he is paid or not, is never without an intriguingly friendly grin on his face and gives as his motto, "Need not Creed." Many are called but

few are chosen and it strikes me young "Mac" was well chosen. If I had half his heart I'd be a better man.

More than four hundred residents packed the Balmain Town Hall last Saturday to pay their respects to missionary and Mrs John McKittrick on their Golden Wedding celebrations. The McKittricks spent thirteen years in Balmain following mission and charity work during the depression and war days. Although now living in Campbelltown this well-known couple are still remembered here for the help they were always prepared to give to those in need. A relative, Samuel McKittrick, who came with his wife from Nelson Bay Baptist Church for the Balmain celebrations, summed up the feelings of those at the Town Hall with the words: "Some ministers preach good sermons, John McKittrick went further than that—he lived them." During his time in Balmain, John McKittrick was well known as a man on a bicycle with a ready smile and helping hand for everyone. Mary on the other hand always held open house for those who were hungry.

Mention should be made of the great ministry of sisters Bladon, Edgar, Mason, and McMillan—great servants of Christ.

A Home to the Homeless: The City Night Refuge

I was visiting Mr Cowley our Treasurer in hospital and he said to me, "Can't you get me help for the Refuge?" Mr McDonald had asked me on two occasions to take the Refuge, but I said not while a certain gentleman was there. This man came from the old set-up of the Refuge before the Mission took over and used to take charge if there was no manager. To say the least, he did not know how to deal with the men. When Mr Cowley said this, it seemed as though God said, "You must!" I went home and said to my wife, "Come and have a look at the City Night Refuge." When she had a look at the place and I told her how I felt God was challenging me to take over the place, she said she was willing to come. I went to our Superintendent and I said I was willing to go to the Refuge. I never even asked about salary. I found later it was sixteen pounds per week with food and accommodation; the whole of the staff's gratuities, as they were called, was under fifty pounds per week; the highest-paid man was the cook who received 6 pounds. The men were happy to have this small money and to have a secure home and they did not get into trouble.

We were to live in the historic old cottage that was next door to and part of the Refuge. Mary went to a Balmain firm which we knew and had special long curtains made for the old lounge room. This was only one of the ways we sought to brighten up the old house; we paid these off by time payment out of our big salary. I will always remember the first day as I went to take over, kneeling down in the old room, literally trembling and committing it all into God's hands.

Movement Four—From Forgetfulness to Transforming Memory

What a task it was! R.G. Henry, one of our missionaries said, "John, you will have to shut it down and commence in a new place, it stinks." And it did stink! The Mission hadn't long taken it over, and the original committee could not get men to run it properly.

Every night at least one hundred men would line up in the street waiting to come in for the evening meal. The Police van would come down and take any man who had too much drink to the cells. This was the first thing we altered. There was an old building in the yard of the Refuge that was used for storing furniture; the furniture was removed elsewhere and I rang a plumber friend to ask when he could put on a new roof. He said straight away, and within a week the men were off the street. They came into this building that we called the Assembly Room at 3.30pm and played dominoes and table games or just talked. My own two youngest boys often played with them.

The second thing was the staff quarters. These men who were supposed to be keeping the place clean were sleeping in a dormitory with about an inch of fluff and cigarette butts on the floor. The first few weeks were hell and it came mainly from the staff. We decided to divide this dormitory up into little cubicles and every man had his own little room with his dressing table, etc. Our own handyman, a very fine old Irishman, did the alterations. This meant we got a better class of man coming to us for work.

There were two big dormitories, each with fifty-two beds. The beds in one were free. In the other two shillings and sixpence was charged per night. This meant that a man out of work could have a free bed till his dole came through, and then he paid for his bed. We had pensioners who came for periods, but they were not allowed to remain permanently.

On the free beds were canvas sheets which were not changed, but white sheets that were changed once a week were on the paid beds. I ordered the canvas sheets to be replaced by white sheets. The old man I mentioned before, who used to sometimes take charge when there was no manager, said, "You'll ruin the place!" The work was very much in the red then, and the extra fifty-two sheets sent to laundry added quite a bit of extra expense. It was not long before we installed our own laundry unit with our own laundryman. Another thing contributing to our being in the red was having to buy quite a lot of the food required, but it was not long before we were in the position of having to buy very little. When we took over, a man with an old horse and cart brought in the food. This man was not too clean, yet he had been a sergeant in the army at one time. He went to the big bakers for food that had been left over from the day before. He would just take the trays of food and tip them into his cart. When he came to the Refuge a big sheet was spread out and the cart was tipped up, the best picked out and the rest went into the piggery bin. This was soon altered. A little motor van was purchased with "City Night Refuge Mission to Men" and our address on the sides, and the horse and cart were sold. The old man was given another job and the manager brought in the food. The food was carefully picked and handled, with the result that much less had to be paid for it, for with the better approach more people were ready to help.

One of the gifts picked up every weekday was sixty pound of meaty bones, the backbones of the ox. These were put on to boil, left overnight and stripped in the morning, and this formed the basis of the stew for the evening meal for over two hundred men. One holiday we had four hundred and fifty men lined up for a meal—one of the other places was shut in the holidays so they all came to us. How did we manage? We always had plenty of tinned soups. At the end of the winter season the big firms sent us in lines that had been left over and these were stored in readiness. We added plenty of soup to the already prepared stew, and it was quite a good meal with two slices of bread and a bun and, of course, the good cup of tea. I always told the cook to make a good cup of tea!

The other daily meal was breakfast: a plate of wholemeal porridge and two slices of bread, one with jam and the other margarine, and again the cup of tea. How did we seat such a crowd? There was seating for one hundred and twenty, and the first one hundred and twenty dinners were on the tables ready. After that the men picked up their dinners from the server, and by that time men were beginning to move out and others were able to take their place at the table. It was a colossal task with a staff of alcoholics and pensioners!

It was seldom a man was turned away without a meal, but it was different with beds—if a man had had too much drink he didn't get a bed. Many a man I lifted bodily from the table for playing up—as he sat in his seat I put my arms round him, pinning his arms to his side, and dragged him out. After the evening meal they went to bed at 6.30pm. This was why the Refuge was commenced in the beginning, I believe, to keep these men off the streets. The bell went at 6.30am in the morning, one hundred and four men locked up for twelve hours and the only man to deal with any unruliness was the manager!

Near the beginning of the ministry I came back from receiving food to find the cook with his face bleeding and his shirt torn; he told how a man had come into the kitchen knocking them all about. I said, "Come and show me him." When we got to him I said, "You cannot come here knocking the staff around, you must go out." He said, "Get the police to put me out!" I said, "We don't do that here," and grabbed him by the arm, the cook taking the other side. As we were taking him out, he said, "I've left my case back in the Assembly Room." I said, "Go and get it." When he got back to the Assembly Room where all the men were, he said, "Come on, McKittrick, I'll have a go at you!" I tried to dissuade him, but he insisted, so I just took off my coat and watch and handed them to my boy and demonstrated what I had learned as a young man in Glasgow. The next morning some of the men said, "I wish I could box like you." It got around that I had been the champion of the Navy! I did not disillusion them, it came in very handy—fellows would want to fight, and then change their minds.

Movement Four—From Forgetfulness to Transforming Memory

No alcohol was allowed on the premises; the penalty if caught was that the bottle was poured down the toilet. One day a man came in with a new bottle of wine; I took it from him and made to the place to empty it, but had not time to get there so I smashed it on the concrete floor. He threw a punch, but immediately was all apologies.

One night when a certain man asked for a bed, Mr Glasby, a retired police officer who was helping in an honorary capacity at the time, said, "We won't give him a bed, he is a stand-over man." What we did if we did not want a man to have a bed was to keep him waiting till all the others had gone off to bed. As this man saw all the others going up to bed he came to the desk saying, "Where is my bed?" We said, "We haven't got a bed for you!" Immediately he threw a punch and when I jumped round the desk to deal with him in the same way, he piped right down—Mr Glasby roared with laughter! (By the way, Mr Glasby took over the management some time after we left and did a very fine job.) We had no difficulty in dealing with such men—God always helped us. Paddy, a wild Irishman, would come up to the desk punching one hand with the other, demonstrating his strength, but he didn't frighten us.

These men, as I said, were closed in their dormitories for twelve hours, and as you could well imagine there were occasional incidents. I used to inspect the dormitories at different times in the night, sometimes at midnight, and sometimes I would find a man with a bottle at his side. I would pick it up and whisper, "See me in the morning"—he invariably lost his bed.

Occasionally there was a fight in the middle of the night; if I was asleep Mary heard them and wakened me to deal with it. One night a fellow picked me up like a baby and was carrying me to the open window. I said something and immediately he dropped me and said, "Oh, it's you Mr Mac." This man was in the DTs—they have extra strength in this condition. I booked him in the following night, but before bedtime he came to say he was going out—some of the men had ganged up against him because of the previous night. How these poor men have to suffer! Another time I was a long time fixing up a fight and when I was coming down the stairs I met my wife coming up the stairs in her dressing gown and a big iron bar in her hand. She thought something must have been happening to her husband.

What prevented a lot of unnecessary trouble of this kind was that a man was stationed at the door and watched that no one came in with a bottle. Sometimes they even fanned the man, that is, running hands down the pockets. This was a job we had big twenty-three stone John doing. One night he closed the door and came hurrying round to me "Mr Mac. there's a big man going to kill me," and sure enough when we got to the entrance door a big man rushed at John saying, "I'll kill the big so and so; I have just done seven years for nearly killing a man, I'll kill him." We were able to fix everything up all right.

On another occasion John came in to me in real distress: one of the men had caught the pocket of his trousers and ripped it right down the side; he looked so funny I just stood and laughed. He said, "It's all right for you to laugh, but it is the only pair

I've got." We were nearly always able to help with clothes, but John's size was a bit of a problem. When he came on to the staff we got a suit made to measure for him, and he paid it off out of his big gratuity.

There was a man in charge of each dormitory and his job was to keep the dormitory and the beds clean, and to watch that there were no lice brought into the beds. The cook, with a helper, was in charge of the kitchen, and there were two outside cleaners and, when we installed our laundry, a laundryman. This unit cut expenses such a lot, as did a new combustion stove. At the time the laundry was built we had a beautiful new bathroom added.

Most of the staff took an interest in the place, but would never take part in dealing with unruliness—that was left to the manager. No doubt they were afraid of repercussions. One night a man rushed down from the bathroom and said, "Mr Mac, there's a man up there and he is full of body lice." I rushed up and, true enough, he was in a dreadful condition. This man had been in the night before so I concluded he must have left them in his bed, and it was so. The dormitory man probably had found the bed made and did not touch it. Everything had to be taken off the bed, and clean blankets and sheets put on, the man's clothes burned, his body completely checked and clean clothes given. This was something we had to constantly watch. It was one of the many acts of kindness given in this place—a man who had been sleeping out and had become infected with body lice, would come and we would put him in a special bath, burn his clothes, and give him a clean rig-out. One old English gentleman had this operation. The next morning I said to him, "How do you feel now?" "Much better," he said and added, "I don't know how I get like that." This dear man had two Christian sisters home in England who wrote to him regularly, he had very poor sight and would come to Mary to read the letters to him. When she came to the part where they would be pleading with him to come to Christ and receive him as Savior, he would say, "That's enough," and would not listen. I felt Arthur had sinned away his day of grace. God had ceased to speak to him. This can happen. God says, "My Spirit shall not always strive with people."

You will no doubt be wondering what the men who came to us were like. Don't think they were all just old deadbeats; there were men who had come from homes of culture and refinement. We had two men who were Etonians. Once we had a doctor. This man sat away by himself and we were in touch with his lovely sister who was broken-hearted about her brother. One night a man said, "Mr Mac. You are not talking to a donkey, you are talking to an officer of the Gurkhas!"—he had been an officer in the Indian army. This man had a special trade in printing and was much in demand, but would only last in a job till he got his first pay.

We had a young man of twenty seven years, the son of a titled man home in England. My heart bled for this young fellow, I tried so hard to help him. Mary had him in our home and in so many ways tried to show him we cared. We lost sight of him for a period, and then I got word that he was in one of the big psychiatric hospitals. I went

Movement Four—From Forgetfulness to Transforming Memory

to see him and the Superintendent said to me he was prepared to let him come out if I would look after him. I told him I would be happy to do that. Just before he came out he received one hundred pounds from his dad; he bought two new suits and all that went with it. When he came to the Refuge, I said to him, "Do not touch the grog, you cannot take even one drink." He said, "I have learned my lesson, I won't touch it." That same afternoon I saw him outside one of the big hotels in Broadway, drunk. I didn't see him again for three weeks, when he turned up at the Refuge filthy dirty and on the verge of the DTs. We took him in and doctored him up (Mary used to say I looked after these men more than I did her!), and when he was right again we let him go, again with a word not to touch alcohol. We did not see him for a period again, and then we heard he was back at the hospital. We thought this was the end for this young man, but he turned up at the Refuge some months later, looking the perfect gentleman. After greetings he said, "It will be different this time, I am engaged to a lovely lady." We thought this might be the answer for him, but he turned up again and we could see he had been drinking. When we asked him about the love affair he said, "It's all off." I had occasion to speak to the lady on the phone and in a beautiful cultured voice she said, "John McKittrick, he is impossible—I caught him drinking metho." The last we heard of him was that his mother had sent his fare for him to go home. We heard this young man learned to drink when an officer in the army and was stationed at a place where there was no duty on the grog.

Another man we tried to help was a brilliant fellow; he was a writer and a sculptor. In his own words he said before he was eight he could play the piano, and before he was twelve he had read as many books as any ordinary man. For over twelve months we had him booking in the men and in charge of clothing. What a disappointment when one night he came in the worse for drink; when he was on it he was truly on it! He was the only man I have known to drink metho without you being able to smell it on him; we never found out what he did. I tried to get him back on his feet again, but he was never the same. We found this out about alcoholics; they seemed to give up easily after a mistake. This man was never arrested for drunkenness. Even in the midst of a bender he would keep clean and dress fairly presentably, and invariably walked along carrying a folded newspaper. When recovering he suffered hell, perspiration would run down his face, and it was easy to see he was in agony. On one occasion taking him for a drive and a chat in the little mission van we went through Northbridge, and he said, "Mr Mac, I used to drive my own beautiful car through this district."

Bill was a lovely fellow who would do anything for you. He helped me to paint the outside of the Refuge on one occasion, and what a job that was with our improvised trestles, etc. Bill was at Lidcombe Hospital for a period. He came back saying, "I am finished with the grog," and told me how in his ward there was a man who had been an international footballer. This man had been in the same ward for about three months yet when he went to the bathroom and came back he did not know which was his bed. The doctor told Bill this man's brain had gone soft through alcohol and added,

"You are going the same way unless you give it away." Poor old Bill, he used to carry around tablets that made the drinker violently ill if he took a drink, but as far as we know he did not come to the only One who could deliver him, our wonderful Savior.

How do men like that get to this awful position? We who know Christ as our own personal Savior know that it is only he who keeps us from this and other evils, because we are sinners by nature and we need to be born again.[1]

Very often it has been some disappointment or other that has just left them discouraged and feeling they cannot face it all. One Sunday two men were standing away by themselves. I said, "Good afternoon, how are you?" "No good," said one, "It is Sunday and we cannot get a drink." I said, "Is that all you live for?" After further conversation one man said, "Do you see this man here? At one time he was one of the best-dressed men in Sydney." I said, "What happened?" and he told this story. His friend was a qualified shopwalker, he had worked for many of the leading stores, but his wife was an alcoholic, and every place he worked at she came in and disgraced him. The last place he worked at was McDowells and he did not tell her where he was working, but one day he was coming down the stairs and bumped into her—that was the end, he gave it all away.

Very few people have any sympathy for these poor people. We had a man who took very ill, and we rang the doctor who came about midnight. I said, "Oh doctor, I could not let you into the dormitory at this time of the night, I would have fifty-two men on my hands all night." He said, "Leave it to me." We quietly went to the man's bed by the light of a torch. The doctor quietly talked to the man, gave him an injection, and said he would be back in the morning. Whilst he was washing his hands the doctor said, "He's been drinking. Has he been drinking metho?" I said, "I don't think Marny drinks metho." Then the doctor said, "You cannot blame these poor fellows." I said, "Oh, doctor?" He said, "Well think about it, all they possess is the clothes they stand up in, no friends, depending on charity for a bed to sleep in."

Poor fellows, I tried to show them love and concern, and they knew we cared. As they were coming down the stairs from the dormitory in the morning I would greet them with, "Good morning, that's a nice clean shirt you have on this morning," or something like that. Then I would stand beside the cook as he dished up the porridge to the ones who came in from outside and greet them too. I should mention here that men who had slept out would very often grab the cup of tea trembling and begin to drink as they walked to the table. That is why I said to the cook, "Always make a good cup of tea."

The police were our friends, but they were not allowed to go through to check the men. If they wanted a man they came to the cottage and said whom they wanted and I went to the man and whispered, "You are wanted at the office," and the poor fellow was not embarrassed in front of the others. One man told me he met fellows all over Australia who knew about our love and concern for these poor men. Some of them

---

1. John 3:3.

Movement Four—From Forgetfulness to Transforming Memory

hiked all over Australia. You may think that we were only interested in giving men a bed and a feed but that is not so: often I called out to the men, "We are here not just to give you a feed and a bed, we are here to point you to Christ our wonderful Savior whom you need." This was our main desire and work, that Christ might be exalted. We believe that our wonderful Savior is able to save such and make them new creatures. "If anyone is in Christ they are a new creation: old things are passed away; behold all things are become new."[2]

A service was held after tea on the Sunday night; different men and parties came to sing and speak. We sometimes had a Bible study during the week, and we were always available to talk with the men. "What results did you see?" you might ask—there were men who were brought to Christ and their lives changed by the power of Christ, but not many; perhaps this was because we had not time to pray as we should have. On deputation to the churches I used to say, "Pray for us, we have not time to pray as we should." "This kind comes out only through prayer and fasting."[3]

Big John was an outstanding case of a man becoming a new creation through faith in Christ. John had a beautiful voice. Before his conversion he would go into a hotel and sing something, and before long the counter before him was filled with pots of drink as men asked him to sing; every night he would be thrown out drunk. One thing stands out in my mind: I was taking him with me to sing at a big men's meeting down the coast. He sat next to me in the front of the van reading an Amplified New Testament, and every now and again he would say, "Listen to this Mr Mac!" He loved his Bible, a sure sign that a person has become a new creation in Christ.

Then there was Charlie, who married a very lovely nursing sister who had helped at the Refuge for a while, and who with his wife lived for Christ to the joy of members of his own family who had prayed for him for years.

Another was Michael, who married a fine lady and had two children. When giving his testimony he would say, "When God can save me he can save anyone." He died later as the result of his past awful life. He is with his Lord.

This was my report, which appeared in the December issue of the Mission Herald, 1955:

> In a ministry of this nature, there are experiences which encourage and which disappoint. It is only by the power of God that human beings can be set free from the sins that enslave, and know the joy of victorious living.
>
> One man, whom we had helped for a long time and of whose future we had eventually despaired, was in a service at a mission hall recently. He has not taken drink for twelve months and consequently he is no longer a vagrant. He has been received back by his lovely wife and they are rebuilding their home life. He is a man of gifts, an artist of outstanding merit and, when free from drink, can easily support his family.

2. 1 Corinthians 5:17.
3. Matthew 17:21.

A man in a dreadful state of drunkenness came while a service was being conducted. In the audience was a man who had been lifted from the depths through faith in the Lord Jesus Christ. This man escorted the enslaved man out and talked with him, telling him of his own experience of the saving power of Christ. He took a taxi, went to a chemist, and purchased a sleeping draught and then brought the man to the Refuge where he was given a bed. This is an incident worth remembering.

Amongst the things that sadden are the deaths that occur at intervals of men who will not accept God's offer of salvation. Someone does not waken in the morning and arrangements have to be made for the disposal of the body, with the knowledge that another has gone out into the dark.

For some months the missionary and his helpers cared for a little man who had no legs. He was carried up and down stairs and looked after in all ways. The doctor had warned him that he was eating too little and drinking too much and prescribed medicine for him. He was found dead in his wheelchair in the street; five days previously the missionary had bathed and shaved him, giving him a change of clothing, and had taken him to Sydney Hospital. He died of pneumonia, a slave to his appetite.

The missionary was requested to attend at the morgue to identify a man who had been sleeping at the Refuge and who had been found in the Harbour. He had been drinking metho with a companion and had either fallen in or had thrown himself in; he was a clever motor mechanic and at one time owned his own garage and a service station. The unutterable sadness of those who lose all, and their souls in addition!

In the August 1, 1956 issue of the Mission Herald this report appeared:

In addition to the work of the Refuge there is an opportunity to go to the wharfies in the early morning for open-air meetings—five hundred men to preach to each week! What a privilege to bring to them the glad message! If prayer backed up this witness, great things could be accomplished. A man came to us last week and said he was a believer, mentioning the church where he worshipped. We have met only two Christians in the eighteen-month ministry on the wharves; pray for these two men and a backslider contacted, pray for a mighty work of God's Holy Spirit amongst them.

This article from June 1957:

A glance at the figures shows that 132,960 free meals were provided (an increase over last year) and 39,420 beds were occupied. Some fifty beds each night are paid for (two shillings and sixpence each), the remainder are free. All sorts and conditions of men turn up for shelter—the uncouth and the refined, the dirty and the clean, the trickster and unfortunately some new Australians. The main reason is economic; they have not sufficient money to get accommodation elsewhere. The Refuge is not a permanent hostel, there is a limit on the nights allowed, but it is always full. Many who seek shelter are in a pitiable condition due mainly to the evils of the drink traffic to which they have fallen. The majority of the men are slowly but surely reaping the full benefits, victims to a degree that would seem beyond recovery. Sin pays its wages! Is there no hope for these men? Ask the missionary in charge and he with flashing eye and Bible in hand will answer that there is hope, and will tell of men who (in this past year) have found Christ and gone out to face the world as new creatures. Mary ably supports John McKittrick in this difficult sphere of service. Thanks are due to Mr R. W. Glasby and others who from time to time are able to help.

Finally an article from May 1, 1957, in which a dear lady who loved the Mission and knew so much about it and its ministry each month had been writing articles about the members of the staff; these were called "spotlighting":

If it is true, as has been said, that the playing fields of Eton have had a decided effect on the conflicts of England then I venture to suggest that the football fields of Glasgow have provided the Sydney City Mission with a man who down through the years (since as a lad of ten chosen to represent the schools of Glasgow at football) has retained the zeal and fighting spirit which fostered his love for the game.

He was a boxer in his day, too, this gentle-spirited, inoffensive servant of all, whose gracious presence has brightened many a sick room; whose faith has infused hope to the hopeless and comfort to the dying. Incidentally he tells me that his experience in the ring is useful occasionally if one of the guests of the City Night Refuge needs a firm hand. But strong-arm tactics are not the usual method employed by missionary John McKittrick in this most heart-breaking ministry of his. I quote the advice that he gives always to young Christian workers as his own rule of life: "Work hard and pray much!"

Work hard? John McKittrick rises before five each morning; spends a hallowed time "in the secret place" and is at work soon after five, superintending the preparation of breakfast for his overnight guests. This of course, is the famous McKittrick wholemeal porridge with bread and jam. At 9.30am the men leave and the missionary's day is spent replenishing stocks from the markets etc., and attending to the continual cleaning operations of the Refuge. At 3.30pm the men return again, waiting in the Assembly Room until their tea of stew and rolls is served before they retire at 6.30pm. One hundred and fifty have breakfast, two hundred and seventy are provided with tea, and one hundred and six beds are provided each night. Quite a family, you will agree.

Though religion is not handed out with the soup, John McKittrick assures me that each man is quietly spoken to about the Lord Jesus Christ and his power to lift the fallen, a Scripture booklet given to all. On Sunday evenings a gospel service is held in the dining room. I suggested that the work must be depressing and frustrating, and his reply was characteristic of the man: "Over and over again when I have talked to the men about salvation and find they are interested only in receiving a shirt, a razor, a meal, or a bed, I go to my room and fall on my knees to cry to God for the souls of these poor beaten men." Oh yes, he works hard and prays much, practicing always what he preaches.

John McKittrick left Scotland in 1924 to see the world and to escape from religion that had surrounded him in his Christian home all through his life. "Religion was for sissies," he argued, "not for pugilists and footballers!" Who can gauge the measure and power of a mother's prayers which, "followed, followed after"? On the high seas he met the Master face to face, and was brought to his knees in his cabin, after locating the Bible that his mother had begged him to read, yet which he had packed away as "not needed on the voyage." One has to be careful that these spotlight articles do not read as character references or funeral orations but I write now, most sincerely that I believe that in that hour of revelation and conversion, a twentieth-century saint was commissioned to move among his fellows, truly as a person "sent from God whose name was John."

For a while John McKittrick worked as a brickmaker in Newcastle assisting in open-air evangelism at every opportunity. The attention of Rev. S. A. McDonald was drawn to this young man with a passion for souls of men and on the recommendation of Dr F. H. Rayward and Rev. A. Jolly, the Superintendent invited John McKittrick to accept appointment with the Sydney City Mission, which he did, as he says, in fear and trembling at the greatness of the task, yet thrilled to be called of God. That was twenty-four years ago. Since then he has served in Millers Point, Paddington, and Balmain with his jolly, self-sacrificing wife, who has counted it a joy to take second place in the heart of her husband, "that Christ may be all and in all." I well remember in his hour of deepest sorrow, how John McKittrick went from the deathbed of his lovely daughter to comfort another broken-hearted father in the same ward who sorrowed without hope. The ward sister stood by with awe—confessing that she felt the presence of God.

On the occasion of his "farewell" from the Paddington district the Municipal Council sent a letter to the Mission Council expressing their appreciation of a splendid ministry.

The new system of radio call-up of wharf laborers has meant the termination of the open-air meetings that John McKittrick conducted summer and winter at 7am at the wharf-laborers' pick-up center. If he has any spare time (which I doubt) he gives it to the work of the Poona and Indian Village Mission of which John McKittrick is the Chairman of the Sydney Council. Aware that the circumstances are dissimilar yet the sentiments the same, I borrow Shakespeare's declaration to pay tribute to a revered missionary and friend:

His life was gentle and the elements
So mixed in him that nature might stand up
And say to all the world—
This was a man.

Movement Four—From Forgetfulness to Transforming Memory

After five years in this taxing ministry we had to ask for a change. Just how taxing it was is known only by God and my dear partner (she got to the stage where she could not sleep at night thinking of these dear men). It was during this ministry that my lovely father took ill and had a cancer operation. The hospital authorities were prepared to put him in a home, but I said, "No, we will look after him." He had a special room to himself and we looked after him. One day he said, "What a son!" I said, "What a father!" He was a mighty man of prayer and we felt the benefit at the Refuge.

It was during this period that one night I booked in an old man whom I could see was very ill, but whom I could not turn away. In the morning he and his bed were in a shocking condition, he had been sick every way. It was my job to clean him up; I could not ask men who were receiving such small money to do such a job. I rang Lidcombe Hospital, and was told they could not take him for several days. I had no hope of looking after the dear old chap, what could I do? I dressed the old man in clean clothes, gave him a cup of tea and a scone, and set him off up the street. It was not long till a man came in and said one of my inmates had fallen down in the street. I did nothing about it, something I found hard to do, something under ordinary circumstances I would not have done, but I was worn out. I knew someone would ring the Ambulance and he would be taken to Lidcombe Hospital, and this is what happened. We tried to follow up cases in hospital, jail, going to Lidcombe, Long Bay, Parramatta, and Maitland.

From Door to Door: Glebe

We went from the Refuge to the Glebe district, and the Mission's best hall—it had wonderful facilities and some very fine workers, some of whom had found Christ there. I will never forget the Sunday morning out in the open-air witnessing, dear John a fine young man with me, when we went into his own street and he literally trembled as he told his neighbors what Christ meant to him. There was a good work done amongst the young people in Girls' Brigade, Boys' Brigade and Sunday School. We picked up children in our van. The tennis court was used to reach many. The men came on Saturdays at 7.30 till 9.30am, then the children, and in the afternoon the young people. I had a strange experience one Saturday afternoon: a dear old lady sent word to me that she had planned to go to the Registry Office in Balmain to be the second witness to her granddaughter's wedding, but was too sick, could I fit in for her? I could not refuse and consented to go. It meant I had to go in my tennis rig-out to Balmain, but fortunately the Registrar knew me and understood I was trying to help. The bride and the bridesmaid were both pregnant; I found out later the young couple did very well together, although I never saw them again.

One Saturday a woman came and said a young lady had come from another State to board with her and she had no friends, could we help? Helen came and played tennis that afternoon, and at night went to a Special Mission in another district where she was converted. She became a Sunday School teacher with us, and later married the Superintendent of a Sunday School in another district and set up a lovely Christian home.

I have, too, a picture in my mind of one of our young men with his open Bible on the sideline, at soccer, helping another young person.

We saw several very fine conversions. A woman in her testimony told how, before she was converted, she used to be cranky and swearing at the children as she was getting them off to school. She would be so sorry and ashamed, and resolve to do better but the next day she was as bad as ever; but when Christ came in it all changed. This dear woman with another young convert went from door-to-door visiting with me.

A mother came to me about her daughter. She said when this girl was growing up her own father said to the girl, "If I had your face and figure I would not work," and that's where she was, a street girl. We prayed for her and one day the mother sent word that she had come home. I went to see her and had the joy of leading her home to Jesus. A few weeks later her brother came and said, "I want what my sister has." I pointed him to Christ. This was one of the evidences that Christ had changed this young woman. She not only started coming to the gospel meetings and the prayer meetings, but she also wanted to become a Sunday School teacher as soon as she was converted.

Another woman came to Christ and what a change came into her life! She began to dress nicely and attend the meetings. Her doctor and many other people were amazed at the change in this dear woman, but she had a bad slip, when an old man friend came to see her (how Satan works!) and in a moment of weakness she took a drink. She ended up with this man in her home, and so far down that both of them could not get out to the out-door toilet; the place was in a terrible mess! My heart bled for her; oh the power of the evil one and the awful things the grog can make a person do! I didn't just leave them to wallow in the mire. I went in, pulled the sheets off the bed and washed them, cleaned up the house, and under God got the dear one back to sanity, though she was never as bright as before. We found this with alcoholics: if they made a mistake it seemed to rob them of their joy in salvation. 1 John 3:9 says, "Whosoever is born of God does not commit [continue in] sin," but we may make a mistake (not deliberately). Thank God in 1 John 1:9 it says, "If we confess our sins, he is faithful and just to forgive us our sins, and to cleanse us from all unrighteousness"—this was written to Christians.

During our Mission ministry we proved God in many wonderful ways in providing our needs. In the staff meeting one morning one of the missionaries said, "It is well-known that John McKittrick is a good touch!" I said I would like to reply to that, and related this story: "About five weeks after I came into the Mission, Mary, the new baby, and the other three children came to join me. Mr McDonald came to the station with his car to transport them to their new home. As we were walking up the platform together Mr McDonald put his hand on my shoulder and said, 'Guard against becoming too hard in dealing with the people, rather be too soft than too hard,' and I have adopted that throughout the ministry."

I have never wanted for the wherewithal to help these needy people. God used strange means at times. When the local SP bookmaker at the Glebe Mission came in one day with a check for one hundred pounds, I rushed into Sister's office saying, "What do I do?" I knew that our Superintendent did not accept monies from gambling sources and I was heartily behind him, but I wanted to reach this man for Christ and I could not snub him. I came back and said, "I will not use it for the preaching ministry, but will use it for relief work." I pulled out my cashbook and showed him that in that very month I had given out nearly one hundred pounds. I tried to keep in touch with this man. I went to see him in another district where he had bought into a hotel. It is recorded of my Savior that he received publicans and sinners and changed them. Another man who looked after parking at the dogtrots sent regular donations. May my dear Lord forgive me if I did wrong in receiving this money.

The Final District: Newtown

Our next district was Newtown with its little narrow, drab streets and almost no backyards—what a challenge! The entrance to the Mission hall had a big iron front gate, just like a prison. My son-in-law and one or two others came one Saturday and pulled it out and transferred the wooden doors from the top of the stairs to the front—what a difference it made! The dear old Sunday School Superintendent said, "You'll never keep the boys out of the hall," but we never had any trouble that way. The old roof looked terrible and was leaking. I asked Rev. N. Reeve, our new Superintendent, for permission to paint it, but it was some time before he gave consent, as a man who had a lot to do with the Mission property said it was not safe. Eventually we got consent and, with a missionary friend home on furlough and a couple of teenage boys, we did a good job stopping the leaks with rags and black jack and painting it; we also painted the outside of the hall and sometime later, the inside. I was on the roof painting when a traveler at a house opposite called out, "It's well seen you haven't got a weak heart." He didn't know I had had a coronary whilst at Glebe!

We had clubs for boys and girls, and Friday was young people's night. We commenced a coffee bar for these young people and our honorary superintendent footed the bill to have our kitchen fitted out with all the facilities for this venture—we supplied hamburgers, ice cream, and soft drinks. For the first few weeks we had over fifty attending each night, but we found girls going off with boys when parents thought they were at the Club. We made a rule that girls who came must not leave the hall till the finish without permission. The number fell quite a bit. The Sunday School grew considerably. We started picking up children in our big Morris van, and on Saturdays in the summer we took the children to Parsley Bay for swimming; in winter we had soccer. If they came to swimming they had to come to Sunday School. We had up to thirty sometimes in our van. One day we parked alongside a man and woman in a big latest-model car, and they stood amazed as our big family piled out. "How many more?" he kept saying. We picked up some children of an Aboriginal woman, but unfortunately not all her children came to the Sunday School—she was the mother of nineteen!

It was so difficult to reach these dear young people for Christ our Lord. Very often when they came to Christ they went home to parents who could not care less. A very lovely lad came to Christ and a few days later I was in the shop at the opposite corner of the Mission when his mother came in and began to relate in front of all the other people how her boy, Stephen, had come home on Sunday night and said, "Mum, I've become a Christian." She said, "I thought this is just some other new fad, he will soon forget all about it, but this was not so, he reads his Bible every night and he is so different." I said before all the people, "Mother, you need to come to Stephen's Savior, he will change your whole household." She did not come to Christ. Stephen later got away from the things of God and what distress and heartache that mother has had because of her family. I pray for them by name very often.

One teenage lad who was a bright Christian told how he had his quiet time with the maggots. He and his mother, brother, and sister lived in a little three-roomed cottage and he had to go to the toilet down the yard to have his prayer time. These young people were helped to know their Bibles and to grow in the Christian life.

Tuesday was Christian Endeavour time and they came for tea, a two-course hot meal that the missionary prepared, then their meeting. We had a lady from another church helping with this meeting. She loved the very natural way some of these young people talked to our heavenly Father in prayer. Some of these young people are still going on with the Lord.

Speaking of help, every Sunday afternoon several students from the Sydney Bible College came to help in the Sunday School. These young people stopped for tea and the evening service, often taking part. After tea we went round the district preaching in the open-air, and this was good for these young people in their preparation for service.

We did quite a lot of open-air work in this district. About 9.30am on Sunday I would pull into a back lane, set up the amplifier, and herald forth the glad tidings. In all the years we did this only one woman objected, and did she object!—she came out of her house screaming and flinging her arms about! I could not go back there again. After this witness I usually went to one of the other churches. We had no morning service at our Mission halls; we encouraged those who came to Christ to go to the church of their choice in the morning. Many of our people became members of other churches. The Mission's job was to reach people who very often would not go to church. One day I said at the staff meeting, "Last night we had a typical mission congregation; we had a man with a bottle on the hip, and stinking of metho and bodily odors, we had a young woman (whom the local welfare officer described as 'a working girl') with two of her girl friends."

One of the beautiful pictures which remain in my mind of this district is of a beautiful young lady worker standing sharing a hymnbook with one of these poor dirty old men—she was trying to show him Jesus cared.

We had a big relief program here helping people with food, clothing, furniture, and in other ways. One day on my way to visit, I met a dear Aboriginal woman on her way to see me—the landlord was going to put her furniture out on the street, could I help? I went and transported the furniture to a temporary place, and arranged for the family too. We had a good ministry here amongst the Indigenous Australians; always there were some in the congregation, some very fine people.

Two fathers in this district got into trouble; one was out of work and the two set off to try to find a job. One of them could not read or write; as children their father sent them out to steal when they should have been at school. Now they stole two TV sets from one of the big firms and were caught. We took the wives (who were respectable women who sent the children to Sunday School) to Maitland Jail to see their husbands. On the day of their trial we took them and some of the children to Taree for the trial. We went up one day and stopped overnight; the wives and children slept in our van and we slept in a friend's place. The magistrate was a very understanding, kind man. I told what I knew about the men and the family, the wives were questioned, and these men were given a bond of two years. The detective in charge of the case came up and said to the men, "I will take a ticket in lottery with you anytime!"—in other words he was amazed that they had been freed on a bond. Prior to this big trial they had been tried for two other offences and fined fifty pounds; this had to be paid before they left the Court. I went to my friend and borrowed the money (they paid it back by installments) and they were free. We came home from Taree in our van, parents and children singing choruses all the way. One father made good, but the other broke his bond and went to prison—one of the many disappointments you get in a work like this.

We were five years in Newtown. It was from this district that we retired from the Mission after thirty-four-and-a-half very wonderful years. We never considered it any hardship to do the many duties involved, and we trust it was all to the glory of God.

A Further Mission: Castlefield

From Newtown we went to a little interdenominational work in Campbelltown. Mr Stan Reeve carried on this fine work. I met him at the Refuge one day when he came in to park his car. His first approach to us was typical of this dear man—"John, what is your most urgent need?" He very soon helped with the request for blankets, and his mother sent one hundred pounds for blankets on another occasion. I rushed out to the disposal shop and purchased fifty at two pounds each, and when I sent her the receipt I said, "The blankets are on the beds"—she was my friend and helper ever after.

I had been out to Castlefield to take a morning service occasionally. One day Stan said, "I would like it if some retired man could come to help and we could continue doing as we do now." All offerings went to various Missions; from the Sunday School alone about $400 each year went to the Bible Society. This appealed to me, and when we retired from the Mission we went there.

We went up into the district of Sherwood Hills, which at that time was not touched by the church. We told the people we were not representing any particular denomination; if their children came to our Sunday School they could take them to their own church at any time. The result was we had children from all churches. We had over one hundred children on the roll and attending regularly. Mr Reeve built the school halls. They were used for Scouts too; a very fine troop was here—several boys gained the Queen Scout's badge.

There was a morning service of worship. In the beginning it was held in a little chapel built by the first priest to come to the district, but later the service was continued in a lovely little modern church built by the Main Roads Department when the chapel had to be removed for the new highway. The chapel is preserved at the monastery further up the road.

Soccer became a big thing here, used to reach boys and parents for Christ our Lord. We tried to have prayer in the center of the field before each game and parents and often members of other teams appreciated this. One year we had ten teams in the churches competition. Mr Reeve made a paddock available as our soccer ground; it was great on Saturdays to see crowds of boys and parents enjoying the fun and fellowship.

After eleven years of happy fellowship and ministry with Stan, his dear wife Margaret and family, and many lovely friends, we were called to another ministry. Before finishing writing about this district and work, however, there is something I am hesitant about recording, but feel it may help some. We used our 1959 Kombi Van to bring in children to Sunday School and to take them to soccer, and Mr Reeve said our van would need to be replaced, so he put four thousand dollars in a special account for that purpose. When we were leaving, I said, "We did not need to use that money, it belongs to you," but he would not hear of it, he said it was ours. I suggested we send it with the interest to the different missionary societies and he agreed heartily. We were prepared to go to Forster in our VW so we cleaned the van up, and put new curtains on the windows, but God had other plans—he knew the old VW would not stand up to it, and sent enough money, with the trade-in, to buy a good second-hand car!

Movement Four—From Forgetfulness to Transforming Memory

Called to Another Ministry: Forster Baptist Church

I went to an interim ministry at Forster Baptist Church, and this too was a happy, fruitful ministry amongst young and old. I rode a pushbike through this beautiful district, visited my people, went from door to door with other workers, made good use of every contact by follow-up, and saw God working in lives. They were a great band of dear praying people, reaching out to the community in the name of Christ our Lord. A very special outreach was to the old people of the district. The church had an afternoon bi-monthly gathering when they went out in their cars and brought these old people to an afternoon of happy fellowship and concert, then sit-down afternoon tea, and a little message from the word of God. About one hundred people came, and these dear old people loved it.

A big factor in our leaving Forster after two years was that I had a back injury caused when an old man did not give way to his right and I slammed into his car on my pushbike.

Mary's Homecoming

On Sunday 28th February we had Rev. D. McKeough as our guest speaker, and he brought a great word from the Lord about family life appropriate to the dedication of Karyn Lynette Zimmerman. It was good to sit in the congregation with my dear Mary—little did I know it was the last time I would sit with her. On the way home in the car she said, "John, it is about time you gave up." She added, "You are getting a bit trembly." I said to her, "My dear, in twelve months time, God willing, I will give it serious thought." She replied, "I will accept that."

In the evening she dressed, ready to come with me, but took an angina turn and said she had better not go. Fortunately Grace, our daughter, was with her, for after I left she got worse. Grace called the ambulance and on the way to hospital the ambulance man gave her oxygen, but when she arrived at Wyong Hospital she passed home to be with the Lord Jesus.

At our evening service I preached on 2 Corinthians 8:9, "For you know the grace of our Lord Jesus Christ, that, though he was rich, yet for your sakes he became poor, that you through his poverty might be rich." After speaking of our Lord's riches and his poverty, I preached about our great riches in him, salvation from the past, in the present, and for the future. I mentioned how Paul speaks in Philippians about putting off the old body and going to be with Christ, which is far better. Little did I know that my beloved Mary was about to do this. When I arrived home I heard she was in hospital and with help from my dear grandson, Wayne, got to the hospital to be greeted by Grace saying, "Mum has gone home."

We had fifty seven happy years together; we had our difficulties and problems, but God always undertook for us, praise his Holy Name. I will miss her so much; she was always by my side in all the service recorded here. At the Refuge especially, the poor men loved to come to our back door to talk to her. I can hear one dear man saying, "Mumsie, come and talk to me." She loved these poor broken men, that was why she got to the place where she could not sleep at night thinking of them, and we had to leave and go back to a district. I thank God for his grace that has been so real at this time. I can say, "The Lord gave, and the Lord has taken away; blessed be the name of the Lord." She is "absent from the body, present with the Lord." What a great life it's been with Christ our Lord and Savior!

Valediction: Home to Glory

John McKittrick's only surviving brother, Samuel McKittrick, wrote the following words after John's death.

And he "walked with God and he was not; for God took him." "And so the time came for his departure," as John Bunyan wrote about Greatheart, the guide and helper of the pilgrims. So it was for our "Greatheart." But his time came with shocking suddenness. On Monday, 23 August 1982, he drove his car to conduct the funeral service of an old friend of his Balmain days, readily responding to a call for help and comfort. Having spent the night with his son Paul, he left for home next morning. There was no indication of any physical weakness, and he confessed to being quite well. That always-ready smile of his was his parting gesture. But in a few hours his earthly life ended, and he was "with Christ." Reports indicate that he suffered a massive heart attack and he died at the wheel of his car. Mercifully, contact with a heavy vehicle and a roadside pole prevented any hurt or damage to anyone else.

So John McKittrick, servant of Jesus Christ, died "on active service," as some of us near to him felt he would, and as it is certain he would have wished. For him there was no discharge, no retirement. The soldier of Christ died, sword in hand, still serving. He could say: "I have fought a good fight, I have finished my course, I have kept the faith."

The family and friends were soon informed, and the news spread widely. There were reports on radio and in the daily papers. A very wide circle of people mourned his "exodus." The funeral took place on the following Monday in the Narara Valley Baptist Church, his last sphere of service. The building was filled to capacity and many listened outside. There were brother ministers, Baptist Union representatives, and people from every place in which he had served, and many others. In their places were his children, grandchildren, and great-grandchildren. At his request, several times repeated, it was my privilege and heavy responsibility to conduct the service. The Minister of the Church, the Rev. Leigh Wedge, assisted me. His son John gave a family tribute. The members of the Boys' Brigade formed a guard of honor. The cortege,

Movement Four—From Forgetfulness to Transforming Memory

of great length and with a police escort, moved to the beautiful Palmdale Cemetery. After a brief service of committal, he was buried beside his wife who had predeceased him by only six months.

In my tribute to my dearly loved, and greatly loving, brother John, I tried to cover in barest outline his outstanding service for others which he gave in the name of his Lord and Master, Jesus Christ. He was born on 17 March 1903 in the city of Glasgow. That was St Patrick's Day, a fitting day for a Scotsman to be born, for that great missionary was born not many miles from the same place. But for some of us, that day has for long been celebrated as St John's Day. His story has already been told, but there are some things he will not have written. As a schoolboy he won distinction in soccer football, and was in line for selection to play for his country. Later he learned the pugilistic art. I remember my pride at seeing the medal he won as runner-up in the amateur welterweight championship competition of Glasgow. He pioneered the way for his family when he immigrated to Australia in 1924.

I can recall the sadness of farewell when he left his young wife and us. But I can recall, even more clearly, the joy when news came of his conversion that took place on the ship. I can remember the tears of joy as my parents, clasped in each other's arms, rejoiced at the answer to their prayers. Soon John was engaged in service in churches and in the open-air, where he learned to preach. In 1933, I was the pastor of a church in Ballarat when my brother wrote to tell me of his call to serve in the Sydney City Mission. So began his outstanding life of service.

Golden words are needed for this final word of farewell. But such words are only in our hearts, in the hearts of hundreds of people all over the city and country who will love to think of him in years to come and to recall those wonderful incidents in which they knew him. But most of all, we shall draw inspiration from his life and ministry. He prayed that through the story of his life there might be those who will yet be led to Christ the Savior whom he preached with such glowing power.

He refused to acknowledge the coming of advancing years. He just lived and served on and on. He continually drew strength and inspiration, through his deep devotional life, from the source of life in Christ. The beautiful description of the Apostle Paul sums up his life. He was simply "a man in Christ." Like his Master, he was completely and utterly selfless. Indeed we could say he was entirely unselfconscious. This was because of his great love for his Lord and his untiring "passion for souls." From this source flowed his infinite capacity for caring, and never a call for help of any kind was unanswered.

Our brother Robert, also a missionary in the Sydney City Mission, was killed in a road accident in 1951. He, too, was in the service of others at the time. Now the brothers are reunited and we, who continue to serve, will remember them till our call comes to join them where there is no death.

So for our Greatheart, brother, companion, and true friend to us and to many, the "trumpets have sounded on the other side." Farewell!

Individual and Corporate Servantship Practices

- Provide space for people to share their story and to hear the stories of others.

- Tell the stories of your congregation, both past and present. Allow space for people to discover what God is doing in and through your congregation through its shared memories, collective stories, and living narratives.

- Look for daily opportunities to practically care for the broken, vulnerable, rejected, and needy. Nurture the same *attitude* of Jesus Christ by *making yourself nothing* and *humbling* yourself. Out of this humility serve with compassion and empathy.

- Pray daily that God would bring broken people into your life, that you might serve them (and serve with them) as though you were serving Jesus Christ.

- Commit to reading biographies, the Gospels, the book of Acts, and historical accounts of the church and its mission, in order to cultivate a transforming memory. Read the biographies of people like C. S. Lewis, Augustine of Hippo, Thomas Merton, Corrie Ten Boom, Jackie Pullinger, Stanley Hauerwas, Therese of Lisieux, Teresa of Avila, John Henry Newman, Martin Luther, and Dietrich Bonhoeffer.

- Over the next thirty days, read prayerfully through the Gospels every day. Journal your thoughts and prayers. Invite God to change your heart, mind, and practices as you cultivate a transforming memory.

Questions for Reflection and Discussion

- What stories inspire you to follow Jesus completely?

- How do these stories help you obey, sacrifice, grow, understand yourself, and witness to Jesus?

- How will people tell your story? Is it time to reshape your story so that it is formed around the mission of Jesus and his concern for the broken and vulnerable?

- How does the servant-heart of Jesus toward the most wounded in society shape your servantship?

22

Epilogue

Following Our Servant Lord and His Mission

Graham Hill

Servantship is essentially about following our Servant Lord and his mission—it is a life of discipleship to him. Authentic discipleship to Jesus shapes a life of service of the triune God, and of service within his church and world. The contributors in this book have outlined some of the theology and practices of radical servantship, and have called us to follow our Servant Lord and his redemptive mission within human history and creation. They have called us to pattern our servantship after the servant nature of Jesus Christ.

In an article outlining the relationship between (1) God's sovereignty in world affairs and in human history, (2) a theology of servanthood, and (3) the mission of the church, Lesslie Newbigin calls the church to service, which means "to obey, to suffer, and to witness."[1] Newbigin describes how God is drawing the peoples of the world into a single history, dismantling the western church's Constantinian position and structures, and dispersing the church through the many peoples of the world. These things remind us that God is in control of human history, and that we are to be his servants, passionately pursuing his sovereign mission and purposes in the world. Just as Jesus was a servant, submitting himself to the Father's will, we are called to serve our Lord and Savior "in response to the realities with which God confronts us." Newbigin presents the church and its servantship with this challenge:

---

1. Newbigin, "Jesus the Servant and Man's Community," 23–33. I have modified this quote so that it uses gender inclusive language (rather than the language of the era).

Servantship

But what does "total commitment to Jesus" mean? It means partnership in his servanthood. It means to obey, to suffer, and to witness. It does not mean being visibly on the winning side. It does not mean a campaign to contain the revolutionary forces of our time. It does not mean success and influence for the church. It means precisely what it has always meant—the obedience of a servant for whom the only thing that matters is to do the master's will; the acceptance of whatever share of suffering is accorded in the doing of that will; and the witness to God's rule which is the hidden but sovereign power shaping all things towards the end for which they were created. We are always tempted to hanker after another role; we look for a kind of authority and influence for the church that Christ neither sought for himself nor promised to his disciples . . .

To share in the servanthood of Jesus means also to be his witness. It is not our service which shapes history or gives it its meaning. History has been given its meaning by God, who created all things in Christ to be summed up in Christ, and it is shaped by him who ceaselessly directs all things to that end. The servant of the Lord is sent to live under obedience to that direction, and to bear witness to it by the manner of our participation in the ever-changing life of the world. But, because our lives will always obscure God's rule at least as much as they reveals it, we are required to bear witness also by the explicit word which points beyond ourselves and our service to God made manifest in Jesus Christ, and to that dying and rising in which the meaning of history was finally disclosed . . .

To share in the servanthood of Jesus means to be committed totally, as he was, to the service of God in and through him. A servant does not choose how and where she or he will serve; a servant accepts the direction of the master to whom the servant is committed . . . Service is not a sort of gesture; it is a response to the realities with which God confronts us . . . The context of the Christian life is the end of the world and the ends of the earth, because Christ is Lord of all. Its center is at the point where the Lord of all was manifest as the Servant of all, giving his life that all humanity might have life, not by seeking it but by surrendering it.

My prayer is that our movement from leadership to radical servantship, from shallowness to dynamic theological reflection, from theories to courageous practices, and from forgetfulness to transforming memory, will give honor to the suffering and glorified Lord and Servant of all.

Bibliography

Agosto, Efrain. *Servant Leadership: Jesus and Paul*. St. Louis, MI: Chalice, 2005.

Alcoholics Anonymous. *Alcoholics Anonymous Big Book*. 4th ed. Online: http://www.aa.org/bigbookonline/en_tableofcnt.cfm.

Amaladoss, Michael. "Mission in a Post-Modern World: A Call to Be Counter-Cultural." *Mission Studies*, 13, 1, no. 2 (1996) 68–79.

Anderson, David A., and Margarita R. Cabellon. *Multicultural Ministry Handbook: Connecting Creatively to a Diverse World*. Downers Grove, IL: IVP, 2010.

Anderson, Ray S. *An Emergent Theology for Emerging Churches*. Downers Grove, IL: IVP, 2006.

Arterburn, Stephen, and Fred Stoeker. *Every Man's Battle: Every Man's Guide to Winning the War on Sexual Temptation One Victory at a Time*. Colorado Springs, CO: Waterbrook, 2000.

Arthur, Sarah. *The God-Hungry Imagination: The Art of Storytelling for Postmodern Youth Ministry*. Nashville, TN: Upper Room, 2007.

Ash, Christopher. *Marriage: Sex in the Service of God*. England: IVP, 2003.

Australia Bureau of Statistics. "What Are Our Qualifications?" In *Hornsby Shire Council Community Profile*. Hornsby: Commonwealth of Australia, 2006.

———. "2006 Census Quickstats: 2114 (Postal Area)." Online: http://www.censusdata.abs.gov.au.

———. "Australian Social Trends: Internet Access at Home." Online: http://www.ausstats.abs.gov.au/Ausstats/subscriber.nsf/0/5A60A933925F7987CA25748E0012ADCF/$File/internet_access_at_home_final_version.pdf.

Australian Government, Department of Foreign Affairs and Trade. "Australia: A Culturally Diverse Society." Online: http://www.dfat.gov.au/facts/culturally_diverse.html.

Bahr, Howard M., and Kathleen S. Bahr. "Families and Self-Sacrifice: Alternative Models and Meanings for Family Theory." *Social Forces* 79, no. 4 (2001) 1231–58.

Banks, Robert, and Bernice Ledbetter. *Reviewing Leadership: A Christian Evaluation of Current Approaches*. Grand Rapids, MI: Baker, 2004.

Baptist Union of Queensland. *Queensland Baptist Code of Ethics—Pastoral Handbook*. Brisbane: Baptist Union of Queensland, 2009.

Barna, George. "Gracefully Passing on the Baton." Ventura, CA: Barna Group, 2009. Online: http://www.barna.org/component/wordpress/archives/77.

Barrett, Lois Y. *Treasure in Clay Jars: Patterns in Missional Faithfulness*. Grand Rapids, MI: Eerdmans, 2004.

Bass, Bernard M., and Ronald E. Riggio. *Transformational Leadership*. 2nd ed. Mahwah, NJ: Lawrence Erlbaum Associates, 2006.

Bauckham, Richard. *Bible and Mission: Christian Witness in a Postmodern World*. Grand Rapids, MI: Baker, 2004.

Bibliography

Bauman, Zygmunt. *Liquid Modernity*. Cambridge: Polity, 2000.

———. *Liquid Times: Living in an Age of Uncertainty*. Cambridge: Polity, 2007.

Bauman, Zygmunt, and Lydia Bauman. *Culture in a Liquid Modern World*. Cambridge: Polity, 2011.

Bausch, William J. *Storytelling: Imagination and Faith*. Mystic, CT: Twenty-Third, 1984.

Beaudoin, Tom. *Virtual Faith: The Irreverent Spiritual Quest of Generation X*. San Francisco, CA: Jossey-Bass, 1998.

Behrstock, Ellen, and Matthew Clifford. *Leading Gen Y Teachers: Emerging Strategies for School Leaders*. TQ Research and Policy Brief. Washington, DC: National Comprehensive Center for Teacher Quality, 2009.

Bell, Rob. *Love Wins: A Book about Heaven, Hell, and the Fate of Every Person Who Ever Lived*. New York, NY: HarperOne, 2011.

———. *Velvet Elvis: Repainting the Christian Faith*. Grand Rapids, MI: Zondervan, 2005.

Berkhof, Louis. *Systematic Theology*. Edinburgh: Banner of Truth, 1959.

Bessenecker, Scott A. *How to Inherit the Earth: Submitting Ourselves to a Servant Savior*. Downers Grove, IL: IVP, 2010.

Bieschke, Marcus D. "Five Succession Planning Values to Keep Your Organization Alive." *Leadership Advance Online*, VI (2006) 1–4.

Billings, J. Todd. "What Makes a Church Missional? Freedom from Cultural Captivity Does Not Mean Freedom from Tradition." *Christianity Today* 52, no. 3 (March 2008) 56–59.

Bjork, David. "A Model for Analysis of Incarnational Ministry in Post-Christendom Lands." *Missiology* 25, no. 3 (1997) 279–91.

Blanchard, Kenneth H., and Phil Hodges. *The Servant Leader: Transforming Your Heart, Head, Hands, & Habits*. Nashville, TN: Thomas Nelson, 2003.

Blier, Helen M. "Webbing the Common Good: Virtual Environment, Incarnated Community, and Education for the Reign of God." *Teaching Theology and Religion* 11, no. 1 (2008) 24–31.

Bliese, Richard H. "The Mission Matrix: Mapping out the Complexities of a Missional Ecclesiology." *Word and World* 26, no. 3 (2006) 237–48.

Block, Peter. *Stewardship: Choosing Service over Self-Interest*. 1st ed. San Francisco, CA: Berrett-Koehler, 1993.

Boatman, Jazmine, and Richard S. Wellins. "Global Leadership Forecast: Time for a Leadership Revolution." *The Talent Management Expert* (2011). Online: http://www.ddiworld.com/glf2011.

Bonhoeffer, Dietrich, and John W. Doberstein. *Life Together*. San Francisco, CA: HarperSanFrancisco, 1993.

Booth, Catherine. *Papers on Aggressive Christianity*. London: Salvationist, 1880.

Bosch, David J. *Believing in the Future: Toward a Missiology of Western Culture*. New York, NY: Trinity, 1995.

———. *Transforming Mission: Paradigm Shifts in Theology of Mission*. Maryknoll, NY: Orbis, 1991.

Bouma, Gary D. *Australian Soul: Religion and Spirituality in the Twenty-First Century*. Port Melbourne: Cambridge University Press, 2006.

Boyd, David. *You Don't Have to Cross the Ocean to Reach the World: The Power of Local Cross-Cultural Ministry*. Grand Rapids, MI: Chosen, 2008.

Bruce, Steve. *God Is Dead: Secularization in the West*. Oxford: Blackwell, 2002.

Brueggemann, Walter. *Cadences of Home: Preaching among Exiles*. Louisville, KY: Westminster John Knox, 1997.

———. *Finally Comes the Poet: Daring Speech for Proclamation*. Minneapolis, MN: Fortress, 1989.

———. *The Prophetic Imagination*. Minneapolis, MN: Fortress, 2001.

Bryan Smith, J. *The Good and Beautiful God: Falling in Love with the God Jesus Knows*. The Apprentice Series. Downers Grove, IL: IVP, 2009.

———. "Why Christians Should Be Strange." In *International Renovaré Institute for Christian Spiritual Formation IV: Living as an Apprentice to Jesus*. Colorado Springs, CO: 2012.

Capon, Robert F. *Kingdom, Grace, Judgement: Paradox, Outrage, and Vindication in the Parables of Jesus*. Grand Rapids, MI: Eerdmans, 2002.

Carey, William. "An Enquiry into the Obligation of Christians to Use Means for the Conversion of the Heathens." In *Perspectives on the World Christian Movement*, edited by Winter, Ralph D., 293–99. Pasadena, CA: William Carey Library, 1792.

Carson, Donald A. *Becoming Conversant with Emergent: Understanding a Movement and Its Implications*. Grand Rapids, MI: Zondervan, 2005.

Carter, Warren. *Matthew and Empire: Initial Explorations*. Harrisburg, PA: Trinity, 2001.

———. *Matthew and the Margins: A Sociopolitical and Religious Reading*. Maryknoll, NY: Orbis, 2000.

Chester, Tim. "Questioning the Incarnation as a Model for Mission." Online: http://timchester.wordpress.com/2010/09/04/questioning-the-incarnation-as-a-model-for-mission/.

———. "Why I Don't Believe in Incarnational Mission." Online: http://timchester.wordpress.com/2008/07/19/why-i-dont-believe-in-incarnational-mission/.

Chu, Jeff. "How Willow Creek Is Leading Evangelicals by Learning from the Business World." Online: http://www.fastcompany.com/1702221/how-willow-creek-leading-evangelicals-learning-business-world.

Clapp, Rodney. *A Peculiar People: The Church as Culture in a Post-Christian Society*. Downers Grove, IL: IVP, 1996.

Cleary, John. "Boundless Salvation: An Historical Perspective on the Theology of Salvationist Mission." Sydney: Salvation Army, 2001.

Clinton, J. Robert. *Leadership Perspectives: How to Study the Bible for Leadership Insights*. Altadena, CA: Barnabas, 1993.

Cohen, David J., and Michael Parsons, eds. *Beyond 400: Exploring Baptist Futures*. Eugene, OR: Wipf and Stock, 2011.

Cole, Neil. *Church 3.0: Upgrades for the Future of the Church*. San Francisco, CA: Jossey-Bass, 2010.

———. *Organic Leadership: Leading Naturally Right Where You Are*. Grand Rapids, MI: Baker, 2009.

Collins, James C. *Good to Great: Why Some Companies Make the Leap—and Others Don't*. 1st ed. New York, NY: HarperBusiness, 2001.

Conradie, Sas. "Christian Community Computer Centers (C4s): Transforming Communities through Information Sharing and Technology." *Transformation* 24, no. 2 (2007) 102–09.

Costas, Orlando E. *Christ Outside the Gate: Mission Beyond Christendom*. Maryknoll, NY: Orbis, 1982.

Cottrell, Stephen. *Hit the Ground Kneeling*. London: Church House, 2009.

Cowell, John. "In Defence of Christendom: The Claim of Christ and the Confidence of the Church." Online: http://www.postchristendom.com/files/In_defence_of_Christendom.pdf.

Bibliography

Cox, Harvey. *God's Revolution and Man's Responsibility*. Valley Forge, PA: Judson, 1965.

Croft, Steven, ed. *Mission-shaped Questions*. London: Church House, 2008.

Cronshaw, Darren. *Credible Witness: Companions, Prophets, Hosts, and Other Australian Mission Models*. Springvale: UNOH, 2006.

Crouch, Andy. "Emergent Evangelicalism: The Place of Absolute Truths in a Postmodern World—Two Views." *Christianity Today* 48, no. 11 (2004) 42–43.

———. "Rekindling Old Fires." *Christianity Today* 46, no. 9 (2002) 56.

Crowdell, Scott. "The Postmodern Church." *St Mark's Review* 168, no. Summer (1996) 14–20.

Daniel, Lillian. "Church Netiquette: Ministry by E-Mail." *Christian Century* 126, no. 13 (2009) 26–28.

Dart, Jonathon. "Identity Crisis: Our Cross to Bear." *The Sun Herald*, 15th November 2009, 42–43.

De La Hoyde, Christopher. "The End of Christendom and Mission in the Local Church." Online: http://www.porterbrooknetwork.org/resource-detail/the-end-of-christendom-and-mission-in-the-local-church/.

Detweiler, Craig, and Barry F. Taylor. *A Matrix of Meanings: Finding God in Pop Culture*. Grand Rapids, MI: Baker Academic, 2003.

Deymaz, Mark, and Harry Li. *Ethnic Blends: Mixing Diversity into Your Local Church*. Grand Rapids, MI: Zondervan, 2010.

Dickson, John. *If I Were God I'd Make Myself Clearer*. Kingsford: Matthias, 2002.

Divine, Miranda. "Church and Family Can Save Kids." *The Sun Herald*, 16 November 2003.

Drane, John W. *After McDonaldization: Mission, Ministry, and Christian Discipleship in an Age of Uncertainty*. London: Darton, Longman and Todd, 2008.

———. "Contemporary Culture and the Reinvention of Sacramental Spirituality." In *The Gestures of God: Explorations in Sacramentality*, edited by Rowell, Geoffrey, and Christine M. Hall, 37–55. London: Continuum, 2004.

———. *Cultural Change and Biblical Faith*. Carlisle: Paternoster, 2000.

———. *Do Christians Know How To Be Spiritual?: The Rise of New Spirituality and the Mission of the Church*. London: Darton, Longman and Todd, 2005.

———. "Looking for Maturity in the Emerging Church." Unpublished Lecture Delivered in Manchester Cathedral, May 2007.

———. "Rebuilding the Household of Faith: Being Spiritual, Human, and Christian in Today's World." Unpublished Address Given at the Churches Together in Britain and Ireland 2002 National Assembly.

———. "The Globalization of Spirituality." Unpublished Lecture Delivered at Regents Park College, Oxford University, November 2006.

———. *The McDonaldization of the Church: Consumer Culture and the Church's Future*. Macon, GA: Smyth and Helwys, 2001.

———. "Who Wants To Be a Leader?" *Talk: the Mainstream Magazine* 4, no. 2 (2007) 7–8.

Drane, John, and Olive M. Fleming Drane. "Breaking through into Dynamic Ways of Being Church." In *Breaking New Ground: The First Scottish Ecumenical Assembly* 2001, edited by Action of Churches Together in Scotland. Edinburgh: Action of Churches Together in Scotland, 2001.

———. "Worship and Preaching." In *This Is Our Story: Free Church Women's Ministry*, edited by Wootton, Janet. Werrington: Epworth, 2007.

Drane, Olive M. Fleming. *Spirituality to Go*. London: Darton, Longmann and Todd, 2005.

Driscoll, Mark, and Grace Driscoll. *Real Marriage: The Truth about Sex, Friendship, and Life Together*. Nashville, TN: Thomas Nelson, 2012.

Driscoll, Mark. *Confessions of a Reformission Rev.: Hard Lessons from an Emerging Missional Church*, The Leadership Network Innovation Series. Grand Rapids, MI: Zondervan, 2006.

Driver, John. *Images of the Church in Mission*. Scottdale, PN: Herald, 1997.

Ebertz, Susan. "Technology for Ministry: Ministry 2.0." *American Theological Library Association Summary of Proceedings* 62 (2008) 316–23.

Economist. "Church as Businesses: Jesus, CEO." *Economist*. Online: http://www.economist.com/node/5323597.

———. "The Lunatic You Work For: If the Corporation Were a Person, Would That Person Be a Psychopath?" Online: http://www.economist.com/node/2647328.

Edgar, Brian. "Multiculturalism Is an Essential Part of the Gospel." Online: http://www.ea.org.au/site/DefaultSite/filesystem/documents/public policy/Christ and multiculturalism.pdf.

Edwards, Gene. *A Tale of Three Kings: A Study in Brokenness*. Wheaton, IL: Tyndale House, 1992.

Edwards, James R. *The Gospel According to Mark*, The Pillar New Testament Commentary. Grand Rapids, MI: Eerdmans, 2002.

Engen, Charles Edward van. *God's Missionary People : Rethinking the Purpose of the Local Church*. Grand Rapids, Mich.: Baker Book House, 1991.

———. "Mission Theology in the Light of Postmodern Critique." *International Review of Mission* 86, no. 343 (1997) 437–61.

Erickson, Millard J. *Christian Theology*. Grand Rapids, MI: Baker, 1998.

Fillebrown, William P. "The Church Meets the Postmodern Era: A Problem or an Opportunity?" *International Congregational Journal* 6, no. 2 (2007) 81–88.

Fitch, David E. *The End of Evangelicalism?: Discerning a New Faithfulness for Mission: Towards an Evangelical Political Theology*, Theopolitical Visions. Eugene, OR: Cascade, 2011.

Ford, Lance. "Do Some Churches Suffer from 'Leadership Immunity?'" Online: http://www.churchleaders.com/pastors/pastor-articles/158167-does-the-church-suffer-from-leadership-immunity.html?p=3.

———. *Unleader: Reimagining Leadership . . . And Why We Must*. Kansas, MO: Beacon Hill, 2012.

Foster, Richard. *Celebration of Discipline*. London: Hodder and Stoughton, 1989.

———. *Money, Sex, and Power: The Spiritual Disciplines of Poverty, Chastity, and Obedience*. London: Hodder and Stoughton, 1985.

———. *Streams of Living Water: Celebrating the Great Traditions of Christian Faith*. Bath: Eagle, 1999.

Foster, Richard, Beebe, Gayle D., and Dallas Willard (eds). *The Life with God Bible: With the Deuterocanonical Books*. New York, NY: Harper Collins, 2009.

Fraker, Anne T., and Larry C. Spears. *Seeker and Servant: Reflections on Religious Leadership*. San Francisco, CA: Jossey-Bass, 1996.

Frame, Tom. *Losing My Religion: Unbelief in Australia*. Sydney: University of New South Wales Press, 2009.

France, R. T. *Matthew: Evangelist & Teacher*, New Testament Profiles. Downers Grove, IL: IVP, 1989.

Frost, Michael. *Exiles: Living Missionally in a Post-Christian Culture*. Peabody, MA: Hendrickson, 2006.

Bibliography

———. *Longing for Love: Gender, Sexuality and Our Experience of God.* Sydney: Albatross, 1996.

———. *The Road to Missional: Journey to the Center of the Church*, Shapevine. Grand Rapids, MI: Baker, 2011.

Frost, Michael, and Alan Hirsch. *ReJesus: A Wild Messiah for a Missional Church.* Peabody, MA: Hendrickson, 2009.

———. *The Faith of Leap: Embracing a Theology of Risk, Adventure & Courage*, Shapevine. Grand Rapids, MI: Baker, 2011.

———. *The Shaping of Things to Come: Innovation and Mission for the 21st-Century Church.* Peabody, MA: Hendrickson, 2003.

Gaebelein, Frank E., et al., eds. *The Expositor's Bible Commentary: Romans through Galatians.* Vol. 10. Grand Rapids, MI: Zondervan, 1976.

Galli, Mark. "From the Printing Press to the iPhone." *Christianity Today*, 64, (2009).

Garman, Andrew N., and Jeremy Glawe. "Succession Planning." *Consulting Psychology Journal: Practice and Research* 56, no. 2 (2004) 119.

Gibbs, Eddie. *ChurchNext: Quantum Changes in How We Do Ministry.* Downers Grove, IL: IVP, 2000.

Gibbs, Eddie, and Ryan K. Bolger. *Emerging Churches: Creating Christian Community in Postmodern Cultures.* Grand Rapids, MI: Baker, 2005.

Gladwell, Malcolm. "Small Change." Online: http://www.newyorker.com/reporting/2010/10/04/101004fa_fact_gladwell?currentPage=all.

Glasser, Arthur F. *Announcing the Kingdom: The Story of God's Mission in the Bible.* Grand Rapids, MI: Baker Academic, 2003.

Gnanakan, Ken. *Proclaiming Christ in a Pluralistic Context.* Bangalore: Theological Book Trust, 2000.

Goldsmith, Martin. *Matthew and Mission: The Gospel through Jewish Eyes.* Leicester: IVP, 2001.

Goldsworthy, Graeme. *Gospel and Kingdom: A Christian Interpretation of the Old Testament.* Exeter: Paternoster, 1981.

Greenleaf, Robert K. *Servant Leadership: A Journey into the Nature of Legitimate Power and Greatness.* New York, NY: Paulist, 1977.

———. *The Servant-Leader Within: A Transformative Path.* New York, NY: Paulist, 2003.

Greenleaf, Robert K., and Larry C. Spears. *Servant Leadership: A Journey into the Nature of Legitimate Power and Greatness.* 25th Anniversary ed. New York, NY: Paulist, 2002.

Greenman, Jeffrey P. "Spiritual Formation in Theological Perspective." In *Life in the Spirit: Spiritual Formation in Theological Perspective*, edited by Greenman, Jeffrey P., and George Kalantzis. Downers Grove, IL: IVP Academic, 2010.

Greig, Pete, and Dave Roberts. *Red Moon Rising.* Winter Park, FL: Relevant, 2003.

Grenz, Stanley J. *A Primer on Postmodernism.* Grand Rapids, MI: Eerdmans, 1996.

———. *The Baptist Congregation: A Guide to Baptist Belief and Practice.* Valley Forge, PA: Judson, 1985.

Guder, Darrell L., "Missional Theology for a Missionary Church." *Journal for Preachers* 22, no. 1 (1998) 3–11.

———. "Walking Worthily: Missional Leadership after Christendom." *The Princeton Seminary Bulletin* 28, no. 3 (2007).

Guder, Darrell L., et al. *Missional Church: A Vision for the Sending of the Church in North America.* Grand Rapids, MI: Eerdmans, 1998.

Gundry, Robert H. *Matthew: A Commentary on His Handbook for a Mixed Church under Persecution*. 2nd ed. Grand Rapids, MI: Eerdmans, 1994.

Gurtner, Daniel M. *Jesus, Matthew's Gospel and Early Christianity: Studies in Memory of Graham N. Stanton*, Library of New Testament Studies. London: T & T Clark, 2011.

Guyon, Jeanne. *Experiencing the Depths of Jesus Christ*. Jacksonville, FL: SeedSowers, 1975.

Hall, Douglas J. *The End of Christendom and the Future of Christianity*. New York, NY: Trinity, 2002.

Hamilton, Andrew. "How Not to Pick a Fight" *The Next Wave, Church and Culture*, no. 81 (2005), Online: http://www.the-next-wave-ezine.info/issue81/index.cfm?id=4&ref=ARTICLES_EMERGING CHURCH_54.

Hammett, John S. "An Ecclesiological Assessment of the Emerging Church Movement." Online: http://www.ateam.blogware.com/AnEcclesiologicalAssessment.Hammett.pdf.

Hanciles, Jehu. *Beyond Christendom: Globalization, African Migration, and the Transformation of the West*. Maryknoll, NY: Orbis, 2008.

Harrison, Jeffrey S., and James O. Fiet. "New CEOs Pursue Their Own Self-Interests by Sacrificing Stakeholder Value." *Journal of Business Ethics* 19, no. 3 (1999) 301–08.

Hauerwas, Stanley, and William H. Willimon. *Resident Aliens: Life in the Christian Colony: A Provocative Christian Assessment of Culture and Ministry for People Who Know That Something Is Wrong*. Nashville, TN: Abingdon, 1989.

Hawthorne, Gerald F., et al., eds. *Dictionary of Paul and His Letters*. Downers Grove, IL: IVP, 1993.

Hay, David. *Something There: The Biology of the Human Spirit*. London: Darton Longman, and Todd, 2006.

Hedlund, Roger E. *The Mission of the Church in the World: A Biblical Theology*. Grand Rapids, MI: Baker, 1991.

———. *Magnificent Surrender: Releasing the Riches of Living in the Lord*. Eugene, OR: Wipf and Stock, 2012.

Helland, Roger, and Len Hjalmarson. *Missional Spirituality: Embodying God's Love from the Inside Out*. Downers Grove, IL: IVP, 2011.

Hiebert, Paul G. *The Gospel in Human Contexts: Anthropological Explorations for Contemporary Missions*. Grand Rapids, MI: Baker Academic, 2009.

Hill, Graham. "An Examination of Emerging-Missional Ecclesiological Conceptions: Missional Ecclesiology and the Ecclesiologies of Miroslav Volf, Joseph Ratzinger and John Zizioulas." PhD diss., Flinders University of South Australia, 2009.

———. *Salt, Light, and a City: Introducing Missional Ecclesiology*. Eugene, OR: Wipf and Stock, 2012.

Hirsch, Alan. "Defining Missional." *Leadership Journal* 29, no. 4 (2008) 20–22.

———. "Reawakening a Potent Missional Ethos in the Twenty-First Century Church." *Missiology* 38, no. 1 (2010) 5–12.

———. "Three Over-Looked Leadership Roles." *Leadership Journal* Spring 2008 (2008) 33.

———. *The Forgotten Ways: Reactivating the Missional Church*. Grand Rapids, MI: Brazos, 2006.

Hirsch, Alan, and Darryn Altclass. *The Forgotten Ways Handbook: A Practical Guide for Developing Missional Churches*. Grand Rapids, MI: Brazos, 2009.

Hirsch, Alan, and Dave Ferguson. *On the Verge: A Journey into the Apostolic Future of the Church*, Exponential Series. Grand Rapids, MI: Zondervan, 2011.

Bibliography

Hirsch, Alan, and Debra Hirsch. *Untamed: Reactivating a Missional Form of Discipleship*. Grand Rapids, MI: Baker, 2010.

Hjalmarson, Len. "Post-Modern Possibilities." *NextReformation*. Online: http://nextreformation.com/wp-admin/articles/postmod1g.htm.

Horsfield, Peter G., and Paul Teusner. "A Mediated Religion: Historical Perspectives on Christianity and the Internet." *Studies in World Christianity* 13, no. 3 (2007) 278–95.

Hunsberger, George R., and Craig Van Gelder, eds. *The Church between Gospel and Culture: The Emerging Mission in North America*. Grand Rapids, MI: Eerdmans, 1996.

Jamieson, Alan. *A Churchless Faith: Faith Journeys Beyond Evangelical, Pentecostal and Charismatic Churches*. Wellington: Philip Garside, 2000.

Jamieson, Alan, et al. *Five Years On: Continuing Faith Journeys of Those Who Left the Church*. Wellington: The Portland Research Trust, 2006.

Jensen, Richard A. *Thinking in Story: Preaching in a Post-Literate Age*. Lima, OH: C.S.S., 1993.

Jenson, Robert W. "How the World Lost Its Story." *First Things* 36 (1993) 19–24.

Kaldor, Peter, et al. "The Role of the Churches in Australia Today." *National Church Life Survey:Taking Stock*. Online: http://www.ncls.org.au/default.aspx?sitemapid=2224.

Keel, Tim. *Intuitive Leadership: Embracing a Paradigm of Narrative, Metaphor, and Chaos*. Grand Rapids, MI: Baker, 2007.

Keener, Craig S. *A Commentary on the Gospel of Matthew*. Grand Rapids, MI: Eerdmans, 1999.

Keller, Timothy J. "Ministry Movements." *City to City Blog*. Online: http://redeemercitytocity.com/blog/view.jsp?Blog_param=203.

———. "Religion-Less Spirituality." *Leadership* Fall (1999) 25–26.

———. "The Missional Church." Online: http://www.columbiapres.org/docs/Missional Church by Tim Keller.pdf.

———. *The Reason for God: Belief in an Age of Skepticism*. London: Hodder and Stoughton, 2008.

Kelly, Gerard. *Retrofuture: Rediscovering Our Roots, Recharting Our Routes*. Downers Grove, IL: IVP, 1999.

Kempis, Thomas à. *The Imitation of Christ: In Four Books*. New York, NY: Vintage, 1998.

Kilpatrick, Joseph W. *A Theology of Servant Leadership*. Pasadena, CA: Fuller Theological Seminary, 1988.

Kimball, Dan. "The Emerging Church and Missional Theology." In *Listening to the Beliefs of Emerging Churches : Five Perspectives*, edited by Webber, Robert, Grand Rapids, MI: Zondervan, 2007.

———. *Emerging Worship: Creating Worship Gatherings for New Generations*. Grand Rapids, MI: Zondervan, 2004.

———. *The Emerging Church: Vintage Christianity for New Generations*. Grand Rapids, MI: Zondervan, 2003.

———. *They Like Jesus but Not the Church: Insights from Emerging Generations*. Grand Rapids, MI: Zondervan, 2007.

Kinnaman, David, and Aly Hawkins. *You Lost Me: Why Young Christians Are Leaving Church . . . And Rethinking Faith*. Grand Rapids, MI: Baker, 2011.

Kirk, J. Andrew. "Following Modernity and Postmodernity: A Missiological Investigation." *Mission Studies*, 17, 1, no. 2 (2000) 217–39.

Konrad, Kai A., and Stergios Skaperdas. "Succession Rules and Leadership Rents." *Journal of Conflict Resolution* 51, no. 4 (2007) 622–45.

Kraft, Charles H. *Christianity in Culture: A Study in Dynamic Biblical Theologizing in Cross-Cultural Perspective*. Maryknoll, NY: Orbis, 1979.

Kreider, Alan. "Beyond Bosch: The Early Church and the Christendom Shift." *International Bulletin of Missionary Research* 29, no. 2 (2005) 59–68.

———. *The Change of Conversion and the Origin of Christendom*. Harrisburg, PA: Trinity, 1999.

Kuhn, Thomas S. "The Structure of Scientific Revolutions." *Foundations of the Unity of Science* 2, no. 2 (1972).

Langmead, Ross. "The Best of Times, the Worst of Times: The Australian Context." Perth: Uniting Church of Australia in Western Australia, 2009.

Laubach, Frank. *Letters by a Modern Mystic*. Colorado Springs, CO: Purposeful Design, 2007.

Law, Eric H.F. *The Wolf Shall Dwell with the Lamb: A Spirituality for Leadership in a Multicultural Community*. St. Louis, MO: Chalice, 1993.

Lencioni, Patrick. *The Five Dysfunctions of a Team*. San Francisco, CA: Jossey-Bass, 2006.

Lewis, Rick. *Mentoring Matters: Building Strong Christian Leaders, Avoiding Burnout, Reaching the Finishing Line*. Oxford: Monarch, 2009.

Liederbach, Mark, and Alvin L. Reid. *The Convergent Church: Missional Worshipers in an Emerging Culture*. Grand Rapids, MI: Kregel, 2009.

Long, Jimmy. *Emerging Hope: A Strategy for Reaching the Postmodern Generations*. Downers Grove, IL: IVP, 2004.

Lundy, J. David. *Servant Leadership for Slow Learners*. Milton Keynes: Paternoster, 2002.

Lynch, Gordon. *Understanding Theology and Popular Culture*. Oxford: Wiley-Blackwell, 2005.

MacDonald, George. *Thomas Wingfold, Curate*. 3 vols. Vol. 3. Whitefish, MT: Kessinger, 2004.

MacIlvaine III, W. Rodman, "What Is the Missional Church Movement?" *Bibliotheca sacra* 167, no. 665 (2010) 89–106.

MacIntyre, Alasdair C. *After Virtue: A Study in Moral Theory*. 2nd Notre Dame, IN: University of Notre Dame Press, 1984.

Mackay, Hugh. *Advance Australia . . . Where?: How We've Changed, Why We've Changed, and What Will Happen Next?* Sydney: Hachette Livre, 2007.

———. "Australia and the World: The Australian Paradox." Centre for Policy Development. Online: http://cpd.org.au/article/australia-and-world:-australian-paradox.

MacLaine, Shirley. *Out on a Limb*. Toronto: Bantam, 1983.

Malphurs, Aubrey. *A New Kind of Church: Understanding Models of Ministry for the 21st Century*. Grand Rapids, MI: Baker, 2007.

Mannoia, Kevin W. *The Integrity Factor: A Journey in Leadership Formation*. Indianapolis, IN: Light and Light Communications, 1996.

Marr, David. "Our Faith Today." *The Sydney Morning Herald*, 19th December 2009.

Mason, Michael C. *The Spirit of Generation Y: Young People's Spirituality in a Changing Australia*. Mulgrave: John Garratt, 2007.

Maxwell, John C. *The 21 Irrefutable Laws of Leadership: Follow Them and People Will Follow You*. Nashville, TN: Thomas Nelson, 1998.

McCrindle, Mark. "Emerging Trends, Enduring Truths." Sydney: McCrindle Research. Online: http://www.mccrindle.com.au.

McGavran, Donald A. *Ethnic Realities and the Church: Lessons from India*. South Pasadena, CA: William Carey, 1979.

Bibliography

McKittrick, John. *Just One of God's Servants: John McKittrick: An Autobiography.* Lawson: John McKittrick, 1983.

McKnight, Scot. *Galatians,* The NIV Application Commentary. Grand Rapids, MI: Zondervan, 2009.

———. "What Is the Emerging Church?" In *Contemporary Issues Conference.* Westminster Theological Seminary, 2006.

McLaren, Brian D. *A Generous Orthodoxy.* Grand Rapids, MI: Zondervan, 2004.

———. *More Ready Than You Realize: Evangelism as Dance in the Postmodern Matrix.* Grand Rapids, MI: Zondervan, 2002.

———. *The Church on the Other Side: Doing Ministry in the Postmodern Matrix.* Grand Rapids, MI: Zondervan, 2000.

McManus, Erwin R. *An Unstoppable Force: Daring to Become the Church God Had in Mind.* Loveland, CO: Group, 2001.

McNeal, Reggie. *The Present Future: Six Tough Questions for the Church.* San Francisco, CA: Jossey-Bass, 2003.

Metaxas, Eric. "Imagination, Culture, and Politics." *Colson Centre for Christian Worldview* 5, no. 14, (2012).

Middleton, J. Richard, and Brian J. Walsh. *Truth Is Stranger Than It Used to Be: Biblical Faith in a Postmodern Age.* London: SPCK, 1995.

Minear, Paul S. *Images of the Church in the New Testament.* London: Lutterworth, 1961.

Moltmann, J. *The Church in the Power of the Spirit.* London: SCM, 1992.

———. *The Open Church: Invitation to a Messianic Life-Style.* London: SMC, 1978.

Morisy, Ann. *Journeying Out: A New Approach to Christian Mission.* London: Morehouse, 2004.

Moritz, Joshua M. "Beyond Strategy, Towards the Kingdom of God: The Post-Critical Reconstructionist Mission of the Emerging Church." *Dialog* 47, no. 1 (2008) 27–36.

Moynagh, Michael. *Emergingchurch.Intro.* Oxford: Monarch, 2004.

Muck, Terry C. *Those Other Religions in Your Neighborhood: Loving Your Neighbor When You Don't Know How.* Grand Rapids, MI: Zondervan, 1992.

Murray, Stuart. "Christendom and Post-Christendom." Online: http://www.missional churchnetwork.com/wp-content/uploads/2010/04/christendom-murray.pdf.

———. *Church after Christendom.* Carlisle: Paternoster, 2004.

———. *Post-Christendom: Church and Mission in a Strange New World.* Carlisle: Paternoster, 2004.

———. "Post-Christendom, Post-Constantinian, Post-Christian . . . Does the Label Matter?" *International Journal for the Study of the Christian Church* 9, no. 3 (2009) 195–208.

———. "The End of Christendom." Online: http://www.nextreformation.com/wp-admin/resources/end_christendom.pdf.

NCLS Research. "Young Adult Retention." In *Extended Church Life Profile,* edited by NCLS. Sydney South: NCLS, 2009.

Nelson, Alan E. *Spirituality and Leadership: Harnessing the Wisdom, Guidance, and Power of the Soul.* Colorado Springs, CO: NavPress, 2002.

Nessan, Craig L. *Beyond Maintenance to Mission: A Theology of the Congregation.* Minneapolis, MN: Fortress, 1999.

Newbigin, Lesslie. *A Word in Season: Perspectives on Christian World Missions.* Grand Rapids, MI: Eerdmans, 1994.

———. *Discovering Truth in a Changing World.* London: Alpha, 2003.

———. *Foolishness to the Greeks: The Gospel and Western Culture.* Grand Rapids, MI: Eerdmans, 1986.

———. "Jesus the Servant and Man's Community." In *Christ's Call to Service Now*, edited by Reeves, Ambrose, 23–33. London: SCM, 1963.

———. *The Light Has Come: An Exposition of the Fourth Gospel.* Grand Rapids, MI: Eerdmans, 1982.

———. *The Open Secret: An Introduction to the Theology of Mission.* Grand Rapids, MI: Eerdmans, 1995.

Newman, Barclay M., and Philip C. Stine. *A Handbook on the Gospel of Matthew.* New York, NY: United Bible Societies, 1992.

Niebuhr, H. Richard. *Christ and Culture.* New York, NY: Harper and Row, 1954.

Nielsen, Jeffrey S. *The Myth of Leadership: Creating Leaderless Organizations.* Palo Alto, CA: Davies-Black, 2004.

Niewold, Jack. "Beyond Servant Leadership." *Journal of Biblical Perspective in Leadership* 1, no. 2 (2007) 118–34.

Nikravan, Lavin. "Ask a Gen Y." *The Chief Learning Centre.* Online: http://blog.clomedia.com.

Northouse, Peter G. *Introduction to Leadership: Concepts and Practice.* Los Angeles, CA: Sage, 2009.

———. *Leadership: Theory and Practice.* 5th ed. London: Sage, 2010.

Nouwen, Henri J.M. *In the Name of Jesus: Reflections on Christian Leadership.* New York, NY: Crossroad, 1989.

Olley, John. "Light and Salt: Christian Participation in Society." Melbourne: Evangelical Alliance, 2004.

Ortberg, John. *The Life You've Always Wanted: Spiritual Disciplines for Ordinary People.* Expanded edition. Grand Rapids, MI: Zondervan, 2002.

Ott, Craig, et al. *Encountering Theology of Mission: Biblical Foundations, Historical Developments, and Contemporary Issues.* Encountering Mission. Grand Rapids, MI: Baker Academic, 2010.

Overman, J. Andrew. *Church and Community in Crisis: The Gospel According to Matthew.* The New Testament in Context. Valley Forge, PA: Trinity, 1996.

Owens, Tara M. "Longing Bodies, Aching Souls: Letting God Reclaim Our Sexuality." *Conversations* 9, no. 1 (2011) 36–42.

Padgett, Alan G. "God Versus Technology? Science, Secularity, and the Theology of Technology." *Zygon* 40, no. 3 (2005) 577–84.

Pagitt, Doug. *Reimagining Spiritual Formation: A Week in the Life of an Experimental Church.* Grand Rapids, MI: Zondervan, 2003.

Pamphilius, Eusebius, and Philip Schaff. "Nicene and Post-Nicene Fathers Series 11." Online: http://www.ccel.org/ccel/schaff/npnf201.iv.vi.ii.xliv.html.

Pratt, Jonathan. "Awake O Sleeper: Disturbing a Denomination at the Crossroads." In *Directions 2012 Research Steering Group*, edited by Heinrich, June. Sydney: Baptist Union of NSW and ACT, 29th April 2009.

Prosser, Stephen. *To Be a Servant-Leader.* New York, NY: Paulist, 2007.

Putman, David, and Ed Stetzer. *Breaking the Discipleship Code: Becoming a Missional Follower of Jesus.* Nashville, TN: B&H, 2008.

Quicke, Michael J. *360-Degree Leadership: Preaching to Transform Congregations.* Grand Rapids, MI: Baker, 2006.

Bibliography

Rand, Lenora. "The Church on Facebook: Why We Need Virtual Community." *Christian Century* 126, no. 13 (2009) 22–25.

Rattray, Paul. "Sacrificial Succession: A Solution to Leadership Transition Crisis." Online: http://www.sacrificialsuccession.com.

Rice, Jesse. *The Church of Facebook: How the Hyperconnected Are Redefining Community*. Colorado Springs, CO: David C. Cook, 2009.

Richmond, Helen. "Struggles in Multicultural and Cross-Cultural Ministry." Online: http://www.uca.org.au.

Richmond, Helen, and Myong Duk Yang. *Crossing Borders, Shaping Faith: Ministry and Identity in Multicultural Australia*. Sydney: National Assembly of the Uniting Church in Australia, 2006.

Riddell, Mike. *Threshold of the Future: Reforming the Church in the Post-Christian West*. London: SPCK, 1998.

Riddell, Mike, and Mark Pierson. *The Prodigal Project: Journey into the Emerging Church*. London: SPCK, 2001.

Rinehart, Stacy. *Upside Down: The Paradox of Servant Leadership*. Colorado Springs, CO: NavPress, 1998.

Robinson, Martin. *To Win the West*. Crowborough: Monarch, 1996.

Rodin, R. Scott. *The Steward Leader: Transforming People, Organizations, and Communities*. Downers Grove, IL: IVP Academic, 2010.

Roxburgh, Alan J. *Missional Map-Making: Skills for Leading in Times of Transition*. San Francisco, CA: Jossey-Bass, 2010.

———. *The Missional Leader: Equipping Your Church to Reach a Changing World*. San Francisco, CA: Jossey-Bass, 2006.

———. *The Missionary Congregation, Leadership, and Liminality*. New York, NY: Trinity, 1997.

———. *What Is Missional Church? An Introduction to the Missional Church Conversation*. Eagle, ID: Allelon, 2007.

Roxburgh, Alan J., and M. Scott Boren. *Introducing the Missional Church: What It Is, Why It Matters, How to Become One*. Grand Rapids, MI: Baker, 2009.

Rusaw, Rick, and Eric Swanson. *The Externally Focused Church*. Loveland, CO: Group, 2004.

Russell, Robert. "A Practical Theology of Servant Leadership." Online: http://www.regent.edu/acad/sls/publications/conference_proceedings/servant_leadership_roundtable/2003pdf/russell-_practical_theology.pdf.

Sample, Tex. *The Spectacle of Worship in a Wired World: Electronic Culture and the Gathered People of God*. Nashville, TN: Abingdon, 1998.

Samuel, Vinay, and Albrecht Hauser. *Proclaiming Christ in Christ's Way: Studies in Integral Evangelism*. Oxford: Regnum, 1989.

Savage, Sara B. *Making Sense of Generation Y: The World View of 15 to 25 Year Olds*. London: Church House, 2006.

Sayers, Mark. "The Weakness of Social Networking Vs Discipleship and Depth." Online: http://marksayers.wordpress.com/2010/10/12/the-weakness-of-social-networking-discipleship-and-depth/.

Schaeffer, Francis A. *The Church before the Watching World*. London: IVP, 1972.

Schnabel, Eckhard J. *Early Christian Mission*. Downers Grove, IL: IVP, 2004.

Scott, Bernard B. *Re-Imagine the World: An Introduction to the Parables of Jesus*. Santa Rosa, CA: Polebridge, 2001.

Scott, Eleonora L. "A Theological Critique of the Emerging, Postmodern, Missional Church/Movement." *Evangelical Review of Theology* 34, no. 4 (2010) 335–46.

Seay, Chris. "East Meets West." *Leadership* Fall (1999) 27–28.

Sellers, Robert P. "Is Mission Possible in a Postmodern World?" *Review and Expositor* 101 (2004) 389–424.

Sheffield, Dan. "Leading a Multi-Cultural Congregation." *McMaster Journal of Theology and Ministry* 5 (2002).

Shenk, Wilbert R. "New Wineskins for New Wine: Toward a Post-Christendom Ecclesiology." *International Bulletin of Missionary Research* 29, no. 2 (2005) 73–79.

———. *Write the Vision: The Church Renewed*. New York, NY: Trinity, 1995.

Siebert, Jared. "The Ecclesiology of the Emerging Church." Online: http://www.jaredsiebert.ca/.

Sims, Bennett J. *Servanthood: Leadership for the Third Millennium*. Cambridge, MA: Cowley, 1997.

Sine, Tom. *Mustard Seed Vs McWorld: Reinventing Life and Faith for the Future*. Grand Rapids, MI: Baker, 1999.

———. *The New Conspirators: Creating the Future One Mustard Seed at a Time*. Downers Grove, IL: IVP, 2008.

Singh, Niti, and Venkat R. Krishnan. "Self-Sacrifice and Transformational Leadership: Mediating Role of Altruism." *Leadership and Organization Development Journal* 29, no. 3 (2008) 261–74.

Skreslet, Stanley H. *Picturing Christian Witness: New Testament Images of Disciples in Mission*. Grand Rapids, MI: Eerdmans, 2006.

Smith, David. *Moving Towards Emmaus: Hope in a Time of Uncertainty*. London: SPCK, 2007.

Smith, James B. *The Good and Beautiful God: Falling in Love with the God Jesus Knows*. Downers Grove, IL: IVP, 2009.

Sonnenfeld, Jeffrey. "Good Governance and the Misleading Myths of Bad Metrics." *The Academy of Management Executive* 18, no. 1 (2004) 108–13.

Spellers, Stephanie. "The Church Awake: Becoming the Missional People of God." *Anglican Theological Review*. (2010) 29–44.

Stafford, Tim. "Mere Mission: N.T. Wright Talks About How to Present the Gospel in a Postmodern World." *Christianity Today* January (2007) 39–41.

Stanley, Timothy. "Speaking Credibly? Communicating Christian Particularism in Postmodern Contexts." *International Review of Mission* 97, no. 384 (2008) 21–30.

Stanton, Graham. *A Gospel for a New People: Studies in Matthew*. Edinburgh: T. & T. Clark, 1992.

Stevens, R. Paul. *The Other Six Days: Vocation, Work, and Ministry in Biblical Perspective*. Grand Rapids, MI: Eerdmans, 1999.

Stoddard, Chris, and Nick Cuthbert. *Church on the Edge: Principles and Real Life Stories of 21st Century Mission*. Milton Keynes: Authentic, 2006.

Stott, John R.W. *Calling Christian Leaders: Biblical Models of Church, Gospel and Ministry*. Leicester: IVP, 2002.

———. *The Living Church: Convictions of a Lifelong Pastor*. Nottingham: IVP, 2007.

Stott, John R.W., and Alister McGrath. *The Cross of Christ*. Downers Grove, IL: IVP, 2006.

Sweet, Leonard. *Summoned to Lead*. Grand Rapids, MI: Zondervan, 2004.

Sweet, Leonard, ed. *The Church in Emerging Culture: Five Perspectives*. Grand Rapids, MI: Zondervan, 2003.

Bibliography

Tacey, David J. *The Spirituality Revolution: The Emergence of Contemporary Spirituality.* Pymble: HarperCollins, 2003.

Tatarnic, Martha S. "The Mass Media and Faith: The Potentialities and Problems for the Church in Our Television Culture." *Anglican Theological Review* 87, no. 3 (2005) 447–65.

Taylor, J. Hudson. "The Call to Service." In *Perspectives on the World Christian Movement*, edited by Winter, Ralph D. 300–304. Pasadena, LA: William Carey Library, 1999.

Taylor, Justin. "5 Questions with Andreas Köstenberger on Excellence." *The Gospel Coalition*. Online: http://thegospelcoalition.org/blogs/justintaylor/2011/10/25/5-questions-with-andreas-kstenberger-on-excellence/.

Taylor, Steve J. *The Out of Bounds Church: Learning to Create a Community of Faith in a Culture of Change.* Grand Rapids, MI: Zondervan, 2005.

Tenney, Tommy. *Prayers of a God Chaser.* Minneapolis, MN: Bethany, 2002.

Thew, J. "My Neighbour Is Korean." Melbourne: Department of Cross-Cultural Ministries, Anglican Church Centre, 1995.

Todd, Eleanor M. "Book of the Month." *Expository Times* 115, no. 11 (2004) 376–78.

Tozer, Aiden W. *The Pursuit of God.* Harrisburg, PA: Christian Publications, 1948.

Troeger, Thomas H. *Preaching While the Church Is under Reconstruction: The Visionary Role of Preachers in a Fragmented World.* Nashville, TN: Abingdon, 1999.

TrueLocal. "West Ryde: 2012." Online: http://www.truelocal.com.au/find/church/nsw/sydney-greater-metro/west-ryde.

Useem, Andrea. "The New Connectivity: How Internet Innovations Are Changing the Way We Do Church." *Congregations* 34, no. 4 (2008) 22–28.

Van den Heever, James. "Web 2.0: Technology for the Postmodern Sensibility and Its Implications for the Church." *Journal of Theology for Southern Africa*, no. 132 (2008) 86–107.

Van Gelder, Craig. "From Corporate Church to Missional Church: The Challenge Facing Congregations Today." *Review & Expositor* 101, no. 3 (2004) 425–50.

———. "Rethinking Denominations and Denominationalism in Light of a Missional Ecclesiology." *Word and World* 25, no. 1 (2005) 23–33.

VanderLeest, Steven H. "Teaching Justice by Emphasizing the Non-Neutrality of Technology." *Journal of Education & Christian Belief* 10, no. 2 (2006) 111–28.

Veith, Gene E. *Postmodern Times: A Christian Guide to Contemporary Thought and Culture.* Wheaton, IL: Crossway, 1994.

Viola, Frank. *Reimagining Church: Pursuing the Dream of Organic Christianity.* Colorado Springs, CO: David C. Cook, 2008.

Volf, Miroslav. *After Our Likeness: The Church as the Image of the Trinity.* Grand Rapids, MI: Eerdmans, 1998.

Wallace, J. Randall. "Servant Leadership: A Worldview Perspective." Online: http://www.regent.edu/acad/global/publications/sl_proceedings/2006/wallace.pdf.

Ward, Angie. "Looking for Leaders: What Does Leadership Look Like in the Emergent Generation?" *Leadership* (2006) 19–22.

Ward, Pete. *Liquid Church.* Peabody, MA: Hendrickson, 2002.

Warren, Robert. *The Healthy Churches' Handbook: A Process for Revitalizing Your Church.* London: Church House, 2004.

Watson, David L. "Salt to the World: An Ecclesiology of Liberation." *Missiology: An International Review* 12, no. 4 (1986) 453–76.

Webber, Robert E. *Ancient-Future Faith: Rethinking Evangelicalism for a Postmodern World.* Grand Rapids, MI: Baker, 1999.

———. *The Younger Evangelicals: Facing the Challenges of the New World.* Grand Rapids, MI: Baker, 2003.

Webber, Robert, et al. *Listening to the Beliefs of Emerging Churches: Five Perspectives.* Grand Rapids, MI: Zondervan, 2007.

Weiler, Angelina. "Information-Seeking Behavior in Generation Y Students: Motivation, Critical Thinking, and Learning Theory." *The Journal of Academic Librarianship* 31, no. 1 (2005) 46–53.

Weston, Paul. "Lesslie Newbigin: A Postmodern Missiologist?" *Mission Studies* 21, no. 2 (2004) 229–48.

Willard, Dallas. *Knowing Christ Today: Why We Can Trust Spiritual Knowledge.* New York, NY: Harper One, 2009.

———. *Renovation of the Heart: Putting on the Character of Christ.* Colorado Springs, CO: NavPress, 2002.

———. *The Divine Conspiracy: Rediscovering Our Hidden Life in God.* San Francisco, CA: HarperSanFrancisco, 1998.

———. "The Gentle Art of Making Disciples." In *DMin Hooding Address.* Fuller Theological Seminary, 2012.

———. *The Great Omission: Reclaiming Jesus' Essential Teaching on Discipleship.* London: Monarch Books, 2006.

———. *The Spirit of the Disciplines: Understanding How God Changes Lives.* New York, NY: Harper One, 1988.

Williams, John N. "Confucius, Mencius, and the Notion of True Succession." *Philosophy East and West* 38, no. 2 (1988) 157–71.

Williams, Rowan. *Mission-Shaped Church: Church Planting and Fresh Expressions of Church in a Changing Context.* London: Church House, 2004.

Willimon, William H. "Postmodern Preaching : Learning to Love the Thickness of the Text." *Journal for Preachers* 19, no. 3 (1996) 32–37.

Wilson, Frederick R., ed. *The San Antonio Report: Your Will Be Done: Mission in Christ's Way.* Geneva: WCC, 1990.

Wilson, Sharon. "Please, Not Another E-Mail! Understanding the Hidden Costs of E-Mail's Demanding Nature." *Congregations* 34, no. 4 (2008) 16–19.

Winter, Ralph D., and Bruce A. Koch. "Finishing the Task: The Unreached Peoples Challenge." In *Perspectives on the World Christian Movement*, edited by Winter, Ralph D., et al., 509–24. Pasadena, CA: William Carey, 1999.

Woolfe, Lorin. *The Bible on Leadership: From Moses to Matthew—Management Lessons for Contemporary Leaders.* New York, NY: MJF, 2003.

World Council of Churches. "Appendix: Mission and Evangelism—An Ecumenical Affirmation." In *"You are the Light of the World": Statements on Mission by the World Council of Churches*, edited by World Council of Churches: World Council of Churches, 1982.

Wright, Christopher J. H. *The Mission of God: Unlocking the Bible's Grand Narrative.* Nottingham: IVP, 2006.

———. *The Mission of God's People: A Biblical Theology of the Church's Mission.* Grand Rapids, MI: Zondervan, 2010.

Bibliography

Wright, N. T. *Jesus and the Victory of God: Christian Origins and the Question of God.* Minneapolis, MN: Fortress, 1996.

———. *The Challenge of Jesus.* London: SPCK, 2000.

———. *The New Testament and the People of God.* London: SPCK, 1992.

Wright, Nigel G. "Post-Denominationalism and the Renewal of a Denominational Witness." In *The Burleigh Conference.* Adelaide, 2001.

Wright, Walter C. *Relational Leadership: A Biblical Model for Influence and Service.* Colorado Springs, CO: Biblica, 2009.

Yates, Timothy. "David Bosch's South African Context: Universal Missiology—Ecclesiology in the Emerging Missionary Paradigm." *International Bulletin of Missionary Research* 33, no. 2 (2009) 72–78.

Young, David S. *Servant Leadership for Church Renewal: Shepherds by the Living Springs.* Scottdale, PA: Herald, 1999.

Yukl, Gary A. *Leadership in Organizations.* 7th ed. Upper Saddle River, NJ: Prentice Hall, 2010.

www.ingramcontent.com/pod-product-compliance
Lightning Source LLC
Chambersburg PA
CBHW060508300426
44112CB00017B/2584